D1125165

Yale Western Americana Series, 36

Editorial Committee
Archibald Hanna, Jr.
Howard Roberts Lamar
Robert M. Utley

Mario T. García

Mexican Americans

Leadership, Ideology, & Identity, 1930 – 1960

Yale University Press   New Haven & London

Published with assistance from the foundation
established in memory of Philip Hamilton
McMillan of the Class of 1894, Yale College.

Designed by James J. Johnson
and set in Times Roman and Cheltenham types.
Printed in the United States of America.

Library of Congress Cataloging-in-Publication Data

García, Mario T.
    Mexican Americans: leadership, ideology, and identity,
1930–1960.

    (Yale Western Americana series ; 36)
    Bibliography: p.
    Includes index.
    ISBN 0–300–04246–9 (cloth)
         0–300–04984–6
    1. Mexican Americans—Politics and government.
2. United States—Politics and government—1933–1945.
3. United States—Politics and government—1945–
4. Southwest, New—Politics and government.   I. Title.
II. Series.
E184.M5G375   1989   303.3'4'0896872   88–33969

*The paper in this book meets the guidelines for
permanence and durability of the Committee on
Production Guidelines for Book Longevity of the
Council on Library Resources.*

10 9 8 7 6 5 4 3 2

To Giuliana Rosa, Mario Giancarlo, and to Ellen

Contents

Part Three: Mexican-American Intellectuals

Conclusion

Acknowledgments

I first conceptualized this study during a delightful year as a Fellow at the Center for Advanced Study in the Behavioral Sciences in Stanford, California. While at the Center my colleague in Chicano history, Professor Albert Camarillo of Stanford University, introduced me to archival collections in the Green Library at Stanford which provoked my perceptions of the Mexican-American Generation and formed the origins of my research on this topic. For this inspiration, I wish to thank Professor Camarillo.

This study is completely dependent on primary sources, which represent the lifeblood of a historian. As such I am indebted to a number of dedicated and generous archivists and librarians who helped me along the way. They include the late Patricia Palmer, Roberto Trujillo, and Carol Rudisell, in Special Collections at the Green Library at Stanford University; Salvador Guereña, of the Colección Tloque Nahuaque at the library of my own campus, the University of California, Santa Barbara; Richard Chabran of the Chicano Studies Library at UCLA; César Caballero of Special Collections at the University of Texas at El Paso Library; Gilda Baeza and Mary Sarbor at the Chicano Studies Collection and the Southwest Collection in the El Paso Public Library; Sarah John of the Institute of Oral History at the University of Texas at El Paso; Laura Gutiérrez-Witt, Carmen Sacomani, Elvira Chavarría, Gerald Poyo, and Juan Rodríguez at the Benson Latin American Library at the University of Texas at Austin; the staff at the Western History Collection at the University of Colorado, Boulder; the staff in the Freedom of Information Section of the Federal Bureau of Investigation in Washington, D.C.; Lillian Castillo-Speed of the Chicano Studies Library at the University of

California, Berkeley; and Irma Silva of Southwest Microfilm in El Paso. Finally, I wish to thank the staff of the Inter-Library Loan department at the University of California, Santa Barbara, for their assistance.

I want to also thank Leonor Varela López, Bert Corona, E. B. León, Luciano Santoscoy, Belén Robles, Humberto Sílex, M. C. González, Judge Albert Armendáriz, Mary Lou Armendáriz, and Henry Martínez, who provided me with access to their own private collections as well as to Juan Aranda and Gabriel Cedillo of the U.S. Steelworkers in El Paso, who allowed me to search their local files for material on the International Union of Mine, Mill and Smelter Workers.

Research assistants who aided my work include Enrique Hermosillo and Ann Joyce at the Woodrow Wilson International Center for Scholars and Martín González, Dina Gutiérrez-Castillo, and Jeff Garcilazo at UC Santa Barbara.

Particular individuals who provided intellectual or moral support, more often both, include my mentor, Ramón Eduardo Ruiz. Professor Ruiz over the years has consistently encouraged me to be the best historian I can be; his intellectual and guiding presence is always with me. I wish to thank my other mentor at UC San Diego, Michael Parrish as well as Richard García; Carlos Cortés; Oscar Martínez; the late Ralph Guzmán; Rudolfo Acuña; Guadalupe San Miguel; Robert Kelley; and Elliot Brownlee. I, of course, want to thank Charles Grench of Yale University Press, who expressed enthusiasm and support for this project. Alexander Metro, my line editor at Yale, provided invaluable assistance, as he did for my first book.

A special gratitude goes to Richard Griswold del Castillo, who read the manuscript in its entirety not only once, but twice and provided valuable suggestions for improvements. For his support on this project as well as on others, I am deeply appreciative.

Institutions that provided financial support and facilities for the development of this study are the Center for Advanced Study in the Behavioral Sciences (NEH Grant No. FC 262787-76-1030); UC Santa Barbara, for a Faculty Development Grant and sabbatical leave; the National Research Council and the Ford Foundation for a 1982–83 fellowship; the Woodrow Wilson International Center for Scholars for an eight-month fellowship during 1984, an experience I will never forget; and the Center for Chicano Studies at UC Santa Barbara for research support and travel expenses. I want to give particular credit to my friends and colleagues in the Department of History at my undergraduate alma mater, the University of Texas at El Paso, especially Professors Carl Jackson and Oscar Martínez, for being gracious hosts during my residence in the Fall of 1982.

Exceptional clerical assistance was provided by María Teresa Boschee, Tracy Hamilton, Jim Vieth, Jane Mahanke, and especially Linda Dorr, who meticulously typed the initial draft of the manuscript. I wish also to thank my administrative assistant, Lucille Coppel, for greatly easing the burdens of my tenure as Chair of the Department of Chicano Studies at UCSB.

Another special thank you to my cousin Rosalva Montelongo of El Paso, who provided bed and board and wonderful companionship during several research trips to my hometown of El Paso, and to Ambassador Raymond L. Telles for graciously consenting to several interviews from which I gleaned information that would have otherwise been unavailable.

Last, I want to pay homage to the men and women of the Mexican-American Generation and others who gave me their time, knowledge, and feelings by reliving for me their pasts. Without them, this study would have been severely handicapped. This is their history and I am proud to reveal it. They include M. C. González; Henry Martínez; Amadita C. Valdez; Judge Albert Armendáriz; Mary Lou Armendáriz; Leonor Varela López; Candelario Mendoza; Dr. Raymond Gardea; Gabriel Navarrete; Luciano Santoscoy; Francisco "Kiko" Hernández; Alfredo "Lelo" Jacques; Ted Bender; Ralph Seitsinger; Richard Telles; David Villa; Ray Marantz; Conrad Ramírez; Ken Flynn; Joe Herrera; Bert Corona; Dorothy Healey; Josefina Fierro; Manuel Ruiz, Jr.; J. B. Chávez; Humberto Sílex; Gabriel Cedillo; Juan Aranda; Alfredo Montoya; Mauricio Terrazas; Clint Jencks; Julia Luna Mount; Belén Robles; Joe Calamia; Rodolfo García; Marvin Shady; Santos de la Paz; Frank Galván; Ernie Craigo; Mario Acevedo; Lucy Acosta; Paul Andow; Margarita Blanco; Salvador Del Valle; Modesto Gómez; E. B. León; and Alfonso Pérez.

CHAPTER ONE

The Mexican-American Generation

We set out to study leadership in order to gain a fresh perspective on the notion of ethnic groups in American society.

—JOHN HIGHAM, 1978

Political generations are a group of human beings who have undergone the same basic historical experiences during their formative years.

—MARVIN RINTALA, 1979

But we are going to come out the winner in this the "Survival War," for we are Americans-all and ours is the course of justice and freedom.

—IGNACIO LÓPEZ,
May 1, 1942

This is a study of ethnic leadership. It concerns what I term the Mexican-American Generation.[1] Between the 1930s and the 1950s, covering the experiences of the Great Depression, World War II, and the cold war, a new generation of community leaders emerged out of the expanding Mexican-American barrios of the Southwest. This generation of leaders organized the first significant civil rights movement by Mexican Americans in the United States. Unfortunately, this civil rights history has received less attention than that of other minorities, most notably Afro Americans. Mexican Americans, of course, are no strangers to this country. The ancestors of some can be traced to the Spanish explorations and settlements in New Mexico, Colorado, Texas, Arizona, and California. Most, however, are of more recent lineage. Thousands of Mexicans crossed the U.S.-Mexican border during the period of the Mexican Revolution of 1910 and throughout this century. Mexican Americans are both an old and a new ethnic group. Despite popular stereotypes that view Mexican Americans as apolitical, marginalized farmworkers, as "illegal aliens," and as a people who selfishly cling to their culture, they have not been isolated from the great struggles and transformations of our age. The present study, as Octavio Romano argued in his seminal essays in *El Grito* during the 1960s, places the Mexican American within the currents of

1

the history of struggles to achieve equal opportunities, respect, and dignity in the United States.[2]

Possessing a complex and heterogeneous history, Mexican Americans have evolved through several historical stages. This study concerns one of these—what I call the Mexican-American Era. On a larger scale than ever before a majority of Mexicans in the United States were now U.S. born and raised.* Of course, after the U.S. conquest of northern Mexico during the Mexican War (1846–48) Mexicans who remained in the Southwest were allowed to become U.S. citizens. These first Mexican Americans numbered no more than about 100,000.[3] By contrast, during the 1930s perhaps as many as 2 to 3 million Mexicans, the majority U.S. citizens, lived north of the border.[4] Recruited and exploited as a cheap labor force, and indispensable to the impressive economic growth of the Southwest during the late nineteenth and early twentieth centuries, Mexican Americans remained rooted in the working class, although their intraclass positions shifted by the 1930s and 1940s to more urban industrial and service occupations. With urbanization came increased education. A rising although limited U.S.-born middle class likewise arose. A middle class existed during the early part of the century but in most places was composed predominatly of immigrants and political refugees.[5] The convulsions of the Great Depression combined with new economic and political opportunities during World War II and with the historic discrimination in the Southwest against Mexicans and rising expectations among Mexican Americans to give birth to a new leadership, cognizant of its rights as U.S. citizens and determined to achieve them. This leadership was not confined to the middle class but included working-class leaders as well as a handful of intellectuals. Mostly liberal, the Mexican-American Generation was also composed of radicals. Together this generation forged a spirited and persistent struggle for civil rights, for first-class citizenship, and for a secure identity for Americans of Mexican descent. Mexican Americans identified with the World War II slogan: "Americans All." This study is a panorama of that leadership.

A word should be said here concerning gender and leadership. In researching the archival sources that provided me with the foundation for this study, I consciously made an effort to locate material pertaining to the role of women within the Mexican-American Generation. I discovered various sources but, unfortunately, of a somewhat limited nature. The focus of this study is on leadership and, as in most other U.S. ethnic communities in mid-

---

*Mexican refers to a person of Mexican descent who is either a U.S. citizen or a Mexican national; Mexican American refers specifically to a U.S. citizen of Mexican descent; *mexicano* refers to a Mexican national residing in the United States, and Anglo refers to a U.S. citizen of European descent.

century, the vast majority of leadership positions were held by men. Although the Mexican-American Generation consisted of both men and women, it was mostly dominated by men. This appears to be particularly true of middle-class organizations. Traditional prejudices toward women limited but did not exclude participation, as exemplified by the role of the Ladies Councils in the League of United Latin American Citizens (LULAC), the most important Mexican-American civil rights organization of this period (see chapter 2). Moreover, representing still predominatly poor Mexican-American communities and a limited middle class, Mexican-American middle-class women did not possess the resources to establish organizations, especially of a political and civic nature, comparable to those of Anglo middle-class women. On the other hand, it is also evident that in the world of Mexican-American radical politics a more enlightened and tolerant political consciousness toward women functioned. This is obvious in the central role of Josefina Fierro de Bright of the Spanish-Speaking Congress (see chapter 6) and in the leadership role of women in the Asociación Nacional México-Americana (ANMA) (see chapter 8). Certain militant CIO unions such as the United Cannery, Agricultural, Packing, and Allied Workers of America (UCAPAWA), as revealed in Vicki Ruiz's recent study, also incorporated Mexican-American women into leadership positions.[6] Finally, although I considered writing a separate chapter on women within the Mexican-American Generation, I decided that such a chapter might be construed as patronizing and incorrectly suggest that women did not participate in the larger movements such as those of the Left. Consequently, I have chosen in this survey to integrate the material on women—scant as it might be in some cases—within rather than apart from the other material.

Political Generations

In examining Mexican-American ethnic leadership I utilize the concept of what sociologists and political scientists have termed a "political generation" or in some cases a "historical generation" or a "social generation." Political generations, according to Marvin Rintala, are "a group of human beings who have undergone the same basic historical experiences during their formative years."[7] A political generation is distinct from a biological generation in that while it possesses, like a biological generation, chronological or age-cohort boundaries, or what Karl Mannheim termed a generation location or a social location, it is not age but politics that determines its character.[8] A political generation consciously and politically reacts to its historical era. "Whatever else it may be," Rintala adds, "a political generation is not the same as a biological generation."[9] Politics and ideology in response to particular historical experiences that accelerate social change—or what can be called an experiential process or the shared experiences of a particular age cohort—not age per se distinguishes a political generation.[10]

Although students of political generations may differ somewhat as to the age boundaries of a political generation, they all basically agree that it is shaped by historical changes—usually convulsive ones, such as wars or revolutions—specific to a certain period which trigger a particular political response or responses by a collection of individuals who come of political age during this time. Julián Marías, for example, notes: "[A] generation must be considered as a political reality, which is to say that it begins at the moment when men arrive at, or are born into, political life."[11] Marías further observes: "Thus, we have to conclude that the setting of generations is society and thence history."[12] If a shared historical experience is a key variable in the making of a political generation, it also is molded by a loosely shared sense among the members of a political generation that their historical time or destiny has arrived. Mannheim alludes to this ingredient in these words: "We shall therefore speak of a *generation as an actuality* only where a concrete bond is created between members of a generation by their being exposed to the social and intellectual symptoms of a process of dynamic destabilization."[13] Alan Spitzer in his analysis of the French Generation of 1820, which defined itself in relation to the Restoration, characterizes a political generation as a social network. The Mexican philosopher Samuel Ramos concurs and notes of this bond: "To deserve the name, a generation must be united by strong spiritual bonds, not simply by motives of expediency."[14] These bonds, however, do not necessarily imply that a political generation is fully cognizant of itself as a generation. Like class consciousness, generational consciousness is also a process. A political generation can be a generation in the process of recognizing itself as a political generation. Ramos cautions: "To me it seems logical to assume that the group itself is the least capable of knowing whether or not it constitutes a generation. Only after the work is done and later evaluated in the perspective of time is it possible to tell whether the spiritual unity of the generation exists."[15]

Moreover, a political generation emerges not just in reaction to history but in order to make history—that is, to produce and consolidate significant social changes in an environment conducive to such changes. Consequently, political generations involve power, the distribution of power, and the possession of power. Quant underlines this in his definition of a political generation: "I would define a political generation in terms of shared political orientations toward the objectives of policy and the uses of power."[16]

Students of political generations also address themselves to various other aspects that influence the composition of a political generation. The question of the boundaries of a generational age cohort is one of these. Some argue that a political generation lasts fifteen years; others suggest twenty-five to thirty years. The importance of age here is that a political generation is composed of individuals who have been born within a reasonable distance from one another, but not necessarily during the same year or even coterminous years. Yet the distance is not so large that a dichotomy between a young and an old generation appears. The age cohort, however, can be liberally defined as long as it has been influenced by the same historical experiences and it has reacted to these in a definite political fashion that marks it off from the past. Stepan in his analysis of military generations in Latin America addresses the issue of the relationship of an age cohort to a political generation: "We can talk about it as a generational experience, but we are not talking about a narrow *age cohort,* but of an *experiential cohort* within which the members' age span will often be as broad as twenty-five years." [17] Defined in this manner, a political generation may in fact include an overlap between biological generations. In the case of the Mexican-American Generation, for example, there is some overlap between those who began to become politically conscious as leaders either due to their participation in World War I, to their experiences during the Great Depression, or to their involvement in World War II. Most, however, were clustered as young adults coming of political age during the Great Depression and World War II. Despite some age differences, all were affected by similar changes and upheavals, as Mexicans in the United States by the 1930s began the transformation on a mass scale from being either immigrant communities or isolated communities deriving from the nineteenth century to Mexican-American ethnic communities. This shared experience overlapping biological generations is termed a "derived experience." [18] Quant notes that in some very unusual occasions there can even be movement from one political generation to another—what he calls "intergenerational mobility" through "adult resocialization." [19]

Still another key aspect of political generations is that while they encompass in broad terms a collection of individuals who share common historical experiences and who react to the politics of their age, a political generation at the same time is not a monolithic phenomenon. Political variations and reactions are not unusual in political generations. Members of a political generation can differ politically and ideologically and compose what Mannheim termed generation units, but they still comprise a holistic political generation because their political responses emanate from the same source or foundation—their shared historical experience. [20] In the case of the Mexican-American Generation one can speak of certain generational units that together form a political generation. These would consist, as the divisions of this study suggest, of a rising middle class, a working class beginning to integrate itself into the labor union movement, radicals connected to the Communist party, and professional intellectuals. These generational units share differences as well as similarities. But together they have been given political birth by the shared historical experiences of the Great Depression and World War II. Despite certain differences, they can understand one another better than they can a later generation. As Rintala observes: "It is worth noting . . . that these different voices within a generation are far more capable of communicating with each other than with members of another generation." [21]

There are, of course, numerous examples of political generations. Alan Spitzer has examined what he calls the French Generation of 1820, which came of age during the Restoration, and Robert Wohl has studied what he terms the "Generation of 1914," a study of those European intellectuals—liberals, Marxists, and fascists—who experiencing the horror of World War I came to identify themselves with this central historical experience. [22] In the history of the United States, historians have referred to the revolutionary generation of 1776, to the Civil War generation, to a New Deal generation, a World War II generation, and more recently to a Vietnam generation. In each case—and there are other examples of political generations in specific national histories—a political generation generally revolves around key historical occurrences such as a major war or revolution. In their reactions and responses they also come to capture what Mannheim called the "spirit of the age" [Zeitgeist] or what Spitzer terms a "generational ideology." [23] Marías correctly adds that historical events such as wars and revolutions per se do not determine a political generation, but they do represent catalysts for the greater manifestation of underlying social changes taking place. [24] I would modify the general characteristics of a political generation as set forth by Mannheim and others by noting that the central experience or experiences, or what Feuer terms generational events, by which a political generation can be defined can likewise be social changes more particular to a specific group. Hence, the Mexican-American Generation is not defined only by its reaction to larger social convulsions such as the Great Depression and World War II, but also by its affinity to the organic changes affecting the Mexican-American communities and the resulting and significant civil rights movement that emanated from these changes.

Further, political generations by definition represent an elite or vanguard—although I do not use the terms here in a pejorative manner—as opposed to the masses. Quant in his discussion of generational change in the Arab world stresses that political generations usually involve an analysis of elites: "[I]n an analysis of political generations it is most useful to look at elites rather than to attempt to speak of a political generation that has some broad mass base." [25] Marías comments on this connection between elites and masses: "In any generation, then, at a historical level, we find a mass or multitude and a guiding minority in which the essence of the generation is revealed and which lends the generation its notoriety and historical relief."[26]

Finally, while the concept of political generation has generally been applied only to national or international movements, it can also, as in this study, be used for a particular ethnic group or national minority. In this case it is an ethnic minority that has been relatively little studied, largely misunderstood, but increasingly important as Hispanics/Latinos come to represent the largest minority in the United States: Mexican Americans. It is not my intention here to indulge in an extended discussion of political generations—others have done it more thoroughly—but rather to suggest that historians can employ the concept as a tool in studying social change and specifically the role of leadership. I should further note that in taking a generational approach to Chicano history I have no intention of imposing an idealistic, as opposed to a materialistic, view of history. A generational approach allows me to better conceptualize Chicano history and to understand class changes within the Mexican-American community, but it does not replace a class analysis which is embedded in this study and, as suggested, in its basic divisions. Class changes and struggles along with race and gender, in the case of racial ethnics, are the motor forces of history, but they can at times be better understood by applying an equally broad analysis such as a generational one.

In whatever context the model of a political generation is used it can be a dynamic application, for political generations actively make history rather than passively note history. As Wohl aptly puts it: "Historical generations are not born; they are made."[27]

Ethnicity and Generation in U.S. Historiography

Any venture into Chicano history should be understood within the larger framework of the history of the United States. Mexican Americans, of course, possess certain characteristics that distinguish them from most other U.S. ethnic groups. For example, Mexicans, like Native Americans and Afro Americans, began their U.S. experience as a conquered population, in their case as a result of the war against Mexico in the 1840s and the subsequent capture of the Southwest. Mexicans, however, have also represented an immigrant population. Yet it is different from European and Asian immigration in that for Mexicans the "sending country" is immediately adjacent to the "receiving country." This situation has lent itself, unlike for other immigrant groups, to a continuous pattern of new immigrant waves. Essential to U.S. society as a working-class population, Mexicans have experienced restrained mobility and have remained a "permanent minority" not only due to class

prejudice but to racial discrimination as well. Mexican Americans
a people of color—*mestizos*.[28] At the same time, Mexican Ameri-
likewise shared certain common experiences with other Ameri-
ᴄᴀɴꜱ. ᴛhese include aspirations and struggles for the full promises of the
American dream as expressed in the Declaration of Independence and the
U.S. Constitution and as learned by every American schoolchild, whether in
integrated schools or in segregated ones such as the Mexican schools of the
Southwest. Despite a common stereotype of Mexican Americans clinging
selfishly to their own separate culture and way of life, in fact, Mexican Americans have, with other ethnic groups, expressed pride in their U.S. citizenship
and have desired to be accepted as first-class Americans. Hence, what is the
relationship of this study to the larger parameters of U.S. history? That relationship can best be understood by focusing on the importance of ethnic history to a society as diverse as the United States.

Although ethnic history has in one form or another always been a part of
the historiography of the United States, it has experienced a major revival
and celebration during the last twenty years. The Afro-American civil rights
struggles of the 1960s, including radical tendencies such as the Black Power
Movement, helped rekindle an interest not only in Afro-American history but
in the role of race and ethnicity in the United States. Revisionist historians
rebelled against the hegemony of the consensus approach embraced during
the cold war years of the 1950s, which stressed "nonideological" consensus
in American life. Instead, revisionists—sometimes referred to as the New
Left—saw conflict, including race and class warfare, rather than consensus
as the driving force in the history of the United States. Uniformity also gave
way to diversity. Pluralism became the historical guidepost. Yet historical
pluralism, as John Higham has suggested, resulted from and produced a dialectic. Pluralism could be used as a base to seek alternative political and cultural models for a more liberated society. Historians of this persuasion Higham
terms the "hard pluralists." At the same time, pluralism in the hands of more
conservative historians—whom Higham refers to as the "soft pluralists"—
became the foundation for a new form of consensus that while acknowledging differences—especially of an ethnic and cultural form—tied diversity to
the fundamental structures of American capitalism.[29] However, within this
dialectic and this new aperture in U.S. historiography—the new ethnic history—historians by the early 1970s began to publish a myriad of books and
articles extolling the ethnic diversity of the country. We all knew, to slightly
revise Oscar Handlin's earlier and famous phrase concerning immigration,
that the history of America was ethnicity, but in the post–1960s period we
came to know it even better.

The new ethnic history, with the exception of Afro-American history, for the most part was for obvious reasons closely tied to what was called the "new immigrant history." Indeed, ethnicity and immigration became seen by many historians as almost one and the same phenomenon. The new ethnic-immigrant history in turn was distinguished from an earlier school by its focus on the value of ethnicity in the immigrant process. Ethnicity here and throughout this study is used to reflect not only particular ethnic cultural artifacts, but institutional life and an evolving sense of community and even peoplehood that functions in a dynamic interplay with mainstream U.S. Anglo-Saxon–derived culture and institutions as well as the proverbial American way of life. Older studies such as those by Hansen and Handlin, steeped in what Rudolph Vecoli terms "Turnerian determinism," had argued that immigrants to the United States had experienced a severe ethnic and cultural shock. While conceding that ethnic retention was part of the adjustment process, the older historiography concentrated more on the dialectical process of "Americanization" that ultimately tied the immigrants to the American consensus. The older school, influenced by Frederick Jackson Turner's stress on the Americanizing effect of the environment, was more concerned about assimilation than about ethnic pluralism. "Because of their expectations that assimilation was to be swift and irresistible," Vecoli notes of this earlier school, "historians and social scientists have looked for change rather than continuity, acculturation rather than cultural maintenance." [30] Revisionist historians, on the other hand, celebrate ethnic retention and the role of ethnicity in cushioning settlement in a new land. Moreover, in an atmosphere of counterculture and alienation from earlier concepts such as the "melting pot" and the Puritan ethic, a new generation of historians in the 1960s and early 1970s looked to earlier ethnic groups and cultures for alternative statements concerning American life. The new ethnic-immigrant historians conceded assimilation but differed as to its pace and certainly as to its ultimate effect.

Yet this revisionist school—with some exceptions—has perhaps been too static in its analysis of the ethnic-immigrant experience and not dynamic enough in interpreting the role of ethnicity in continued social change. Having made the case for ethnic pluralism, historians, as Higham further suggests, need to return to the relationship or synthesis between assimilation and ethnicity. [31] Hence the problem that I am interested in here is the relationship of ethnicity to generational change. The new ethnic-immigrant history, including my own earlier study of Mexican immigrants, [32] has tended to concentrate almost exclusively on pioneer-immigrant generations. Consequently ethnicity is immigration and ethnics are immigrants. Yet ethnicity, as sociologists more than historians have urged, is not a one-generation phenomenon.

In a refreshing and notable study of second-generation Jewish Americans in New York City, Deborah Dash Moore describes how a rising Jewish middle class negotiated the integration of American middle-class values with an adapting Jewish identity. "At home both in American urban culture and immigrant Jewish culture," she writes, "second generation Jews could synthesize the two." To one degree or another, ethnicity influences succeeding biological and political generations. But ethnicity changes as much as generations do and hence takes different forms in different historical periods. Some ethnic groups retain more ethnicity than others. Whereas sociologists and other scholars argue over whether European-derived ethnics still maintain an ethnic variable, this is hardly an academic question for racial-ethnic groups such as Mexican Americans who continue to perpetuate evolving ethnic traditions while at the same time suffering the effects of ethnic, cultural, and racial prejudices.[33] The problem—to put it in more social scientific terms—for this study concerns the role that ethnicity plays in the transition from either first-generation immigrants or those Mexican Americans native to the Southwest who had been mostly isolated from mainstream currents to a second, U.S.-born generation or a generation (composed of both children of immigrants and of those descended from the nineteenth-century communities) that on the whole began to understand that it was part of U.S. society and that it had to compromise between its ethnic roots and full incorporation and assimilation into American society. Olivier Zunz has recently stressed the importance for ethnic historians to transcend their concentration on the immigrant process and to view ethnicity from a larger perspective. "Enclaves exist," he writes of ethnic communities, "but they are only temporary, and this ethnicity is best understood within a framework of generations."[34]

The problem of ethnicity and generational change in turn touches on still larger issues in American life. For embedded in this research problem is the issue of the distribution of power and rewards. Ethnicity in a capitalist society with its class-racial-ethnic-gender divisions that are fundamental to its survival assumes a role in the distribution of power and wealth. In the struggle for power and wealth, my question is what role does ethnicity play in this drama? How does ethnicity, for example, manifest itself in class terms both outside and inside an ethnic group? How does ethnicity influence political movements aimed at narrowing the gap between the haves and the have nots? How does ethnicity affect political ideologies such as that embedded in the American dream, which, on the one hand, sustains the hegemony of the ruling class and, on the other, provides the ideological impetus whereby the exploited seek to modify if not overthrow this hegemony? How does ethnicity mediate class consciousness and generational consciousness? How does ethnicity affect acculturation and assimilation—the American way of life—

which can likewise be used to dominate but can also be a rallying cry for the politics of rising expectations? And what is the relationship between ethnicity and identity in a society that upholds equality but uses ethnic and race differences to assure class divisions? These are some of the questions directly and indirectly probed in the present study.

Yet while I have framed these questions in the form of a social science approach, I concede that I provide answers more in the form of a narrative historian. "The two essential ways in which narrative history differs from structural history," Lawrence Stone notes in observing the revival of narrative history in the 1970s, "is that its arrangement is descriptive rather than analytical and that its central focus is on men [and women] not circumstances."[35] I am ultimately more interested in active human beings and their *mentalité* than I am in passive and static social science models and graphs. To me, history is people. People make history even under the most difficult circumstances. Hence, I have chosen to emphasize the human dimensions while at the same time providing reflections on the larger questions involved. Narrative history, of course, is not devoid of analysis, as Stone adds: "The kind of narrative which I have in mind is not that of the simple antiquarian reporter or annalist. It is a narrative directed by some 'pregnant principle' and which possesses a theme and an argument."[36] This narrative and commentary examine the specific variable of ethnic leadership. Consequently, I hope that my work, in addition to providing insights on the evolving role of ethnicity in U.S. history, will make a contribution to the genre of ethnic leadership studies. I chose a study of ethnic leadership to reflect what I perceive to be new substantive changes affecting the Mexican-American communities by the 1930s and into the 1940s and 1950s not only because archival materials for this period lent themselves better to such a study, but because I came to agree with John Higham's point that studies on ethnic leadership could in fact be appropriate conduits for the understanding of broader social changes within ethnic communities. In his 1978 edited volume *Ethnic Leadership in America* (which regrettably did not contain a section on Latinos), Higham stresses the importance of examining ethnic leadership as a strategy for capturing the essence of the role of ethnicity in American life. "We set out to study leadership in order to gain a fresh perspective on the nature of ethnic groups in American society," Higham writes of the work of his co-contributors.[37]

Higham also raises questions which my study likewise seeks to illuminate: "What roles have leaders played in the history of America's ethnic groups? What objectives have they employed, what styles exhibited, what problems faced, what results achieved?"[38] Higham, at the same time, mollifies a concern that became evident to me as I pursued my work on ethnic leadership. That is, as I began to present some of my early findings, inevitably someone would question the relevance or need to study the elite. After all, were we as Chicano Studies scholars not part of a new generation of ethnic studies scholars who had condemned the history establishment for mostly concentrating on the "great man" approach to U.S. history to the exclusion of the people's history? And what of history from the bottom up? These are valid concerns and Higham addresses them in this way. First of all, he acknowledges that in the field of ethnic history, for the above reasons, there has been too little stress on leadership. "Leaders must in a sense stand above the rank and file and move in a larger world," he notes. "That is why the problems and tasks of leadership are easily neglected in ethnic studies today." [39] Yet Higham believes that this neglect has in fact created a significant gap in ethnic history. For history is not just the masses but the leadership or vanguards that rise from them. In a statement that I myself would qualify, Higham adds that in a sense "ethnic groups in an open society are, in some degree yet to be specified, the creation of their leaders." [40] I would qualify Higham's words in order not to be misunderstood as to the nature of my study. I am not per se suggesting that the social changes and evolving ideologies resulting from the emergence of a new leadership—the Mexican-American Generation—were in all cases pursued and perceived by rank-and-file Mexican Americans. This remains an examination of leadership, albeit a leadership that must be understood in its tense interaction with the masses. Evidence of the consciousness and actions or reactions of the masses is more difficult to obtain, especially if the focus is on the politics of a community, and hence my study can only infer that due to the viability of certain movements generated by the leadership something resembling a larger social movement was occurring. In any event, it is the Mexican-American Generation that as a dynamic political entity imposes on its historical period a particular temper and mentality. As Mannheim notes:

> If we are speaking of the "spirit of an epoch," for example, we must realize, as in the case of other factors, too, that this *Zeitgeist,* the mentality of a period, does not pervade the whole society at a given time. The mentality which is commonly attributed to an epoch has its proper seat in one (homogeneous or heterogeneous) social group which acquires special significance at a particular time, and is thus able to put its own intellectual stamp on all the other groups without destroying or absorbing them. [41]

In practical terms, Higham goes on to observe correctly that the study of ethnic leadership is fundamental because of what he terms the amorphousness of ethnic groups. As ethnic groups evolve, as they undergo the process of change within U.S. society, as they move from being immigrants to American ethnics, the difficulty of gauging these changes becomes a more difficult undertaking for the historian.[42] It is certainly easier to isolate and study a pioneer-immigrant generation with its more visible and notable ethnic cultural artifacts and institutions. But what of the intergenerational changes? This becomes a more difficult task in dealing with the retention of ethnic culture, ethnic politics, and ethnic consciousness. Yet by exploring the leadership component of an ethnic community and the changes that they represent and help bring about, the historian may be in a better position to understand changes within the larger community. "Accordingly we may find in configurations of leadership a distinctiveness and clarity that disappears when we look at the group as a whole," Higham concludes. "Leaders focus the consciousness of an ethnic group and make its identity visible."[43]

A Generational Approach to Chicano History

If my study can be read for larger implications concerning the role of ethnicity and specifically ethnic leadership in U.S. history, what is its place in the relatively new and developing field of Chicano history? In my earlier study of Mexican immigrants, *Desert Immigrants: The Mexicans of El Paso, 1880–1920* (1981), I examined the life and culture of the first large wave of Mexican nationals who crossed the border seeking a better life and a haven from economic and political instability. Once in the United States, and concentrated in the Southwest, Mexican immigrant workers formed the labor base for the developing extractive economy of the region, which was characterized by an extensive railroad network, mining, smelting, agriculture, and ranching. Exploited as cheap labor and facing racial as well as cultural prejudice in a relationship described by some scholars as "internal colonialism" or a "segmented labor market" and never fully considering themselves as genuine immigrants, *mexicanos* nostalgically continued to look southward.[44] They hoped, like many other immigrants, to return home eventually. For Mexicans who traversed an open desert rather than an ocean to reach the United States, the practicality of return was more a reality than a dream. Many returned. Others returned but only to come back. Still others never returned. In any event, the great migration from Mexico between 1900 and 1930, when more than a million Mexicans crossed the border, transformed earlier nineteenth-century Mexican communities (with the exception of northern New Mexico) into predominantly immigrant communities. This study is an attempt to explore the political, social, and cultural changes affecting those communities by examining the succeeding Mexican-American Era as exemplified by the leadership of that period: The Mexican-American Generation. To a degree, it is a study of the children of the "desert immigrants." In exploring this transition we can acquire a better understanding of the movement from immigrant life and culture to that of American ethnics.

A key in conceptualizing this transformation concerns the fact that since the annexation of the Southwest following the Mexican War, Mexicans in the United States have not fully shared in many of the benefits of American society despite their significant economic and cultural contributions. Faced with a legacy of conquest as well as class, racial, and cultural prejudice, Mexican Americans have also experienced serious identity problems. Are they Americans or Mexicans? What does it mean to be Mexican American? Are Mexicans white or people of color? Yet Mexican Americans did not engage in significant civil rights protests related to their status and identity in the United States until the 1930s due to their particular history.

Like American Indians and Afro Americans, Mexicans initially became Americans not through voluntary immigration but through conquest and annexation. Although Mexicans received U.S. citizenship after the Mexican War of the 1840s, Anglo Americans rapidly dispossessed them of their lands and treated them as second-class citizens. This period I term the Conquest Era. The decline of the Mexican landed and political elite, moreover, left many native communities devoid of leadership. Those who politically survived either pursued an accommodationist, nonconfrontational strategy, such as the Californio elite and the "ricos" of New Mexico, or else participated in the politics of protest, or what Navarro terms "insurrection politics," as manifested in such violent uprisings as the California bandit activity, the Cortina War in south Texas, the El Paso Salt War, and the movement of Las Gorras Blancas in New Mexico. Together this accommodationist and rebellious leadership, reacting to their shared central historical experience of the U.S. conquest, could be considered the first political generation in Chicano history: the Conquered Generation. Forced into defensive enclaves, Mexicans during the last half of the nineteenth century were too economically weak, politically marginal or compromised, geographically isolated, and not sufficiently acquainted with U.S. traditions, ideology, and language to launch a civil rights offensive.[45]

Massive immigration from Mexico, what Rodolfo Álvarez has termed in a biological sense the "Migrant Generation," during the first two decades of the twentieth century and what I term the Immigrant Era augmented and revitalized the Mexican presence north of the border but did not create the conditions for a civil rights movement either.[46] Nineteenth-century Mexican communities now became predominantly immigrant ones. At no other time in Chicano history have Mexican immigrants and refugees so totally dominated the Spanish-speaking Mexican condition in the Southwest and elsewhere. Hired as cheap laborers for the booming industries of the Southwest, and later the Midwest, Mexican immigrant workers possessed a limited stake in U.S. society despite their indispensable economic contributions: to find work, save money, and hopefully return to a better life in Mexico. Immigrants protested against the most overt forms of labor and racial exploitation and oppression but adjusted to difficult working and living conditions. Immigrant workers as well as political refugees from the Mexican Revolution of 1910 were grateful for a haven in the United States, comparing it to economically depressed and revolutionary-ridden Mexico. Immigrant leadership, or what could be termed the Immigrant Generation, expressed itself as a political generation in relation to the central experiences of this period: immigration and the Mexican Revolution of 1910. Leadership was located in the heads of immigrant mutual benefit societies, mexicano patriotic associations, the Mexican consuls, the various political factions in exile during the Revolution of 1910, refugee newspaper publishers and editors, and a small number of labor leaders. Together the Immigrant Generation viewed itself as "México de afuera"—Mexico of the Outside. *Mexicano* leaders, along with the immigrant masses, for the most part saw their experiences north of the border as transitory. They hoped to return to *la patria* and a better life. They possessed a Mexican dream, not an American dream. They adjusted to life in the United States by attempting to reproduce a Mexican world for themselves. Having just enough time and energy to make a living, unwilling to give up their Mexican citizenship, living adjacent to their homeland, and seeing themselves as temporary sojourners, Mexican immigrants were not ripe candidates for a protracted civil rights struggle.[47]

However, by the 1930s the political climate among Mexicans, especially the children of immigrants, began to change. This was partially caused by a major demographic shift. Owing to a high birth rate among Mexican immigrants, plus the curtailment of immigration from Mexico during the Great Depression, native-born Mexican Americans rose to majority status among the Mexican population. Although undoubtedly undercounting people of Mexican descent, the 1930 U.S. Census revealed that 56.6 percent of the 1,422,533 Mexicans enumerated were native-born U.S. citizens.[48] Growing up in this country, Mexican Americans were increasingly more acculturated, bilingual, and, as a result, more politically functional. Formally educated to a greater extent than ever before, they became better socialized to their rights as U.S. citizens. Mexican Americans expressed pride in both their U.S. citizenship and Mexican heritage, although not without degrees of insecurity regarding identity. Coming of political age during the reform period of the New Deal and experiencing the patriotic idealism generated by World War II, Mexican Americans expected more from American life than immigrants. For Mexican Americans, there was no going back to Mexico. The United States was their home. They hungrily pursued the American dream. Generational changes among Mexican Americans, of course, were not uniform, as sociologist Joan Moore suggests. One's geographical position (urban or rural) often determined one's level of acculturation. Yet on the whole, more Mexican Americans were experiencing acculturation or Americanization by the 1930s than ever before.[49]

At the same time, despite more education, increased industrial jobs, and urbanization, Mexican Americans still faced persistent conditions of poverty, discrimination, and cultural alienation. Even those who through initiative, luck, or family circumstances had achieved middle- or lower-middle-class status remained, with few exceptions, economically vulnerable due to their dependence on a poor Mexican community and clientele as well as without access to political power. While the inspirational leadership of Franklin Roosevelt sustained Mexican Americans in their belief in the American dream, the New Deal failed to uplift most Mexicans, along with many other Americans, out of their economically underdeveloped state or their second-class political position. Renewed production during World War II did not accomplish this either. Not only were more Mexicans migrating to urban areas, but increased immigration from Mexico by the 1940s added to an already poor population living in congested neighborhoods and characterized by greater social and cultural dislocation and alienation, especially among youth. What was different in this period of increased aspirations but continued poverty and discrimination was the emergence of a political generation of middle-class and working-class leaders who were determined to wage protracted struggles for change in the Mexican communities and who demanded a rightful place for Mexican Americans in U.S. society. This was the Mexican-American Generation.

Unfortunately, in Chicano history the period of the 1930s through the 1950s—the Mexican-American Era—has not received much scholarly attention. Attracted to what were perceived as more authentically Mexican periods and in search of roots, most of the key studies in the still youthful genre of Chicano history have focused on either the nineteenth century or the Immigrant Era of the early twentieth century. Notable exceptions have been the work by Guadalupe San Miguel on educational issues and Richard García on San Antonio's Mexican-American community. Still others have acknowledged some labor struggles during the 1930s, but on the whole the Mexican-American Era has not been considered a rich research period in Chicano history. Rather than being appreciated for its own complexity, the period has generally been seen as only a transition between the Immigrant Era and the better-known Chicano Movement or Chicano Generation, which captured national and international attention in its militant struggle for self-determination and a new ethnic identity during the 1960s and early 1970s. Barrera, for example, uses terms such as "complex," "explosion of political activity," and "development without parallel in Chicano history" to describe the Chicano Movement, thereby implying that all previous historical movements were simply "antecedents"—to use his term—for the ultimate climax of the Chicano Movement.[50]

Mexican Americans revises the general impressionistic views of those scholars who, despite few studies of this period and generation, have too quickly classified many Mexican-American leaders between the 1930s and 1950s as "accommodationist" (in the worst sense) and as people who accepted negative views of themselves as pronounced by a hostile Anglo community. Political scientists and sociologists such as Álvarez, de la Garza, García, Navarro, Cuellar, and Guzmán, for example, have scolded much of this leadership for pursuing the "politics of adaptation" or the "politics of accommodation."[51] Álvarez patronizes what he also refers to as the Mexican-American Generation by charging that it failed to comprehend the economic subordination of Mexicans in the United States: "Lack of education meant that the Mexican American did not have sufficient understanding of the nature of the society in which he lived and its economic system to even know that he was being treated unfairly."[52] Incorrectly suggesting that the politics of the Mexican-American Generation was exclusively a middle-class phenomenon, Barrera refuses to see any goals besides integration and assimilation as characterizing this period and unfairly criticizes this generation's lack of concern for "community." Romanticizing the concept of a "lost homeland" among Chicanos, Chávez accuses members of the Mexican-American Generation of selling out their heritage. "The person who could shed his ethnic background, move out of the *barrio,* even out of the Southwest," he writes, "was to be regarded as a success."[53] Moreover, these writers erroneously suggest that a clear division exists between Mexican-American politics of the 1930s and that of the post-World War II years. They categorize the first period as "apolitical" and the second as a politicized one. "The politicization of Mexican American communities in the Southwest," Cuellar wrongly proposes, "dates only from the years following World War II."[54] Guzmán classifies the leaders of the Mexican-American Era, especially those who began to come of political age prior to World War II, as "expressive" or interested only in playing symbolic roles rather than engaging in "purposive goal-oriented activity."[55]

Yet a closer reading of the Mexican-American Era suggests a different history. The actual record reveals a generation much more complex in its makeup and in its goals. The Mexican-American Generation, including those members who became politically involved in the 1930s, was uncompromising in its demands for first-class citizenship and pursued these goals through a variety of tactics, including direct action. Furthermore, World War II rather than dividing links the struggles of the 1930s with those of the 1940s. Both the Great Depression and World War II can be seen together as forming the twin central historical experiences for a political generation committed to actively struggling for civil rights and first-class citizenship for Mexican Americans. World War II, with its stress on the preservation of democracy, intensifies this movement but does not give birth to it. The Mexican-American campaign for civil rights and a new identity envelops the entire period from the 1930s into the 1950s. The Mexican-American Era is set apart, on the one hand, from the Immigrant Era with its stress on the politics of immigration and a continued orientation toward Mexico and, on the other, from the succeeding and separatist-oriented Chicano Movement of the 1960s. While certain tendencies still flow from one to the other, nevertheless there exists between each what might be called "generational disequilibrium." [56] The dominant political generation of each era revises the goals of its predecessor and pursues different strategies to deal with the Mexican problem. Each period possesses a distinct spirit, mentality, or Zeitgeist. Each era or generation to one degree or another, as Feuer suggests, "deauthorizes" the previous one. [57]

Resorting to presentism (the mechanical interpretation of the past from a present-day perspective), or what Aileen Kraditor refers to as "relevance historians," various Chicano Studies scholars, particularly nonhistorians, have further misread and miscalculated the meaning and significance of the Mexican-American Era by indicting its leadership for succumbing to "assimilationist tendencies" at the expense of Mexican identity and culture. Alvarez, for example, incorrectly and unfairly writes of Mexican Americans of this period: "Because of his psychic identification with the superordinate Anglo, he abandoned his own language and culture and considered himself personally superior to the economically subordinate Migrant Generation." [58] And Chávez adds: "Trying to escape the discrimination aimed at their group, these Mexican-Americans disassociated themselves from anything Mexican, at times even boasting of their inability to speak Spanish." [59] Yet, as this study also reveals, the Mexican-American Generation experiencing the frustrating tensions between loyalty to ethnic background and Americanization resorted to embracing not full assimilation (if by assimilation here one means the unconditional surrender of one culture or way of life to another), or what Joshua Fishman calls "de-ethnization," but cultural pluralism, or what Higham terms "pluralistic integration" and a pluralism as much as possible on Mexican-American terms. [60] The Mexican-American Era represents a clear transition to the Chicano Era of the 1960s but it is more than a transition. It possesses a character of its own, a richness of political struggle, and a deep search for identity. Scholars must come to terms with it on its own grounds.

Organizing community movements in different areas of the Southwest, the Mexican-American Generation attempted to rectify the contradictions affecting Mexican-American life. Active in organizations such as the League of United Latin American Citizens (LULAC), the Mexican-American Movement, the Spanish-Speaking Congress, the Unity Leagues, the Community Service Organization (CSO), La Asociación Nacional México-Americana (ANMA), and the American GI Forum, as well as CIO locals and the Communist party, this political generation of Mexican Americans was, despite shared experiences, still too segmented by class, region, and level of acculturation to comprise a unified, much less monolithic, movement. These differences resulted in Mannheim's generation units. Middle-class reformers, for example, feared the influence of radicals, especially those associated with the Communist party.

Besides generation units comprised of such groupings as the middle class, the working class, radicals, and intellectuals, the Mexican-American Generation possessed other cleavages. One can distinguish what Feuer calls "multiple levels." [61] Hence the precursors of the Mexican-American Generation who became politicized due to their participation in World War I and who experienced the growing anti-Mexican prejudice of the 1920s comprise the first level. Mexican Americans who came of political age during the Great Depression form the second level. And, finally, what Camarillo has called the G.I. Generation—those who returned from the war determined to bring about social changes—constitute the third and last level. [62] Despite an age difference—bridging in some cases two biological generations—in political and ideological terms, these levels represent a political generation in their commitment to achieving first-class integration and a new identity for Mexican Americans in a period shaped by the Great Depression and World War II. They shared not only certain common experiences (not just major historical crises but the indignities of discrimination at the same time they were becoming aware of their rights as U.S. citizens), but also similar hopes and disillusionments with older forms of political responses more appropriate to an immigrant population. Generation units and multiple levels within the Mexican-American Generation can be illustrated by the accompanying table.

As a political generation, then, the Mexican-American Generation possessed several distinguishing characteristics. This was a generation composed predominantly of native-born Mexican Americans and led by lower middle-class professionals and businessmen, as well as those of working-class backgrounds in the case of labor unions and radical organizations. This was a generation that viewed itself as a permanent one in the United States.

TABLE 1. *The Mexican-American Generation*

Multiple levels	Generation units			
	Middle class	*Working class*	*Radicals*	*Intellectuals*
Precursors: World War I	×	×	×	×
Great Depression cohort	×	×	×	×
World War II cohort	×	×	×	×

The recognition of permanency and the fact that Mexican Americans were more highly Americanized than Mexican immigrants led to an understanding that the Mexican-American struggle had to be for integration rather than separation from U.S. society. This was a generation that gave high priority to the achievement of civil rights for all Mexicans in the United States. For Mexican Americans economic success was unthinkable without full civil rights. Socialized into believing in American democracy by their training in U.S. schools, by their gravitation to the Democratic party under Franklin Roosevelt, and most important by their participation in World War II, the Mexican-American Generation realized better than any previous political generation of Mexicans in the United States the contradictions between American ideals and practices. However, they believed that these contradictions could be overcome or tempered until a later and more propitious time for greater fundamental change through peaceful reforms.

Moreover, the Mexican-American Generation believed not only in achieving civil rights but in protecting and advancing them by engaging in a process of political integration. This included participation in the electoral process through voting, through endorsing candidates and issues which would support the interests of Mexican Americans, through encouraging Mexican Americans to run for political office, and through promoting Mexican-American political organizations. The Mexican-American Generation aspired to achieve integration into the political mainstream but at the same time realized that ethnic politics was perhaps the most effective vehicle to obtain its goal. As Michael Parenti correctly observes of the relationship between ethnicity and politics, "ethnics can . . . sometimes behave politically as ethnics while remaining firmly American." [63] Through their concentration on civil rights issues and the electoral process, members of the Mexican-American Generation supported the development of community and ethnic consciousness: Mexican Americanism. Not only did this generation organize new forms of political associations among Mexicans in the United States, but it utilized preexisting ones such as mutual benefit societies as a basis for political organization. Centered in a Mexican world composed of both Mexican

Americans and Mexican immigrants, the Mexican-American Generation sought broad consensus. It employed both Mexican and American cultural traditions to develop a form of Mexican-American enlightenment. Through a strong emphasis on the uplifting and integrating character of formal education, the Mexican-American Generation encouraged all Mexicans to dream beyond their current more menial conditions and to use education as a major means for self and community improvements. Finally, the Mexican-American Generation possessed a world view of a culturally pluralistic society in the United States. Proud of their Mexican origins and of their ability to function in two cultural worlds, Mexican Americans—the term popularized during this period in itself is symbolic—looked to an eventual synthesis and co-existence between the culture of their parents and their desire to be fully accepted as U.S. citizens. This synthesis was not peculiar to Mexican Americans. As one observer of Italian Americans noted in 1942: "[L]ife in the Italian Community today is not Italian, but Italian-American, and Little Italy, or what remains of it, is not an alien offshoot on American soil, but a merging of two cultures, with the American increasingly predominating over the Italian." [64]

Forged by particular historical experiences, the Mexican-American Generation brought forth formidable leaders. Although only partially successful in their objectives due to the intransigence of institutionalized forms of class and racial discrimination against Mexicans and the inability especially of middle-class Mexican-American leaders because of their class biases and "false consciousness" to comprehend the true nature of the U.S. class structure and of American racism, members of this political generation helped advance under very difficult and hostile conditions the historical struggle by Mexican Americans for self-determination. Mexican-American organizations, for example, achieved the desegregation of some of the Mexican schools in the Southwest. They also forced the desegregation of public facilities such as theaters and swimming pools. During and after World War II, they aided in removing certain discriminatory practices toward Mexicans in war-related occupations and in housing. Moreover, it was the Mexican-American Generation that achieved increased political representation as more Mexican Americans won public offices. In labor struggles, Mexican-American leaders played important roles in unionizing Mexican-American workers in particular industries. Such reforms by no means removed Mexican Americans from a subordinate position, nor did they completely eliminate the crisis of identity. Nevertheless, seen as part of a historical process of change, these reform struggles served notice that Mexican Americans would no longer accept second-class citizenship. As such, this movement predated the better-known mobilization of Chicanos in the 1960s and 1970s.

Conclusion

This study is a panorama or what Wohl calls a "collective biography" of the Mexican-American Generation.[65] It is not intended to be inclusive of every single political leader, organization, or movement that sprang out of the Mexican-American communities between the 1930s and 1950s. Some organizations such as the American G.I. Forum in Texas have already been specifically examined even if uncritically so.[66] Still others, such as the Community Service Organization (CSO), do not apparently possess sufficient archival sources. Instead, my study evolves out of the search and location of archival sources that allow a more detailed and substantive analysis of the Mexican-American Era and more specifically of the Mexican-American Generation. The discoveries of archival collections, along with oral histories, convinced me that an anthology on the Mexican-American Generation—in this case an anthology written exclusively by me—was possible. I use the term "anthology" deliberately because I believe that each chapter can stand on its own as a case study of this political generation. Hence, I have compiled a number of case studies of the Mexican-American Generation based on specific groups of leaders, organizations, or issues pertinent to the time. Three sections comprise the study. The first, "The Middle Class," deals with those Mexican-American leaders who, mediated by their middle-class positions and consciousness, struggled for fundamental civil rights, ethnic respectability, cultural pluralism, and effective political representation. The second section, "Labor and the Left," examines those Mexican Americans of working-class roots who emerged as labor leaders in the CIO struggles of the period and who interpreted first-class citizenship in working-class terms. In addition, this section concerns the complementary emergence of radical Mexican-American leaders closely connected with the Communist party, who, pursuing a Popular Front strategy, sought to achieve practical reforms for a working class still in the process of recognizing itself as a class. The third section, "Mexican-American Intellectuals," studies the role that three of the most prominent Mexican-American intellectuals of their time played and their contributions to what Richard García has aptly called the "making of the Mexican-American mind." [67] It is my hope that this panorama of the Mexican-American Generation will stimulate other studies on additional topics concerning this generation and its historical period. Finally, it is my hope that other scholars of American ethnicity will benefit from this study, which seeks to understand the changing character of ethnicity.

PART ONE

The Middle Class

CHAPTER TWO

In Search of America: The League of United Latin American Citizens (LULAC)

Respect your citizenship and preserve it; honor your country, maintain its tradition in the spirit of its citizens, and embody your self into its culture and civilization.

Love the men of your race, be proud of your origins and maintain it immaculate, respect your glorious past, and help to defend the rights of your own people.

—The LULAC Code, 1929

The search for America and their place in it shaped the consciousness and politics of the Mexican-American Generation. Mexican Americans, however, did not define "Americanization" in the patronizing and ethnocentric terms characteristic of many Anglo-American educators and welfare workers. They interpreted Americanization in light of the perceived need to forge a movement that would help break the economic, political, and cultural isolation of Mexican Americans in the United States during the early twentieth century. The Mexican-American Generation aspired to move into the mainstream of American life. They recognized that Mexican Americans could no longer adequately function in the marginal ethnic enclaves of the Southwest that had survived the nineteenth century or in the immigrant culture superimposed after 1900 as thousands of Mexicans crossed the border seeking work and political asylum. Instead, the Mexican-American Generation sought to advance from their past and to see themselves as permanent citizens of the United States with all the rights and privileges of American citizenship. They sought to synthesize their experience based on their relationship to their Mexican roots, their Mexican-American reality, and their search for an American future. No Mexican-American organization better exemplified this search for America than the League of United Latin American Citizens, founded in 1929 and the oldest Mexican-American civil rights association in the United States.

Origins of a Political Generation

The Mexican-American Generation, as a political entity, began to come of age in the 1930s, but its embryo can be detected in the Roaring Twenties. In this decade, Mexican Americans already stressed the need for a new political direction for themselves based on two basic needs: the importance of instilling a new consciousness among Mexican Americans—to develop a "new Mexican" in the United States—and the need to organize new forms of political and civic organizations—a "new politics"—that would best serve their interests separate from those of Mexican immigrants. The confluence of these two needs can be seen in south Texas, the cradle of the Mexican-American Generation.

The importance of a new political movement for Mexican Americans in south Texas was emphasized by the economic and social transformations affecting the region. Increased agricultural production during World War I integrated south Texas into the market economy of the United States. Possessing a year-long warm climate, south Texas became the "winter garden" of the nation, producing a variety of commercial fruits and vegetables. Economic development along capitalist agricultural lines in turn changed the class structure of south Texas. Texas-born Mexican-American farmers and ranchers as well as sharecroppers found themselves unable to compete with agribusiness and some lost what small family lands they possessed. In their place, or alongside them, came thousands of Mexican immigrant wage-workers to pick the crops produced by the new mode of production. The introduction of this large immigrant work force plus the need to segregate Mexican immigrants and dislocated Mexican Americans as a cheap agricultural labor force responsible for producing surplus value intensified earlier patterns of discrimination and racial hostility toward people of Mexican descent.[1]

Indeed, the "Mexican problem" emerged in the 1920s. Anglos adversely affected by the rise of agribusiness vented their resentments and frustrations toward Mexican immigrants, whom they characterized as an economic and social threat to Texas and the rest of the country. They charged mexicanos with introducing crime, illiteracy, and diseases and with mongrelizing the social-ethnic base of American society. Critics of Mexican immigration, while unsuccessfully calling for restrictions and a quota on immigration from Mexico similar to those imposed on southern and eastern Europeans, made no distinctions between Mexican immigrants and native-born Mexican Americans. "Those who favor the restriction of incoming Mexicans," one observer wrote, "are inclined to put all Texas-Mexicans into one category and to characterize them generally as ignorant, slothful, unclean, dangerous, and incapable of assimilation or of good citizenship." [2]

Such antagonisms in conjunction with labor exploitation directed at people of Mexican descent during the 1920s, plus a previous history of racism in Texas and elsewhere, created objective conditions for efforts toward Mexican-American political unity.[3] M. C. González, one of the original founders of LULAC, categorized five types of discrimination faced by all Mexicans in Texas during the 1920s. These included (1) public school segregation of Mexican-American children; (2) segregation and discrimination in public facilities such as restaurants, movie theaters, swimming pools, and barbershops; (3) the establishment of "white man's" primaries to prevent blacks and Mexican Americans from exercising their right of suffrage; (4) discrimination in housing by not allowing Mexicans to purchase real estate in certain sections of towns and cities such as San Antonio; and (5) discrimination in the administration of justice by preventing Mexican Americans from serving on juries.[4] In addition, Mexicans, regardless of nationality, suffered much violence directed against them. "The killings of Mexicans without provocation is so common as to pass almost unnoticed," the *New York Times* commented about Texas in 1922.[5] Much of this violence came at the hands of the infamous Texas Rangers. Of course most Mexicans also faced job discrimination. Both rural and urban employers profited from Mexicans as cheap unskilled labor and refused to jeopardize such a lucrative labor pool by supporting educational and job opportunities.

Yet, despite heightened discrimination against Mexicans in south Texas, economic development plus the needs of an expanding Mexican population produced some advances and even relative prosperity for a few Mexican Americans in the growing towns and cities of the region. Those whose families had previously been merchants or who had recently migrated from the rural areas with sufficient capital to open small stores shared, although unequally, in the south Texas boom. Most catered to the Mexican communities—the "Mexiquitos"—and hence experienced mobility within a Mexican-American context. A few *comerciantes*, especially along the border, expanded enough to also service Anglo customers. An even smaller number with better opportunities for education became lawyers, teachers, journalists, and politicians. In effect, a small Mexican-American middle-class emerged or survived from an earlier period.[6]

The Mexican-American middle class, however, confronted a contradiction. It participated in the new prosperity of south Texas but still faced racial, cultural, and social discrimination. The notice No Mexicans Allowed affected them just as it did immigrant workers. Hence, the Mexican-American middle class sowed the seeds of discontent over the magnitude and persistence of racial discrimination and called for its eradication. Yet the middle class recognized that the struggle against racism would have to take a different form and have a different emphasis than before. Mexicans through older forms of organization such as mutual aid societies and through Mexican consulates had historically protested against discrimination. But antidiscrimination was never effectively linked with the issue of integration. This was mainly because previous generations of both native-born citizens, still living in a predominantly Mexican world, and recent immigrants from Mexico did not share an interest in Americanizing their experiences. Many, including the older native-born, still saw themselves first and foremost as mexicanos and found little attraction in Anglo-American culture. In addition, their exposure to racism repelled them from thoughts of integration, much less acculturation. Post-World War I young Mexican-American leaders saw things differently. "The Mexican mind was 'Porfirista'"; historian Richard García distinguishes between the intellectual and political world of Mexican political refugees and the new generation of Mexican Americans. "[T]he Mexican-American was 'Rooseveltian.' The former was conservative, the latter liberal."[7] It was not enough to cry out against discrimination. Mexican Americans also had to learn the culture, language, and political system of the United States in order to effectively wage their political struggles and to integrate into the system. There was no other way to overcome discrimination and underdevelopment.

This new approach conformed to the reality of a new generation of Mexican Americans. Young Mexican Americans were not only more Americanized through greater exposure to Anglo education, but some had fought for American democracy in World War I. If they were good enough to risk their lives for their country, they believed they had a right to all the benefits of American citizenship.[8] Believing in their destiny as American citizens, middle-class leaders hoped to convert their less politically conscious fellow Mexican Americans. "He [the Mexican American leader] realizes full well," O. Douglas Weeks of the University of Texas and a close student of Mexican-American politics in the 1920s observed, "that the greatest stumbling block in the way of accomplishing this end is the Mexican-American himself, who possesses no very clear conception of the significance of the privileges and duties of his American citizenship."[9] Part of this new socialization had to involve a sober recognition of and acculturation to the Anglo-American transformation of south Texas.[10]

Besides a change of consciousness, a "new politics" was in order. Unlike the older generation of Mexican-American politicos who subordinated themselves to Anglo political machines, purchased the Mexican-American vote, and literally herded Mexican Americans to the polls, those involved in the "new politics" hoped to cleanse Mexican-American politics by stressing nonpartisan civic action and avoidance of machine politics. A new direction would be followed. "I feel that no longer are we to go forward along the lines set by our fathers in these varying times and constantly changing conditions," M. C. González observed, "and we must seek new, and let us hope, better ways."[11] This new consciousness and new politics would give birth to a new citizen: the Mexican American.

The Formation of LULAC

The initial effort at a new political movement among Mexican Americans commenced in 1921 with the organization of the Sons of America in San Antonio. Comprised of mostly lower middle-class professionals, the Sons stressed socializing Mexican Americans to their rights as U.S. citizens and obtaining equal rights for them. Unfortunately, personal rivalries within the Sons soon splintered the organization. Some dissidents formed the Sons of Texas while still others founded the Knights of America led by attorney M. C. González.[12] When still a fourth Mexican-American organization, the League of Latin American Citizens, appeared in 1927, Mexican-American leaders became alarmed over the level of fractionalization. To remedy the situation and redirect efforts toward political unity, Ben Garza of Council No. 4 of the Sons of America and González of the Knights took the lead in advocating a merger of the different organizations. They convinced prominent attorney Alonso S. Perales as head of the League to commence negotiations with president James Tafolla of the Sons. The possibilities of unity between the League and the Sons in San Antonio at first appeared bright. Regrettably, the unity movement sputtered as Tafolla soon attacked the other organizations as traitors and insisted that unity could come only by all other groups joining the Sons of America. When Tafolla and Council No. 1 of the Sons refused an accommodation with the other organizations, Ben Garza of Council No. 4 of the Sons proposed instead a merger of his council, the Knights, and Perales's League. Perales, writing from Nicaragua, where he was serving as part of a special U.S. mission for the State Department, applauded Garza's suggestion and stressed the urgency of unification. With Perales's support as well as that of González and the Knights, Garza and Council No. 4 formally separated from the Sons and called for a unity convention to be held in Corpus Christi on February 17, 1929, for the purpose of founding a new Mexican-American association.[13]

Twenty-five designated delegates attended the convention held in Obreros Hall. An additional 150 Mexican Americans participated as nonvoting members. They came from throughout south Texas: Brownsville, La Grulla, Encino, McAllen, Alice, Robestown, Austin, Corpus Christi, Harlingen, and, of course, San Antonio. The leading figures included Ben Garza, self-educated restaurant owner and head of the Corpus Christi delegation; attorney Alonso Perales, educated in Washington, D.C., one of the most important Mexican Americans in Texas, and a recent envoy to Central America; M. C. González, an attorney who represented the Mexican consulate in San Antonio and the head of the Knights of America; Judge J. T. Canales of Brownsville and a former state legislator; and Professor J. Luz Sáenz of McAllen, a leading educator in south Texas. Other delegates appear to have been additional professionals and small merchants. Symbolizing a belief in God and country, one delegate commenced the proceedings by reading a prayer written by George Washington.[14]

The convention unanimously agreed to fuse all three represented organizations and to form what delegates called the League of United Latin-American Citizens (LULAC). The convention also agreed to restrict its membership to U.S. citizens of Latin extraction. English would be the official language of LULAC.[15] Moreover, delegates adopted a code that contained LULAC's general beliefs. Bridging the past, present, and future, LULAC proposed a synthesis of Mexican, Mexican-American, and U.S. experiences and traditions. Key aspects of the code included:

> Respect your citizenship, conserve it; honor your country, maintain its traditions in the minds of your children, incorporate yourself in the culture and civilization;
>
> Love the men of your race, take pride in your origins and keep it immaculate; respect your glorious past and help to vindicate your people;
>
> Study the past of your people, or the country to which you owe your citizenship; learn to handle with purity the two most essential languages, English and Spanish.[16]

The convention ended its deliberations by inviting delegates to a constitutional convention to be held in Corpus Christi on May 18 and 19.[17] At the Corpus Christi constitutional convention, the assembled delegates further pledged their commitment to LULAC as the vehicle for the elimination of discrimination and the achievement of full citizenship rights for Mexican Americans. They elected a Supreme Council with Ben Garza as first president general and took an oath "to be Loyal to the Government of the United States of America, and support its Constitution and to obey its laws and . . . teach [their] children to be good, loyal, and true American citizens."[18] The adopted constitution outlined the aims and purposes of LULAC. Noting that Mexican Americans had now been "roused from our slumber," LULAC proposed to join "the enlightened races of today."[19]

Mexican Americans were to be socialized to U.S. citizenship. The goal was "to develop within the members of our race the best, purest and most perfect type of a true and loyal citizen of the United States of America." However, Mexican Americans could not assume their rightful place alongside other Americans as long as they faced discrimination. LULAC committed itself to a campaign, if not crusade, against such un-American practices. Reforms would be achieved not by radical measures but within the confines of the law. Americanization for LULAC meant struggling within the system not outside it and certainly not against it. Of course, Americanizing the Mexican-American experience also involved a cultural question. LULAC emphasized a dual cultural approach. For one, LULAC emphatically reiterated its support of English as the organization's official language and noted that only by learning English could Mexican Americans be integrated as full citizens. Yet, organizers of LULAC believed that they were of such an ethnic, class, and cultural background that they did not have to apologize for their Mexican roots and cultural traditions. Lulacers were not begging for integration. They were proud middle-class Mexican Americans who at the same time understood the need to adapt to American conditions. Consequently, Americanization was not perceived as a one-way street. Anglo Americans would also have to accommodate to the best of middle-class Mexican-American life. "We solemnly declare once and for all to maintain a sincere and respectful reverence for our racial origin of which we are proud." The LULAC constitution reaffirmed the need to maintain bilingualism and ethnic pride.[20]

Despite the affirmation of their ethnicity, or what Conzen regards as the invention of ethnicity, Lulacers still recognized the controversial nature of their exclusion of Mexican nationals and their adoption of English as LULAC's official language. Indeed, the exclusion of Mexican nationals had not been a unanimous decision. M. C. González, for example, had argued that ethnic unity required inclusion of Mexican nationals and that LULAC could utilize the support of the Mexican consulates along with mexicano self-help organizations such as the Comisiones Honoríficas and the Cruz Azul. LULAC leaders shortly after the constitutional convention felt obliged to elaborate on these aspects of the constitution. Alonso Perales stressed that exclusion of Mexican nationals was based solely on pragmatism. Mexican Americans continued to feel an ethnic and cultural affinity with Mexican nationals in the United States, but at the same time believed that only an organization composed of U.S. citizens could achieve the social reforms desired by all Mexicans, irrespective of citizenship. Perales observed that the past efforts to relieve discrimination by mutual aid societies, which contained many Mexican nationals as members, and through the Mexican consulates had proved fruitless. State and local authorities, especially in Texas, did not respect or fear groupings of noncitizens. Perales argued that only an association of U.S. citizens, such as LULAC, could effectively pressure and lobby for concrete reforms. Practicality also involved a recognition that Mexican Americans and Mexican nationals possessed certain distinct political interests that separated them. Whereas Mexican nationals looked toward their eventual repatriation to Mexico, Mexican Americans hoped for integration within the United States. Consequently, Perales feared that mixed organizations would pull in different directions and only confuse other Americans as to the nature and goals of such an organization. The dilemma of the relationship between Mexican Americans and Mexican nationals, of course, was enhanced by persistent immigration from Mexico and the propinquity of Mexico to the Southwest.[21]

On the question of the use of English, Lulacers reemphasized that this did not imply an abandonment of Spanish. Instead, *La Verdad* of Corpus Christi, a LULAC supporter, advocated bilingualism and called on Mexican Americans as well as Mexican nationals to retain their knowledge of Spanish. English, however, could not be avoided. It was indispensable for adjusting to life north of the border and it behooved Mexicans—of whatever nationality—to learn it. Moreover, Mexican Americans would be aided in their efforts to secure their rights and privileges as U.S. citizens by learning English and the customs of the country. The acquisition of their rights in turn would have a trickle-down effect and advance the protection of the rights of Mexican "aliens." Yet neither set of rights could be obtained without degrees of acculturation. One Mexican-American newspaper observed (not quite accurately but its point was well taken) that 75 percent of all Mexicans in the United States were American citizens. It chastised those Mexican Americans who remained skeptical that they could accommodate to the use of Spanish and English as well as adjust to dual cultures. If Mexican Americans did not claim their American citizenship, they would be doomed to remain "conquered people."[22]

Finally, the Corpus Christi constitutional convention underscored the need for Mexican-American unity. Without it, LULAC efforts to remove the barriers excluding Mexican Americans from full participation in American life would come to naught. "We should resist and attack energetically," the constitution proclaimed, "all machinations tending to prevent our social and political unification."[23] Weeks accurately concluded after attending the convention that LULAC represented a pioneer movement by a new generation of Mexican Americans to answer the question What does it mean to be an American of Mexican descent? Just as de Tocqueville and other European observers had witnessed efforts by earlier ethnic groups in the United States to wrestle with the issue of identity and status in the new American nation, so too did Weeks record a similar effort by Mexican Americans.[24]

From a few initial chapters in south Texas, LULAC expanded throughout the 1930s. By the commencement of World War II, it included more than 80 councils in Texas, New Mexico, Arizona, California, and Kansas. "Tejanos" with their more numerous councils, however, continued to dominate the organization. Indeed, most of LULAC's principal issues and activities took place in Texas until the postwar period. LULAC suffered during the war as many members left for military service. "LULAC's best and most active men, in its best and most active councils," the *LULAC News* observed in 1940, "are going forth to military camps and military expeditions for training against the grave hour that faces our nation."[25] LULAC rebounded after the war and by the 1950s possessed close to 100 councils throughout the Southwest and Midwest and with several thousand members became the largest and most influential Mexican-American organization.

Americanization

As pioneers searching for a Mexican-American place in the American sun, LULAC leaders attempted to define what Americanization meant to them. This involved both the evolution of a set of principles, what one historian has termed the "Mexican-American mind," as well as a praxis through particular struggles.[26] Mexican Americans in LULAC desired integration and acceptance as U.S. citizens but at the same time wanted to negotiate maintaining their Mexican heritage, or portions of it. Could such a pluralistic assimilation be accomplished? This was one of the questions faced by the initial LULAC generation. This and other issues were magnified by the pressures and transforming conditions of the Great Depression, World War II, and the cold war. LULAC's responses to these historical periods set the tone for much of the politics of the Mexican-American Generation. Although more radical Mexican Americans would challenge LULAC for political hegemony, they supplemented rather than replaced LULAC's basic reformism. Reform not revolution characterized Mexican-American politics. Moreover, despite its indictment of being too conservative by later Chicano scholars, LULAC's reformism has to be understood in its regional as well as in its class context. Devoid of a radical political culture such as existed in California, which was characterized by the greater activism of white radicals as well as a more militant labor movement, Texas proved to be less than fertile ground for a more radical form of Mexican-American politics such as would develop in southern California with the Spanish-Speaking Congress (see chapter 6). Fundamental to LULAC's reform initiatives was the stress on Americanization, or

LULAC's interpretation of Americanization, for the purpose of preparing Mexican Americans for their roles in American society and proving to other citizens the assimilable character of people of Mexican descent. Americanization for LULAC revolved around the following issues: (1) adjustment to American values and culture, (2) political socialization, (3) cultural pluralism, (4) desegregation, and (5) education.

Believing in the American system, LULAC sought to acculturate Mexican Americans to the prevailing social and cultural values of the United States. "Education, union and quick adaptation to the prevailing customs and usages of the best citizenry of this country," the *LULAC News* editorialized in 1931, "will steer us safely over the sea of racial discrimination and injustice to our proper place as citizens of this country," [27] In meetings, conventions, and through its monthly publication, the *LULAC News*, LULAC instructed its members about the foundations of American government. It stressed, for example, the democratic origins of the United States in the Magna Charta of thirteenth-century England. From the Magna Charta sprang the American Declaration of Independence. No document better expressed the political philosophy of the young nation than the U.S. Constitution. Lulacers could relate to the Constitution, Alonso Perales observed, because they themselves had struggled with the writing of their own LULAC constitution.[28] "Yes, the Constitution," the *LULAC News* inspired its readers, "the charter of Human Freedom, the heart of our nation, the guarantee of our civil liberties, the fortress of our institutions, the bulwark of our security, and the inspiration of our American way of life." [29] Besides being expected to acquire knowledge of American principles and institutions, Mexican Americans were encouraged to capture the spirit of Americanism. "It is upon the proper understanding of the spirit of America," one Mexican American pointed out, "that proper and natural assimilation into the life blood stream of this great nation can be accomplished." According to the Reverend James L. Navarro, this spirit involved fair play, sportsmanship, goodwill, human dignity, and individual rights.[30]

Fundamental to LULAC's effort to assimilate American democratic ideals was the need to reinforce the idea among Mexican Americans that they were as American as anyone else in the United States. Mexican Americans did not reject Mexican cultural traditions, but they were cautioned by LULAC not to participate in organizations that stressed mexicano nationalism. One LULAC leader in Corpus Christi warned members to avoid the local Mexican Chamber of Commerce, which he considered to be a "foreign organization." [31] Mexican Americans had to see themselves as Americans not Mexicans. LULAC rejected any suggestion that "real Americans" belonged to a particular ethnic group. "When Columbus came here he brought with him our forefathers," one LULAC official wrote, "but he did not bring a blood. Later, when Americo Vespucius named the country America, he had no particular racial blood in mind. So therefore we are all Americans because we live in America, and don't let anyone kid you." [32] No basic human differences existed between the average Mexican American and the average Anglo American. [33]

LULAC accentuated the inherent Americanism of Mexican Americans but still had to confront ethnic labeling. This involved the term "Latin American." The *LULAC News* acknowledged that the term had been a compromise to accommodate the particular position of Mexican Americans in the Southwest. LULAC needed a term that would not offend Anglos but at the same time convince them that Mexican Americans were American citizens and not just "Mexican." To stress the transitory nature of the term "Latin American," LULAC in 1936 approved eliminating the hyphen in "Latin-American." Addressing the "Question of the Hyphen," LULAC proposed that only one type of citizen existed in the United States "and that is the *American citizen,* and all other words used to describe that citizen of the United States are merely descriptive, participating of the qualities of an adjective and not of those of a noun." LULAC dispensed with the hyphen in its title in order to subordinate "Latin" and ascend the term "American Citizen." Some Lulacers suggested going even further. Council No. 132 of El Paso, for example, attempted to eliminate altogether the term "Latin," believing that it suggested self-segregation, invited discrimination, and confused the issue of American citizenship. Resisting a name change for fear that it would harm its already successful organizing, LULAC instead reacted to criticism by explaining that LULAC was an authentic American organization and that each letter in its name expressed patriotism: *L* stood for love of country; *U* for unity as American citizens; *L* for loyalty to country; *A* for advancement; and *C* for citizenship. [34]

The "American character" in particular attracted LULAC. It believed that the "genius" and "quality" of Americans had made the United States great and that Mexican Americans should develop such virtues. These included individualism. LULAC maintained that only in the United States could citizens progress and retain their individuality. Individualism was not foreign to the "Mexican character," but it could be refined and enhanced in an American context. Warning fellow Lulacers to beware of what he termed "Dependicitis," Nick Martínez noted in 1940 that Mexican Americans relied too much on federal relief measures such as the WPA. [35] The American character likewise included "American know-how." "I have lived long enough,"

Judge Canales wrote in 1932, "to see that part of our country, in California, Arizona, Colorado and New Mexico, which was then called The Great American Desert, turned into a very fertile region through American ingenuity."[36] However, American know-how could be of functional value only if Mexican Americans accepted the Puritan work ethic. "It becomes unpleasant for me to state that in the attainment of discipline we, the American Latins, have a late start," a LULAC official lamented.[37] Only through hard work and discipline could Mexican Americans achieve integration. Finally, Mexican Americans needed to accept the American idea of progress. Everything and anything was possible if one applied oneself.[38]

Acculturation also meant rejecting competing ideologies. During the 1930s, LULAC condemned both fascism and communism. In an editorial entitled "Beware of Communism," M. C. González pledged that LULAC would not only be an agent of Americanization, but that it enlisted in the combat against "communistic propaganda that is so destructive of the basic principles of Democracy and of American ideals."[39] At its 1938 convention in El Paso, LULAC furthered its antitotalitarian posture by adopting resolutions opposing "all seditious propaganda courting our subscription to the un-American doctrines of Communism, Nazism, fascism, and all other 'isms' detrimental to the present and future well-being of all Americans."[40] World War II, of course, proved the most important opportunity for LULAC and thousands of Mexican Americans to display their patriotism by defending the country against fascism. In late 1940 LULAC observed that the war raging in Europe was of vital interest to all Americans. This was no ordinary war. It was an ideological one pitting dictatorships against democracy, and the United States could not stay aloof from it. Following Pearl Harbor, Mexican Americans proudly enlisted in the military. Many lost their lives. Although depleted of younger members, LULAC councils continued to function and support the war effort at home. Some, like El Paso Council No. 132, formed Special Committees on Defense that instructed Mexican Americans on civilian defense. Lulacers also sold war bonds and collected gift packages for Mexican-American members of the armed forces.[41] For LULAC, the war not only proved Mexican-American patriotism but served as a major Americanizing experience. "The primary or general objective of the League, to teach Americans of Latin American origin to be better and more loyal citizens has been accomplished by war," the *LULAC News* editorialized in 1945.[42]

With the onset of the cold war, LULAC again stressed its fidelity to Americanism and reaffirmed its antagonism to communism. Influenced by the anticommunist hysteria of the period, LULAC attacked communism's "failures." "There is nothing that Communism can do for the world that democracy isn't already doing better," national president Albert Armendáriz wrote in 1953. He asserted that communism could not provide a higher standard of living than American democracy. What communism could deliver was fear and insecurity. Strongly anticommunist, LULAC nevertheless resisted efforts to compel members to certify that they were not or had not been members of the Communist party. This was unnecessary because LULAC's anticommunist record was clear.[43]

As part of its effort to Americanize the Mexican-American image, LULAC upheld middle-class role models. "Most of us in LULAC enjoy a fairly good standard of living," the *LULAC News* reported in 1954, "bringing about our desire to 'keep up with the Jones.'"[44] Both middle-class and working-class Mexican Americans joined LULAC, but the middle class dominated leadership positions at the local and national levels. Attorneys, for example, formed the overwhelming majority of national LULAC presidents. In addition, the *LULAC News* extolled the life histories and achievements of its middle-class leaders. A composite picture of such role models included the following characteristics: American born, rising from poor backgrounds to achieve education, veterans of World War I or World War II, high school or college graduates, and professionally either a lawyer, teacher, physician, or government employee. In all, LULAC equated Americanism with middle-class success and believed that true leadership could emanate only from the middle class.[45]

Although an organization of Mexican Americans, LULAC also aimed to Americanize Mexican nationals. Mexicanos could not be official members of LULAC, but they could become honorary members and some apparently joined under this status. LULAC in Victoria, Texas, in 1944 sponsored a meeting chaired by the Mexican consul of Corpus Christi that discussed discrimination against Mexican nationals and organized a committee composed of Mexican nationals to investigate the situation. Moreover, LULAC through the Spanish-language sections of the *LULAC News* during the 1930s counseled Mexican nationals about adjustment to life in the United States.[46] It organized English and citizenship classes for Mexican nationals. LULAC councils in south Texas in the post-World War II period, for example, expressed shock at the number of Mexican nationals who failed citizenship examinations due to lack of both English and a knowledge of American civics. Consequently, Laredo Council No. 12 commenced its own adult night school for Mexican nationals. In 1953 the school taught English and citizenship to more than two thousand persons.[47] LULAC teachers provided citizenship classes in both English and Spanish. "I teach them in English hoping they will pick up the language," one teacher in El Paso told a reporter about his students, "and I teach Spanish to be sure they learn the essentials of the American form of government in which they will be tested when they apply for naturalization." [48]

LULAC Women

Acculturation also led LULAC to adjust to a greater degree of "freedom" for women, although still in a subordinate role to men. Middle-class women in Mexican communities in the United States had historically always possessed active social lives steeped in charitable work outside the home, but few appear to have pursued careers outside the home. Unlike many working-class women who had to work to help sustain their families, most middle-class women did not. LULAC accepted this social pattern when it incorporated women's auxiliaries in 1932.[49] Most men in LULAC conceded women a role within the organization as long as it did not get out of hand. "The foundation of society rests on its homes," one male member asserted. "The success of our homes rests in the wives." [50] However, middle-class-oriented Mexican-American women coming of age by the 1930s proved less accommodating than their predecessors. They did not threaten male hegemony in LULAC, but they did struggle for greater independent roles. They possessed more education than earlier middle-class Mexican women and many were determined to have working careers of their own. Like Mexican-American men, the women were also influenced by modernizing trends in the United States and hoped to adapt the traditional role of Mexican women to an American context. In a 1937 article in the *LULAC News* entitled "Women's Opportunity in LULAC," Mrs. F. I. Montemayor commented on some of the American influences affecting Mexican-American women. "The female gender of the species is making her way into the function of all phases of world activity as solidly as the men who have held the spotlight for a good many centuries." Montemayor encouraged women to identify with such role models as Carrie Nation, Secretary of Labor Frances Perkins, Eleanor Roosevelt, Amelia Earhart, and Helen Hayes. In LULAC, Mexican-American women could emulate these Anglo women. "The LULAC is as much a vital organ to the Latin American women," she concluded, "as it is to the Latin American men." [51]

Unfortunately, not all LULAC men agreed. One year later, a *LULAC News* editorial admitted that some male members had proposed terminating the Ladies Councils, first organized in 1934 and offering women equal rights in LULAC, or reassigning them as auxiliaries. The malcontents argued that most of the women's councils were inactive and hence contributed little. A more enlightened *LULAC News* disagreed and pointed out that women were as active as men and that the real source of male discontent lay elsewhere. "The real cause of apprehension among those who favor the move," it observed, "is the aggressive attitude which some of our women members have adopted and shown in the conduct of our League's affairs." Some males feared that women would replace them in leadership positions. These feelings, the *News* noted, were un-American and should be dispelled. "[S]ome of our would be leaders and members can not get over that Latin way of thinking that in civic affairs and administrative fields men are superior to women." [52] LULAC did not disband the Ladies Councils; instead, they spread throughout the Southwest. Although almost all men's and women's councils remained separate by choice, a few contained both men and women.

As with the men, LULAC projected an image of the "LULAC Woman." Middle-class, educated, and working outside the home, the LULAC woman was as aspiring as her male counterpart. Biographies published in the *LULAC News* during the 1930s revealed some of the backgrounds of early women in LULAC, especially those in leadership positions. The most prominent woman in LULAC was Mrs. J. C. Machuca of El Paso. Mrs. Machuca, believing women should have equal rights and privileges within LULAC, formed the first Ladies Council. She served as Ladies Organizer General and assisted in founding other Ladies Councils. Jennie M. González, president of Ladies Council No. 17 in Albuquerque in 1938, possessed a B.A. degree from the University of New Mexico and worked as a school supervisor. Susie Chávez of Las Vegas, New Mexico, taught school and had previously worked in the state legislature. Mary Baca Romero, also of Las Vegas, had acquired an M.A. and taught on the faculty of the New Mexico Normal University Training School. Tomasa González of El Paso, a high school graduate, worked as a bookkeeper. Elvira Chaparro graduated valedictorian of her high school in Roswell, New Mexico, obtained a B.A. magna cum laude from Baylor University, and in 1939 served as vice president of Ladies Council No. 9 in El Paso. [53]

While LULAC male members accommodated to more aspiring Mexican-American women and even encouraged them to be like their Anglo female counterparts, they did not share authority equitably with the women. Some women were elected to national positions but never to dominant executive ones. Still, within this type of second-class position, the women made important community contributions, although in activities still closely related to "women's work." Women, of course, were not averse to engaging in purely social affairs among themselves. However, they likewise directed much of their energies to work in the barrios. This included assisting in orphanages and health clinics, sponsoring youth activities, and collecting and donating toys and clothes to underprivileged children. Along with the men, they registered voters, raised money for college scholarships, and taught English and citizenship to Mexican nationals. All this did not make LULAC women feminists but instead revealed the emergence of a new, more Americanized Mexican-American woman.

Political Socialization

Although LULAC's constitution prohibited councils from engaging in electoral politics, still, men and women members were encouraged to participate in politics. However, they had to do so in a nonpartisan fashion. LULAC believed that it would lose effectiveness if perceived as a partisan front for a political party. According to M. C. González, given the hostile climate against Mexican Americans in Texas, LULAC could organize politically only by stressing citizenship and Americanism and avoiding being labeled as "political agitators." [54] Hence LULAC reacted strongly to implications that it was a political organization. When the *Harlingen Morning Star,* in noting the formation of a LULAC council in this south Texas city, referred to it as a "Vote League," the neighboring Brownsville LULAC council quickly refuted the statement. "This is absolutely wrong," officer Federico Recio wrote the Chamber of Commerce. "The League of United Latin American Citizens is not a political organization, it stands for something better and higher than that; it is a Civic and Patriotic Organization." [55] Shunning the label of "political club," LULAC insisted that members as individuals actively work in local, state, and national politics. In doing so, they should be guided by LULAC principles. T. G. Giron of El Paso stressed that nonpartisan political activity conformed to the need for a new political direction and abandonment of machine politics that had characterized much of Mexican-American politics, especially in Texas. Under the "old politics," politicians saw Mexican Americans only as commodities to be bought or sold during election time. This was also the politics of "old Mexico" and it had to change and become Americanized by Mexican Americans acting independently in politics. [56]

LULAC considered voting to be the most important political act. Voting was a right and a duty for citizens. For Mexican Americans, it was also an Americanizing exercise. Good citizenship was more than fighting to protect one's country in war or being patriotic in time of peace. Good citizenship also involved participating in the making of the country's laws. Citizens did this through voting and electing their representatives. Mexican Americans could not take their rights and privileges for granted. "The people from countries under communist domination would give their right arm to be able to have a voice in their government," Virgilio Roel asserted in the *LULAC*

News in 1956. "It is time that we shed our shell of indifference and become full-fledged citizens." To Roel only two types of citizens existed: the first class who voted and the second class who did not. Failure to vote was "Un-American." [57]

In Texas, however, voting was no simple matter. Like other southern states, Texas required a poll tax until the 1960s. The tax in the South prevented blacks from voting, but in Texas it likewise discriminated against thousands of poor Mexican Americans. Some counties excluded Mexican Americans from voting in "white primaries" of the Democratic party until the 1930s. LULAC detested the poll tax but faced a dilemma. It could boycott the tax and attempt to eliminate it or it could encourage Mexican Americans to pay the tax and build up Mexican-American political strength. Recognizing that not to pay would be the greater evil, LULAC organized Poll Tax Committees and conducted voter registration drives. [58]

Besides expressing citizenship, voting effected social change. At one level, LULAC encouraged negative voting by Mexican Americans to prevent adversity. This included voting against politicians who would be prejudicial against Mexican Americans. In other cases, LULAC supported negative voting in local bond elections. Council No. 81 in Taft, Texas, reported in 1938 that the Mexican-American vote had defeated a recent school bond proposal because it would harm Mexican-American interests. Pressured by the Mexican-American opposition, school board members reintroduced a new proposal that Mexican Americans endorsed. [59] LULAC mobilized positive voting through the election of representatives who would benefit the Mexican-American community. Marfa Council No. 26 in west Texas understood positive voting when it organized the Latin American Civic Club, which successfully increased the number of registered Mexican-American voters. "When school board elections were in order," the *LULAC News* noted in 1932, "our Latin Americans held the balance of power and they did not hesitate to use it choosing who was to represent them in the school board in order to put a stop to segregation in our public schools." [60]

Voting also assumed importance in encouraging Mexican Americans to run for office. LULAC acknowledged that one of the main political problems faced by Mexican Americans was their lack of representation. However, Mexican-American candidates had to run free of entangling alliances with machine politics. M. C. González, who unsuccessfully campaigned in San Antonio for the Texas legislature in 1930, sought votes under the banner of the Citizens League, a reform political movement. "It is obvious from my name that I am of Mexican descent," González told a reporter during the campaign. "I was born and raised in Texas, however; I served my country during the war. I am an American and am proud of it." [61] Other Mexican-

American candidates ran for office and failed, but in time some succeeded. LULAC celebrated the election in 1932 of Mexican-American Griff Jones as county commissioner of Maverick County in south Texas. "As he is Vice President of the Eagle Pass Council of LULAC," the *LULAC News* observed of Jones, "rumor has it that LULAC is responsible for his election, as all the Eagle Pass Lulacers supported him individualby [*sic*]." [62] Mexican-American politics accelerated in the postwar period as veterans returned inspired by the struggle to defend the Four Freedoms. Important electoral victories included the election of Raymond Telles as mayor of El Paso in 1957 (see chapter 5) and the election of Henry B. González of San Antonio to the Texas State Senate in the mid-1950s. LULAC members enthusiastically supported both candidates. [63] LULAC recognized that Mexican Americans remained underrepresented in southwestern politics as of the 1950s but believed it had helped achieve a political voice for Mexican Americans.

LULAC's efforts at political socialization finally consisted of getting Mexican Americans to become interested and involved in state and national politics. The economic crisis of the 1930s, of course, and the activist response by President Roosevelt's New Deal attracted Mexican-American adherents, as they did Afro-American and other previously unrecognized minorities, to FDR and the standard of the national Democratic party. LULAC furthered the nationalization of Mexican-American politics by passing resolutions at its national conventions endorsing federal legislation that would benefit Mexican Americans. [64] In all, LULAC through its political socialization sanctioned the Mexican-American Generation's need to engage in a new type of politics in the Southwest aimed at its integration into American life.

Cultural Pluralism

LULAC defined Americanization as acculturation but did not imply thorough cultural assimilation. Mexican Americans in LULAC desired political and economic integration but preferred cultural pluralism. Interpreting their particular history and culture in middle-class terms, Lulacers stressed that they derived from a background that was compatible with Anglo America and not in conflict with it. They genuflected—like most other Americans—to the concept of the "melting pot," but like other ethnics, including Afro Americans, and perhaps even more so, Mexican Americans defined "melting pot" as a state of ethnic pluralism rather than the "melting" of different ethnic ingredients and the production of a syncretic "new American." Historical antecedents in the Southwest prior to the American conquest in 1848, sustained immigration from Mexico, and the propinquity of Mexico to the Southwest created the objective conditions for such an approach. To be sure, LULAC's reaction to the cultural question contained certain ambivalences and even contradictions. What is certain, however, is that Lulacers, despite the insistence of later Chicano scholars to the contrary, hoped to achieve some functional balance between mainstream Anglo-American culture and the culture derived from their Mexican roots. In this sense, LULAC's development of a Mexican-American ethnic identity corresponded to what Padilla terms "political ethnicity." [65]

Cultural compatibility began with the issue of ethnicity. Despite or because of the racism directed against Mexican Americans, especially in Texas, Lulacers emphasized both for internal as well as external consumption that Mexican Americans derived from a proud and ancient people who were worthy of being accepted into American society. Judge Canales noted, for example, that owing to their Latin backgrounds Mexican Americans could lay claim to the splendor and glory of ancient Rome. Canales, at the same time, considered Anglo Americans to be the "new Romans" because like Romans they had constructed a new civilization, the industrial world. Hence, Mexican Americans and Anglo Americans shared a common "Latin" foundation for ethnic cooperation. "Latins," of course, had contributed to Anglo-Saxon culture through the Norman conquest of England. Canales observed that the "Latin race" had contributed its share of great artists, sculptors, musicians, singers, intellectuals, and political leaders. These included El Cid, Bonaparte, Bolívar, Marconi, and Galileo. Mexican Americans further praised their descent from highly civilized and enterprising Spaniards and laid claim to notable figures such as Cervantes, Cortés, and Fray Junípero Serra as well as other famous conquistadores and explorers. As descendants of Latins and Spaniards, Lulacers also claimed "whiteness." Mexican Americans as "whites" believed no substantive racial factor existed to justify racial discrimination against them.[66]

Lulacers, however, did not turn their backs on their Mexican-Indian (mestizo) character. They acknowledged this fact of history but as "mixed bloods" still believed they qualified as "whites." [67] Terming the Spanish period of the Southwest "Mexican," Andrés de Luna proudly lectured to a meeting of the Daughters of the American Revolution about the contributions of Mexicans to American society. "[I]t was from civilized Mexico," he pointed out, "that the Missionary teachers pushed there [*sic*] way through the then uncivilized territories of Texas and Arizona, New Mexico and California." De Luna reminded the Daughters that years before the Pilgrims landed at Plymouth Rock the ancestors of Mexican Americans had introduced the first printing press in the New World and established the first university on the continent. Moreover, in an article in the *LULAC News* entitled "The Nobility of Our Indian Heritage," Alberto García of Council No. 85 in Austin encouraged Mexican Americans to be proud of their Indian forefathers. Indians of both North and South America had contributed to the struggle for freedom. "The will to freedom is essentially Indian," García wrote. "Europeans learned much of it from the Indians." Avoiding the Spanish role in creating the symbol of the Virgin of Guadalupe, García advanced the questionable suggestion that the Virgin represented the Indian struggle for freedom against colonialism. Mexican Indians also possessed qualities that Mexican Americans could be proud of and seek to emulate. These involved patience, a conformity with both life and death, self-governance, truthfulness, and moral virtue. Unfortunately, García fell prey to stereotyping and outlandish conclusions. He proposed, for example, that Mexicans in Texas had the lowest incidences of venereal diseases because they had inherited the Indian's emphasis on high morals. García and other Lulacers, of course, concentrated (as would later Chicanos) on "high" Indian civilizations such as those of the Aztecs and Mayas. Advanced cultures in both Spain and Mexico together had produced a race and culture worthy of being integrated into American society. García called on Mexican Americans to reconcile their dual racial heritage and be proud of it.[68]

Integral to LULAC's pursuit of cultural pluralism was Mexican cultural retention. Maintenance of the Spanish language symbolized this effort. LULAC promoted Spanish and bilingualism through the bilingual publication of the *LULAC News* during the 1930s. LULAC members wrote and published poems in Spanish for the *News* that expressed pride in the Mexican-American experience and in LULAC's role. One such poem in 1932, entitled "A la liga Latino Americana y a sus Héroes" [To the Latin American League and its Heroes] by Margil López honored LULAC's founders, such as Perales, González, and Canales. "El Texano," a poem by Santiago Tafolla, stressed in 1940 that Mexican Americans in Texas—the Texanos—feared neither Hitler nor Mussolini and that they would go to war to preserve the American union.[69]

Spanish symbolized more than culture for Lulacers; it served as a practical tool. Many Mexican Americans, including LULAC members, still spoke Spanish as their primary langauge. Consequently, although later Chicano scholars would castigate LULAC for its stress on English, LULAC could not enforce its own rule that English be used as the organization's official language. In a Spanish-language essay in 1932, Mauro Machado warned that LULAC was losing members who could not easily speak English. Machado advocated the use of Spanish in those councils containing mostly Spanish-speaking members. He noted that the American Legion had succeeded in New Mexico because it organized in Spanish. Machado believed LULAC could do the same.[70] LULAC did not officially change its language requirement, but it did permit Spanish in recruiting new members and in conducting meetings, especially during the 1930s, when language differences among Mexican Americans remained minimal. "There was no way we could go out there and talk to them in English," M. C. González recalls of LULAC's organizing tactics. "We would open by a Pledge of Allegiance to the flag because there would be a Deputy Sheriff or somebody around there. We would sing America. Then we'd start speaking in Spanish. That's how we broke the ice." [71] LULAC also used Spanish to inform both Mexican Americans and Mexican nationals about its various programs and benefits. Council No. 34 of Albuquerque, for example, distributed in 1940 several hundred copies of a Spanish-language social security publication. The *LULAC News* informed Mexican Americans about jobs necessitating bilingual abilities. Although the employment of Spanish declined after World War II as most LULAC members became more functional in English, still LULAC supported bilingualism. In 1941 the El Paso Council endorsed the teaching of Spanish in the public schools but shied away from compulsory Spanish-language instruction. However, ten years later the same council backed a resolution by the Texas Good Neighbor Commission that called for compulsory teaching of Spanish in the public schools. In all these cases, LULAC insisted that correct Spanish be spoken and not the slang of the barrios. [72]

Besides promoting Spanish, LULAC favored retaining various Mexican cultural traditions. Arthur L. Campa of the University of New Mexico in an essay in the *LULAC News,* for example, noted the elitist and misguided effort to differentiate between New Mexican and Mexican folklore. In fact, Campa pointed out, folklore from Santa Fe to Chihuahua had always been considered Mexican and possessed no major differences. In a much later essay in *LULAC News,* Campa acknowledged the contributions of Spanish-Mexican *vaqueros* to the folklore of the American cowboy. The cowboy represented a folk hero who revealed the coexistence of Mexican and Anglo cultures (see chapter 11). In addition, LULAC celebrations generally included Mexican music, songs, and dances performed by Lulacers and their families as well as the serving of Mexican cuisine. [73] "Some of us, even though we were American citizens, born here . . . we still had our Mexican culture," recalls Amadita Valdez of LULAC's participation in El Paso's 16th of September celebrations (Mexican Independence Day). [74] Finally, although LULAC formed a mostly middle-class organization, it did not entirely eschew Mexican-American barrio culture. In the 1950s, the *LULAC News* published short stories by Arizona writer Mario Suárez that sensitively brought to life barrio and "chicano" culture in Tucson. [75]

In all, LULAC projected a world view based on pluralism. Society rather than melting differences would permit degrees of cultural differences to survive within the framework of a more generalized American culture. One could be proud of being of Mexican and Latin American descent and remain a loyal American citizen. "We are Latin Americans, within the all-embracing term of 'American Citizen,'" noted LULAC official Ezequiel Salinas in 1937.[76] Lulacers did not seek cultural conflict but rather hoped to integrate Mexican cultural traditions within mainstream American ones. Cultural pluralism, however, would be effective only when certain positive attitudes took hold. "The essence of Americanism," George I. Sánchez of the University of Texas emphasized, "is tolerance." Sánchez also warned against efforts by some under the guise of patriotism to force an artificial and dangerous uniformity on others. "Failing to understand the American pageant of peoples and cultures," Sánchez criticized such ethnocentric individuals, "they would appoint themselves as the 'true Americans' and promulgate their narrow conception of culture as *the* American way" (see chapter 10). Finally, as one Lulacer expressed it as late as 1960, even if Latin Americans chose not to identify as Latins, they would still be treated as "others" as long as racial prejudice continued. Consequently, since Latin Americans could not avoid being treated as different, they should express pride in their heritage and be "proud to be a big part in the American way of life."[77]

Desegregation Struggles

Desiring to be integrated as first-class citizens, Mexican Americans in LULAC, like their middle-class Afro-American counterparts in the NAACP, struggled against various forms of racial discrimination. Lulacers did not ask for special concessions, privileges, or programs aimed specifically at them as a minority group. They constituted a minority, but they did not want to be treated as one. They did not want to be singled out for discrimination or for patronization. All they aspired to was equal access to the rights enjoyed by other Americans. Lulacers believed that Mexican Americans were entitled to first-class citizenship not only under the Constitution but also under the guarantees of the Treaty of Guadalupe Hidalgo (1848), which ended the Mexican War. The treaty annexed northern portions of Mexico to the United States and offered U.S. citizenship to the resident Mexican population. LULAC did not see Mexican Americans as a colonized people as a result of the American conquest of the Southwest as did more radical Mexican Americans. However, LULAC used the treaty of 1848 to buttress its civil rights demands. It believed that the disparities between constitutional and treaty promises and the second-class status of Mexican Americans could be rectified within the prevailing system. Yet for this to occur, Anglos would have to acknowledge Mexican Americans as worthy of integration and differentiate between them and Mexican nationals who hoped to return to Mexico. Not all people of Mexican descent were the same. David Montejano in his study of south Texas argues that Lulacers indeed possessed a class bias in their desegregation efforts. They sought to eradicate discrimination that particularly affected their hopes for greater mobility as more middle-class-oriented Mexican Americans. Yet if we concede a class bias for Lulacers, the fact remains that their desegregation efforts did affect to one degree or another the mostly working-class Mexicans. At best, it represented a challenge to the culture of race and ethnic repression that touched all Mexicans. Finally, Lulacers possessed few illusions that the Anglo establishment would voluntarily deliver full civil rights to Mexican Americans. These would be won only by persistent struggles.[78] "The defense of our RIGHTS and IMPROVEMENT of conditions amongst our people must be stimulated by ourselves," one Lulacer correctly observed.[79]

LULAC in particular protested against discrimination in public facilities, considered a major affront to Mexican Americans. Not shy about resorting to the courts, LULAC preferred diplomacy and pressure group politics to achieve desegregation. As such, LULAC leaders, certainly the dominant male element, represented what Daniel Thompson in his study of black leadership refers to as "Race Men." Lockhart Council No. 38 in Texas, for example, after hearing in 1938 that a new movie theater was going to segregate Mexicans and blacks in the balcony, vehemently objected to the management and succeeded in desegregating the theater, at least for Mexican Americans.[80] One year earlier in San Angelo, LULAC had had to go further in desegregating a local theater. The theater management, in hosting a benefit involving the Mexican Típica Orchestra of Mexico, encouraged the local Mexican population to attend and announced that the balcony would be reserved for them. Learning of this segregated policy from its San Angelo council, the LULAC national office protested to the mayor of the city. Unsatisfied with the response, LULAC notified the orchestra about the segregation and solicited their support in the protest. "We consider this a vicious and malicious insult to our people," LULAC President Frank Galván wrote to the orchestra's director, "and more especially to you and your Company who are of our race." Galván obtained the orchestra's pledge not to perform in San Angelo until Mexicans could sit wherever they pleased in the theater. Threatened with the benefit's cancellation, the management conceded that no special areas would be reserved for Mexicans. The Mexican Típica Orchestra played in San Angelo and Mexican Americans attended in large numbers.[81]

On certain occasions diplomacy and pressure group politics had to include the threat of an economic boycott to achieve desegregation of public facilities. In 1940 LULAC again protested in San Angelo over the efforts of a new movie theater to segregate Mexicans along with blacks in the balcony. President General A. M. Fernández at first counseled firm diplomacy. He advised LULAC's newly created Public Relations Board headed by E. D. Salinas to investigate the issue and "courteously" request that the theater drop its segregated policy toward Mexicans. Fernández also proposed publicizing this local affront to Mexican Americans by linking it with the harm such a case of prejudice did to President Roosevelt's efforts to advance the Good Neighbor Policy. If the management still demurred, Fernández proposed appealing to Washington, where Senator Dennis Chávez, the lone Mexican American in the Congress, and other supporters of the Good Neighbor Policy might be able to intervene. These political channels would first be exhausted before possibly pursuing adjudication. Yet diplomacy had to be reinforced by more direct action. Fernández called on Mexican Americans to boycott the theater until its segregated policies ended. LULAC's strategy succeeded. The management agreed to seat Mexicans throughout the theater and publicly apologized for the controversy. Besides theaters, LULAC protested, in many cases successfully, the segregation of Mexican Americans in swimming pools, restaurants, hospitals, and other forms of public accommodations.[82]

In these antisegregation efforts, LULAC rejected any attempt to segregate Mexican Americans as a nonwhite population. Mexican Americans expressed ambivalences about race identity and possessed their own prejudices against blacks. However, they also recognized that irrespective of how they saw themselves, reclassification as colored, especially in Texas, would subject Mexicans not only to de facto segregation but to de jure as well. This was intolerable. Lulacers consistently argued that Mexicans were legally recognized members of the white race and that no legal or physical basis existed for racial discrimination. Lulacers specifically objected to Anglos excluding Mexican Americans from the political process because Mexicans were colored. In 1937 Council No. 69 in Wharton, Texas, successfully stopped the county tax collector from designating Mexican Americans holding receipts as "colored." The official insisted that he had been pressured to do so by the "White Man Union" that wished to eliminate Mexican Americans from county politics. LULAC pointed out that the term "Mexican" was appropriate if it meant one's nationality or citizenship, but not if it referred to race and especially with the intent to discriminate. The *LULAC News* reminded its readers that some years earlier the attorney general of Texas had ruled that persons of Mexican descent would be considered white. LULAC likewise pressed local enumerators to include Mexicans as white. Council No. 1 in Corpus Christi negotiated an agreement with the chamber of commerce to terminate classifying Mexicans either as "Mexicans" or as "English-speaking

Mexicans." They would now be listed only as "Americans." Other efforts included getting local radio stations and newspapers to cease distinguishing between whites and Mexicans. By the 1950s, LULAC still remained vigilant over racial classification intended to discriminate. In 1954 LULAC officials overturned the segregation of Mexican-American prisoners at the Texas State Prison in Huntsville. Although the practice was illegal, prison officials also had classified Mexican Americans as "American Latin American." In addition, in 1957 through the efforts of ex-national president Luciano Santoscoy of El Paso, LULAC forced the State Department of Public Health no longer to list Mexicans as a special category apart from whites.[83]

Public discrimination against Mexican Americans likewise involved the exclusion of Mexican Americans from juries in Texas. Although this practice had a long history, Mexican Americans in LULAC vowed to eliminate this blatant type of discrimination. Despite earlier efforts to achieve proportional representation on grand juries in Texas counties with significant Mexican-American populations, by 1951 LULAC concluded that only through court action could jury discrimination be abolished. In September of that year, LULAC lawyer Gus García agreed to represent Pete Hernández, a laborer charged with murdering another Mexican American in Jackson County, Texas. García defended Hernández not only because he believed that authorities were determined to condemn the 26-year-old to the electric chair, but because García concluded that he could use the case to combat the systematic exclusion of Mexican Americans from jury commissions, grand juries, and petit juries in Texas. Exclusion could be attacked as a violation of the Fourteenth Amendment, which insisted on equal protection of the law. With the assistance of Houston lawyer John J. Herrera, who also served as first national vice president of LULAC, García defended Hernández in his preliminary hearing and in the initial trial. García moved to set aside Hernández's indictment by establishing that a systematic exclusion of Mexican Americans from jury service existed in Jackson County. He documented that no Mexican Americans had served on any jury or been called for jury service in at least twenty-five years. This was obvious discrimination since qualified Mexican Americans lived in Jackson County. According to García, Anglos treated Mexican Americans as a separate class of people. Despite García's and Herrera's labors, a Jackson County jury, containing no Mexican Americans, found Hernández guilty and sentenced him to life imprisonment.[84]

Not discouraged, García and Herrera filed a motion for a new trial with the Texas Court of Criminal Appeals. In the appeal process, Carlos Cadena, a law professor at St. Mary's University in San Antonio, assisted García and Herrera. The court heard the Mexican-American arguments but still rejected

Hernández's request for a new trial. It argued that the Fourteenth Amendment did not apply to the case. The amendment, so the court asserted, recognized only two classes under its equal protection of the law clause: whites and blacks. Mexican Americans were considered whites, hence they could not claim that they had been discriminated against in jury selection. As long as other whites served on these juries, Mexican Americans were represented. It rejected Hernández's contention that in fact Mexican Americans rather than being treated as whites were subject to discrimination as a specific class of people. Following its decision, the court of appeals refused to rehear the case.[85]

Despite some misgivings over the case, García and Cadena filed an application for a writ of certiorari (review) with the U.S. Supreme Court on January 19, 1953. "We had little hope that it would be approved because every year hundreds of applications are submitted but only a few are granted," García recalled. "Much to our surprise, our petition received favorable consideration on October 12, 1953, Columbus Day, or better known throughout Latin America and Spain as 'El Día de la Raza.'" To cover initial costs of arguing the case before the Supreme Court, LULAC Council No. 2 in San Antonio shifted $900 from its scholarship fund to meet the lawyer's expenses. Other LULAC councils, the American G.I. Forum (composed of Mexican-American veterans), the Texas Good Relations Association, and private individuals raised additional funds. In all, $3,000 was accumulated.[86]

On a cold and blustery January 11, 1954, in Washington, D.C., Gus García and Carlos Cadena argued the Hernández case before the U.S. Supreme Court, assisted by John J. Herrera. In what is widely regarded to have been a marvelous discourse, García contended that jury discrimination against Mexican Americans in Jackson County had prevented Hernández from obtaining a fair trial by a jury of his peers. He disputed the court of appeals interpretation of the "two classes" theory contained in the Fourteenth Amendment. Not only did this interpretation restrict the protective arm of the Fourteenth Amendment to other discriminated groups, but it could be used to justify de facto segregation of Mexican Americans in schools, housing, parks, and other public places by the argument that no segregation existed since Mexican Americans were whites. García and Cadena agreed that Mexican Americans were white, but that as whites Mexican Americans were still being discriminated against as a separate class of people. Documenting their case and articulately presenting it, the Mexican-American lawyers won the case. The U.S. Supreme Court on May 3, 1954, in a decision written by Chief Justice Earl Warren, overturned the Texas Court of Appeals and ruled that Hernández had not received a fair trial due to jury discrimination against Mexican Americans depriving him of the equal protection of the laws under the Fourteenth Amendment. Warren and the Court rejected the "two classes" theory and stated that the Fourteenth Amendment did not restrict itself to whites and blacks.[87]

The Hernández decision represented a major legal victory for Mexican Americans. Although Hernández received another trial that still convicted him of murder, attorney Cadena stressed the larger implications of the Hernández case. Not just in Jackson County but wherever else Mexican Americans faced jury discrimination the Hernández decision could be applied. The Supreme Court's rejection of the "two classes" theory under the Fourteenth Amendment meant that other ethnic groups besides blacks could appeal for protection under the amendment. The Hernández decision, Cadena further noted, could even be used against gender discrimination in jury service. Finally, to quiet fears on the part of some Mexican Americans who believed that the Hernández decision could be manipulated to reclassify Mexicans as nonwhites, Cadena reassured them that the decision had been based not on race but on national origin. However, rather than using *Hernández* to dissociate from blacks, Cadena wisely proposed that Mexican Americans seek an alliance with blacks. "Mexicans should be proud to be identified with other minority groups," he stated, "including the ultra-progressive Negro-Americans, instead of attempting to build a cultural fence around themselves and live in a vacuum."[88]

Besides acting against discrimination in public facilities and on juries, LULAC struggled against varied forms of job discrimination. It investigated charges of discrimination in WPA jobs during the 1930s depression. LULAC also protested efforts to exclude Mexican Americans from skilled jobs. In 1941 El Paso Council No. 132 expressed anger over the Southern Pacific Railroad's refusal to provide skilled apprenticeships to Mexican Americans. LULAC members called for vigorous opposition similar to the kind that had recently forced the local telephone company to hire Mexican-American women or face the threat of an economic boycott by LULAC. During the war certain councils pressured defense industries to hire Mexican Americans. As veterans returned following the conflict, LULAC worked to ensure equal job opportunities for them. In addition, LULAC consistently supported the enforcement of state and federal labor laws, especially the right to a minimum wage and the right of Mexican Americans to organize in unions. LULAC opposed the involvement of Mexican Americans in certain unions considered to be "radical" but encouraged unionization in moderate labor organizations, especially after the merger of the AFL and CIO in the early 1950s.[89]

As part of its concern over job discrimination, LULAC paid special attention to the plight of Mexican-American migrant agricultural workers. It voiced apprehension concerning the dangerous and unsanitary travel conditions affecting such workers and sustained by labor contractors and agribusiness. LULAC protested the violation of child labor laws, a common practice in agriculture. It advocated adequate wages for migrant workers and coverage by federal minimum wage laws. Other supported reforms included welfare benefits for migrant workers and their families, decent and sanitary housing facilities, adequate diets, and the elimination of public discrimination against Mexican-American migrant workers in communities where they labored. LULAC also endorsed state aid for migrant workers through agencies such as the Farm Extension Program. In particular locations, individual LULAC councils assisted migrant workers and their families by providing recreational programs at the migrant camps. Moreover, LULAC backed the right of migrant workers to form unions. It dismissed growers' contentions that such unions could lead to crippling strikes at harvest time by noting that low wage scales together with intolerable working conditions could bring equal financial disaster to migrant families.[90]

Directly related to the conditions of Mexican-American farmworkers was the persistent migration of Mexican wage laborers across the border. LULAC, shortly after its formation, attacked racist measures to restrict Mexican immigration on the basis of racial and cultural inferiority. However, by World War II LULAC opposed two forms of immigration from Mexico: the Bracero Program and the entry of "wetbacks." The Bracero Program, negotiated by the United States and Mexico as a wartime labor emergency measure, provided temporary contract labor primarily for agribusiness. In 1942 LULAC called for its termination because of the overt exploitation of the braceros, expecially in Texas. In the postwar era, the Bracero Program continued and LULAC extended its opposition to include the argument that such contract labor took jobs away from Mexican Americans and domestic farm laborers besides creating unfair and unequal economic competition. In addition, LULAC objected to what it called the "fearful problem": the increased entry of undocumented workers from Mexico who, unable to enter under the contract labor system, crossed in large numbers anyway. As with the Bracero Program, LULAC favored the restriction of wetbacks because of the exploitation they faced and the dislocation they caused Mexican-American workers, especially in agriculture. Yet wetbacks along with Mexican-American workers were the victims. LULAC correctly blamed others for this state of affairs, including Mexico for being unable to correct its unemployment crisis, U.S. agribusiness for knowingly hiring wetbacks, and the U.S. Immigration Service for being lax about illegal entries. The presence of wetbacks increased not only labor exploitation but also racial discrimination against all persons of Mexican descent. Frustrated, LULAC in 1954 unfortunately supported mass arrests and deportations of wetbacks by the Immigration Service in Operation Wetback. It also unsuccessfully supported legislation to penalize employers for hiring "illegal aliens." Moreover, concerned about deportation abuses, LULAC opposed that same year the McCarran Immigration Act, calling it oppressive and unjust. LULAC in particular objected to provisions that would permit immigration officials to deport "illegal aliens" who had permanently resided in the country for many years as well as those parents of U.S.-born children.[91]

Education and the Mexican American

Yet eliminating discrimination would not mean much unless accompanied by education. Consequently, education became basic to LULAC's ideology and the foundation of its Americanization program. As political liberals, Lulacers perceived education as the key solution to the social problems facing Mexican Americans. LULAC linked its commitment to education to the belief that Americans possessed a universal right to education with no limit to individual educational achievement. Mexican Americans would no longer accept, as they had experienced for many years, limited education in inferior Mexican schools throughout the Southwest. Such an education reproduced a low-skilled work force and kept Mexican Americans in a state of economic underdevelopment. LULAC stressed, as one of its educational principles, education as a means to economic progress for Mexican Americans. Education would materially benefit Mexican Americans not only as a group but also as individuals. Education would expand a professional-managerial Mexican-American class, but LULAC in a pragmatic vein also endorsed advanced vocational education that would produce Mexican-American skilled workers. In turn, the economic advancement of Mexican Americans at all levels would enrich the entire community, both Mexican Americans and Anglos.[92]

LULAC also visualized education as a means of developing permanent leadership for the Mexican-American community. This leadership would, of course, be based on a professional middle class. The linkage of education with leadership, however, would require access to university education. Carlos Castañeda of the University of Texas expressed delight with the increased number of young Mexican Americans studying at Austin in the 1930s. He especially noted the importance of many of them studying law. "This is essential to the best interests of our Latin American citizens," he wrote to lawyer M. C. González. "What we need most of all in this state is a group of well trained and representative Latin-American lawyers to whom our people can go for legal advice and who can defend their rights when these are trampled upon."[93]

Embracing education as perhaps the chief vehicle for the integration of Mexican Americans, LULAC at the same time understood that Mexican Americans would have to wage desegregation struggles to achieve quality education. Although LULAC observed that a good education was not a privilege in the United States but a child's birthright, it likewise noted that Mexican-American children faced de facto segregation in inferior Mexican schools, especially in Texas. LULAC critics condemned the maldistribution of school resources whereby Mexican schools generally received less support than those in Anglo neighborhoods despite housing a large percentage of all schoolage children. Consequently, the Mexican schools remained overcrowded, unsanitary, and provided a limited number of school years for the pupils in comparison to their Anglo counterparts. Not surprisingly, they also contained inexperienced and inferior teachers (see chapter 3).[94]

LULAC in particular expressed discontent over the segregation of Mexican-American children. This was unjust and un-American. Many Lulacers agreed with Professor H. T. Manuel's assessment in 1931 that some form of separation, especially on the basis of language differences and perhaps health conditions, might be temporarily justified, but not on a long-term basis. Segregation inherently meant inferior education. Moreover, Manuel charged that segregation as practiced in Texas was irrational because it involved students whose separation could not be justified. "A school board, for example, will set up a rule prescribing that Mexican children attend a separate school because of lack of knowledge of English and then will take no cognizance of the fact that there are individuals in the group who know English as well as Spanish." Finally, segregation undercut one of the primary aims of education: the preparation of children for future cooperation as citizens. Manuel reiterated that language difference was perhaps one of the few reasons for justifying a minimum of separation involving Mexican-American children, but that such separation should certainly not go beyond the second or third grade, as in fact existed in many Texas school districts. "The important consideration is that pedagogical wisdom rather than prejudice should prevail."[95]

LULAC pursued dual strategies in its attempt to achieve educational integration and quality education for Mexican-American children. It first sought through a combination of protests, negotiations, and community pressure to convince school authorities to institute changes voluntarily. LULAC councils, for example, investigated charges by Mexican parents concerning discriminatory acts by teachers against their children and when warranted brought such incidents to the attention of the proper authorities. Councils also publicized the unequal distribution of educational resources between schools predominantly attended by Mexican Americans and those attended by Anglos.

Moreover, councils protested against de facto segregated schools for Mexican-American children. In particular cases, local community pressure by itself succeeded in desegregating the schools. In 1934, Goliad Council No. 21 assisted by Lulacers from San Antonio obtained the integration of Mexican-American students into the primarily Anglo Goliad High School. Five years later, Council No. 2 of San Antonio achieved the desegregation of the high school in Beeville, Texas. Still other actions involved meetings with state educational authorities concerning desegregation and increased resources for Mexican-American students as well as the hiring of attorneys to investigate segregated conditions. Some of these efforts resulted in reforms, while others encountered more obstacles.[96]

Because of the difficulties in eradicating de facto school segregation in Texas and throughout the Southwest, LULAC also pursued a policy of instigating or assisting in legal actions. In 1930, one year after its formation, LULAC organized its first school desegregation case in Del Rio, Texas. Jesús Salvatierra and several parents, assisted by LULAC lawyers M. C. González and Judge Canales, requested and obtained a local injunction from a state court prohibiting the Del Rio School District from using recently approved bond monies to construct new facilities that Mexican Americans claimed would only further the existing segregation of Mexican-American children. Three elementary schools functioned in Del Rio. School officials designated one of them the Mexican or West End school and reserved it specifically for Mexican Americans up to and including the low third grade. Mexican-American parents complained that this was deliberate segregation based on race and hence unconstitutional. The district superintendent responded that he had no intention of such segregation. Only Mexican Americans attended the West End school, but this was necessary because of other conditions. These included that fact that most Mexican-American children enrolled late in the year when their farmworking parents returned from the fall harvest. To enroll these children late in the other elementary schools attended by Anglos would be disruptive and place the Mexican-American children at a distinct disadvantage. Moreover, the superintendent justified separation on the basis that Mexican-American children predominantly spoke Spanish. In their own schools, Mexican Americans could get special attention commensurate with their educational retardation and their language problems. Finally, the superintendent argued that the Mexican-American children tended to be older than Anglo students and that to integrate them in the same classrooms would pose problems. As the superintendent put it: "I have been told that it is true that a Mexican child will reach puberty stage sooner than an American child, and that people originating in torrid climates will mature earlier; it's owing to the climatic conditions." Yet all these reasons for separation, the superintendent concluded, were instructional in nature and had nothing to do with racial discrimination. In fact, he added, the Mexican school was "the best equipped and most pleasant elementary school situation we have." In their own separate schools, Mexican-American children could concentrate on their "innate talents." [97]

After hearing the arguments, a local trial court ruled in favor of Salvatierra and the other Mexican-American appellants and issued an injunction restraining the school district from expanding the de facto segregated Mexican school. However, on appeal the court of appeals in San Antonio overturned the injunction. The court in the Salvatierra case dismissed the contention by the appellates that the Del Rio school district deliberately segregated Mexican-American children on the basis of race. It agreed with the school superintendent that what separation existed had been done on an instructional basis. Consequently, the courts had no jurisdiction over such an administrative matter. LULAC salvaged a partial victory when the appeal court also ruled that although not applicable in this case, any school segregation founded purely on the basis of race was unconstitutional and would entitle the courts to overturn decisions by local school districts. Unable in this initial effort to achieve school desegregation, LULAC nevertheless accepted the opinion of the appeal court on the unconstitutionality of school segregation based on race as a moral victory. The Salvatierra case had displayed LULAC's ability to lead in this matter and to organize support. Numerous individuals as well as local LULAC councils throughout Texas contributed to the legal defense fund. The Salvatierra case became the first step in a legal campaign for school integration. [98]

Sixteen years later, in 1946, LULAC helped achieve a major legal breakthrough in the Westminster case in California. Undoubtedly, the improved social climate due to wartime unity efforts plus a more liberal political temper in California influenced the decision. LULAC endorsed and supported a class suit by Gonzalo Méndez and other Mexican Americans against the school districts of Westminster, Garden Grove, El Modeno, and Santa Ana of Orange county. Mexican Americans alleged that these districts' policies of segregating Mexican-American students throughout most if not all of the elementary grades was discriminatory and a violation of the Fourteenth Amendment. They filed suit with the U.S. Federal Court in San Diego on behalf of some 5,000 persons affected by such segregation. David C. Marcus of Los Angeles, representing the National Lawyers Guild and the American Civil Liberties Union, argued the case for the Mexican-American community. The plaintiffs charged that the school districts discriminated against Mexican Americans by not allowing them to attend other schools in their district composed predominantly of Anglo students. In some cases, Mexican-

American children living in proximity to an Anglo school had to attend a Mexican school in another part of the district. The petitioners requested an injunction to prohibit the continuation of such practices. The issue did not rest on whether the districts sponsored an overt form of racial separation or even that the Mexican schools might be inferior to the Anglo schools. The issue concerned the claim by Mexican Americans that the de facto segregation of their children based on a language criterion—the idea that Mexican Americans had to be taught separately because they were predominantly Spanish speaking—and their prohibition from attending the Anglo schools were unconstitutional.[99]

The Federal District Court agreed and ruled that such segregation not only violated California educational laws that prohibited segregation of Mexican-American children, but also violated the Fourteenth Amendment of the U.S. Constitution. The court conceded that the only tenable grounds for segregation lay in the language deficiencies of some of the Mexican-American children. However, these conditions did not justify, as existed in Orange County, the segregation of Mexican-American students through the sixth and eighth grades. On the contrary, the court observed that segregation retarded the learning of English. The court further observed that no credible language tests existed to determine the segregation of Mexican-American children on their inability to speak English. Moreover, records revealed that even those Mexican-American students who achieved outstanding grades, learning in English, could still not transfer to an Anglo school.[100]

On appeal the Ninth Circuit Court of Appeals one year later affirmed the decision in the Westminster case. Closely resembling the more famous Brown case in 1954, in which the U.S. Supreme Court declared separate schools for blacks unconstitutional, the Westminster case signaled a major victory for Mexican Americans and for LULAC, which had helped provide the funding support for the adjudication of the case. In the appeal, Mexican Americans were aided by the National Association for the Advancement of Colored People (NAACP), the American Jewish Congress, the Japanese-American Citizens League, as well as the ACLU and the National Lawyers Guild. Attorney Marcus hailed the Westminster decision as the "greatest opinion since the emancipation of the slaves and the writing of the 14th Amendment."[101]

The Westminster case had a ripple effect and in 1948 LULAC sponsored and funded a similar legal challenge to school segregation in Texas. In *Delgado v. Bastrop Independent School District,* a federal district court again ruled, as in the Westminster case, that the segregation of Mexican-American pupils violated the Fourteenth Amendment. The Delgado case went one step further and specifically declared unconstitutional the segregation of Mexican Americans in separate classrooms within "integrated" schools. The court, as in Westminster, allowed that Mexican Americans could be separated because of language differences but that this could be done only in the first grade while the pupils learned English. The separation could not be done on the basis of race, but only after the application of scientific and standardized tests equally given to all students, both Mexican American and Anglo. Despite the *Delgado* decision, many Texas school districts procrastinated in desegregating their schools and in some cases attempted to circumvent integration by keeping Mexican-American children segregated in their own classrooms in schools attended by both Anglos and Mexican Americans. To specifically attack this practice, LULAC with the aid of lawyers Gus García and James De Anda supported a suit by Mexican-American parents against the Driscoll School District in south Texas in 1957. García and De Anda observed that Mexican-American children were segregated in the first and second grades on the claim by school authorities that they spoke only Spanish. In addition, officials administered no scientific tests to all students to determine their proficiency in English. A federal district court again agreed with the plaintiffs and ruled that the Driscoll system violated the Fourteenth Amendment rights of Mexican Americans by arbitrarily segregating them as a separate class. This constituted race discrimination. The court, as in other cases, agreed that some initial separation based on language could be practiced, but that this had to be determined on individual abilities calculated by scientific tests and not arbitrarily on racial or ethnic distinctions.[102]

Successful in their own legal efforts against school segregation, Lulacers likewise applauded the 1954 Brown case. "Minority groups all over the United States have for years fought to end segregation," one Lulacer commented about the historic Supreme Court decision, "and it has taken all these years to finally bring about equality of educational opportunity for all races in our country."[103] Yet the Brown decision along with the Mexican-American cases did not immediately transform segregated education into integrated education. More legal battles and civic protests would still have to be waged in later decades. In Texas, for example, LULAC vigorously condemned legislation in the late 1950s intended to avoid the Brown case and continue school segregation, especially of black students. Lulacer Pete Tijerina reminded his colleagues in 1957 that Mexican Americans together with blacks would have little choice but to rely on federal intervention to ensure compliance of constitutional rights. LULAC's legal battles did not end educational underdevelopment for many Mexican Americans. They continued to face inequalities in comparison to Anglo students. Still, LULAC's path-breaking litigation forced the southwestern education system on the defensive and obtained the force of law behind Mexican-American efforts to achieve educational equality. It also furthered the "nationalization" of Mexican-American politics through

LULAC's reliance on the powers of the federal courts to institute changes for Mexican Americans.[104]

Conclusion

For over thirty years LULAC served as the principal and most visible Mexican-American organization in the United States. Although founded in Texas and initially concentrating on Mexican-American issues in that state, LULAC by 1960 had become a national organization with councils throughout the Southwest and Midwest, the regions containing the majority of Mexican Americans. In later decades it would spread even more and include other Latino peoples such as Puerto Ricans and to a lesser extent Cuban Americans. As one of the few organizations working on basic civil rights for Mexican Americans, LULAC, despite its idealistic faith in the ability of the American system to reform itself, provided a degree of ethnic protection for Mexican Americans and through its struggles achieved breakthroughs in advancing civil rights. Yet the end of the 1950s and the commencement of the 1960s marked the end of one period of LULAC's history and the start of another.

Since its formation LULAC had sought to integrate Mexican Americans into the mainstream of American life. In doing so, it sought to break down discriminatory barriers and to stress the similarities between Mexican Americans and other groups. It fostered cultural pluralism as a symbol of cultural coexistence rather than of cultural defiance. Pluralism was Americanism. Above all, LULAC shunned identification as a minority organization, although it pragmatically organized around Mexican-American issues. It did not favor special programs aimed at Mexican Americans. Instead, it sought to integrate Mexican Americans into existing institutions that had either consciously excluded Mexican Americans or had not been sensitive to Mexican-American participation.

However, under the administration of Félix Tijerina of Houston (1957–61), LULAC supported the concept of special programs exclusively for Mexican Americans, signaling the evolution of LULAC into a self-acknowledged minority organization. Tijerina recognized the language problems faced by thousands of Spanish-speaking children as they entered school, and he believed it important for LULAC to devise a program to teach English to these children as preschoolers. As a result, Tijerina organized the Little School of 400 in 1957, which LULAC supported through its own resources with the endorsement of local school districts. These preschools for Mexican-American children sought to teach them 400 basic English words. The hope was that this would lessen the cultural and linguistic shocks that Spanish-speaking children generally experienced as they began their education. The Little School of 400 in itself was not necessarily a major departure for LULAC, since it had previously sponsored English classes for Mexican nationals. Moreover, Tijerina and his supporters did not consciously conspire to introduce ideological changes within LULAC. Still, what made the Little School different was Tijerina's successful efforts to get the Texas state government to fund the project and hence recognize by legislation a special program for Mexican Americans. In 1959 LULAC, with the help of friendly Anglo legislators, acquired passage of legislation to provide state funds for school districts wishing to establish preschool English classes for Mexican Americans. The Little School of 400 as a state project became the model for the federally funded Head Start Program during the 1960s.[105]

Yet not all Lulacers agreed with Tijerina. The Little School introduced the first major ideological crisis in LULAC's history. Integration, as defined by LULAC, had been the cornerstone of Mexican-American efforts to achieve first-class citizenship. Dissenters from the Little School concept claimed that they now were being told that some separation in education was acceptable. This was anathema on both ideological and instructional grounds for some Lulacers. Judge Albert Armendáriz, past president of LULAC, recalled the questions that the Little School created among the LULAC leadership: "The basic concept of the LULAC leadership was that integration was the answer to equality of opportunity in schools and nothing less will ever suffice." Despite their objections, Armendáriz and other opponents failed to counter successfully Tijerina's new orientation. Consequently, many of the more traditionalist leadership either left LULAC or more often were relegated to a subordinate role. Armendáriz still believes that the Little School concept of stressing separate education was wrong. "Integration is what they will not give us," he concludes. "They'll give us three millions of dollars for special education, but they will not integrate the schools."[106]

The Little School did not ostensibly affect LULAC's goal concerning the Americanization of Mexican Americans. Yet although not necessarily abandoning integration as a principle, LULAC now began to favor special compensatory programs for Mexican Americans. Separation rather than integration for particular remedial purposes became acceptable. In the 1960s LULAC acknowledged that Mexican Americans were different from Anglos in certain ways and that these differences had to be dealt with before full integration could occur. "In 15 years from now," Tijerina observed of the importance of the preschool program, "the children of Latin American descent will be equal to other Americans because of this English language instruction."[107]

If the Little School of 400 inaugurated a new direction for LULAC, the reform programs of the New Frontier–Great Society during the 1960s accelerated the minoritization of LULAC. As the black civil rights movement advanced and through bitter struggles achieved civil rights reforms, including compensatory programs for blacks, Mexican Americans demanded similar opportunities from the federal government. Moreover, the growing recognition of Mexican Americans as an important political group plus the federal largess that accompanied that recognition proved to be quite seductive for LULAC and other more mainstream Mexican-American organizations. A separate identity from other Americans in conjunction with separate programs now came to be seen as legitimate. Consequently, the Johnson administration through its War on Poverty campaign targeted and funded specific Mexican-American projects. Federally funded job-retraining centers for Mexican Americans through Operation SER (Service, Employment, and Redevelopment), for example, became integral parts of LULAC's program. Special federal housing for Mexican Americans likewise came under LULAC's jurisdiction. LULAC further endorsed federal legislation for bilingual, bicultural education. In addition, LULAC supported President Johnson's formation of a special Inter-Agency Committee on Mexican-American Affairs and called for a department of Mexican-American affairs within the U.S. Civil Rights Commission.[108]

All of this did not fundamentally alter LULAC's basic principles aimed at achieving first-class citizenship for Mexican Americans. It did, however, symbolize a recognition by LULAC that the road to full integration would be lengthier than first thought and that in the meantime it would not be enough to call attention to the basic similarities between Mexican Americans and other ethnic groups. If special programs for Mexican Americans as a minority group were possible, then LULAC had to accept them in the hope of widening the bases for the Americanization of Mexican Americans through economic and educational reforms. In the process, the minoritization of LULAC alienated the older leadership—the Mexican-American Generation—which had refused to compromise on the issue of integration and what it believed to be the negative stigma of a minority. Hence, the 1960s witnessed the augmentation of earlier LULAC pluralist concepts, which had focused on culture, to include political and economic issues. In addition, the emergence of a militant Chicano Movement by the mid-1960s, with its emphasis on cultural nationalism and political self-determination, pressured LULAC to meet this challenge for political hegemony in Mexican-American communities by becoming more nationalistic. In all, LULAC did not abandon the search for America in the 1960s, but it did begin to take a different route.

CHAPTER THREE

Education and the Mexican American: Eleuterio Escobar and the School Improvement League of San Antonio

An illiterate cannot defend himself, his community or his country.
—ELEUTERIO ESCOBAR (autobiography)

The Mexican-American Generation regarded educational reform as its most important social issue. LULAC, of course, attacked de facto school segregation in the courts. At the community level, other Mexican Americans pressured authorities for improvements in the Mexican schools. Education, as LULAC leaders stressed, was the key to integration and social mobility. Hence, the battle over the schools was a logical arena of protest, especially for the aspiring lower middle class. The schools symbolized, on the one hand, Anglo institutions of authority and control and yet, on the other, the promise of upward mobility if Mexican Americans could help change their direction. As sóciologists Piven and Cloward correctly argue, "people experience deprivation and oppression within a concrete setting, not as the end product of large and abstract processes, and it is the concrete experience that molds their discontent into specific grievances against specific targets." [1] Lacking access, for the most part, to political offices and unlike Mexican-American workers who could strike and unionize to express their discontent, lower-middle class Mexican Americans as community leaders focused on school issues as a natural forum for their social protest. Schools affected their children's chances for the American dream as well as serving as a community issue bringing together all sectors of the barrio. This chapter examines the politics of educational reform in San Antonio initiated by Eleuterio Escobar and the School Improvement League.

Escobar and the league, composed of a small number of dedicated community leaders, from 1934 to 1956 carried on a persistent crusade to improve and expand educational facilities for thousands of Mexican-American children in the the west-side barrio of San Antonio. While other Mexican-American leaders of this period sought social reforms through the courts, politics, or labor struggles, Escobar and the league took on the local school board and organized a grassroots resistance to a legacy of educational injustice.

Eleuterio Escobar

Eleuterio Escobar came to educational reform out of his own life experiences. Born in 1894 in Laredo, Texas, to working-class parents, Escobar faced educational discrimination and segregation growing up in south Texas. Years later he wrote:

> When I first attended school (in Pearsall), I was segregrated along with other children with a Spanish surname. There were three elementary schools. One for Anglos made of permanent construction with several acres of play ground, one for Mexican Americans, a dilapidated one room frame building to serve first, second, and third grades. During these years I attended school in and out and some years after I never saw that any of my mates ever reached the sixth grade. The other school was for colored children.[2]

Most Mexican-American children worked on ranches performing a variety of tasks. The combination of limited and inferior schools as well as poverty produced, as Escobar observed, "a great number of families in which their sons, parents and grandparents were completely illiterate and many of them died in frustration, poor and without enjoying equal educational rights." Escobar, himself, never went much beyond the third grade and at age thirteen became the male head of the house after his father died. He and his mother worked at a ranch close to Charlotte, Texas. As a farmhand, Escobar received forty cents a day. Later as a foreman, he noted numerous children working alongside their parents instead of attending school. "Many children," he remembered, "were making nearly as much as some grown people." Determined to rise above his position, Escobar abandoned fieldwork and with his small savings established in 1912 a bicycle repair and rental shop in Pearsall. However, the big city attracted him and he soon left to become a traveling salesman working out of San Antonio. Selling quilts and blankets, Escobar traveled throughout south Texas.[3]

Escobar succeeded as a salesman despite his customers' poverty. Moving from town to town he observed the inferior conditions under which the resident Mexicans lived and worked. Most customers could not sign their names to his receipts. They could only make their mark. Families lived in dilapidated and congested shacks. Children rarely went to school and when they did received a limited education in segregated facilities.[4] As economist Paul

Taylor would later note, the Anglo establishment of south Texas would finance and provide only restricted education for Mexican-American children
since farmers needed them to reproduce the agricultural labor force.[5] Nevertheless, Escobar was always received warmly and with much hospitality by
his Mexican-American clientele despite their difficult lot. They saw Escobar
not just as a merchant but as a friend. "Being in their homes I could see
clearly what these people were up against," he wrote in his autobiography:

> I believe that with twenty thousand dollars in those days I would never have
> learned what I learned just for the price of trying to make a living. This
> touched me very much, because I had to go through their experience and I
> could feel their suffering because I am one of those unfortunates who was
> denied an equal education, and my human and constitutional rights were
> denied and infringed by our highest state and school officials. Their frustra-
> tion and suffering caused mothers to shed many tears. I said to my God,
> "God if I ever am in a position to help these unfortunate children in my
> humble way, I am going to do it." [6]

In 1918, after the United States entered World War I, Escobar enlisted
in the infantry and saw service in Europe. He returned one year later and
again traveled as a salesman. He wanted his own business and with credit
opened the San Antonio Mercantile Company with his friend and partner,
Antonio Martínez. They worked hard to satisfy their Mexican customers, and
Escobar's retail business flourished during the Roaring Twenties. In 1924 he
left Martínez with the business and formed the Escobar Furniture Company
in the west-side barrio of San Antonio. With his wife, whom he had married
the previous year, Escobar again succeeded in his enterprise. "Since this was
the only furniture store owned by a Mexican American," he remembered, "it
attracted the attention of the vast Mexican American colony." Besides acquiring his store, Escobar purchased property on the west side. "Everything
went well," he later wrote, "until 1929 when the depression broke out." He
could now barely pay his creditors, and his own customers and tenants de-
faulted on their payments. As the depression deepened, Escobar—like most
everyone else—struggled to survive.[7]

Yet, more fortunate than others, Escobar in both good and bad times
participated in community life. In 1927 he had helped organize the Mexican
Casino in San Antonio, composed of about sixty Mexican-American and
mexicano businessmen and professionals. The casino served as a social and
cultural center and apparently also sponsored charitable work.[8] Escobar
joined the Knights of America, one of the predecessors to LULAC. As a representative of the Knights, Escobar attended the 1929 Corpus Christi convention that founded LULAC. Always interested in youth, the San Antonio mer-

chant promoted athletic activities for Mexican-American boys by providing baseball equipment and converting some of his property into a baseball diamond that came to be called Escobar Field.[9] Although educational reform as an organized activity would in time become Escobar's primary civic activity, he did not come to it in a vacuum. Along with other Mexican-American political novices, Escobar evolved politically. At the height of the depression, he and a few other Mexican-American leaders, including prominent civic leader Alonso Perales, organized to participate in electoral politics. The depression, plus increased racial tensions, spurred them in this direction. In 1930, for example, some Texas Democrats had unsuccessfully attempted to ban Mexican Americans from primaries by arguing that Mexicans were not whites but Indians.[10] Lack of effective Mexican-American political representation in San Antonio also encouraged electoral politics. "At that time Mexican-Americans did not have a voice in the city, county, or state governments," Escobar later explained, "and the only representatives that we had were a few policemen, street sweepers, and garbage collectors." Composed predominantly of business and professional men, many of whom had never participated in electoral politics, the Association of Independent Voters selected Escobar as its president.[11] The association stressed the endorsement of candidates who possessed no prejudices against "people of Latin descent," who would deal with Mexican Americans on an equal basis with Anglos, and who would provide fair representation on juries and in governmental affairs.[12]

Unfortunately, the association soon divided on whether it should endorse state candidates, especially for governor, or just local ones. Irreparably split, the association collapsed. Escobar and other founders abandoned it and, according to Escobar, "the Association of Independent Voters . . . died . . . of natural causes."[13] In a postmortem, Alonso Perales optimistically noted that despite the association's demise it was only the initial phase of a more concerted Mexican-American political movement in San Antonio. The challenge was to maintain unity among the people. "This is the problem," Perales told Escobar, "and you and I will have to study this issue and see what we can do."[14]

Educational Struggles during the Great Depression

Escobar's political evolution led him to the cause that would come to occupy much of his active civic life: the campaign to provide educational opportunities for Mexican-American children. Deprived of an education himself, although self-taught, Escobar fervently embraced this struggle.[15] Escobar witnessed the increasing poverty of Mexican Americans in depression-ridden San Antonio and believed that only increased educational opportunities could alter such an uninspiring future. He wrote:

> In 1933 . . . the economic and educational situation was desperate. Thousand[s] of San Antonio families in order to survive were compelled to work shelling pecans for very low wages. Some of them were making as low as 15 cents a day. This made it very difficult for the family to feed, clothe, and educate the children.[16]

Few possessed a chance for a better life. The 1931 San Antonio city directory, for example, listed only five Spanish-surnamed lawyers. In addition, the difficulty with English plus lack of knowledge concerning their civil rights handicapped many Mexican Americans and mexicanos. Still, parents coveted education for their children and cried for help. "Many mothers swallowed their tears," Escobar recalled, "some were imploring with their cries for human justice. Others murmured with trembling voices, 'My children are not attending school.'"[17]

Escobar and other Mexican-American leaders concluded that only education could lift Mexican-Americans out of poverty. Consequently, they organized to improve the schools in San Antonio's west side. In early 1934 Escobar worked as a member of LULAC Council No. 16 and became chair of the council's Committee for Playground and School Facilities. The committee at first engaged in what some scholars term "action research": documenting the unsuitable nature of the Mexican schools with the intent of affecting public policy. Escobar astutely understood that his most formidable strength would be documentation not rhetoric.[18]

Over a period of weeks and months, mostly through Escobar's research in school and municipal records, the committee compiled an impressive array of data about the depressed and inadequate state of west-side schools. Escobar focused on the inequities surrounding the Mexican schools and compared them to the Anglo schools in other parts of San Antonio. An almost equal number of students attended both types of schools. The west-side schools contained 12,334 students while 12,224 studied in the non-Mexican schools. However, the students on the west side were cramped into only 11 schools, while 28 schools serviced the other sections. The Mexican schools contained less physical space and grounds: 23 acres for the 11 west-side schools to 82 acres for the other schools. Two-hundred and fifty-nine rooms were contained in west-side schools, while 368 rooms were in the other schools. The average number of students per room on the west side came to 48, while the average in the other sections was 23. Two-hundred and eighty-six teachers taught in the Mexican schools, while 339 taught in the Anglo ones. The school board averaged a direct cost of $24.50 per pupil on the west side, while spending an average of $35.96 per pupil elsewhere. Finally, Escobar observed that west-side schools contained 34 temporary frame rooms, while only 10 such rooms could be found in other schools.[19]

As the comparative data indicated, overcrowdedness posed the biggest problem for west-side schools: too many children and not enough facilities. The 11 schools had 259 rooms with a capacity for 9,065 pupils; yet 12,334 students were already attending. Crockett School, for example, had 1,430 students, but room for only 1,050. Barclay School with a capacity for 1,120 received 1,717 students. Navarro School had 1,822 with a total capacity for 1,330. And Brackenridge Memorial School hosted 2,004 children but could comfortably accommodate only 1,435. In all, the 11 schools had an excess of 3,269 students.[20]

Additional research revealed particular problems among individual schools. The committee reported that in Brackenridge Memorial, 14 children not yet registered but attending classes had to stay in the school auditorium due to lack of rooms. "They wait their turn until there is room for them," the committee observed, "and they are then permitted to be registered and to attend regularly." In the Barclay School, 53 fifth-graders were found in one room with only 40 desks. To accommodate all of them, the teacher sat 26 children 2 to a chair. At the Lanier Junior High School, administrators assigned the cafeteria, auditorium, library, dining rooms, and cooking and sewing rooms as classrooms.[21]

Bulging with students, the west-side schools had to resort to only half-day classes for many of the children. The committee discovered that about 1,000 first-graders attended school only half-day on double shifts. "For this reason," it noted, "it takes these children twice as long to complete a grade." With not enough room for them, as many as 6,000 school-age children on the west side did not attend any school. "Occasional inquiries have been made of children on the streets," the committee recorded, "and they say they are not in school because there is no room for them."[22]

The committee concluded that a direct link existed between overcrowded conditions and the discriminatory appropriation of funds for west-side schools by the school board. Besides providing less money per pupil to west-side schools, the school board did not spend the entire amount of monies apportioned for the Mexican schools. The total income for these schools based on both state contributions and property taxes came to $799,152.00. Yet the total expenditures for the eleven schools amounted to only $422,203.48. A surplus of $376,948.52 remained that the school board chose to spend elsewhere despite the poor conditions of the west-side schools.[23]

Utilizing these data, Escobar and the committee proposed that much more could be done by the school board to alleviate overcrowded and inadequate conditions for Mexican-American children. The committee was not prepared to directly challenge the de facto segregated status of the Mexican schools, but it called for at least making them equal to Anglo schools. It suggested a minimum of 5 new elementary schools with a total of between 82 and 94 rooms to service an additional 3,269 students. At least one more junior high was also needed. The construction of these new schools could easily be financed within the existing school board budget. The committee pointed out the contradiction of the school board's ability to finance the construction of new schools and facilities in Anglo neighborhoods but not in the west side. This money would be better utilized, the committee reasoned, in meeting the congested west-side school problems.[24]

Besides documenting the uneven development of the Mexican schools, the committee organized the ideological arguments for remedying the situation. Justice, for one, demanded that these educational inequities be corrected. It was not just for Mexican-American schoolchildren to be deprived of a good education. Educational reform would breed sound citizenship, which would benefit the entire San Antonio community. The committee contradicted malicious rumors that its proposed reforms were intended to foster self-segregation. Rather, these reforms were practical corrections to deplorable conditions harming more than just Mexican-American children. Twenty-five percent of the schoolchildren in the west side were Anglos, "and they are being discriminated the same as the others." The committee insisted that it fought for all children regardless of race, color, or creed. Finally, and perhaps more important, good and equal education for Mexican-American children was not only a moral issue but a constitutional one. Under the law, Mexican Americans were entitled to such education. The committee concluded that 82 additional rooms in the form of 5 new school buildings were needed by the opening of the new school year.[25]

Their data collected and their arguments sharpened, the LULAC committee headed by Escobar presented its case to the school board. The board listened and agreed to review the west-side situation but at the same time became defensive. Escobar and the committee attended various other meetings only to receive no response or delays.[26] On one occasion, R. S. Menefee, the president of the board, even suggested that the only reason behind the committee's proposal to build new schools consisted of Escobar's hopes to profit from selling his west-side property to the board. The committee quickly rebuffed Menefee, and Escobar reminded the board that the committee's sole desire was to achieve a good education for west-side children. The problem lay not with the committee but with the board's refusal to upgrade the west-side schools and instead spending money intended for them elsewhere. Escobar noted that mothers in the west side loved their children as much as mothers in other districts and "are interested in seeing that their children get their just due at the hands of this Board."[27] Supporting Escobar, attorney Alonso Perales appeared before the board and categorically denied Menefee's unfounded allegations. "The truth is," Perales stressed, ". . . that each and every member of Council No. 16 of the League of United Latin American Citizens is sincerely and honestly interested in the welfare of all our school children." Escobar had been selected to chair LULAC's committee on education not because he owned west-side property but because of his leadership qualities and his willingness to spend the time gathering the facts of the case. Perales charged that it had been Menefee who had first raised the issue of Escobar's property by offering to buy it if Escobar dropped the proposal for improving west-side schools.[28]

To appease the committee and to neutralize the issue of west-side reforms, the board announced the immediate authorization of an additional school for the west side. However, this amounted only to purchasing 15 abandoned frame rooms from the Peacock Military Academy and moving them to the west side, where the board declared the completion of Lorenzo de Zavala School. Not deceived, the committee denounced the board's action as a deliberate attempt to mislead public opinion. "The said frame dwellings are inadequate and unsafe," the committee declared.[29] Perales reiterated that 88 new rooms were needed and that these had to be in permanent and fire-proof structures: "We do not want shacks."[30] Besides its meager effort in "establishing" Zavala School, the board proposed a survey of west-side school conditions by a University of Texas committee. Escobar sensed delay but hoped that the outside investigation would prove productive. He welcomed this concession and promised to provide the survey committee with his own data.[31]

Dissatisfied with the school board's response and fearful of losing momentum, the committee solicited public support to achieve its objectives. It appealed for endorsements from other organizations and invited them to the committee's meetings. It shared its data on west-side schools with other interested parties.[32] Escobar encouraged supporters to send letters to the school board concerning the west-side issue. "Your effort in their behalf," Escobar explained, "will mean happiness for thousands of school children who are not attending full sessions now for lack of space."[33] Escobar also personally contacted a variety of both Mexican-American and Anglo organizations, labor unions, and many in San Antonio's religious community. In all, the committee claimed support from 73 civic, social, labor, and religious organizations. Mexican-American groups endorsing the committee included the Alianza Hispano-Americana, the Baptist Good Will Center, the Democratic Club, Federación Obrera Latino-Americana, Home of Neighborly Service,

Cámara Mexicana de Comercio, Mexican Ministries Alliance, Mexican Protestant Social Workers, Order Hijos de América, Sociedad Benito Juárez, Unión de Barberos Latino-Americanos, Unión de Empleados y Dependientes, Unión de Jornaleros, and Unión de Panaderos.[34]

With strong community support, especially among Mexican Americans, Escobar went above the heads of the school board by appealing directly for school relief to State Superintendent of Public Instruction L. A. Woods.[35] Woods agreed to investigate the west-side conditions and would inspect the area himself. "I assure you," he promised Escobar, "that I am not going to be a party in hurting the Latin-American children of San Antonio."[36] Capitalizing on Woods's favorable response, the committee mobilized to host Woods at a mass rally where it could impress upon the state superintendent the urgency of school reform and of the community's support for it. Scheduled for October 24, 1934, at Sidney Lanier Junior High School, the evening meeting was hailed as an opportunity to hear Woods's proposals for relieving the congested school conditions. Besides asking Woods, the committee invited other prominent speakers including the Reverend C. Tranchese, a leading Mexican-American religious leader and the pastor of Our Lady of Guadalupe; James Tafolla, president of LULAC Council No. 2 of San Antonio; Orlando F. Gerodetti, president of LULAC Council No. 16; Ermilio R. Lozano, president general of LULAC; Alonso Perales; local attorney Carl Wright Johnson; Mrs. María Hernández, secretary of Orden Caballeros de América; Carlos E. Castañeda, librarian-historian at the University of Texas and superintendent of the San Felipe School District in Del Rio, Texas; P. H. Dickson, a member of the state legislature; and Franklin Spears, also of the state legislature. Escobar, of course, would likewise speak.[37] In his autobiography, Escobar recalled the problem of enough seating for the many families expected. From his store, he lent the arrangements committee 2,500 chairs. As the ceremony commenced, Escobar observed thousands of people marching into the outdoor meeting place. "That was the most impontant [sic], impressive and emotional scene that I have ever seen," he wrote. Escobar estimated the audience to be between 10,000 and 13,000. *La Prensa* had announced before the meeting that it would be the largest ever held by Mexicans in San Antonio.[38]

During the speeches, the crowd interrupted each speech with rounds of applause. Attorney Johnson drew an enthusiastic response when he stated: "There is no question about it that those West Side children are being deprived of an adequate education by our state school board officials and are victims of abuse and discrimination and these injustices should be corrected." Finally, Superintendent Woods addressed the meeting. He praised the committee and the audience for their interest in the schools and did not deny the charges concerning the west-side schools. He concluded: "I promise after I investigate, that I will see to it that your school children's problems will be corrected." The crowd was ecstatic and so was Escobar.[39]

One week later, Escobar informed supporters that he had received a letter from Woods in which the superintendent agreed to support the committee's efforts. Woods conceded the truthfulness of the committee's depiction of the west-side schools. He noted that both the president of the San Antonio School Board and the local superintendent of schools admitted the deficiencies of the Mexican schools. However, the situation could be remedied by utilizing some $900,000 in bond money available to the district. If the school board refused to do this and instead spent it elsewhere, Woods suggested that the committee resort to the courts to prohibit such action. "Frankly," he told Escobar, ". . . I am of the opinion that the first thing the School Board should do is to remedy the terrible school conditions that exist in the west-side, and I believe that if you continue your work the Board will concede your just demands." A delighted Escobar welcomed Woods's opinion as the first moral victory of the school campaign and believed that with the superintendent's intervention the struggle would go forward.[40]

Taking full advantage of Woods's letter, Escobar sent a summary of it along with supporting data to some of the city's leading Anglo leaders. To Escobar's surprise, many of them, including the mayor, responded with letters of support. Still, despite such favorable response to the committee, the school board refused to deal with Escobar. Board President Menefee told a reporter that he saw no necessity of working with LULAC since the board on its own was moving to make reforms. "(If) we could be free of outside intervention," Menefee was quoted as saying, "we could make the correction much easier." A disappointed Escobar now believed that as long as he headed LULAC's school committee, Menefee would have nothing to do with it. Escobar offered to resign.[41]

The School Improvement League

Escobar's offer of resignation was also indicative of internal strains within LULAC. On at least two occasions, Escobar had complained about the unwillingness of various LULAC members to support wholeheartedly the school campaign.[42] These tensions plus the reluctance of the school board to negotiate with Escobar led Council No. 16 to appoint a new school committee excluding Escobar. The council also designated the new committee without first conferring with the various organizations supporting the school issue. Insulted and angered, representatives of these other groups denounced the council's actions and moved to organize their own school committee with Escobar as its president. Informed of such action, Escobar approved it and agreed to head the alternative committee. Named La Liga Pro-Defensa Escolar (the School Improvement League), the Liga quickly claimed the support of more than 70 organizations representing approximately 75,000 persons. With such response, the Liga now spearheaded the struggle for better schools and superseded the LULAC committee, which self-destructed.[43]

Early in 1935 the Liga mobilized support from Anglo politicians. Most of San Antonio's representatives to the state legislature, undoubtedly sensitive to increasing political activism by Mexican Americans, endorsed the Liga as did two members of the school board who publicly admitted the depressed school conditions on the west side. Confident of both community and political backing, the Liga moved to pressure the school board by initiating a bill introduced by Representative J. Franklin Spears that would reduce a San Antonio School Board member's term from six to two years. The Liga believed that much of the problem with the school board concerned board members feeling immune from public pressures due to their long terms.[44] Board members apparently felt less sensitive to Mexican-American pressures because of exceedingly low turnout of voters, including Mexican Americans, for school board elections. The bill passed the house but stalled in the education committee of the senate. To impress upon that committee, especially Senator Ernest Fellbaum of San Antonio, the level of community support for the bill, the Liga encouraged supporters to send telegrams to Fellbaum. "Our organization composed of more than five hundred members requests you support bill number three forty-six shortening term members School Board," the Sociedad De La Unión informed Fellbaum.[45] Over 200 telegrams reached Fellbaum and the committee. In addition, Liga members headed by Escobar attended a public hearing sponsored by the education committee. Escobar once again revealed the deplorable school conditions for Mexican-American children. Legislators questioned Board President Menefee, who under pressure conceded the Liga's arguments and promised to upgrade the Mexican schools. He would recommend the construction of at least two new schools and the addition of 50 new rooms. Additional property on the west side would also be purchased for school playgrounds. Menefee further agreed to hire sufficient teachers for the west-side schools. With Menefee's concessions, the education committee shelved the bill.[46]

Not willing to relax its campaign after the Austin hearings, Escobar and the Liga sought to solidify community support and to establish an information network. It commenced publication of a bilingual newspaper, *The Defender (El Defensor De La Juventud)* to keep both its Spanish-speaking and Anglo supporters informed of Liga activities and issues. *The Defender* re-

inforced the arguments for the citizens of San Antonio to support the movement for better schools. It was their duty as parents, as taxpayers, and as
concerned citizens interested in the welfare of youth. It was the moral thing
to do. The Liga reiterated that it would maintain pressure on the school board
until Mexican-American children received justice.[47] In its English-language
section, *The Defender* also appealed to concerned Anglo citizens for support.
Besides its community newspaper, the Liga utilized other methods to reach
out to the public. In March 1935 it announced plans for a large fiesta at the
Municipal Auditorium. Escobar obtained as headliner Mexico's foremost
composer and singer, Agustín Lara. Held on April 10, the fiesta proved a
success. The Liga mixed entertainment with consciousness raising by publishing a fiesta program containing data about the school problem. In addition, Carlos Castañeda from the University of Texas explained the Liga's role
and objectives. The fiesta attracted large numbers of people and raised more
than $700 for the Liga. Other community events sponsored by the Liga in-
cluded athletic field days for the children of the west side.[48]

The Liga received its most important success, however, a few months
later in July 1935, when the University of Texas survey committee completed
its report of west-side school conditions. It confirmed the findings of the earlier LULAC research and recommended construction of new schools plus ad-
ditions to existing ones in the west side. The school board accepted the recommendations and together with Menefee's previous pledges authorized the
building of three new elementary schools during the next three years in addition to maintaining Zavala School with its wooden barracks.[49] Yet these concessions, after over a year's struggle, would only partially improve west-side
conditions. Unfortunately, the Liga affected by the economic pressures of the
depression, found it difficult to maintain momentum. Moreover, the dawn of
World War II completely set aside the school campaign and ended the first
chapter of the School Improvement League.

The Postwar Struggles

The war over, a still-committed Escobar believed it propitious to
launch another protest movement concerning west-side school conditions.
The school board had made some additional modifications but had done
nothing substantial to relieve congestion on the west side while the number of
schoolage children increased. On sound personal economic footing after the
war, Escobar now plunged back into the school struggle. In August 1947,
representatives from more than thirty Spanish-speaking organizations along
with certain Anglo supporters reconstituted the School Improvement League
with Escobar as its president. "Before the war we fought a bitter campaign in

order to obtain a mere dole of four schools of varied and inadequate construction from the San Antonio School Board," Escobar reminded delegates. "With the onset of the war all of our efforts were then enlisted in behalf of victory. Our campaign for educational justice remained dormant."[50] The war had been won and Mexican Americans intensified their demands for opportunities equal to those of other Americans.

The league's ideological argument for quality education was enhanced by the experience of the war. "Our fight to preserve our way of life from the endangering and hostile forces of the world has ended victoriously," the league stressed, "and we now face the task of rebuilding our own community." The war, by enlisting Mexican-American efforts in the struggle to preserve American democracy, had accelerated the acculturation of Mexican Americans. Consequently, the league more intensively defended Mexican-American children not as "Latin Americans," "México-Texanos," or "Indo-Latinos" but as Americans. "If in the trenches of Europe and the Pacific we were equal and we demonstrated our loyalty and love for the Stars and Stripes," the league noted, "then in civic life we also desire equality." The league sought no special privileges, just equality: "We simply want the same opportunity given our children in education as the equal duty that was given them to figh[t] and die for our country."[51]

Having reorganized the league, Escobar sought to capture media attention, revitalize the issue of the west-side schools, and once again put the school board on the defensive. He astutely accomplished this by focusing attention on the "fire traps"—the temporary wooden buildings—housing many west-side children during school hours. In interviews with local newspapers, Escobar charged that the lives of more than 2,000 schoolchildren were being endangered by having to attend classes in these buildings. "In the event of fire any one of these school buildings would result in our children dying like rats," he told the *San Antonio Evening News*.[52] Drawn to the sensationalism of this story, the same newspaper published photographs that supported Escobar's charges. One revealed an abandoned pecan shelling plant reconverted to classrooms at Sidney Lanier High School. Another showed an old abandoned wooden church serving as a music hall for the same school. Still a third exposed two worn outdoor tables at Zavala School that substituted for a cafeteria. Escobar reminded readers that the entire Zavala School consisted of old frame buildings that should be condemned. Already a fire in 1945 had destroyed part of Zavala.[53] Asked to comment on Escobar's charges, Superintendent of Schools Thomas B. Portwood declined to debate the School Improvement League in the media. The league exploited this publicity by announcing that it would not be satisfied until such wooden structures were replaced by permanent ones and additional schools built in the west-side. "We don't want any more shacks," Escobar insisted.[54]

To effectively argue, as in the 1930s, that it spoke for the Mexican-American community, the league again concentrated on obtaining broad public support. Many of the older Mexican-American organizations once more enthusiastically endorsed the league, as did certain Anglo welfare and religious groups. In addition, younger Mexican Americans, many of them "veteranos" recently returned from the war, received their political baptism by joining the league. The league expanded its support base even more in the postwar period by securing the formal encouragement of the Catholic hierarchy in San Antonio through the Archdiocesan Office for the Spanish Speaking. More than eighty organizations ratified the league's objectives.[55]

Public support was also solicited by the reestablishment of an information network. Besides its own newspaper and reliance on sympathetic publications such as the *San Antonio Light* and the Spanish-language *La Prensa*, the league this time made use of radio as a consciousness-raising and information-disseminating tool. Several San Antonio radio stations, especially Spanish-language ones, offered free radio time. For example, Raul Cortez, owner of KCOR, allowed Escobar 15 minutes each Monday at 1 P.M. for the league's program. KITE through its daily afternoon program "La Voz de México" (The Voice of Mexico) granted the league 15 minutes each day.[56] Reaching thousands of people on a daily basis, the league used radio to further four basic objectives. First, it strongly counseled parents to keep their children in school in spite of difficult school conditions and the economic hardships faced by families. The situation was underscored by the large number of migrant farmworking families who resided in the city during the nonharvest season, but who left during the picking season to utilize all family members, including children, as a working unit. These parents were told that by not keeping their children in school they irrevocably harmed them. "The money that your children can earn in one year of farmwork," the league stressed to parents, "cannot justify ruining their futures by a lack of education."[57] Second, the league used radio to socialize Mexicans in San Antonio, especially parents, to the league's educational philosophy. Education raised children from a state of ignorance and made them better sons and daughters as well as future parents and citizens. It prepared them to cope with life. Education was both a human and a constitutional right. Mexican-American children were entitled as U.S. citizens to an education and no one could deny them that opportunity. Third, through the air the league informed parents about its activities and of basic facts concerning the schools. Escobar estimated that about 80 percent of Mexicans in San Antonio did not know their educational rights. Some did not know at what age their children could attend school or what school district they belonged to. Finally, Escobar used time on English-language broadcasts to reach Anglos and convince them of the league's cause.[58]

To justify additional schools and facilities as well as to educate the public about the west-side school problem, the league once again engaged in "action research." It formed a special research committee to compile data.[59] Although the basic inequities between Mexican schools and Anglo ones had not changed, the committee discovered that the disparities of resources had widened. Overcrowded conditions still plagued west-side schools. The league estimated that 11 west-side elementary schools did not possess adequate classroom space for over 7,000 students. In some cases, 50 or more students occupied one classroom. "The state law requires that there shall be no more than 35 students to each teacher," Escobar observed, "but on the West Side there are more than that—In West Side classrooms, in some instances, 65 to 75 pupils per teacher." Overcrowded conditions forced many children to attend only half-day classes. In five elementary schools alone more than 1,800 students were restricted to half-day classes. Thousands of others attended schools out of their district for lack of space. Those fortunate enough to attend were not only cramped in classrooms but did not have proper recreational areas. While 25 elementary schools in Anglo sections contained over 70 acres of recreational space to serve 9,225 students, on the west side 4 elementary schools, as an example, only possessed 13 acres of playgrounds to care for 4,087 students. Escobar calculated that over 15,000 west-side schoolchildren had unsuitable playgrounds.[60]

Overcrowded and confined in space, many of the Mexican schools also represented firetraps. More than 2,000 children occupied temporary frame rooms. The league stressed the dangers of this condition by arranging an on-site inspection of these facilities by the San Antonio Fire Department accompanied by league members and representatives of the school board. In its report, the fire department substantiated the league's concerns. Of Zavala School, the report read: "buildings are situated within 20 feet of each other, thus creating an exposure hazard to all buildings." And of the one-story wooden annex at Sidney Lanier, it noted; "Wallpaper is rotten and loose. This constitutes a very serious fire hazard." The fire chief recommended immediate evacuation of the annex. The Lanier music hall—the old wooden church—had no fire extinguishers. Even west-side schools built of brick, such as J. T. Brackenridge, possessed no fire extinguishers.[61] "Imagine a city that lays claim to be counted as modern," the league chastised San Antonio, "having to admit that hundreds of its little people are closeted for hours daily in school buildings which have been proved to be positive fire traps!"[62]

The league concluded its postwar survey of school conditions by formally petitioning the school board on November 12, 1947, for changes. Escobar and league officers demanded the immediate elimination of the worst aspects of the west-side schools and the commencement of a new school construction program. League spokesman Manuel Castañeda stressed to the board that crowded classrooms and congested playgrounds retarded the intellectual and physical health of children. "The combination of these two evils, namely stunted mental growth and inferior physical conditions," he warned, "in turn creates fertile conditions for the existence of warped social complexes, vice, and inevitable juvenile delinquency and criminality." [63] The league insisted that all temporary wooden buildings—the firetraps—be vacated and replaced by permanent structures. It also called for acquisition of new playground acreage for west-side schools. Escobar noted that these immediate changes would pose no undue financial burdens on the board since, according to his research, it possessed more than adequate and unused building funds. The league called for the construction of the following specific items: six to eight new elementary schools, one junior high school, one senior high school, and one vocational school. [64]

Receiving the league's demands, School Board President Harry Rogers thanked the league for coming to the board rather than to the newspapers. Yet unwilling to concede past board failures concerning the west side, Rogers defensively insisted that the board already had initiated its own improvements for schools in the area. These included condemned property adjoining some schools, such as Sidney Lanier, that could be purchased by the board for new buildings and playgrounds. As for the wooden buildings, Rogers concluded that they could not be closed immediately. "Would you rather we close these 'firetraps' and have more half-day sessions?" he challenged league members. "Yes," responded Castañeda. "They're nothing but firetraps." "Well," reacted Rogers, "these firetraps have been there for 25 years and we've never had a child burned to death." Despite the heated exchange and Rogers's display of insensitivity, both sides agreed to appoint subcommittees and negotiate league demands. The league had won round one by forcing the board to consider their petition and accept negotiations. Assuming the moral high ground, the league gained additional public sympathy. "Apologies for existing conditions as well as vague promises of improvement are out of order," the *San Antonio Express* criticized the board. "There is work to be done, for which the entire community must share responsibility even as it will share the benefits of the achievement. How about ditching the talk—and getting on with the job." [65]

In its follow-up meeting with the board's subcommittee, the league presented specific proposals for immediate action on the firetraps and overcrowded conditions. They included the abandonment of the old pecan shelling plant used as a schoolroom annex at Sidney Lanier; the purchase of the city block south of Sidney Lanier and the construction of a new annex composed of classrooms and a gymnasium; the building of a new Zavala School to replace the barracks; the authorization of a new elementary school on 20 acres at the intersection of Barclay and Arizona streets; the addition of eight new classrooms to Brackenridge School; and the acquisition of four sites for new elementary schools. Faced with the league's pressure plus public concern over the firetraps, the school board acquiesced to some of these demands. It would acquire the city block south of Sidney Lanier and build additional classrooms and a gymnasium. The old pecan shelling plant at Lanier would be closed and students temporarily transferred to other schools. A new Zavala School would replace the barracks. However, Zavala students would remain in the frame building until the new school became available on adjacent property. Brackenridge School would acquire eight new classrooms. Finally, the board, in subsequent action, approved construction of two new elementary schools at a total cost of $400,000. An elated but cautious Escobar informed the Mexican-American community that this success was only the beginning of a new struggle over the schools. Much still remained to be done.[66]

Escobar's cautiousness was not unwarranted. Although the board in principle agreed to most of the league's initial demands, it procrastinated in fulfilling them. Instead, it accelerated new school construction in Anglo neighborhoods or in nonpopulated suburbs where they hoped to entice new housing developments.[67] Dissatisfied with the board's slow response to reforms plus believing that the public did not fully appreciate the magnitude of the west-side school problem, Escobar and the league gathered and presented additional evidence. More than 10,000 students did not have access to adequate schooling. Of those attending school, over 7,000 were cramped "like sardines" in fewer than 200 classrooms. West-side schools averaged more than 40 pupils per room, while those in other sections averaged fewer than 30. At Collins Garden School, for example, 901 students attempted to learn in 25 rooms averaging 32 to 39 per room. The league estimated that even with the construction of the proposed four new elementary schools on the west side they would still not be able to accommodate all of the schoolage children. Critically affected were the hundreds of first and second graders who attended only half-day classes. In four west-side schools alone with a total of 3,621 students, almost 1,500, or 41 percent, went to half-day sessions due to lack of space. When the *San Antonio Light* reported that some educators did not believe half-day classes retarded students since all they lost was recreation time, Escobar countered: "If half-day classes do not retard education why don't these educators put all children on half-day classes so that all children will receive equal education, instead of picking on underprivileged children?"[68]

The league called further attention to the deplorable facilities provided to west-side children. Some schools possessed limited or no cafeterias. At both the Sam Houston and Hood schools no cafeterias had ever been built in twenty years. The children ate off the floor. At Sidney Lanier a cafeteria with a seating capacity of 120 serviced a student body of over 1,700.[69] Many students had to eat their lunches on the school grounds. "This creates a problem of sanitation since food particles are dropped on the yard which attract rats, mice, roaches, and flies."[70] The Lanier senior and junior high school library, for example, only could accommodate 125. Of course, the use of wooden classrooms continued to plague the west side. Despite the board's pledge to eliminate the firetraps, many still functioned as classrooms. Out of 67 such rooms in all San Antonio elementary schools 55 were located on the west side. The barracks courted disaster. In 1948 another fire broke out in one of Zavala's frame buildings that fortunately injured no students. Two years later, a third fire at Zavala engulfed and destroyed two classrooms along with two offices and a library. No permanent classrooms had as yet been built by the school board. Miraculously, the fire occurred on a weekend with no students in attendance.[71] Calling Zavala a "possible funeral pyre," Escobar castigated the board for its "criminal negligence": "We hope that it will not be necessary to see that two or three hundred children are burned to death before we see to it that the School Board does something to correct completely this menacing situation." Escobar and the league insisted on the completion of the projects already agreed upon plus at least one more elementary school and one junior high school.[72]

Seemingly unable to get action from the school board despite persistent and confrontational attendance at board meetings, the league appealed again to public opinion. It utilized its radio program to disseminate information and to request funds and volunteers. In 1948 the league mobilized support for the election of lawyer Gus García to the school board. Several thousand Mexican Americans went to the polls and elected García.[73] In addition, Escobar attempted to duplicate the 1934 mass rally. The highlight of this demonstration would be to show photographic evidence of decaying west-side school conditions. "This [*sic*] slides will show once and for all that our children have not only been deprived of equal school facilities, advantages and opportunities," a league leaflet read, "but that no amount of money would ever be able to repay them for the tremendous loss in morale and physical wellbeing that they have had to suffer."[74] With the meeting scheduled for August 31, 1948, Escobar hoped to use the occasion, as in 1934, to appeal to State Superintendent Woods for school relief. Labeling Superintendent Portwood a "menace" to the welfare of children in San Antonio, Escobar called on Woods to authorize a survey of west-side school conditions.[75] Escobar likewise invited members of the school board: "Mr. President, and everyone of you ladies and gentlemen are invited to attend that meeting, so that you can see in pictures the way that you have neglected, abused and punished helpless children."[76]

Three thousand people attended the rally and heard main speaker Carlos Castañeda decry the fact that schools attended by Mexican Americans in Texas were in worse shape in 1948 than they had been in 1934. "The inferior schools are not a matter of discrimination or segregation but a plain case of social injustice and a violation of the state school law," Casteñeda charged.[77] The league displayed photographic slides that, among other things, revealed pictures of a dead dog that had lain in front of the Brackenridge cafeteria for three days before being removed, of children eating on the ground at Zavala, and of a young boy at Lanier practicing his music in a bathroom for lack of proper space. Although Woods could not attend, Escobar nevertheless used the rally to urge him once more to intervene in San Antonio.[78]

Woods this time did not intervene. However, faced with the league's persistence and its ability to solicit public sympathy, the board itself proposed a survey of the west side. In 1949 it authorized Dean T. H. Shelby, head of the Extension Department of the University of Texas, to head the study. Escobar attacked the survey as incomplete, but the Shelby Committee did note that San Antonio faced an acute shortage of facilities at the same time that its school-age population was expanding. The committee went further and recommended that a minimum of $15 million would have to be expended within five years if the city was going to realistically confront its educational problems. The Shelby Committee's report, however, found little support among school board members. Historically biased against upgrading the west-side schools due to their perception of the "limited educational needs" of the Mexican Americans, the majority of the board desired to spend as little as possible on the Mexican schools and instead use its funds for the equally expanding Anglo neighborhoods. Board President Rogers in early 1950 established still another survey in the hope of soliciting a lower price tag. Rather than staffed by academicians, this committee consisted of citizens approved by the board. The Citizens' Survey Committee would study not just the west side but all San Antonio's schools and propose changes. Rogers suggested that one of these might be a $5 million bond issue. Chaired by Superintendent Portwood, the committee included nine members but only one Mexican American: Bennie Cantú of the Mexican Chamber of Commerce.[79]

Following four months of investigation, the Citizens' Survey Committee issued its report at a special board meeting. It surprised Rogers by advising a $9.3 million bond issue to cover the construction over five years of new schools and improvements and additions to old ones in all parts of San Antonio. For the west-side schools, the committee recommended a new 24-room Zavala School as well as new classrooms and additions at other schools plus cafeteria improvements. It further supported the building of a new junior high school on the west side and the expansion of Sidney Lanier High School. However, the committee chose not to target specific expenditures to particular projects. It believed that this would better be served by the board.[80] Prepared to address the committee's report, the league stacked the board meeting with between 50 and 75 members. "The West Side School Improvement League," one reporter observed, "took to the floor at the outset of the open discussion and held the floor almost the entire evening." Spokesman Richard Sánchez replied that the league found the report satisfactory except for its "discrepancies in the western part of the city." Sánchez proposed three new elementary schools and supported a bond issue, but only if the amount adequately met school needs. When Sánchez and other league members discussed individual schools on the west side, including the firetraps, they drew the ire of President Rogers. "We will not destroy good sound buildings because a few individuals do not know the difference between a good school and a bad one," he angrily addressed the league. Rogers added that, rather than constantly criticizing the board, Escobar and his followers should go out and support the bond issue. And, in a direct attack on the league that exposed Rogers's biases, he concluded: "We can't keep building schools for transients who go to school only three months out of the nine." Not intimidated, league members forced one committee member to admit that even under the report's recommendations some frame rooms would still be utilized on the west side. The board member received catcalls from league partisans when he defended the barracks by insisting that Zavala was the safest school in the district.[81]

The league countered the Citizens' Survey Report by issuing its own based on its most recent research. It found the citizens' report incomplete and incorrect and noted that its recommendations would only partially solve the problems. "We have lived on the Westside and we know the people, their hopes and aspirations," Escobar addressed the citizen's committee. "We feel that we speak for these people in warning you that your report and your request is not ample, and that in a very short time the citizens of San Antonio will again be called on to rectify some of the mistakes which are being made." Escobar observed that the citizens' report called for the construction of new schools in certain northern, eastern, and southern sections of the city where league research revealed nearly 100 vacant classrooms. Some schools in these predominantly Anglo neigborhoods, instead of being used as schools, were being occupied by administrative offices. Three such buildings could accommodate close to a thousand students. "Why does the Board propose to build more school rooms in some sections of town, when there is a total of 57 vacant rooms already in these schools?" inquired Escobar. On the other hand, minority neighborhoods cried out for new schools and improvements. Escobar pointed out that the survey overlooked black requests for a much-needed vocational school in the eastern portion of San Antonio. On the west side, Escobar stressed that the survey had completely failed to provide for such needs as adequate playground space, cafeteria facilities, auditoriums, and additional classrooms. Escobar concluded by insisting that the board commit a certain percentage of the bond money for specific proposals, especially on the west side. Board member Gus García believed that at least $3 million of the $9 million bond issue was needed for west-side schools. The league promised to endorse the bond issue, but only if the board reciprocated by allocating certain monies for west-side needs.[82]

Shortly before the bond election, both the School Improvement League and the local branch of the NAACP requested at a board meeting that the board agree to allocate specific portions of the bond to the Mexican and black schools within the district. Attorney Alonso Perales supported these requests by introducing a letter from Archbishop Robert E. Lucey calling attention to the inadequate school facilities in the poorer parts of the city. Undaunted, President Rogers responded that much was already being done in these neighborhoods and that he could not agree to the pledge desired by Escobar and the NAACP. "This board is not going to be pushed around," he told Escobar. The league president replied; "You talk like you own the school board. I say the (Citizen Survey) committee's report is a lot of misinformation."[83] Faced with a recalcitrant board, the league refused to endorse the bond issue but did not counsel supporters on how to vote. The league declared that it would not campaign against the bond measure and that it would leave the decision up to the voters. In a small turnout, the $9.3 million bond issue passed. A satisifed board asserted that although it was not bound by the citizens' survey it woud comply with most of its recommendations. Accordingly, it approved new plans for a permanent Zavala School plus other construction and improvements outlined for the west-side schools.[84]

Conclusion

Relentless in its campaign against the school board, the league continued its struggle into the 1950s. Unfortunately, it never fully achieved its objectives of equal and adequate educational facilities and opportunities for Mexican-American children. Yet, as with many poor community movements, it succeeded in forcing the issue of the west-side schools on the school board and on the conscience of San Antonio. Through its dedication to cause and by a display of keen organizational skills, the league also gained some concrete results. The new schools and improvements first promised and partially reaffirmed following the 1950 bond issue were in time completed. In 1952 the Zavala firetraps—long the symbol of the league's struggle—were finally torn down and a new permanent structure opened its doors.[85] Because of the league more Mexican-American children could attend school. The league continued to function, although less actively until at least 1956. By then not only were other community organizations engaged in educational issues, but Mexican Americans in San Antonio were achieving a greater voice within the educational structures of the city as teachers, administrators, and representatives to the school board. A legacy of inferior education had not been eliminated, but the league had commenced the movement by Mexican Americans to gain control over educational resources and to assert the rights of their children as U.S. citizens to equal schooling with other Americans. This movement would expand in later decades to include not only the desegregation of Mexican schools as a means to equal education but also the need to restructure curriculums to account for the bilingual, bicultural traditions of Mexican Americans. As if to crown Escobar's and the league's pioneering efforts, a new junior high school was dedicated in 1958 in the name of Eleuterio Escobar: "This gesture of recognition that I gladly accept," Escobar noted at the dedication,

> is really due not to my efforts alone, but to the efforts of all of you—the groups, friends, and organizations—who, side by side with the School Improvement League, joined in the struggle for educational emancipation until the rights of our children were recognized and respected with equality and justice.[86]

CHAPTER FOUR

Mexican-American Muckraker: Ignacio L. López and El Espectador

> El Espectador is not a combative newspaper, but it is vigilant about reason and justice.
>
> —IGNACIO L. LÓPEZ,
> El Espectador, Feb. 17, 1937

Mexicans in the United States possess a long and rich tradition in journalism. Since the U.S. conquest of the Southwest in 1848, numerous Spanish-language, English-language, and bilingual newspapers have been edited and published by Mexicans north of the border. Some quickly disappeared. Others, like *La Prensa* (San Antonio) and *La Opinión* (Los Angeles), have been read for many years. These newspapers document the Mexican experience in this country and reveal a persistent search by Mexican Americans for identity and community. Among the Mexican-American Generation, Ignacio L. (Nacho) López (1908–1973) was perhaps the best-known journalist. Born in Guadalajara in 1908 but raised in the United States, López, the son of a Protestant minister, published and edited *El Espectador*, a Spanish-language weekly, from 1933 to 1961 in the San Gabriel Valley of Southern California, which is east of Los Angeles and was characterized by Anglo-dominated agribusiness and a labor base composed predominantly of Mexicans.[1] López through his editorials, essays, and investigative muckraking in *El Espectador* both reflected and shaped a Mexican-American consciousness. This world view was influenced both by López's ideas on what it meant to be a Mexican in the United States and by his own participation in the Mexican-American struggle for civil rights and integration. López articulated in his newspaper and writings certain basic concepts and goals which helped guide the Mexican-American movement in the San Gabriel Valley. These included the concept of permanency, the struggle for human dignity and civil rights, the need for political integration, and a belief in cultural pluralism.

Permanency

López did not directly address himself to the concept of permanency, but it is one that can be extrapolated from his writings. Permanency here means the understanding, conscious and unconscious, that for Mexican Americans there was no retreat to Mexico. The return to Mexico might be an aspiration of immigrants from Mexico, part of their Mexican dream, but it had no relevance to most Mexican Americans. Born and/or raised in the United States, citizens of the Colossus of the North, Mexican Americans sought their place in the sun north of the border. For them, the American dream was the goal. As a naturalized citizen of the United States, and proud of it, López appreciated permanency. He had come of adult and political age not in Mexico but in California. He had been socialized in American schools, graduating from Pomona High School in 1927 and then attending Chaffey College in Ontario, California, a year before going to Pomona College in Claremont, where he received his degree in 1931. He may have attended the University of California, Berkeley; however, no record appears to exist. As a student, López's interests lay in sociology, political science, and education.[2]

Attending American schools, as most other Mexican Americans, and wanting to make something of himself in his adopted country, López absorbed many of the values and ideals of the United States. He came to accept them as his own. Although he, like so many others of his generation, did not reject his Mexican cultural traditions, still much of López's politics were shaped by a U.S. experience and not a Mexican one. López and most of his generation can be seen as political sons and daughters of the New Deal of the 1930s and of the American involvement in World War II. In seeing himself as part of a political generation engaged in a campaign to overcome the obstacles to complete equality and integration for Mexican Americans, López helped advance the idea that the struggle was here in the United States. Through his participation in Mexican-American issues such as the desegregation of public facilities, the desegregation of Mexican schools, the movement by Mexican Americans into electoral politics, as well as various others, López spoke more for the attainment of the fruits of the American Revolution than the Mexican Revolution. Hence the concept or sense of permanency—the United States being the home country—and the recognition that one was an American citizen with all the rights pertaining to such citizenship strongly influenced the political ideology and activism of Mexican Americans.

Civil Rights Struggles: Public Facilities

Discrimination against Mexicans in public facilities represented one of the most objectionable forms of prejudice challenged by López and the Mexican-American leadership of the San Gabriel Valley. This type of exclusion singled out Mexicans on a very personal level for inferior treatment. Movie theaters, for example, made Mexicans sit in the least comfortable sections, such as the side aisles and balcony. Some Mexicans in time refused such second-class treatment. In early 1939, López reported a complaint made by two Mexican Americans against the Upland Theater in Upland. After purchasing their tickets, the two young adults proceeded to the center section of the theater. Before they could sit down, the assistant manager intercepted them and ordered them to sit only in the front seats closest to the screen. The Mexican-American male protested and inquired if the center section cost more and if so he was prepared to pay the difference. The assistant manager insisted that if they did not take the front seats, he would escort them out of the theater. "In such a rigid manner," López commented, "the management of the theater humiliated this Mexican couple, refusing them to sit where they desired, not because they were poorly dressed or because of poor manners, but because they were Mexicans." [3]

Following the incident, the two Mexican Americans approached López with their complaint. To confirm their story he interviewed the assistant manager at the theater, who explained that Mexicans could be seated only in the first fifteen rows of the theater. López then consulted his lawyer, who counseled that a legal case would be difficult and protracted but that a better strategy might be direct action involving a boycott of the Upland Theater by Mexicans. López accepted his advice and called upon other Mexicans, in particular the older mutual benefit societies, composed of both Mexican nationals and Mexican Americans, to support such a boycott. "*El Espectador* is not a combative newspaper," López stressed, "but it is vigilant about reason and justice." López added that he did not advocate that ill-mannered and rowdy Mexicans be given equal treatment in the theater. Management had a right to refuse service to any disturbing element, regardless of race. But this was not the case here and, as López pointed out, the Upland Theater did not distinguish among Mexicans; it segregated all of them. However, Mexicans were not defenseless. They had recourse to the boycott. This was a powerful weapon and López encouraged all Mexicans to use it, not only against the theater but against all other merchants who had business with the Upland Theater. "*El Espectador,*" López promised, "will support every action to combat this insult to our racial dignity, but we need the support of *Every One* of our readers." [4]

One week after the incident the Mexican-American community of Upland, led by the Comisión Honorífica Mexicana (a Mexican mutual society sponsored by the Mexican consul) organized to carry out the boycott until the theater agreed to thoroughly integrate its facility. Clearly worried, the theater manager at first proposed to the Comisión Honorífica that he would allow Mexicans to seat themselves up to the center seats. The Comisión refused this proposal and announced that until the theater allowed Mexicans to sit wherever they pleased the boycott would continue. López observed that many Anglos in Upland supported the Mexican cause. Some had even protested to the theater and threatened to withdraw their patronage unless the segregation of Mexicans ended. "What this demonstrates to us," López emphasized, "is that we are not alone in our struggle for recognition and racial equality." The editor once again called on Mexicans to remain united and to recognize that they had the economic power to force change. The boycott succeeded and the theater agreed to complete integration. "In this manner the first step is taken," López concluded, "in the Mexican community's defense of its dignity and in its struggle for civil rights." [5]

Discrimination at public swimming pools represented another personalized and direct insult toward Mexicans, regardless of citizenship. In 1940 an angry López, in an article entitled "Quien Es El Culpable?" (Who is to Blame?), noted that a Pomona newspaper had recently carried an announcement that Mexicans would be permitted to use the local Ganesha Pool only on Fridays. The rest of the week would be reserved for Anglos. Who was to blame for this affront toward all Mexicans, including U.S. citizens? López asked. As he would on numerous other occasions in his weekly Spanish-language column, López chastised the Mexican communities for not doing enough to eliminate discrimination. Perhaps an accusing finger should be pointed, he stated, at the leaders of the mexicano and Mexican-American organizations in Pomona and at the Mexican population in general for allowing such discrimination to exist due to their weakness and timidity in defending "the dignity of the Mexican community and the rights permitted by democratic laws to all residents of the country." An accusing finger might be pointed, but López would not do so in the hope that this particular case of discrimination might motivate Mexicans to defend their rights. However, over two months later, López regretted that no effort had been made to desegregate the pool. He had personally met with local Anglo officials who had promised to desegregate, but as yet nothing had been done. Instead, the superintendent of pools had hosted an aquatic carnival for Mexican children at the pool, but still under segregated conditions. López simply could not understand why Mexican parents tolerated such a public display of prejudice. Owing to the apathy of the parents, he could not blame officials for their duplicity but he could blame the Mexicans. "The only ones to blame for these insults perpetuated against us," López concluded, "are ourselves."[6]

During the early 1940s, *El Espectador* publicized other cases of discrimination against Mexicans in public swimming pools in communities such as Riverside, Colton, and San Bernardino. In Riverside, officials agreed to desegregate after confronted by local Mexican-American leaders and by the Mexican consul. In others, such as Colton, officials agreed that Mexicans had a right to use any community pool but suggested that it would be better if they stayed in their own neighborhood ones. Yet the only pool in the Mexican barrio was a private one, and for Mexicans to remain in their neighborhoods would amount to submitting to discrimination in public facilities.[7] Faced with recalcitrant officials, Mexican-American leaders, including López and Eugenio Nogueras, publisher of *El Sol de San Bernardino,* went to federal court in 1943 with the goal of using San Bernardino as a test case to force desegregation of public swimming pools. "Last Tuesday afternoon Reverend J. R. Nuñez and three of the Mexican children of his parish were refused admittance to the San Bernardino Municipal Plunge because they were Mexicans," López had earlier written. "They were refused the use of a swimming pool which displays a bronze plaque that says 'no one is to be refused admittance because of race or color,' and which was built with WPA money."[8] López, Nogueras, and other leaders filed a suit on behalf of more than 8,000 Mexican Americans and Mexican nationals and against the mayor and city council of San Bernardino as well as other local officials for their complicity in segregating Mexicans in public pools. After hearing the case, Federal Judge Leon Yanckwich ruled on behalf of López and the other plaintiffs and declared the segregation of Mexicans in local swimming pools to be unconstitutional and a violation of the Fourteenth and Fifteenth amendments. Mexicans as taxpayers were entitled to the use of public facilities. *El Espectador* commented that the successful challenge had also been the result of Mexican Americans in San Bernardino organizing a local defense committee, the Mexican-American Defense Committee, to eliminate discrimination not only in the public pools but in other places as well. It noted that the city council had recently ordered merchants to remove from their windows signs saying White Trade Only.[9]

Although Mexican Americans always faced obstacles in their struggle for civil rights, López through *El Espectador* and through his own example consistently encouraged them to stand up for their rights. In 1938 López helped lead a boycott against a bar in Ontario for its discriminatory treatment of Mexicans. "This is the only way, a quiet way, without insults or violence," López wrote of the boycott, "that the Mexican community of Ontario has finally found the most effective strategy and what most hurts those who abuse people of our race." [10] The following year, López in an open letter strongly criticized the organizers of the Mexican Independence Day celebrations in Azusa for agreeing to hold the festivities in a dirty and unsafe park. He could not understand how Mexican parents could get aroused about inferior and segregated schools for their children, as they had recently done, and then accept segregated and inferior parks in their community. [11] Public discrimination, unfortunately, did not even stop at death, as López pointed out in rebuking the segregation practices against blacks and Mexicans by a San Bernardino cemetery. "In this 'friendly city,'" he sarcastically wrote, "not even in the tomb can one escape racial prejudice." Whoever had said that death eliminated differences had never dealt with the Mountain View Cemetery. López met with the owners of the cemetery to convince them to abandon their refusal to bury Mexicans. They admitted that their practices were antidemocratic and anti-Christian but that they still could not go against public opinion in San Bernardino. [12] When the power of persuasion failed, López returned to the boycott. In 1946 he called for a blacklist of certain merchants in Pomona and Chino who discriminated against Mexicans. He reminded his readers that they did not have to stand by passively and accept prejudice in public places, but that through measures such as an economic boycott they could force changes. [13]

School Desegregation

Besides fighting segregation in public facilities such as theaters and swimming pools, López and *El Espectador* aided in Mexican-American struggles to desegregate Mexican schools. After World War II, *El Espectador* covered and supported school desegregation drives in the San Gabriel Valley encouraged by the landmark Westminster case, in which a federal judge ruled that the de facto segregation of Mexican-American children over several grades on the basis of language difference in several Orange County schools violated the Fourteenth Amendment. Following the decision in early 1946, schools in the San Gabriel Valley moved to comply with the court's interpretation and to integrate Mexican-American and Anglo pupils. Through the summer of 1946 *El Espectador* alerted readers that school districts in Chino, Ontario, Upland, and Azusa had agreed to integrate. Mexican children would no longer have to attend the Mexican schools. "The 16th of September, a glorious day for those of Mexican descent who honor Mexican independence," *El Espectador* enthusiastically pronounced concerning school desegregation in Ontario, "this year will have additional significance for the children attending the public schools of this city, for when the schools open on that day, Mexican students will be able to attend the school closest to their home and not have to go to a segregated school." López praised the school board. Many benefits would accrue due to desegregation. Mexican Americans had won a significant victory in their struggle to obtain full constitutional rights, but López reminded them that they faced an obligation to cooperate with officials in carrying out school desegregation in a lawful and orderly manner. One week after school opened in September, *El Espectador* observed that in both Chino and Ontario integration had proved a success despite some lingering opposition.[14]

Mexican Americans in the Pomona area best expressed their concerns over equal and quality education in the successful efforts to finally desegregate South Fontana schools. In early February 1948, *El Espectador* reported that a group of Mexican parents, apparently both citizens and noncitizens, representing more than seventy families had organized the South Fontana Civic Club to protest the continuation of segregated school facilities for their children. Although a segregated Mexican school had existed for some time in South Fontana, this protest movement originated after the local school district constructed a new school intended predominantly for Anglo children. After meeting with the superintendent of schools, the civic club announced that he supported the desegregation of South Fontana schools. To obtain the approval of the school board, the club outlined an involved strategy. It would present a written demand to the board of education calling for desegregation. Club officials would personally attend the next board meeting to discuss the demand. At the same time, the club would circulate a petition in support of desegregation in the Mexican-American community. Club members also encouraged as many people as possible to be at the next board meeting to impress upon that body the interests of Mexican-American parents. Finally, the club would continue to sponsor community meetings to keep residents informed of the struggle.[15]

In its written demand to the board of education, the civic club clearly enunciated the views of many Mexican Americans concerning the schools. Segregated education was not only unjust but unequal. Segregation deprived Mexican-American children of the very best possible education. Only through mixed schools could Mexican-American children be fully integrated into American society. The only distinctions should be those of merit and achievement. Social change was not easy, the civic club admitted, but it was inevitable and it demanded that the board implement an integration plan by the next school year. Claiming that it had been planning such a move anyway, the school board defensively agreed to the demands of the South Fontana Civic Club and promised integration by September. Both Mexican-American and Anglo children would then attend the same schools.[16]

The achievement of school integration, primarily during the 1940s, by

Mexican Americans in the Pomona area did not terminate unequal and inferior education for many Mexican-American children, as *El Espectador* would note during the next decade.[17] Racial discrimination in the schools and in other social areas would not vanish that quickly. However, this struggle revealed a deeply ingrained Mexican-American belief that the opportunity to learn amounted not only to a basic human right, but a right emanating from being a U.S. citizen. To integrate, especially economically and politically, Mexican Americans had to obtain access to integrated education.

Police Abuse

Police brutality and the maladministration of justice represented a particularly frustrating area of civil rights concern for López and other Mexican-American leaders. López believed the American judicial system to be largely fair but recognized that police committed abuses, especially in minority communities. He publicized accounts of police brutality toward Mexicans in the San Gabriel Valley and throughout Southern California. Unfortunately, reforms in police-community relations were not as forthcoming as in other civil rights issues.

In 1937 *El Espectador* reported that in a case of mistaken identity three Anglo policemen in Ontario had beaten a young Mexican man, Antonio Camacho. Camacho had been drinking with several companions that night. One of them, Lorenzo Espinoza, left the group to see his ex-wife and proceeded to assault her. In responding to her call for assistance, the police encountered the other youths and mistook Camacho for Espinoza.. The police attacked Camacho and arrested him along with another of his friends. In jail Camacho received no medical attention. The following day both Mexicans were released and the court suspended any penalties since they had been mistakenly arrested. In an editorial, López pleaded for justice in this case: "El Espectador as the only Mexican newspaper in this community and as the defender of all Mexicans calls for the ending once and for all of these types of violent acts." He informed his readers that he had personally talked with Ontario officials, who had assured him that an investigation would be conducted. López approved this and suggested that the policemen involved should possibly be punished. No policeman had the right to use unnecessary force.[18]

Over ten years later, in 1949, *El Espectador* provided wide coverage of the Ríos case in San Bernardino. This incident involved the death of a young Mexican American, Ramón Ríos, at the hands of police officer Johnnie Epps. *El Espectador* investigated Ríos's death and discovered that he and several companions had confronted Epps at a dance in the San Bernardino

Auditorium. Believing the Mexicans to be causing a disturbance, Epps, as the officer assigned to the dance, attempted to disperse them. He chased Ríos and shot him in the back. Ríos died at the scene. Epps was arrested but released on bail. He claimed that he had shot in self-defense after being attacked by the Mexican Americans. In his column, López called for action to protest this additional case of police brutality and hoped that this tragedy would awaken the Mexican-American community of San Bernardino from its lethargy. "Johnnie Epps is not to blame," López scolded his audience. "The guilty ones are all of us, who permit the police to become the executioners of those they are supposed to serve. . . . We are the criminals." Ríos was dead but López believed that similar future cases could be averted if the Mexican-American community insisted that Ríos be avenged and that justice be served. López called for a full investigation. The district attorney tried Epps on a charge of murder, but in the meantime he remained free on bail, although suspended from the police force. During Epps's trial, Mexican Americans in San Bernardino led by the Veteranos Católicos (the Catholic Veterans) and the Mexican-American members of the American Legion joined with other veteran organizations in a call for a systematic reorganization of the police force.[19]

During the trial, López, despite the death of Ríos, called on Mexican Americans to have faith in the American system of justice. For his part, López promised not to try Epps in *El Espectador.* In the United States a person remained innocent until proved guilty. Regrettably, the court found Epps innocent and declared that he had killed Ríos in self-defense. An angered and disappointed López decried the decision and blamed an inept and prejudiced district attorney for not vigorously prosecuting the case. "His office," López promised in reference to the district attorney, "will have to be judged by society."[20]

In cases of police injustices, López consistently attacked infringements on the civil rights of both Mexican Americans and Mexican nationals. It was the people, López instructed his readers, who were the source of authority. In the Jeffersonian tradition, López emphasized that the people came first, then the government. If government abuses the people, the people have the right through elections to change it. No conflict should exist between society and the state. Rights emanated from the people, which government translated into laws. López abhorred police mistreatment because of his concern that all humans should be treated with dignity and because of his understanding of the democratic system in the United States. Police abuses particularly alarmed López and other Mexican Americans because they directly set one arm of government against the rights of people of Mexican descent—indeed of all citizens or residents. Government, whether in the form of the police or the public schools, should not prevent the full achievement of civil rights; it should promote them.[21]

Housing Integration

As in other Mexican-American communities in the United States, Mexican-American residents of the San Gabriel Valley lived mostly in inferior housing and in de facto segregated barrios. During the 1940s and 1950s, however, Mexican Americans accelerated efforts to eliminate such conditions. Because decent nonsegregated housing represented both a human and a civil right, López endorsed various efforts to reform the living conditions of Mexican Americans. In 1940 he praised initiatives in Upland, Ontario, Guasti, and Cucamonga by Anglo community leaders to conduct a census of the Mexican barrios to estimate the extent of dilapidated houses. Large numbers of homes contained families of ten or twelve persons residing in two- or three-room houses. In the postwar period as federal housing aid became available, López promoted the participation of San Gabriel Valley communities in these new programs as a way of improving housing for Mexicans. Unfortunately, some cities refused federal support for new home construction. In the valley, the city of Chino became a test case for Mexican-American efforts to persuade local governments to avail themselves of federal assistance. Initially the Chino city council endorsed in 1949 the submission of a proposal to Washington for federal financing to construct between 150 and 200 new low-cost houses. The council also ordered a census in Chino to determine the extent of dilapidated housing. López backed the Chino proposal and offered the assistance of Mexican Americans in conducting the census. "Our only suggestion," López cautioned, "is that local Mexican-American leaders be alert so that the new housing project will not be built in a location which will only perpetuate the existing segregated state of Mexican housing." Despite its preliminary plans, the Chino city council several weeks later voted not to submit a proposal to Washington for $20,000 to cover the census. An angered López blamed this reversal on Andrés Morales, the Mexican-American councilman who according to *El Espectador* submitted to pressures from local Anglo business interests which opposed the housing project. Labeling Morales a traitor to the Mexican-American voters who had put him in office, López lamented Morales's failure to adequately represent the needs of Mexican Americans. As head of the city's Commission on Health, Morales more than anyone else recognized the acute housing shortage in the Mexican-American community. "Morales had betrayed us," López concluded. "We have bred a buzzard who has attacked our eyes." [22]

Disturbed and perplexed by the city council's change of heart, the

Mexican-American community debated the pros and cons of a federal housing project for Chino. Councilman Morales claimed that many Mexican Americans rejected it, but López countered by alleging that most Mexican-American leaders supported the idea. Proving the publisher correct, Mexican-American leaders along with several Anglo ones exerted sufficient pressure to succeed in getting the city council, including Morales, to vote again to submit the proposal for the census to Washington. The pro-housing coalition rebutted the council's argument that the project would be too expensive by stressing that the persistence of poor housing led to more crime, illness, and generally unhealthy conditions in the barrios, which would be even costlier to the city. In 1951 *El Espectador* announced that the Chino city government had granted the first contracts for the construction of new federally subsidized low-cost housing. One year later the initial units became available to Mexican-American residents.[23]

Besides supporting better homes for Mexican-Americans, López attacked housing discrimination. Most Mexican-Americans lived in de facto segregated tracts, but after World War II many, especially returning veterans, attempted to purchase homes in new residential areas. Some realtors and developers, however, refused to let them. In 1949 López paid particular attention to such a case in Upland. When Salvador Vera and his wife investigated buying a house in the new Campus Gardens tract, the realtor inquired if Vera was of Spanish descent. When the Veras stated that they were Mexican Americans, the realtor refused to negotiate with them, insisting that if he sold homes to Mexicans, the Anglo residents of the tract would cancel their contracts and leave. Since this new housing development was primarily for veterans, López indignantly noted that Vera had served two and a half years in the Pacific defending American democracy and for his valor in combat had been decorated. Led by the predominantly Mexican-American Veterans of Foreign Wars Unit No. 73 in Upland, Mexican Americans launched protests against what *El Espectador* termed the "fascist restrictions" of the Carlton Corporation, builders of the development.[24] The issue aroused considerable controversy, as expressed in a letter to the editor which appeared in an Ontario paper and which López reprinted in *El Espectador*. Calling the author of the letter a racist, López pointed out: "Our objective in publishing this letter is to show the gross ignorance of this domestic fascism, that like Satan, cites the Bible to support its racist beliefs." In the letter, the author could not understand why Mexicans and blacks would force themselves on whites. "Are we white people looked upon as gods that these people want to be right at our right hand in everything?" he queried. God had deliberately created separate races and the writer insisted that Mexicans would be happier if they stayed among their own and did not try to integrate with whites who did not want them.[25]

A week after republishing this letter, *El Espectador* carried a lead story revealing that the Carlton Corporation, while not altering its policies in Campus Gardens, had agreed to integrate the adjacent tract scheduled for development. This arrangement had come, however, only after Mexican-American veterans had threatened to petition the Upland city council to deny Carlton the permit to construct the tract. Although not a complete victory, Mexican Americans had forcefully voiced their belief that they had a right to live wherever they pleased.[26]

Indeed, to López the issue of housing involved more than better homes for Mexican Americans, even though this might entail de facto segregation. López opposed any form of segregated housing. A year after the Upland incident, he editorialized against construction of a housing tract in Whittier exclusively for Mexican-American veterans. Admitting that some Mexican Americans supported such housing because it meant better homes, López aligned himself with those who opposed it on the principle that segregation was unacceptable. Moreover, this constituted an effort to pacify Mexican Americans while denying them the opportunity to purchase homes in Anglo neighborhoods. Offended by this discrimination, especially when the country was calling for unity because of the Korean conflict, López concluded:

> It is not the anglo-saxon who will reap the repercussions of this case of segregation . . . it will be those of us who have yet to understand that the only way to end discrimination and segregation is for us to integrate fully into society . . . making us part of the community and not trying to live in an exclusive world reserved only for ourselves.[27]

Braceros and the Undocumented

Civil rights for Mexicans in the United States also encompassed the treatment of Mexican nationals working in this country, particularly those who beginning in 1942 entered as braceros. From 1942 to 1964, when the program ended, employers promised braceros good working and living conditions. In most cases, however, employers failed to fulfill their contract terms. Paying low wages and providing only minimal living conditions, growers prospered by having a regulated labor supply. *El Espectador* published numerous accounts detailing the plight of the braceros. Besides protesting low wages, braceros often complained of inadequate food and medical care, and of police harassment whenever they ventured beyond their camps. In some states, notably Texas, racial discrimination against braceros became so pronounced that the Mexican government rescinded contract agreements with employers. Despite such problems, López likewise understood the dilemma which pushed Mexican workers into the United States. As long as economic underdevelopment and labor-exploiting conditions remained in Mexico, Mexican nationals, both as braceros and as undocumented workers, would continue to cross the border seeking jobs and a better life.[28]

Besides reporting bracero conditions in other areas, *El Espectador* exposed some of the specific problems braceros encountered in the San Gabriel Valley. López worried, for example, about braceros receiving protection by law enforcement officials and equal treatment by the courts. This was especially important because braceros at times were subject to being robbed, beaten, and even killed as they moved around the valley. *El Espectador* covered events in 1952 surrounding the most publicized local case of violence toward braceros, the murder of Ricardo Mancilla Gómez, a bracero working in the Cucamonga area. Gómez had been murdered in a bar after engaging in a brawl with four Mexican-American teenagers. As a result of the murder, and the fact that another bracero had also been murdered in Cucamonga less than three months earlier, the Mexican consul recommended that all braceros in the vicinity be removed. López lamented that Gómez had died at the hands of people of his own "blood." If such murders continued, the "Mexico of the Exterior" (México de afuera) would exterminate the "Mexico of the Interior" (México de adentro). The murder and other violence committed by Mexican-American youths did not surprise López. He pointed out that besides being affected by ignorance and vice, some Mexican-American youngsters in the valley exhibited the spiritual and moral poverty afflicting the entire United States. Much of this malaise derived from the specter of atomic war brought on by the recent construction of the atomic bomb. The four Mexican-American youths might be convicted for killing one man, López concluded, but it would be done by a government itself capable of killing millions with these new weapons of destruction.[29]

At the consul's urging, the Mexican government removed all braceros from Cucamonga and insisted that they would not return until local officials could adequately protect them. Disturbed, area growers claimed they would suffer irreparable damages. Resident Mexican Americans, especially merchants, feared not only a loss of business due to the removal of bracero consumers but a rising anti-Mexican sentiment from some Anglos who sought to blame the Mexican-American community for the loss of bracero workers. Certain Anglos already claimed that all Mexicans were by instinct criminals and perverts and that all carried knives. Accusing Mexican Americans of Cucamonga of being timid in facing up to such charges, López called for unity in the Mexican-American community to combat these false allegations. Several Mexican-American organizations heeded López's call and conducted meetings with local officials, Anglo community leaders, and growers on how to prevent violence. After authorities promised a reinforcement of police protection for braceros, the Mexican consul announced that the workers would be returned. López welcomed the braceros and called them "ambassadors in overalls" but warned them that even though most Mexican-American residents accepted braceros as members of La Raza, there were some Mexican-American youths who, being negatively influenced by Anglo culture, had become gang members and committed acts of disorder and violence. To prevent a repetition of the Gómez murder, López provided braceros with a list of seven recommendations. He suggested, for example, that they should dedicate themselves completely to their work; that they should avoid altercations in bars; that they should establish good relations with local families; that they should insist on equal treatment and wages with local workers; and that they should not be used to replace local workers. Such recommendations would prevent future bracero removals and give a good name to Mexico and Mexicans.[30]

Although sympathetic to their plight, López objected to braceros and undocumented workers being used to replace and dislocate resident Mexican-American workers. The right to a decent job was both a human and a civil right, and López found himself defending local workers against Mexican nationals in certain cases. In the San Gabriel Valley and throughout California, unscrupulous employers pitted one set of workers against the other and where possible employed the cheaper braceros or "alambristas" (the undocumented). Employers consistently declared that they could not find enough domestic agricultural workers and hence the need for braceros. Yet this claim always worked against Mexican-American farmworkers. When local growers requested braceros in February 1949, López replied that in his opinion braceros were not needed due to the availability of domestic workers, who often had to go without work during certain seasons. There were not enough jobs for both Mexican Americans and braceros. Often when braceros arrived and discovered insufficient work, they abandoned their camps and sought employment illegally. However, the biggest problem was that braceros lowered wage standards, especially for Mexican Americans, who could not compete with the cheaper labor.[31]

In many instances, rather than braceros harming Mexican-American interests, it was undocumented workers employed by local growers. *El Espectador* noted various cases of employers illegally hiring alambristas and of an illicit contraband traffic in what the newspaper termed "human meat." López supported the elimination of undocumented immigration and questioned the neutrality of immigration and border patrol officers, who often seemed invisible when growers desired undocumented workers. "The only ones who can solve this problem," López proposed, "are the resident workers of this region who must take this issue to the highest officials and have them understand that this problem is one of the gravest facing labor in California and is the problem of thousands of Mexican Americans who live exclusively by doing farm labor." [32] Committed to the right of Mexican-American farmworkers to have decent and well-paying jobs, López lamented that this apparently could be accomplished only by opposing the employment of Mexican nationals in those cases where Mexican-American interests were harmed. López believed this dilemma to be a modern and tragic version of the Cain and Abel biblical story. Yet Mexican nationals were being used to replace Mexican-American workers and López called for an end to this displacement. [33]

Political Integration

Realizing the permanent position of Mexican Americans in the United States and supporting their struggle for human and civil rights, López naturally advocated their political integration. The achievement of civil rights was not enough; Mexican Americans had to become integral and active members of the American body politic to advance and defend their gains. A strong patriot committed to American democratic beliefs, López consistently urged Mexican Americans to exercise their right to vote and to use it effectively. Like other Mexican-American leaders of his time, López astutely recognized the usefulness and necessity of ethnic politics. He supported bloc voting by Mexican Americans, the election of Mexican-American candidates, and the formation of Mexican-American local, regional, and national political organizations. Political integration was the objective, but the means was ethnic politics, in this case a distinct Mexican-American politics.

With many others of his political generation, López fully embraced American democracy. He endorsed democracy in general but in particular believed that as practiced in the United States it represented the highest form of political achievement. López's belief in American democracy obviously originated prior to 1939, but it was World War II and later the Korean War and the cold war which crystallized his views on American democracy. Commenting in 1939 on the importance of Cinco de Mayo, the Mexican national holiday celebrating the defeat of the invading French army in 1862, López warned that Hitler and Mussolini, no less than the French in the nineteenth century, posed threats to democracy. And in noting Franklin Roosevelt's victory in the 1940 election, López suggested that despite the political divisions generated by an American presidential election, all Americans, including Mexican Americans, now had to unite to show the totalitarian states that democracy truly functioned in the United States.[34] World War II, of course, marked a significant watershed for Mexican Americans. It mobilized their support for American democracy. They accepted the war as a struggle for the preservation of democracy. Like Afro Americans and other racial minorities, Mexican Americans sought not only to protect democracy, but to expand it to include groups such as Mexican Americans, who had previously been excluded from most of its fruits. "American Negroes took advantage of the war," one historian writes and the same could be said of Mexican Americans, "to tie their racial demands to the ideology for which the war was being fought." This goal particularly applied after thousands of young Mexican Americans returned from the war. "It is quite encouraging to notice the interest of our Mexican-American citizens in civil affairs," López wrote in 1945. "They seem to have rediscovered America."[35] In *El Espectador*'s English-language section in 1949, one Mexican-American veteran called on his generational cohort to take advantage of the opportunities that American democracy offered and to assume their responsibilities as U.S. citizens. "This is our country, too," this veteran concluded, "but unless we give to her what she is giving to us we can't rightfully claim her. The rights we claim are solidified only by the obligations we fulfill."[36]

The cold war and the fear of communism in the United States gave Mexican Americans an additional opportunity to declare their loyalty to American democracy. López, like his counterparts in LULAC, during the early 1950s voiced his total opposition to communism, which he believed offered no solution for the problems of Mexican Americans. His antipathy to communism, or what he interpreted to be communism, derived from his aversion to all forms of totalitarianism. Having just concluded a war against fascism, López believed it to be a contradiction for anyone in the United States to follow communism. To López communism negated liberty because in true cold war fashion he believed that communism dehumanized people and made them into cogs of a godless state. Democracy not communism was the correct ideology of the Americas. "We are men of America," López editorialized, "and we should be faithful to the fundamental principles of the politics of this Continent."[37] Because he was anticommunist, López also strongly opposed any inequalities in the American system. "Just as we are fighting against the absurd theory that comes from Moscow," he insisted, "we are ready to fight against anything that appears to us to curtail individual liberty, against whatever spirit of regimentation appears, against whatever lessens human dignity, and in our special case, the dignity of the Hispanic community of California."[38]

Anticommunist, López objected to any form of totalitarian practice. Consequently, despite the intimidating atmosphere of the cold war, he protested the red-scare tactics of Senator Joseph McCarthy. He attacked McCarthyism for its indictment of liberals as being soft on communism and for being fellow-travelers. "Being a liberal or a democrat," López countered, "or to fight for the most basic democratic rights cannot be equated with communism." [39] López opposed legislation to outlaw the Communist party in the United States not because he was soft on communism but because it could be used indiscriminately to trample the civil liberties of other Americans. López added: "We know how easy it is to call any man who disagrees, a Communist—and throw him in jail." [40] He called on all Americans to renounce McCarthyism and to reaffirm their support of American democracy, in particular the Constitution and the Bill of Rights. In an editorial entitled "Democracy Lives," López encouraged Mexican Americans to rally behind the American way of life, which was rooted in the basic dignity of the individual, regardless of race, nationality, religion, or social background. To protect their way of life, however, Mexican Americans along with other citizens would have to fully integrate themselves into the political system and help correct the problems of American democracy, such as racism. Despite his anticommunist position, but due to his civil rights commitments López was subject to FBI surveillance. [41]

A fervent disciple of American democracy, who was convinced of the importance for Mexican Americans to integrate into the political system, López consistently encouraged his readers to vote. Voting expressed citizenship. During World War II, López reminded Mexican Americans that the war and the preservation of democracy would be won both on the battlefield and in the polling booth. Through voting, Mexican Americans could better assimilate into the political life of the nation. Unfortunately, many Mexican Americans possessing the right to vote did not do so. [42] Yet López viewed voting in more than idealistic terms. He astutely realized that through voting Mexican Americans could advance their working and living conditions. In 1938 López editorialized on what Mexican Americans could do to improve their lives north of the border. Mexicans had two choices. They could either accept their second-class status, as many had done for almost 100 years and through at least five generations, or they could struggle to achieve equality. For López, the time had arrived to demand the Mexicans' rightful place in American society. He observed that demographically Mexicans now formed a sizable population in the Southwest, particularly in Southern California. Statistics, however, would not generate changes. Mexican Americans alone could do this and they could best accomplish this by directly participating in politics and, in a word, by voting. In California Mexican Americans could be the swing vote. López even suggested that Mexican nationals in California seriously think about becoming American citizens so that through voting they could improve their material status. Only by voting in large numbers would Mexican Americans achieve respect and reforms.[43] "The vote is our most sacred right," López sermonized, "and at the same time the most powerful political weapon."[44] Politicians only understood organized political pressure. If Mexican Americans could achieve this through voting, they would be surprised by the "miracles" their votes would bring: paved and lighted streets, better police and fire service, better treatment by public officers, and more Mexican Americans in government.[45]

To more directly integrate Mexican Americans into the political mainstream, López encouraged Mexican Americans themselves to run for office. In the San Gabriel Valley, the most notable example of Mexican-American electoral politics was the formation of the Unity Leagues between 1946 and 1948. In February 1946 *El Espectador* reported that a group of fifty young Mexican Americans, many of them World War II veterans, had met in Pomona and organized the Pomona Unity League for the purpose of aiding the Mexican-American community by engaging in civil-political affairs. Candelario "Candy" Mendoza, a colleague of López's, recalls that the editor was the catalyst behind the league. According to one of its new officers, the Unity League had been established because Mexican Americans who had gone to war to preserve world liberty could not return home and see that liberty deprived to Mexican Americans. Besides Pomona, Unity Leagues sprang up in Chino, Ontario, San Bernardino, and Redlands. Involved in various activities, the Unity Leagues' most important role consisted of organizing local political campaigns for Mexican-American candidates.[46]

Commencing in 1946, Unity Leagues in both Chino and Ontario launched the first political campaigns by league members. They selected as candidates two local Mexican-American merchants, Andrés Morales of Chino and Herman Moraga of Ontario, and sought to elect them as councilmen in the April elections. "For the first time in the history of these communities," *El Espectador* proudly emphasized, "candidates of Mexican descent are competing for public offices." It noted that the two candidates had been chosen for their qualifications as potential officeholders. Moreover, their campaigns would stress good citizenship and honorability. The Unity Leagues believed that their candidates could win, but López considered it already a moral victory just having two candidates from the Mexican-American community.[47]

Both the Chino and Ontario Unity Leagues employed several campaign tactics. They correctly stressed the vital importance of registering Mexican-American voters. Without a strong Mexican-American turnout at the polls neither candidate stood a chance of succeeding. Voters won elections,

López advised, not words or promises of good intentions. He observed that Unity League members two months prior to the elections had been visiting the homes of eligible Mexican-American voters to ensure that they were registered. In Chino, five league members registered 150 Mexican Americans several weeks before the election. A similar handful of league activists enrolled 300 Mexican Americans in Ontario. League members facilitated voter registration by dividing themselves into block committees responsible for registering certain areas of the barrios. The Unity Leagues also solicited support for their candidates by appealing to all sectors of the Mexican-American community. They invited not only Mexican Americans but Mexican nationals to participate in league activities. They encouraged women to become league members and several played leading roles in registering voters. Fund raising represented a third area of league involvement. To finance and publicize the campaigns, the league needed money which they obtained from individuals, Mexican-American merchants, and from both Mexican-American and Mexican national organizations. At one meeting of the Ontario Unity League, for example, donations of $15 apiece were received from the Pomona Unity League, the Asociación de Madres (the Association of Mothers), and Lodge 142 of the Alianza Hispano-Americana. The Club Vecino, a social group, gave $10. To stimulate additional support and create a sense of community, both leagues sponsored dances and other social affairs.[48]

In their tactics, the Unity League effectively utilized the appeal to ethnic loyalty. They urged Mexican Americans to vote for Morales and Moraga on the basis of ethnic ties. The Unity Leagues welcomed Anglo support but waged ethnic campaigns in these city-wide elections. "We were organized because we wanted to elect some Mexicans to office," Candy Mendoza recalls, "and the only way we were going to do this was through unity and voting for our own."[49] The highest vote getters would win office. League organizers believed that if they could capture the entire Mexican-American vote and obtain some minimal support from Anglo and black voters, they would win. The Mexican-American campaigns displayed so much enthusiasm that López observed that the Anglo political establishment of both Chino and Ontario was worried over the introduction of a Mexican-American variable in San Gabriel Valley politics. Some traditional politicians regarded league activities as merely the work of a few agitators, but others took the league more seriously and wondered how they could control it or at least divide the Mexican-American vote. Hoping to maintain a united front, López cautioned league members and all Mexican Americans to be vigilant during the remaining days of the campaign lest reactionary forces succeed. López again stressed that Morales and Moraga could be elected only if Mexican Americans voted for them. In their campaign publicity, the two candidates discreetly pledged to represent all sectors of the population if elected but paid particular attention to Mexican-American voters through their Spanish-language ads in *El Espectador.* "Elect one of your own," a Morales advertisement in Spanish read, "who feels and understands your needs and problems."[50]

On election day, Unity League members delivered the Mexican-American vote. Organized in squadrons, they used their cars to drive voters to the polls. The results: Morales won in Chino, and Moraga, although losing, gathered over 900 votes. Morales polled 427 votes out of 780 and along with two successful Anglo candidates would take his council seat: the first Mexican American elected to a city council in California since the nineteenth century. In Ontario, where Moraga lost to two Anglo candidates, López believed a moral victory had been achieved due to the large vote for the Mexican-American candidate. Both Unity Leagues promised to wage other campaigns and to continue their work in the community. Nogueras, writing in *El Espectador,* believed that the election marked only the beginning of a new day for Mexican Americans in politics. Extolling Morales's victory, he called for other Mexican-American communities to emulate the example. Such future campaigns would lead to the main political objective: "Just representation for those people now being represented by politicos who care nothing about the condition of the Hispanic community." The Unity League election, in particular Morales's success, had only planted the seeds of Mexican-American political self-determination.[51]

While Morales's stunning election in 1946 proved the highlight of the Unity Leagues' efforts, López assisted and promoted other league candidates. The Chino Unity League one year later selected Alicia Cortez, a teacher and wife of a Mexican-American merchant, as its candidate for the Chino School Board. As in the Morales campaign, the league believed that Cortez could triumph only by capturing the Mexican-American vote. This did not materialize and Cortez lost. Receiving 401 votes, she placed third. López praised the league's effort but blamed the apathy of those Mexican Americans who failed to maintain their registration and harmed Cortez's chances. Not discouraged, the Chino Unity League campaigned the following year to elect a second Mexican American to the city council. Mexicans comprised 35 percent of Chino's population and the league believed that they deserved more than one representative. The league again stressed ethnic solidarity and selected as its candidate Samuel Calderón, a young instructor of Spanish at Beulah College in Upland. Calling Calderón an example of the "new American," López predicted that besides receiving Mexican-American votes Calderón would be supported by other teachers and by certain Anglo merchants. López, however, criticized some older Mexican Americans who had attempted to discourage Calderón's candidacy because they feared an Anglo backlash. They believed that such a campaign for a second council seat should wait until Mexican Americans had dispelled Anglo fears that Mexican Americans intended to capture political power in Chino. In an article entitled "Overcoming Our Fear," López admonished these critics for their timidity and praised the courage of the younger generation for nominating Calderón.[52]

Although the league announced four days prior to the election that it had registered 650 voters, Calderón experienced a disappointing defeat. He received only 401 votes and lost by 156 votes. The league had failed to increase the size of its vote since the previous year's campaign. In analyzing the election, López partly attributed the victory of the two Anglo candidates to their more effective organization and to their ability to attract some Mexican-American voters. López reserved his more critical comments for the league. "The defeat was not Calderón's fault," he wrote, "but his organization's." It had failed to display spirit, energy, and conviction. Nothing could be done to recoup the defeat now, but league members could at least learn from their loss.[53] The 1948 election, however, proved to be the last formal appearance by the Unity league in San Gabriel Valley politics. The leagues had initiated a distinct Mexican-American participation in electoral politics, but they themselves disbanded and members channeled their efforts into other organizations and individual campaigns.

Between 1946 and 1960, López supported numerous other Mexican-American candidates for local office. Finding a more politically hospitable climate during this period, a good number succeeded in getting elected.[54] In his involvement with Mexican-American politics in the San Gabriel Valley, López over the years drew certain conclusions. Perhaps his most important one involved his views about the proper conduct of Mexican-American candidates and elected officials. He encouraged and supported Mexican-Americans to run for office and valued ethnic politics, but he disagreed that Mexican Americans should avoid publicly criticizing one another. López spoke out against Mexican-American public officials if in his opinion they did not properly discharge their duties. Besides being honest, Mexican-American politicians had to be effective as politicians. They needed to inaugurate reforms or at least make an effort to do so. Victory at the polls was not enough; Mexican Americans had to prove themselves in office. "Editorially, *El Espectador* has always supported Mexican candidates for public office," López wrote in 1959. "But with one condition—that they be well prepared and disposed to faithfully and diligently serve the community." He regretted that in some cases Mexican Americans had proved incompetent. "What we once referred to as a lack of experience," López noted about these

Mexican-American politicos, "we now understand was in fact a lack of talent." [55]

Applying his litmus test to Mexican-American officials in the San Gabriel Valley, López was not shy about criticizing them. The most notable case involved his running battle with Andrés Morales, whom López had helped elect to the Chino City Council. Three years after Morales's election, López labeled him a traitor to the Mexican-American community. He not only lambasted Morales for voting against federal support for low-cost public housing but called the councilman lazy, incompetent, and ineffective. López reminded Morales that he had been elected to serve the community and not his personal interests. "Three years 'our councilman' has served in his post," López wrote of Morales. "But during this time he has done nothing of value for the community, except chewed a lot of gum during crucial sessions, smiled condescendingly, and never criticized nor protested the views of the other council members." [56] Morales was not only inept, but he was becoming harmful by siding with reactionary forces in Chino. Morales was a tragic figure because he failed to recognize his own ignorance. In opposing Morales's reelection in 1950, López baited the councilman by suggesting that his platform consisted only of the following promises: to be punctual at each council session in order to get the most comfortable seat in which to doze better during council meetings; to chew plenty of gum and loudly enough to inform others of his presence at council sessions; to nod his head affirmatively at proposals against the interest of Mexican Americans and to shake his head negatively whenever Mexican Americans requested anything for their benefit; and, finally, to make sure he collected his per diem for every council session he attended. [57] Calling Morales's election in 1946 a qualified victory for Mexican Americans and his tenure as councilman a disaster, López explained that while Morales was a "good" man, he was not a "good" councilman. López advised Mexican Americans to be sophisticated enough to judge Morales on his record, or, as he put it, his lack of a record. He appealed to voters not to make the same mistake by reelecting Morales, and he criticized a suggestion made by Morales's campaign manager that Mexican Americans vote for the councilman because he also was Mexican American. Dismissing this as a "fascist" tactic, López qualified his support for ethnic politics and rejected the proposal that Mexican Americans vote solely for Mexican Americans on the basis of ethnicity. Ethnic loyalty was important, but in Morales's case his reelection would only harm the community. Morales survived the 1950 election but went down in defeat four years later to López's delight. [58]

Despite the Morales case and his frustration with other Mexican-American politicos, López concluded that the experience in ethnic politics was worthwhile. He remarked in 1958 that in twelve years more than twenty-five Mexican Americans had been elected in the San Gabriel Valley and had given Mexican Americans a voice in municipal politics. "No one can deny that the experiments begun in Chino and Ontario have not been of positive value," he wrote, "in that they have proven to ourselves and to others that within the Hispanic population there are persons with talent and abilities who can serve their fellow citizen." [59] The campaigns had shown, contrary to misinformed public opinion, that Mexican Americans could successfully organize and achieve electoral success. Their triumphs, moreover, revealed that Mexican Americans could play a decisive political role and in time represent a force to be reckoned with in California politics.

Cultural Pluralism

Political integration, however, involved a cultural question. Mexican-American leaders such as López supported integration into the mainstream of American society, but not at the full expense of cultural heritage. López, like other Mexican-American leaders, rejected the melting pot concept and noted that in his travels throughout the United States he had never witnessed the melting pot. "People are human beings," he wrote. "As such they have more similarities than they have differences. Nevertheless, we are the creatures of our culture and our environment. We are the children of our habits. And the beauty and the strength of our America lies not in being alike but in our differences." [60] The Mexican-American Generation took pride in being of Mexican descent and while it understood the necessity of cultural compromise, it also believed in cultural retention. In a Mexican community such as the San Gabriel Valley, comprised of both Mexican Americans and Mexican nationals, common cultural traditions bound one group to the other. Moreover, López proposed that racial and cultural discrimination, which bred ethnic insecurity among all Mexicans, especially Mexican Americans, had to be countered by ethnic pride. "Respect and pride for one's heritage," he advised young Mexican-American graduates in 1957, "is essential in order to feel proud in being an American." [61] López strove to cultivate a bicultural world view among all Mexicans in the San Gabriel Valley. He promoted Mexican cultural traditions while supporting a process of acculturation that would pave the way for integration. Fearful of too much acculturation, especially among youth, López recognized cultural pluralism as a viable alternative. As one writer in *El Espectador* put it: "Continue united for unity builds strength and continue to be proud of being born in the United States and of having Mexican blood in your veins." [62]

López advocated Mexican cultural retention in several ways. He encouraged the continuation of the older immigrant-based mutual societies not only because they served the Mexican community but also because they advanced cultural pride. Linguistically, López affirmed the use of Spanish and the development of a bilingual population. *El Espectador,* itself, represented a predominantly Spanish-language organ. So Mexican-American children could learn Spanish, López in 1938 endorsed the opening of a private Mexican school in Cucamonga. "The cost is minimal," he noted of the instruction, "and it is expected that many parents in Cucamonga and neighboring vicinities will take advantage of this opportunity to provide their children with instruction in our beautiful language." [63] *El Espectador* also served as an outlet for local poets who published their Spanish-language poems and *corridos* (ballads) in its pages. [64] "Journalism has been my mission in life," López proclaimed in 1956. "And I have nothing to complain about. In publishing a Spanish language newspaper we have contributed in a small way to fostering among our readers a love of our beautiful language and of our culture which gives it life." [65]

Annually, *El Espectador* paid particular attention to the celebration of the 16th of September—Mexican Independence Day—and the Cinco de Mayo, the Mexican victory over an invading French army in 1862. López consistently prompted the Mexican-American communities to organize festivals for these key Mexican holidays and often served as the featured speaker. [66] Mexican patriotic holidays were to López occasions for Mexican nationals living in the United States to rededicate themselves to their mother country and for parents of Mexican-American children to instill in them respect for Mexican culture and ethnicity. In a special 16th of September edition of *El Espectador* in 1949, López hailed the dedication with which mexicanos in the San Gabriel Valley celebrated Mexican independence. It appeared to him that they displayed greater enthusiasm for this holiday than did their counterparts in Mexico. "This is because," López explained, "love for one's country assumes greater importance when we live outside of it than when we are there." Mexican nationals, of course, always had in mind returning to Mexico even if only to be buried. "They conserve a love for their language," López observed, "their national heroes, their customs and their Mexican traditions." Honoring the 16th of September likewise helped to prevent the loss of culture among Mexicans born in the United States. "The most important gift that we can leave our children," López editorialized, "is pride in being Mexican." He insisted that if parents retained their cultural traditions and if they passed them on to their offspring that the "Mexican soul" would survive north of the border. [67]

López promoted various other forms of Mexican cultural expression. Groups specializing in Mexican music, art, and theater frequently received attention in *El Espectador*'s pages. In 1938, for example, the paper reported that a number of artists, musicians, and actors had formed the Tehuantepec Mexican Actors Guild in Upland to foster interest in Mexican folk culture, especially among youth. The different Spanish-language plays and pageants performed by the Mexican Players at the Padua Hills Theater in Claremont received publicity over the years in *El Espectador*. The newspaper also accepted advertisements for theaters exhibiting Mexican movies in the area. As the largest distributor of such films in the valley, Azteca Films called itself a "purely Mexican business." "This company," its promotion stressed, "supports the effort to insure that neither the Spanish language, traditions, customs, nor Mexican culture dies out in the United States." To further maintain an interest in Mexico, López published a series of articles commencing in 1949 entitled "Conoce Usted México?" (Do You Know Mexico?), which described various geographic, historical, and political features of the southern republic.[68]

López hoped to maintain Mexican culture in the United States but understood the importance and, indeed, inevitability of Americanization. *El Espectador* reflected and even influenced this acculturation process. The paper's periodic use of a bilingual format underlined the cultural and language changes experienced by Mexican Americans. Between 1938 and 1959, López launched at least five bilingual versions of *El Espectador*. Each ran for several months before reverting again to a Spanish-language copy. Bilingualism in *El Espectador* consisted of an English-language page aimed at the growing number of Mexican-American youths in the public schools. "These young adults and children," López wrote in 1938, "preferring to read in English, in order to understand it better, and also because many cannot read in Spanish, have no interest in our newspaper. Hence, it is our intention [by publishing this English section] to interest our Mexican youth in *El Espectador*."[69] López expected that this section, by concentrating on educational issues, would encourage students to remain in school. Nine years later, Larry Probasco, a World War II veteran and the second editor of the newspaper's English section, stressed the value of learning English. It represented the common denominator linking all ethnic groups in the United States. You spoke English, Probasco suggested, not just out of necessity but because it was a privilege.[70]

López clearly understood the advances English was making among Mexican Americans. If he and other leaders desired not to lose this younger generation, then English rather than Spanish had to be used as a generational bridge. "*El Espectador* also intends to reform itself into a bilingual newspaper," López stated in 1956 in announcing various publishing changes. "In this way we can better serve those of the second and third generations of Mexican descent, who day by day find it more difficult to read in the language of their parents."[71] Jay Rodríguez, another of the English-language editors, affirmed López's sentiment. "Many of the third and fourth generation of Mexican descent find it difficult to read the Spanish language," he wrote, "your writer is among this group. The editors felt that due recognition should be given to the younger group of Spanish speaking people in a language they are more familiar with."[72]

Besides employing English, *El Espectador* taught its readers U.S. history by publishing periodic civic lessons in both Spanish and English. López advised recent immigrants on how best to adjust to life north of the border. This included information on annual alien registration, naturalization, and civil rights provided by Mexican-American attorney Richard A. Ibañez in his weekly column "Sus Derechos" (Your Rights). To answer inquiries concerning domestic life and, in particular, male-female relations in the United States, López inaugurated in 1956 a personal advice column written in English by "Martita." Finally, he acknowledged the emergence of a Mexican-American youth culture by accepting advertisements for concerts aimed at Mexican-American youth and featuring American musical influences. One such ad during the 1940s noted that Tommy Vásquez and his Swing Companions would play for a youth dance in Chino. A 1948 notice alerted readers to a dance in Pomona with the music of Raúl Díaz and Don Tosti, the foremost exponents of the Pachuco Boogie. And in the 1950s, ads appeared for concerts highlighting the new musical craze: rock and roll.[73]

Supporting Mexican cultural traditions while recognizing the attraction and pragmatic necessity of acculturation, López proposed a type of dual cultural citizenship. Mexican Americans could and should benefit from both cultures. To convince Mexican Americans of such an approach, López, like others of his political generation, stressed the similarities rather than the differences between Mexico and the United States. Mexican Americans need not be ambivalent, for example, about celebrating both the 16th of September and the Fourth of July because both celebrations honored liberty and democracy. One complemented the other. "The true spirit of Democracy lives on," López wrote in 1940, "as the Mexican colonies of the Valley prepare to celebrate the National Independence of their mother country in the only haven in the world, the United States of America."[74] Dual cultural citizenship, however, required dual responsibilities. Just as López encouraged the celebration of the 16th of September, he called on Mexican Americans to join in Fourth of July festivities. While promoting a sense of Mexican cultural community, he also advised Mexican Americans not to be sectarian. They should participate with their Anglo neighbors in joint community ventures. The United States was a pluralistic society composed of diverse groups descended from immigrants, López reminded his readers; and while they all remained loyal to their cultures and roots, they likewise had united for the collective good of the United States. Mexican Americans had to follow suit.[75]

Dual cultural citizenship to López represented not only a goal but a growing reality. Older Mexican Americans remained highly loyal to their language and culture, but among the young various forces were pushing Mexican Americans to accept cultural compromises. However, cultural compromise, or what López termed "naturalization," need not be feared. He explained that cultural naturalization came easy for Mexican Americans since they had been native to California before the Anglos arrived. Consequently, Mexicans immigrating to California were in fact only returning home and undergoing a process of naturalization. Yet this remained distinct from forced Americanization, which had been tried earlier and failed. López opposed forced Americanization but accepted acculturation as inevitable and pointed out that customs, diet, marriage, education, jobs, and even wars all constituted centripetal pressures Americanizing Mexicans.[76]

Acculturation was not wrong, but it had to be balanced. It should not deprive Mexican Americans of their cultural heritage or of their ethnic identity. It should not consist of what López called "cultural amnesia."[77] Acculturation could and should not be prevented, but López believed that a sensitivity on the part of both Mexican Americans and Anglos to the benefits of cultural pluralism would help the transformation. If World War II had proved anything, López editorialized in 1946, it was that people and nations had to cooperate and to treat one another with respect. This also had to apply domestically in the postwar era. "The great hope for realization of a better world, instead of a planet of shattering holocausts," he wrote, "lies in our will to merge viewpoints and differing customs—to come to know its varying people as friends and neighbors. To have such opportunities here in our own communities is something we should seek ardently."[78] López recalled the unique cultural roots of California and of the distinct Spanish-Mexican heritage of the state. Cultural pluralism was real in California, but it was and had to be more than simply the stereotypical "colorful Mexican." Mexican Americans had to be accepted as full citizens and integrated into all levels of California society. Only in this manner could a viable cultural pluralism flourish. Only through cultural pluralism could a united society be forged or the "one world" López referred to:

> The time has come—indeed it had to come—for "one world" in our home communities. It is the time for friendliness and courtesy, for the merging of viewpoints and differing customs, for the sharing of civic responsibilities

and problems. Not as newcomers, but as co-workers over many decades of community history, the descendents [*sic*] of Spain and Mexico, bearers of a great cultural heritage, come to take their place in civic life. They are ready to help bear its burdens and rejoice in its triumphs.[79]

Conclusion

By 1961 López concluded his career as a muckraking journalist. After twenty-eight years, *El Espectador* closed publication. During the turbulent 1960s and with the ascendance of the more militant and youth-oriented Chicano Movement, López found greater economic security through employment in the federal antipoverty and minority programs created as a response to the decade's social pressures. Ironically, the militancy of the Chicano Movement with its greater antiestablishment direction achieved for some of the middle-class fraction of the Mexican-American Generation what had previously eluded many of them: recognition, integration, and status. Consequently, New Deal liberals and muckrakers like López became more acceptable to ruling circles than Brown Power advocates. Possessing more limited goals steeped in integration and pluralism plus acceptance of much of cold war culture steeped in anticommunism, the middle-class unit of the Mexican-American Generation reaped personal benefits during the 1960s and 1970s as the establishment sought out less challenging leaders from the Chicano communities. It is not totally surprising, then, that López found himself in 1972 spearheading the Mexican-American campaign for Richard Nixon in Los Angeles. For his support, López received an appointment as Spanish-Speaking Coordinator for the Department of Housing and Urban Development (HUD). One year later López died.[80]

Yet López's contribution to and significance in Chicano history lies in his role as a muckraking publisher, editor, and chief reporter for *El Espectador*. The guiding light for one of the longest-running Mexican-American newspapers, López underscored the value of organic institutions within the Mexican-American community. Yet unlike older institutions such as mutual societies and even newspapers such as *La Opinión* of Los Angeles, which essentially represented an immigrant generation, *El Espectador* represented a Mexican-American institution. It helped bridge the needs and interests of Mexican immigrants with those of a more ambitious and aspiring Mexican-American generation. López, however, left no doubts of his loyalty to his generation. Through his campaigns against humiliating forms of public discrimination, for greater and more authentic Mexican-American political representation, for educational integration, and for a pluralistic society, López represented well the particular interests of the Mexican-American middle class. Not radical, this fraction accepted the American system on its own terms but called for and even demanded that it create room for Mexican Americans. At the same time, López and others of his generation did not deceive themselves as to the natural force for social change. López understood that reforms could be achieved only through struggles led by Mexican Americans themselves. As a hungry middle class rather than a complacent one (more characteristic of the 1980s), the middle-class fraction did not shy away from struggles. Ignacio López as a journalist proved to be one of the few voices able to articulate the changing political temper affecting Mexican Americans by the 1930s. Yet López the muckraker not only reflected but helped shape the contours of the Mexican-American Generation in Southern California.

LULAC Constitutional Convention, Corpus Christi, May 19, 1929. Courtesy
Benson Latin American Collection, University of Texas, Austin.

Ben Garza, LULAC, 1929.
Courtesy Benson Latin American Collection,
University of Texas, Austin.

Alonso S. Perales, LULAC, 1930s.
From Perales, *En Defensa de mi R[*
(1937).

M. C. González, LULAC, 1930s.
Courtesy Benson Latin American Collectio[
University of Texas, Austin.

Mrs. J. C. Machuca, LULAC, 1930s.
Courtesy Benson Latin American
Collection, University of Texas, Austin.

Officers of Ladies' LULAC Council No. 17, Albuquerque, New Mexico, 1939.
Courtesy Benson Latin American Collection, University of Texas, Austin.

Eleuterio Escobar, School
Improvement League, 1930s.
Courtesy Benson Latin American
Collection, University of Texas,
Austin.

Raymond L. Telles, April 11, 1957.
Courtesy *El Paso Herald-Post.*

Ignacio L. López,
September 16, 1945.
Courtesy Leonor Varela.

Luisa Moreno,
Spanish-Speaking Congress,
ca. 1940. Courtesy Bert Corona.

Josefina Fierro de Bright,
Spanish-Speaking Congress,
ca. 1940. Courtesy
Bert Corona.

Spanish-Speaking Congress, Los Angeles, ca. 1940.
Courtesy Bert Corona.

Humberto Sílex (right), Mine Mill, El Paso, with
Vicente Lombardo Toledano, El Paso, 1943.
Courtesy Humberto Sílex.

J. B. Chávez, Mine Mill, El Paso, ca. 1940. Courtesy
Western History Collection, University of Colorado.

Mine Mill Local 501, El Paso, 1948. Courtesy U.S. Steelworkers, El Paso.

**Alfredo Montoya, ANMA, ca. 1950.
Courtesy Western History Collection,
University of Colorado.**

Carlos E. Castañeda, ca. 1940.
Courtesy Benson Latin American
Collection, University of Texas, Austi

George I. Sánchez, ca. 1940.
Courtesy Benson Latin American
Collection, University of Texas, Austi

Arthur L. Campa, 1943. Courtesy Special
Collections Department, General Library,
University of New Mexico.

CHAPTER FIVE

The Politics of Status: The Election of Raymond L. Telles as Mayor of El Paso, 1957

> We had to make . . . a start someplace. We thought Telles was the best man for that position. . . . We wanted a qualified man.
>
> —GABRIEL NAVARRETE, 1982
>
> I'd say that probably 98 percent of the Mexicans really wanted to do something for the man. They saw him [Telles] probably as an image for the *mexicanos.*
>
> —ALFREDO "LELO" JACQUES, 1982
>
> We started feeling the pressure of social justice. We wanted a little cut of the pie.
>
> —RICHARD TELLES, 1982
>
> I don't think that there has ever been as high a participation in any political campaign of a Mexican-American community as we experienced on this day when we elected Raymond Telles.
>
> —ALBERT ARMENDÁRIZ, 1982

The election of Raymond L. Telles as mayor of El Paso in 1957 was a major breakthrough in the Mexican-American Generation's quest for political representation and status in the United States. A personal triumph for Telles, his election also symbolized a political victory for the entire Mexican-American community of this key southwestern border city. After over one hundred years of limited and inadequate political participation in local affairs, Mexican Americans concluded in 1957 that the time had come for electing one of their own as mayor of a city numbering almost 250,000 with one half the population being of Mexican descent.[1] Telles became the first Mexican American to be elected mayor of a major southwestern city in this century. His election and subsequent administration (1957–1961) stimulated additional Mexican-American electoral initiatives and, more important, gave Mexican Americans a growing confidence in themselves as American citizens and as political actors. Hence, the Telles story is part of the larger

113

and ongoing struggle by Mexican Americans to eliminate a legacy of second-class citizenship. This chapter is a case study of the 1957 election.

El Paso and the Politics of Status

The historic labor exploitation of Mexicans in El Paso and throughout the Southwest supported by race and cultural discrimination had led to their second-class political status. A small number of acculturated and better-off Mexican Americans did participate in early El Paso politics, but as political ward bosses for the Democratic ring that controlled local politics during the nineteenth and early twentieth centuries. Most Mexicans possessed no real political representation. Of course prior to the 1930s many maintained Mexican citizenship. Still, they contributed to El Paso politics by being paid to vote by unscrupulous Anglo politicians acting through Mexican-American intermediaries. Mexicans received slight patronage as city laborers out of this political arrangement, but on the whole their involvement only supported a political system that reinforced their economic oppression. Mexican immigrant workers undergoing a process of proletarianization struggled to protect themselves, but their vulnerable political status as aliens and their personal desires to return to Mexico did not lend themselves to long-lasting protest movements.[2]

The 1930s and World War II, however, proved to be political watersheds for Mexican Americans. Repulsed by overt forms of social discrimination, Mexican Americans before and after the war chose first to confront segregation in public facilities such as schools, theaters, swimming pools, restaurants, and housing tracts and in access to elective offices. The efforts to force respect for Mexican Americans by pursuing an integrationist strategy involved what Ladd in his study of black politics in the South terms "status goals," as opposed to "welfare goals" intended to obtain material improvements without disturbing race-ethnic divisions.[3] For Mexican Americans, as for many blacks, especially after the war, "status goals" meant abolishing those forms of public discrimination that called attention to their racial and ethnic differences. Consumed by a desire to be treated as full-fledged American citizens, Mexican Americans engaged in the "politics of status." "The demand for integration" Ladd notes, "is essentially the attempt by a group which has been branded inferior in quite literally a thousand ways by white Americans to gain recognition as a truly equal partner in the American democracy."[4] Reformist by nature, the politics of status did not directly combat the root cause of Mexican-American underdevelopment in the Southwest: the need by capital to expand by maintaining most Mexicans as pools of cheap and surplus labor. The altering of this relationship would entail more fundamental struggles, encompassing both sides of the border, that most Mexican-American leaders were both ideologically and politically unprepared to undertake. They believed that the system was capable of reforming inequities. Nevertheless, the politics of status, including the struggle for democratic political rights, marked a forward step in the political evolution of Mexican Americans. The rising expectations generated by this movement, as well as its accompanying frustrations, would result in even more challenging efforts by a succeeding generation.

In El Paso, Mexican Americans interpreted status goals predominantly in electoral political terms. Unlike other parts of Texas, where Mexicans faced de facto racial discrimination in public facilities, Mexican Americans in the border city did not and had historically possessed access—if they could afford them—to theaters, restaurants, stores, and other forms of public facilities. Even schools and housing tracts were not strictly segregated in El Paso. The Anglo power structure had early learned that it made little economic sense to exclude Mexicans from public facilities because of their importance as a source of labor and as consumers. Moreover, discrimination against Mexicans would jeopardize El Paso's relations with Mexico, especially the border city's role as a labor center and as a wholesale and retail outlet for northern Mexican customers. However, not confronting a system of overt public discrimination, Mexican Americans still lagged behind Anglos in jobs, wages, education, and political representation.[5] "El Paso's discrimination," one report on El Paso politics concluded, "is based primarily on the belief, or rationale, that Latins are 'not qualified' (primarily because of lack of education) for various jobs."[6] In 1950, for example, the Spanish-surnamed population in El Paso composed more than half the city's total population. Of these, almost three-fourths of Mexican Americans were born in the United States. Despite their numbers, Mexican Americans constituted only 1.8 percent of high white-collar occupations, only 26.4 percent of low white-collar occupations, and only 11.2 percent of skilled blue-collar ones. Only seven Mexican-American lawyers practiced in El Paso.[7] Hence, by mid-century Mexican Americans still formed, despite certain gains, a predominantly working-class population excluded from access to political and economic power in El Paso. Two El Pasos continued to coexist as they had since the nineteenth century: one more affluent and predominantly Anglo in the northern section of the city and the other poor and predominantly Mexican "south of the tracks."

Under such circumstances, Mexican Americans in El Paso—experiencing both poverty and degrees of progress—viewed the attainment of effective political representation as the first step in equalizing their status with Anglos. Not having to struggle, as in other parts of Texas, for the right to integrate public facilities—already achieved in El Paso—Mexican Americans in the border city instead saw their lack of access to electoral offices as the most significant affront to their status as American citizens. No Mexican American had ever been elected mayor or served on the city council between 1900 and 1950.[8] Moreover, the existence of a poll tax in Texas added to the political disenfranchisement of many Mexican Americans. After the war Mexican-American leaders vowed to change this. "The Spanish speaking group is ripe for organized action and has an endless list of social grievances, many of which date back fifty years," Carey McWilliams wrote of El Paso in 1948. "It has only begun to achieve real political maturity, but leaders are emerging and the day of political reckoning cannot be long deferred."[9] This was especially true for the aspiring lower middle class, which considered politics not only as an avenue of personal mobility but more important of collective respectability. These Mexican Americans believed that the most symbolic way of acquiring status as full-fledged American citizens was through electoral success, which included winning the mayor's office. It is in this context that the political ascendance of Raymond Telles can be appreciated.

Raymond Telles and Mexican-American Politics

Who was Raymond Telles and why did the Mexican-American leadership of El Paso consider him to be the most "electable" Mexican? Born in 1915 in the barrio of south El Paso, Telles, unlike most other Mexican Americans, received a good elementary and high school education in Catholic schools. Graduating from high school in the midst of the Great Depression, Telles attended business school and worked for the Works Progress Administration until moving to a better clerical job at the federal correctional institution at La Tuna, Texas, just north of El Paso. Being drafted into the army two years later in 1941 only accelerated Telles's personal mobility besides providing helpful background experience for his future political career. Telles entered as a private and returned home a decorated major in the Army Air Force.[10] Back in El Paso, Telles's father, Ramón, who had always been involved in south-side politics along with Telles's politically ambitious younger brother, Richard, and a number of returning Mexican-American veterans—the *veteranos*—saw in Raymond Telles their hopes for political influence if not power. In 1948 they convinced a reluctant Telles to run for the position of county clerk. In a heated race in which his incumbent opponent stooped to racial baiting, Telles achieved a stunning victory with a slim margin of 563 votes. He swept the south-side and Lower Valley barrios as Mexican Americans turned out in large numbers, but he likewise received good support from the Anglo north side. For nine years, Telles proved to be a model administrator and was repeatedly reelected without opposition. In the meantime his Mexican-American admirers continued to promote his image as a civic leader. While county clerk, Telles held high offices in organizations such as the Boy Scouts, Girl Scouts, the El Paso Tuberculosis Association, the El Paso Boys Club, and the Southwestern Sun Carnival Association. He also joined the chamber of commerce.[11] Tall, not particularly dark-skinned, elegant in appearance, an impeccable dresser, thoroughly bilingual, a modest man by nature but with a warm and generous personality, a happily married man and the father of two daughters, Telles stood out as *the* candidate for an aspiring Mexican-American community.

The election of Telles as county clerk in 1948 in turn seemed to increase Mexican-American political involvement. Mexican Americans, as in the past, continued to run and be elected to lesser county positions, such as justice of the peace. More important, they enhanced their total political presence. Mexican Americans formed supportive blocs for particular mayoral candidates both liberal and conservative. In the 1949 election, for example, a group of Mexican-American leaders headed by Modesto Gómez, long-time LULAC activist, endorsed the candidacy of incumbent mayor Dan Ponder over Dan Duke. In both the 1950 and 1954 congressional elections, Richard Telles organized south-side voters on behalf of liberal candidates. In turn, Anglo politicians began to include Mexican Americans on their campaign staffs and on their tickets. In the 1951 city elections, Fred Hervey chose Mexican-American businessman Ernest Ponce as one of his aldermanic candidates. Although not a community activist, Ponce was perceived by the Hervey campaign as their ethnic candidate. To run against Ponce, as alderman for parks and recreation, the opposing ticket of Dan Duke selected Moisés Flores. Ponce easily defeated Flores and swept into office with Hervey.[12] Mexican Americans strengthened their political presence in El Paso by likewise increasing their number of registered voters. In 1951, LULAC Ladies Council 9 won the sweepstakes poll tax contest involving civic clubs. "We have been getting out the vote every year," declared Mrs. Joseph Rey, chairwoman of the LULAC poll tax campaign, "but it has been a telephone campaign in the past. This is the first time we actually sold poll tax receipts. Most of the women in our club work days but get on the phone in the evening. Friday night we will take poll lists and begin calling to get the voters to the polls."[13]

Mexican-American political activity pressured the Hervey administration in the early 1950s to carry out certain improvements in the south side and to appoint Mexican Americans to relatively high city positions. They included Joe Herrera as city clerk, Nick Pérez as city engineer, and Dr. M. D. Hornedo as city-county health director. Luciano Santoscoy, a president of

LULAC at the time, recalls that LULAC presented Hervey with a petition from south-side residents that helped convince the mayor to pave some sidewalks and streets in the area.[14]

More acculturated, more educated, and slightly more occupationally mobile than their parents, young Mexican-American adults aspired for full integration into the civic life of El Paso. Repulsed in their attempt to secure authentic political representation by electing candidates from their own ranks, they particularly hoped for electoral success. Yet they desired to play politics on their own terms and not as an ethnic group manipulated by either Anglo or Mexican politicos as in the past. "It is about time," wrote activist Aurora Mata in 1955,

> that the citizen of El Paso awaken to the fact that the Latin American people of South and East El Paso are intelligent enough to decide any issue on the facts or their sincere beliefs. Some of these citizens (including myself) may not speak English fluently, or understand it in general, but they can decide an issue for their own betterment, for the city, and for problems that exist solely in their neighborhood. They are not a herd of cows that have to be led by so-called leaders.[15]

Believing that their time had come to achieve the highest elective office in El Paso, Mexican Americans also turned to Raymond Telles.

The 1957 Mayoral Primary

In 1955 Mexican-American leaders (excluding Ramón Telles, who had died in 1950) encouraged Raymond Telles to run for mayor.[16] Telles, however, expressed ambivalence about the prospects of a Mexican-American candidate and concluded that the political climate was not right. "In other words," he recalls, "for me to win, there had to be a very special issue, an issue whereby people would vote against the other group and not necessarily in favor of me. So at that time I decided that the issue wasn't there."[17] One year later Mexican Americans again assessed their chances of winning the 1957 mayoral election. "We were hungry to get one of our men to be a mayor of the city," "Kiko" Hernández of LULAC explains. "We had that burning desire. You know when people have that burning desire that's when they get hot."[18] The veteranos, LULAC officials such as Alfonso Kennard, Richard Telles, and others, again approached Telles. "I wanted to see Raymond become mayor," Lulacer Lelo Jacques notes, "because I knew that if Raymond would be mayor that some day Raymond would be a congressman."[19]

Telles agreed this time. He now believed conditions to be propitious for two reasons. First, the city's annexation of the Lower Valley, downriver from El Paso, initiated by the Hervey administration and concluded by the incumbent one, had produced anger and discontent among Lower Valley residents. This protest might effectively be organized into a solid bloc of voters. Second, Mayor Tom Rogers had not been elected by the voters and probably was vulnerable. Rogers, a businessman, had been appointed mayor by the city council in consultation with the city's Anglo business and financial elites— the so-called kingmakers—after Mayor W. T. Misenhimer resigned following his election, citing health reasons. "I decided at that time that it was possible [to win]," Telles remembers his decision. "I knew it wasn't going to be easy. I knew it was going to take a lot of money, which I didn't have and it was going to be very difficult getting people to run with me." [20] Telles had lingering trepidations but by late 1956 was in the race.

Albert Armendáriz, one of the few Mexican-American lawyers and a past national president of LULAC, recalls being present at a strategy meeting with Telles in November 1956. One crucial discussion concerned getting Mexican Americans to pay their poll taxes. Telles, however, was the perfect candidate to excite Mexican-American voters. If Mexican Americans would not vote for Telles, they would not vote for anyone else. Yet the Mexican-American vote would not be enough. Telles would, as in 1948, need some Anglo support. Mexican Americans, such as Armendáriz, believed Telles could appeal to Anglos and not threaten them. "We chose him [Telles] because he's diplomatic-looking; he's light-skinned; he's impeccable; he speaks perfect English," Armendáriz notes. "I mean here was a qualified Mexican American to be mayor. And that was the thing we were looking for. We didn't want to postulate a person for mayor that was going to be rejected on the basis: 'Hey, he's not qualified.' " [21]

The issue of qualifications, of course, had been a particularly aggravating one for Mexican Americans in El Paso and elsewhere. They had nurtured and cultivated Telles so that when the time came to advance him for mayor, no one could question his qualifications. If El Paso accepted Telles, it would accept other qualified Mexican Americans in politics as well as in other fields. "You have to understand the basis for Raymond Telles in this community," Armendáriz stresses:

> Our leadership had been told time after time again that the reason we didn't go up was because we weren't qualified. . . . And this was a term that was not only used against us but it hurt. It ruffled our dignity as a group. . . . It was a system; it was a *modus operandi:* "you're not qualified." And in doing this for Raymond we were able to . . . present an entirely qualified candidate. None of us were foolish enough to believe that we could put Raymond Telles in as anything—dogcatcher—if we did not sway a substantial section of the Anglo community to vote for him. This was basic in our thinking. [22]

In organizing his campaign, Telles began with a strong family foundation including his wife, Delfina, and his two brothers: Joe, who ran the family business, Ramón's Transfer, and, of course, Richard. The youngest Telles brother, a key to Raymond's election in 1948, would be invaluable again through his political and business contacts among Mexican Americans. Richard had inherited from his father an astute political instinct along with a combative personality. In the 1948 campaign, he had masterminded a strategy for getting Mexican Americans to the polls. A nonveteran, Richard, unlike Raymond, had gone into business for himself and operated both a cantina [bar] and a vending company (juke boxes, pinball machines, and cigarettes) serving other bars in the south and southeast barrios of El Paso. Through his business contacts and as Democratic precinct chairman in the south side, Richard organized an informal political network that in later years would come to be referred to by his political enemies as the "organization." The 1948 campaign had allowed him the opportunity to apply his political talents at the service of his older brother. "You had to be tough in those days to exist," Richard recalls of this first political battle.[23]

Outside the family, the veteranos stood ready to literally march once more for Telles. Indeed, the 1948 election had inaugurated a new force in Mexican-American politics in El Paso that influenced Raymond Telles's political future. Returning from a war to save democracy, Mexican-American veterans resolved to have democracy at home. Victims of discrimination before being drafted and encountering it again on their return, especially on job applications, the veteranos organized to achieve equality of opportunity for Mexican Americans in El Paso. "We came back with new ideas," veterano leader David Villa remembers.[24] As part of their reform program the veteranos hoped to build effective Mexican-American political representation in local government. They wanted to break with the older tradition referred to by historian John Higham as "received leadership," in which Anglo politicians handpicked accommodating Mexican Americans to act as "leaders" for the Mexican-American community. Instead, they sought a more authentic or "internal leadership" that emanated from within the people.[25] To achieve this the veteranos led by Gabriel Navarrete, David Villa, and others formed the Segura–McDonald branch of the VFW (named after two Mexican Americans from El Paso killed in the war). Although prohibited from directly engaging in politics as a VFW group, they engaged in political action on an individual basis. When Telles announced for county clerk, the veteranos mobilized to support their fellow veteran not only because he was Mexican American but because they believed he could do the job. "We had to make . . . a start someplace," recalls Navarrete, a school friend of Telles'. "We thought Telles was the best man for that position. . . . We wanted a qualified man."[26]

In addition, a more active LULAC through both the men's and women's councils could assist in registering voters.

Finally, Telles could count on the support of the *El Paso Herald-Post* and its editor, Ed Pooley. Without the support of one of El Paso's two newspapers, Telles believed that his campaign would get nowhere and simply be dismissed as a nonviable ethnic effort. Representing a loose coalition of liberal small businessmen, professionals, and union leaders, Pooley and the *Herald-Post* desired to democratize El Paso politics. Liberalism in El Paso generally meant supporting a more open political process in local government and greater attention by local government to the needs of the masses in the city. The conservative liberal dichotomy also contained an ethnic dimension. Most Mexican Americans supported liberal rather than conservative political candidates. "Now the man that I owe a lot, and I'll never forget, is Mr. Ed M. Pooley," Telles recalls.[27]

As in 1948, Telles started with a Mexican-American base. He could not possibly win without a large Mexican-American vote not only south of the tracks, but in the central districts now housing many Mexican Americans who made it out of the barrio. Mexican Americans would have to be mobilized and registered to pay their poll taxes. Moreover, with the Lower Valley annexation, Telles could expand his base to include this area, containing at least 50 percent Mexican Americans, which he carried in the 1948 county election. If he could win big in Mexican-American precincts and in the Lower Valley, Telles knew he had a chance to be mayor. However, he likewise recognized as in 1948 that he could not run an open ethnic campaign. Such a strategy would undoubtedly cause a backlash among Anglo voters. Telles did not deceive himself. He understood that most Anglos would perceive him as a Mexican-American candidate regardless of what he did. But if he accented the ethnic appeal, even more Anglos would register to vote just to keep a Mexican out of the mayor's office. He would also risk the chance of scaring away those Anglo liberals and moderates he hoped to attract. "I realized," he recalls, "that the odds were very much against me because my name was Telles." He believed that the odds would be even greater against him if he ran an ethnic campaign. Hence, Telles decided on a "People's Ticket campaign." He would stress that he stood for El Paso's common man against the elite "kingmakers." Telles the populist could appeal to both Mexican Americans and Anglos. Finally, Telles would conduct an issues-oriented campaign while relying on Pooley's *Herald-Post* to aggressively and polemically attack the Rogers ticket. "See, the name of the ticket was the People's Ticket," Telles explains, "and we wanted to give the impression that we were dealing with all the people not just one sector, cause if we had ever given the impression that we were there representing only the Mexican

Americans we would've been killed. I mean, we would've never gotten anywhere." [28]

Telles and his supporters concluded that three objectives had to be achieved in the carrying out of their strategy. First they had to select a ticket that would complement the populist theme and help Telles with Anglo voters. Second, as in 1948, Telles would run a nonethnic "public" campaign stressing his administrative background and proposals for reforming city government. Finally, as he had done nine years before, Richard Telles would operate an ethnic "non-public" campaign. Richard would mobilize the Mexican-American vote and turn it out on election day. The Telles campaign would consequently possess different personalities in different areas of El Paso. Telles would appeal as an American populist throughout the city, while in the southern precincts Richard would ensure that ethnic loyalty tied Mexican Americans to his brother. As in 1948, this strategy did not translate into a split personality or opportunism on Telles's part. He personally found no comfort in running as an ethnic candidate and believed it more appropriate to present himself as an American citizen who believed in a democratic form of city government. At the same time, he astutely realized that to win he or his supporters had to specifically organize Mexican Americans.

The selection of a ticket proved to be no easy task. Few Anglos desired to run on a ticket headed by a Mexican American. Telles hoped to entice businessmen candidates to counter Rogers's emphasis on a business approach to city government. Telles: "So I tried gaining these men, but I found it was not possible. 'Cause I approached several of them and several of them said yes and then a couple of days later they came back and said sorry." [29] Consequently, he turned to citizens with less prominent business backgrounds. Ernest Craigo, an insurance man, agreed to be on the ticket. Telles had known Craigo in the Air Force Reserve. Jack White, a service manager for a local auto dealer, also joined the campaign. More important, Telles acquired the services of Ted Bender, a local television and radio personality, and Ralph Seitsinger, a Lower Valley businessman. El Pasoans knew Bender as the "friendly weatherman" and could identify with him. His daily radio and television appearances would indirectly publicize the campaign. Seitsinger turned down being on the ticket at first but agreed to locate a suitable candidate from the Lower Valley. He could not. "Don't get on that Mexican ticket," he heard Lower Valley bankers tell potential candidates. Unable to find a running mate for Telles, Seitsinger joined the ticket himself. Telles had wanted Seitsinger all along. Seitsinger likewise proved an asset by contributing $3,000 to the campaign and by getting a Lower Valley contractor, Joe Yarborough, to substantially fund Telles's efforts. Telles complemented the

Seitsinger selection by naming Ray Marantz as campaign manager. Marantz possessed no political experience but had Lower Valley contacts through his insurance business.[30]

Having chosen a ticket and organized a campaign structure and strategy, Telles formally announced his candidacy on January 22, one day before the filing deadline. "Ours is the People's Ticket," his announcement emphasized, "and if elected, it will be a City Government by the people and for the people of El Paso. We shall bow to no bosses." Telles pledged that his administration would more effectively represent all the people of the city. "Ours will be an administration that serves no special interest or particular area; rather we propose to offer conscientious service to the entire community." Telles reminded voters that as county clerk he had fulfilled all his campaign promises.[31]

Voter Registration and Campaign Issues

Formally in the race, Telles swiftly mobilized to register Mexican-American voters before the poll tax deadline on the last day of January. Voter registration had been done earlier, but Telles's announcement triggered off a frenzy of activity. From campaign headquarters in downtown El Paso, the Telles organization plotted their voter registration drive. Campaign manager Marantz remembers that they stressed registering those Mexican Americans who had never voted, including the elderly. Telles estimated that he would need at least 90 percent of the Mexican-American vote. Voter registration consisted of various methods. The LULAC people, although barred by their constitution from endorsing political candidates, assisted Telles by feverishly selling poll taxes to Mexican Americans. LULAC Council 132, for example, hosted a dance and charged the price of a poll tax for admission. It also sponsored films at the Colón Theatre in south El Paso, where admission was purchase of a poll tax. Lulacers likewise set up poll tax booths in southeast El Paso as well as going door to door. They got Mexican-American merchants and grocers to become deputy registrars and to sell poll taxes in their stores. Francisco "Kiko" Hernández, who sold poll taxes at his drugstore in southeast El Paso, remembers that he and other Lulacers helped those who could not pay their poll taxes by finding work for them.[32] Lulacers further went to barrio churches and sold poll taxes after Sunday masses. Conrad Ramírez, LULAC official at the time, notes receiving much support on poll tax sales in southeast El Paso from Los Compadres, a community group of Mexican Americans working out of our Lady of Light Church and led by people such as Mrs. Frank Maldonado. Mexican-American women, especially members of LULAC Ladies Councils 9 and 335, were particularly active in voter registration. Lucy Acosta, for example, recalls selling poll taxes along with other women in front of the local Sears and J. C. Penney's as well as the Popular and the White House department stores. In all, LULAC sold 4,378 poll taxes and won the Junior Chamber of Commerce Poll Tax Contest. At Smeltertown, where hundreds of Mexican Americans worked at the ASARCO plant, Mexican-American officers of the International Union of Mine, Mill and Smelter Workers registered voters for Telles. *El Continental,* the city's Spanish-language newspaper, aided Telles's voter registration drive by alerting voters to where they could pay their poll taxes.[33] Finally, Richard Telles and his veterano allies, as in 1948, gathered poor Mexican Americans and assembled a formidable bloc of pro-Telles voters.

Telles's candidacy electrified the Mexican-American community and with the untiring work of supporters led to a significant increase in Mexican-American registration.[34] "I'd say that probably 98 percent of the Mexicans really wanted to do something for the man," Lulacer "Lelo" Jacques recounts. "They saw him [Telles] probably as an image for the *mexicanos.*" Lucy Acosta recalls that Mexican Americans needed little if any encouragement to pay their poll taxes with Telles in the race. "That was a *mexicano* running and it was Raymond Telles."[35] Total registered voters in the city numbered 42,542 as compared to 40,735 in 1956 and only 30,412 in 1955. The most impressive increase occurred in Mexican-American areas. In south and southeast El Paso, precincts 10 through 19, 1,627 more voters registered than in 1956. Poll tax increases in eight south El Paso precincts accounted for more than 65 percent of the 2,196 gain in 36 precincts experiencing voter increases. Precinct 12, Bowie High School, went from 285 voters to 461. Precinct 13, Alamo School, went from 439 to 668. Precinct 16, Beall School, went from 720 to 908. In precinct 17, Jefferson High School, Mexican-American registration increased from 1,084 to 1,508. By contrast, registration in Anglo or mixed neighborhoods went up slightly or not at all. Seven north El Paso precincts increased only from 4,225 to 4,241. In fourteen northeast precincts, with mostly Anglo voters, registration went only from 11,626 to 12,104. Combining the number of registered voters in predominantly Mexican-American precincts, Telles could begin with a reliable vote of 7,960. The balance to win would have to come from Mexican Americans in northern precincts, a minority of Anglo voters, and the Lower Valley. The total number of Lower Valley voters was 9,515.[36] *Herald-Post* columnist Dr. B. U. L. Conner observed that the rival *Times*—which he referred to as the "Morning Crimes"—had suggested that some El Pasoans had been illegally registered.[37]

Having registered voters, the Telles "public" campaign developed issues to stimulate interest in Telles, differentiate his ticket from Rogers's, and showcase Telles's grasp of city government. Telles chiefly emphasized that his administration would be oriented toward people as compared to the elitism of the Rogers administration. Mayor Telles's door as well as that of his aldermen would always be open to the public. "We have no bosses but the people," Telles's platform read. No secret meetings would be held to decide any policy. A Telles administration would solicit the views of all El Pasoans by regularly scheduling neighborhood meetings. "There is a fundamental difference between the two tickets," Ted Bender stressed. "It is that we of the People's Ticket believe in the rights of the individual while members of the opposition seem to believe that their strength comes from wealth." Telles hammered at the democratic approach of his ticket. A vote for him was a vote for "government of the people, for the people, and by the people." Telles emphasized that the Lower Valley annexation only reinforced the undemocratic character of the previous administration, which paid little heed to the wishes of the people and to the needs of poorer neighborhoods.[38]

Lacking a large campaign fund, Telles carried his issues in person to the voters while Rogers made use of television. "I would go to a building, for example," Telles remembers, "one of these office buildings, like the El Paso National Bank with 20 floors, I would walk every floor and go and visit the people. I'd walk all over the Lower Valley and walk over the areas in El Paso that I thought were very vulnerable." He told people that he wanted to be their mayor and that he hoped they would give him the opportunity to do so. Telles and his ticket had a better opportunity to discuss issues at numerous candidates' meetings organized by social clubs including Mexican-American ones. At the meetings, Telles and his aldermanic candidates proclaimed their platform and commented on issues along with the Rogers ticket. As he expected, Telles encountered close scrutiny and pressure at Anglo-sponsored assemblies. Opponents circulated preplanned questions before Telles spoke in the hope of embarrassing the county clerk. Telles: "I was always concerned about it, but I felt that I got along pretty good, and that my aldermen even though they were inexperienced and young, they did very well."[39]

The tables were turned, however, when both tickets attended evening meetings or rallies in south El Paso or in the Lower Valley: Telles territory. Unlike Rogers, who could speak only in English, Telles addressed these gatherings in both English and Spanish. Telles, of course, resisted an open ethnic campaign; yet, his use of Spanish served both as a form of communication with Mexican Americans and as an ethnic symbol. Telles had to be bilingual to reach different sectors and generations of the Mexican-American community. In south El Paso, Telles, besides offering his general platform, promised to improve depressed housing conditions, especially in the old tenements, and to possibly eradicate some of them. Such promises and Telles's appearance in the barrios produced much emotion for Telles. "People were very excited about Raymond," Albert Armendáriz recalls.[40]

The Rogers Campaign and the Press War

Tom Rogers and his ticket avoided making a direct issue of Telles's ethnic background. Like other Anglo political and business leaders they feared that overt racial animosity could only harm the border city's economy, so dependent on Mexican labor from both sides of the border and on commercial and tourist relations with Mexico. Moreover, ethnicity was circumscribed by Ernest Ponce being on the Rogers ticket. Instead, the Rogers campaign replaced ethnicity with what Eisinger in his study of white resistance to black rule in Detroit and Atlanta refers to as "neutral-sounding criteria of evaluation that function in effect as code words, masking unacceptable modes of thought and expression for both users and their audience."[41] As such, Rogers concentrated on the virtues and accomplishments of his administration and on portraying Telles as totally inexperienced for the job. Rogers ran not as a politician but as a businessman who brought experience, stability, and efficiency to the city. As the general manager of the Consumer's Ice & Fuel Company and as a former president of the chamber of commerce, Rogers insisted that he knew more than Telles knew about management and business.[42]

Rogers accused Telles of being unprepared to be mayor on several counts. First, Telles lacked financial experience. Hence, Rogers hinted that if elected Telles would harm El Paso's economy. Rogers's emphasis on business experience resembles what Eisinger discovered of white opposition to black rule in Atlanta. By defining the mayor's job in business terms, whites by definition excluded blacks from serious political consideration since whites dominated the business world.[43] The same held true for El Paso. Besides charging that Telles lacked business experience, the Rogers campaign painted the county clerk as being devoid of character. Rogers particularly jumped on Telles's charge of the administration's fraudulent loss of taxpayers' money. He accused Telles of irresponsibility by resorting to such tactics. Alderman Fletcher challenged Telles to prove the charge and noted that Telles had made an "irresponsible slur on the honesty of City employees."[44] The Rogers campaign attempted to cast still other doubts about Telles's candidacy. Alderman Kolliner, for example, suggested that Telles's opposition to police roadblocks indicated that the county clerk was soft on law and order issues. Rogers also claimed that Telles was "not his own man," but simply a puppet of Ed Pooley and the *Herald-Post*. "It is no secret that the editor of the afternoon newspaper wants to run the city," Kolliner charged. "Why doesn't he run himself instead of getting candidates who are ready to front for him." Rogers further indicted the Telles ticket of crass opportunism and of being unresponsive to the voters by refusing to debate the mayor on television. Telles replied that nothing could be debated since only the People's Ticket had a platform.[45]

While fierce, the Telles–Rogers race was tame by El Paso political standards, but only because both sides could rely on their newspaper support for the more hard-hitting issues. The 1957 mayoral election only intensified a long-standing rivalry between the *Herald-Post* and the *El Paso Times*. The editors wrote what the candidates chose not to say in public.[46] Following Telles's announcement to run for mayor, *Herald-Post* editor Pooley quickly editorialized his endorsement. He categorized the Telles ticket as a group of successful and competent Americans. Independent men, they would not be controlled by the kingmakers. Pooley's own campaign strategy consisted of attacking the Rogers ticket as puppets of the kingmakers, of representing only the wealthy, and of being antidemocratic. Rogers, Pooley contended, had been handpicked by the kingmakers in 1955 to succeed Misenhimer. "This is an important election," he stressed. "It will decide whether the people or the bosses shall be in control at City Hall, and whether there shall be a government of, by, and for the people of El Paso, or a government of, by, and for the bosses." As a candidate of the rich, Rogers had twice as much money for the campaign as did Telles. Two weeks before the election, Pooley publicized figures revealing Rogers had spent $5,284.04 to Telles's $3,019.68. Rogers had received more contributions and in larger sums. Individual contributions to Rogers averaged $100.00 compared to $41.50 for Telles. Powerful and rich, Rogers and the kingmakers, Pooley charged, had taken government away from the people.[47]

Over at the *Times*, editor W. J. Hooten responded to Pooley's anti-Rogers campaign by his own attacks on Telles. "There followed one of the roughest and toughest campaigns in the history of El Paso," Hooten wrote later in his memoirs. "The candidates, Rogers and Telles, never said particularly unkind things about each other, but the *Times* and the *Herald-Post* fought each other tooth and toenail."[48] Hooten concentrated on three charges: (1) Telles's lack of experience, (2) Telles's campaign tactics, and (3) Telles's character. Like Rogers, Hooten did not directly refer to Telles's ethnicity but instead used code words—experience, character, and so forth—that cast doubts on Telles's abilities and indirectly on those of all Mexican Americans. In the first case, Hooten contrasted Rogers's business career and his two years as mayor with Telles's lack of business experience and what Hooten consid-

ered his minor administrative duties as county clerk. Hooten warned voters
that they would be taking chances with their tax dollars if they elected Telles.
Telles was a "very nice young man," Hooten patronizingly concluded, but
he had no business running for mayor. Hooten also portrayed Telles as a
scheming politician who would do anything to become mayor. Telles, of
course, was only Pooley's puppet. Devoid of a concrete program, Telles relied on appeals to ethnic loyalty and on constructing a political machine.
Never openly raising the Mexican issue, Hooten instead suggested that Mexican Americans in south El Paso might foolishly disregard what Rogers had
done for them and vote emotionally and "blindly, as a bloc" for Telles.
Hooten indirectly warned the Telles machine and alerted the public to Telles's
"tactics" by publicizing the stiff penalties for illegal use of poll taxes. No
doubt with Telles's Mexican-American supporters in mind, the *Times* warned
that any assistance at the polls had to be conducted only in English. Anyone
using a language other than English could be fined up to $500 and receive a
jail term of one year. Buying votes or lending money for poll taxes was illegal and carried a fine up to $500. Inexperienced and opportunistic, Telles
in Hooten's eyes further lacked character. He attacked Telles for being weak
and for attracting those who did not believe in strict law enforcement as well
as unruly elements. Having exhausted his charges against Telles, Hooten on
election eve resorted to redbaiting the People's Ticket:

> Does the constant hammering on "people" recall any haunting memories of
> other parts of the world where there are "People's Governments" and
> "People's Courts?" When you have nothing to sell the voters you can al-
> ways set yourself up as the champion of the "people." [49]

Hooten's attacks on Telles, while in keeping with El Paso's tradition of
rough political battles, could not help hinting at what in fact was the unspoken issue in the campaign: Could and should a Mexican American be
elected as mayor? No one had overtly made Telles's ethnic background a
campaign issue, as had occurred in the 1948 county clerk race. However, no
one could avoid the implications of Telles's candidacy. Mexican Americans
saw in Telles a crusade for political representation. Many Anglos, on the
other hand, worried that Telles, if elected, would favor Mexican Americans
over Anglos and would corrupt local government. Rumors floated during the
early campaign, for example, that Telles would make wholesale personnel
changes in the police department and replace Anglos with Chicanos. Albert
Armendáriz recalls leaflets passed out in northeast El Paso, not necessarily
by the Rogers campaign, suggesting that Telles as mayor would "fill the
courthouse with Mexicans." One Anglo leader, according to Ted Bender,
stated that Telles would "Mexicanize" El Paso politics: "That all the evils

that Mexican politics is heir to would be vested upon El Paso." To Bender the anti-Mexican feeling in the election was clear but hard to pin down: "You could feel it, but you couldn't grab it. It's like a ghost." [50]

Richard Telles and Barrio Politics

If Raymond Telles conducted his public campaign in organized political forums and in the newspapers and television, he approved of his unofficial campaign being carried out in the streets, alleys, cantinas, community centers, and homes of the barrio. There, Richard Telles put his organizing talents to work and proved indispensable to his brother's campaign. "Richard was *the man.*" Ted Bender recalls. And Lelo Jacques of LULAC notes that Richard was the "Mexican Lyndon Johnson—master politician." [51] Intensely loyal to Raymond and harboring his own political ambitions, Richard understood that ethnicity was the name of the game in the election. Raymond might officially present himself as a public servant above ethnicity, but Richard mobilized the Mexican-American hunger for the election of one of their own as mayor. Mexican Americans were tired of being treated as second-class citizens and hoped that through the electoral process they could achieve political respectability and eliminate barriers to equal opportunities. "We started feeling the pressure of social justice," Richard explains. "We wanted a little cut of the pie." [52]

Richard concentrated solely on the Mexican-American neighborhoods in south and southeast El Paso in establishing his own campaign organization separate from official Telles headquarters in downtown El Paso. "We stayed away from it completely," he recalls. "We knew what we had to do, and we did it from our office in South El Paso." He ran the Mexican-American campaign out of his own business quarters at 8th and St. Vrain, in the same house his father had built for the family. Here, veterano Navarrete explains, the nuts and bolts of the campaign took place. "He knew precincts," Ralph Seitsinger says of Richard, "he knew who was there, he knew who were the workers." Only a massive Mexican-American turnout would elect his brother, and Richard believed only he could organize the vote. Marantz might be the official campaign manager, but Ritchie Telles was the unofficial one and as he puts it: "When it came down to strategy and all that very few people knew how to handle South and East El Paso." [53] He might have added that he was one of the few.

As in the 1948 campaign, Richard Telles's first task consisted in registering Mexican Americans to vote. With the veteranos of the Segura–McDonald VFW club along with additional veterans from the southside Marcos Armijo VFW unit, Telles again assembled a sophisticated political organization in the best tradition of American ethnic politics. He and the veteranos overcame the discriminating poll tax by appealing everywhere for money. "The money was the number one thing," Richard emphasizes. "We hocked our souls." To legitimize these and other campaign operations, Richard organized out of his office the Southside Democratic Club, composed primarily of veteranos who could not officially engage in politics as a VFW group. A diversity of sources contributed funds. Kiko Hernández recalls that many Mexican-American merchants, like himself, gave out of their own pockets. Even the mayor of Juárez, René Mascarenas, who had attended Cathedral High School in El Paso with Raymond, provided financial assistance. With these funds, Richard and over 700 Mexican-American members of the two VFW clubs along with other volunteers fanned throughout the barrios to register voters and assist those who could not afford the poll tax. As in 1948 the Telles forces made use of Richard's business contacts in the cantinas and used these establishments as organizing centers. "It was the easiest way to organize," Richard says of the cantina strategy. At the cantinas, Mexican Americans could purchase their poll taxes, or if they did not have the $1.75 Telles supporters gave it to them. In addition, Richard selected district coordinators and precinct captains who supervised door-to-door contacts encouraging registration. The veteranos likewise held dances where Mexican Americans purchased admission by buying a poll tax. The Women's Auxiliaries of the VFW aided these efforts as well as by selling poll taxes at community halls.[54]

To publicize the campaign, Richard took advantage of border culture by purchasing time on Juárez radio stations across the border that provided cheaper rates than in El Paso. The Spanish-language political advertisements easily reached across the narrow Rio Grande and into Mexican-American homes. These ads, along with the campaign in general, also made Raymond Telles something of a political hero in Juárez. Moreover, in his headquarters Richard stored posters and bumper stickers which volunteers distributed widely two weeks before the election. Richard, along with coordinator David Villa, also personally visited local community organizations such as PTAs in south-side schools, where he called on Mexican-American parents to vote for his brother and to "stand up and be counted." Besides organized efforts, word-of-mouth spread news of the Telles campaign. Druggist Hernández remembers talking to his customers about the election as well as displaying Telles posters in his windows.[55]

Registering voters and publicizing the campaign, Richard likewise educated Mexican Americans on the process of voting. Voter education became doubly important because city officials for the first time employed voting machines in the city election. Richard believed that the use of the machines in an election with a Mexican-American candidate was no coincidence. He saw it as an attempt to intimidate potential Mexican-American voters. To overcome these obstacles, Richard ingeniously devised mock voting machines out of empty refrigerator boxes. He placed these samples at every precinct before and during election day to demonstrate to the people how to operate the machines. The mock-ups resembled a regular machine and volunteers instructed voters how to pull the correct lever alongside each of the People's Ticket candidates. "Don't be scared," Ray Marantz recalls instructors telling voters, "go ahead and vote. You have the privilege and the right to vote." In addition, Ted Bender remembers that some Mexican Americans received a string with knots like a rosary. Telles supporters instructed voters to take this string into the regular voting machine, hang the string alongside the names of candidates, and pull the lever where the knots corresponded to one of the People's Ticket candidates. Other voters memorized a nonexistent telephone number provided by the Telles people each of whose figures matched the correct placement on the ballot of each candidate of the People's Ticket. Although these tactics undoubtedly disturbed the Rogers campaign, it put up no serious challenge to them. "I don't see how they let us," Kiko Hernández still wonders about the mock-machine outside Jefferson High School, "but we did it." [56]

On election day, Richard finely orchestrated his organization to deliver the vote. From his command headquarters in his office, he observed on a big board the total number of registered voters in each Mexican-American precinct and the actual number voting as the day progressed. Telles broke down a list of all registered voters and delegated his volunteers to be responsible not only for particular areas but specific individuals. Every registered Mexican American received individual attention from a volunteer. "We had no computer or anything," Telles recalls. "We'd take those lists, take the names down, break this into streets, break them into numbers, and go from there. It was a hell of a job!" In a separate room at headquarters, David Villa operated three telephones connecting him with district coordinators and precinct captains, who would request information on which precinct a particular voter was eligible to vote in. In the field, volunteers including veteranos and Lulacers contacted people in their homes to see if they had voted. Others drove voters to the polls. Mary Lou Armendáriz recalls taking her children along with her as she drove voters to the polls throughout the entire day. Each volunteer reported to a precinct captain who, along with district coordinators, reported regularly to central headquarters. Still others, including young Mexican women sent over to help by Juárez Mayor Mascarenas, passed out sample ballots at each precinct. "We made sure that every man who had a poll tax went out to vote," Richard explains. "We physically picked the people up from their homes and brought them to vote." As he supervised the election turnout both from his office and in the streets, Richard grew confident that his brother had won.[57]

With the help of the veteranos, the Lulacers, and countless others plus the excitement of his brother's candidacy, Richard Telles masterminded the most impressive Mexican-American vote in El Paso's history. Whether Raymond won or lost, Richard had displayed the political strength of Mexican Americans when organized. "I don't think that there has ever been," lawyer Armendáriz stresses, "as high a participation in any political campaign of a Mexican-American community as we experienced on this day when we elected Raymond Telles."[58]

Election Day

With the flurry of activity on election day, the campaign came to an end. Only the results awaited. Campaign manager Marantz believed that Telles and Rogers were even although no scientific polls existed. In its afternoon edition, the *Herald-Post* headlined a Telles lead determined from polling voters in certain precincts. The paper estimated that the rest of the People's Ticket held substantial margins over their opponents. El Pasoans voted in record numbers. The *Herald-Post* predicted a final vote of at least 30,000, almost double that in the 1955 city election. The polls closed at 7 P.M. and Telles, exhausted from the campaign, waited for the returns at home. He believed he had failed to get the vote out and had lost. Early returns from pro-Rogers precincts only darkened his mood. Telles reconciled himself to possible defeat. However, precinct returns from the south side soon lifted Telles's hopes. "Then I decided well, gee whiz maybe I better go down to the Court House and see what's going on." At the court house, both Telles and Rogers supporters clustered around to hear the returns from the last precinct boxes. "I knew how far behind we were, of course," Telles recalls, " 'cause they were being counted-tabulated all the time and I knew that we had certain precincts of ours which would come in pretty heavy for us, you know, and it started coming in and sure enough before too long after that we pulled up side by side and then we starting pulling away." By 10 P.M. officials finished the count and announced the results. With a record city election vote of 34,883, Telles upset Rogers by 2,754 votes: 18,688 to 15,934 (53.97 percent of the vote for Telles). Moreover, the entire People's Ticket won with even larger margins. Telles supporters celebrated well into the next day. Veterano Navarrete remembers that he and other elated volunteers paraded around the court house and staged a brief victory march into south El Paso.[59]

Telles won because his strategy worked. His sterling military and political record, his dignified personal appearance, and his avoidance of an ethnic public campaign disarmed all but the most racist Anglo voters. The opposition could not isolate him as a threat to the city's interests or portray him as a radical Mexican American. Consequently, Telles gained a certain percentage of Anglo voters while conceding to Rogers only a minute fraction of Mexican-American ones. With Pooley's help, Telles instead placed Rogers on the defensive by exploiting issues such as the Lower Valley annexation. At the same time, Telles remained calm when his opponents counterattacked. Moreover, through the work of Richard Telles, the veteranos, and the Lulacers, Telles effectively mobilized Mexican-American voters. "That was a revolution, not an election," one Mexican American exclaimed.[60]

To win, Telles needed landslide margins in south and southeast El Paso. He had to win or do very well in precincts just north of the tracks that were mixed but becoming predominantly Mexican American. He also had to win with solid margins in the Lower Valley. Finally, Telles had to pick up enough Anglo voters throughout the city to deprive Rogers of comparable victories in Anglo precincts. The Telles campaign accomplished all these goals. In south and southeast El Paso, Telles achieved his landslide: 5,211 to Rogers's 602. Telles won almost 90 percent of the vote (89.6) in these precincts, exactly the percentage he had figured would be needed to win office. Telles supporters turned out 82.5 percent of registered voters in these 10 precincts. In the Lower Valley, Telles won all 9 precincts with a vote of 5,498 to Rogers's 2,768. Telles here received 66.5 percent of the vote. The Lower Valley, according to Ralph Seitsinger, proved to be the swing vote. Together, south and southeast El Paso along with the Lower Valley provided Telles with 10,709 votes out of his total of 18,688, or 57 percent of his total. Telles combined these votes with good success in northern precincts containing growing numbers of Mexican Americans. In the Upper Valley he won precinct 4, Smeltertown, where the Mexican-American local of the Mine, Mill and Smelter Workers delivered 288 voters for Telles to Rogers's 29. In west El Paso, Telles won precincts 7 and 8 in the Sunset Heights district. In the lower portions of northeast El Paso he took 3 precincts and in northwest El Paso (including the central downtown district with significant numbers of Mexican Americans) Telles won 6 out of 8 precincts with a vote of 1,517 to Rogers's 1,410, or 51.8 percent of the vote. In all, Telles won 31 out of 53 precincts. Additionally, he cut into Anglo precincts and denied Rogers landslide victories of his own by winning 30.3 percent of the vote in those northern precincts won by Rogers (4,609 votes to Rogers's 10,595). Albert Armendáriz believes this Anglo percentage for Telles represented liberal Democrats.[61]

Rogers's loss did not lie in his inability to turn out Anglo voters. He amassed as high a turnout percentage of Anglo voters as did Telles among Mexican Americans. In Rogers's strongholds of northeast El Paso and the exclusive Kern Place district he won 16 out of 19 precincts and drew out 80.7

percent of the voters. In the end, however, Rogers failed to match the large Mexican-American vote in both the south side and in those mixed northern precincts along with Telles's sweep of the Lower Valley. The *Times* conceded that these areas gave Telles a runaway lead that Rogers could not overcome. Telles's victory, of course, was sweetened by the election of his entire ticket. Underscoring Telles's more controversial candidacy, all his aldermen by contrast won by substantial margins. Craigo won by 5,777 votes; Bender by 5,268; Seitsinger by 7,989; and White by 7,625 votes.[62]

Telles, relieved and grateful, acknowledged his victory in the Democratic primary and looked forward to being officially elected in the normally uncontested general election. An equally ecstatic Pooley congratulated the victors and in true Rooseveltian tradition proclaimed a "New Deal" at City Hall. On the other side, Rogers expressed pleasure at the record turnout of voters, thanked the people for supporting him during his tenure as mayor, and extended his best wishes to the new administration. Not all El Pasoans, however, proved as gracious as Rogers in defeat. Hooten and the *Times,* for example, congratulated Telles but planted doubts about his votes. Hooten complained that too much flexibility had been allowed in the sale of poll taxes. He specifically objected to the number of private individuals who sold poll taxes. He publicized three "glaring situations" that had been brought to his attention concerning poll tax irregularities. One man reported that he possessed two poll tax receipts. He had bought one and had been given another by a "friend." In a second case, a man living across the border in Juárez claimed to have obtained a poll tax by giving an El Paso address. Finally, Hooten alleged that a south El Paso woman had phoned him and reported being allowed to vote at Aoy School even though her name was not on the voting list because she had a poll tax receipt. "I'm not saying that there was any intentional violation of the law," Hooten proposed. "Those things were either through ignorance of the law or occurred during the excitement. But I do say that the system ought to be changed."[63] Nevertheless, Hooten's charges of irregularities—despite no formal complaints or indictments during or after the campaign—indicated a reluctance to accept the Telles victory and indirectly encouraged a movement to deny him the mayor's office in the general election scheduled for April 9.

The General Election

Victory in the Democratic Party was tantamount to election in El Paso as well as elsewhere in Texas. Few registered Republicans functioned at the local level. Consequently, Telles believed that the general election as in past years would simply be pro forma and that he and his ticket would be unopposed. But Telles was no ordinary candidate. He was a Mexican American. Rumors of a write-in campaign increased as the general election approached. Most prominently mentioned for a write-in challenge was, of course, Mayor Rogers. However, three days before the election, Rogers squelched rumors by stating that though asked to consent to a write-in he disassociated himself from such efforts. Nevertheless, with just two days before the election, M. R. Hollenshead, an unsuccessful independent candidate for alderman in the primary, agreed to a write-in campaign on his behalf. A former assistant superintendent of El Paso schools, Hollenshead owned a sash and door company plus an insurance agency. The *Times* noted that thirty young business and professional men, who declined to publicly identify themselves citing fears of economic reprisals, along with several women's organizations initiated the write-in. They claimed that they had several hundred volunteers and that a large-scale telephone and mail drive would be conducted. Only Telles, and not his aldermen, would be challenged. They charged that Telles would establish machine politics in El Paso and hinted that Telles as a Mexican American would not represent all El Pasoans.[64] Taking the Hollenshead write-in seriously, Telles expressed displeasure at the open effort to deprive him of his primary victory. No other mayoral candidate had ever been challenged outside the primary. "I wasn't exactly happy about it," he recalls. "I couldn't help but believe . . . they were doing it because they didn't want me in there."[65] The Telles forces responded by going on the attack and by mobilizing their own supporters. Pooley as usual led the verbal assault by labeling Hollenshead's supporters as nothing but a cowardly "yellow gang" that lacked the courage to publicly endorse Hollenshead. The *Herald-Post* editor addressed the unspoken issue of the campaign. He accused the Hollenshead write-in of being racist and anti-Mexican. "They are waging an un-American campaign of bigotry and prejudice. They are hurting and dividing its people." Pooley called on El Pasoans to reject this type of politics: "Vote American! Vote Telles!" *El Continental* seconded Pooley's charge of racism by noting that only Telles faced a write-in challenge and not his Anglo aldermanic candidates. "The only conclusion that can be reached," it editorialized, "is that this campaign is discrminatory, anti-Latin, and—why not say it—anti-Catholic." Mexican-American community leader Cleofas Calleros added in a letter to the *Herald-Post* that Hollenshead as a past school administrator had been associated with officials who had discriminated against Mexicans and who were now supporting the write-in.[66]

Besides criticizing the write-in, the Telles camp once again mobilized. "We reorganized the whole campaign stronger than before," Richard Telles remembers the bitterness he felt toward the effort to deny his brother the election. "We were now fighting mad." Rank and file Mexican Americans likewise responded and once again rallied to Telles's cause. They would not be denied their victory. Telles received almost unanimous support in the Mexican-American precincts and duplicated his primary success, even carrying 7 precincts won by Rogers. A record 26,345 voters went to the polls in this unprecedented contested general election. In the 1955 general election only 1,118 votes had been cast. More El Pasoans voted in two hours in 1957 than had voted in the entire 1955 election. Telles received 17,080 votes to Hollenshead's 8,961 and carried 38 of 53 precincts. South and southeast El Paso almost matched their total primary votes for Telles. He received 5,178 votes to Hollenshead's 205, close to 400 votes fewer than Rogers. Telles increased his percentage of the vote in these precincts by obtaining 96.19 percent of the total cast. In precinct 12, Bowie High School, Telles completely shut out Hollenshead 373 to 0. In the Lower Valley, considered vulnerable by the write-in, Telles won by an even larger percentage than in the primary. He gathered 4,528 voters to Hollenshead's 1,410, or 76.25 percent of the total. Of the 7 new precincts Telles won, 2 were in west El Paso, 4 in northeast El Paso, and 1 in northwest El Paso. Telles won in these precincts by apparently picking up more Anglo voters. In the 15 precincts that went for Hollenshead, Telles received 36.44 percent of the total vote, up over 6 percentage points from the primary. In all, Telles won a substantial 65.58 percent of the total vote cast, a significant increase from the 53.97 percent in the primary. "It can be said," *El Continental* concluded, "that Telles' triumph this time was more solid than in the primary and, what is more, it was not totally determined by voters from the Mexican barrios, but from both sections of the city." [67]

On April 11, 1957, Raymond L. Telles officially became the first Mexican-American mayor of El Paso. *El Continental* appreciated the historic moment and headlined: Telles, Alcalde Paisano—Telles "Our" Mayor. [68]

Conclusion

Reelected in 1959, Raymond Telles served four years as mayor of El Paso. During this period, he symbolized the Mexican-American search for political status and recognition. This search crossed class boundaries among Mexican Americans but clearly was pronounced among more upwardly mobile and aspiring Mexican Americans. Those who led the Telles victory saw in it an opportunity to assert their American citizenship and the hope to be accepted into the mainstream. By possessing moderate goals, Mexican-American electoral politics contained the seeds of its own limitations and, indeed, ultimate frustration for a succeeding generation. Mexican Americans who believed in the politics of status did not interpret electoral politics as one way of fundamentally transforming El Paso's historic class-racial system, which relegated most Mexicans to exploitative working-class status. Instead, Mexican-American leaders idealistically believed that electoral politics, without more intense community struggles, could open the doors to equal opportunities for Mexican Americans and translate political equality into economic and social equality. Telles's election widened the culture or arena of opposition that Mexican Americans in El Paso had created over the years to advance their struggle for justice and equal opportunities, but it did not directly jeopardize the city's class-racial system and inaugurate economic democracy for Mexican Americans.

Pursuing the politics of status rather than what might be termed the politics of reconstruction, that is, a direct challenge to the city's class-racial system, the Telles administration is perhaps better known for the political recognition and rising expectations it provided Mexican Americans than for substantive socioeconomic changes. By definition, the search for status involved acceptability by Anglos and hence discouraged more challenging ethnic politics. Telles stressed that he was mayor of all El Pasoans and shied away from appearing to favor Mexican Americans. Nonetheless, Mexican Americans, after yearning to elect one of their own as mayor and only beginning to explore electoral ethnic politics, expressed pride in Telles's administration and exerted no extraordinary pressures on the new mayor. "[W]hen he went into the southside I found him being treated very warmly, with a great deal of respect, with a great deal of admiration," *Herald-Post* reporter Ken Flynn comments on Telles's relationship with Mexican Americans. "I think that Raymond achieved something that everyone in the Mexican-American community was proud of, and I think that most of the people that I talked to . . . kind of treated him as a hero." [69] Telles pursued a moderately successful reform program that for the time satisfied most Mexican Americans. Above all, Mexican Americans identified with Telles. His success was their success. Telles made Mexican Americans believe in themselves and in their own capacities and those of their children to make it in America. Richard Telles assessed his brother's election and administration: "The people knew that we could do it. We were part of the establishment." [70]

If Telles's personal success as mayor can be explained at one level by the continued support he received from Mexican Americans, it can also be understood by the reaction of El Paso's Anglo elite. The kingmakers quickly perceived Telles's moderate objectives and administrative capabilities and hence, rather than remaining opposed to him, shifted to cooperating with the new administration. They came to understand that Telles posed no threat to their interests and that he needed their support to run the city. Eisinger in his study of the election of black mayors in Detroit and Atlanta in the early 1970s observes that the politically displaced white elites faced five possible responses to black political rule: cooperation, maintenance, subversion, contestation, and withdrawal. In both cities white elites, as in El Paso, favored cooperation. Eisinger identified several reasons for this cooperative response, including the stakes that white elites had in these cities, the dependence of the new political elites on cooperation from the old elites, and, most important, the limits within the United States on the use of politics for fundamental socioeconomic changes.[71] "Electoral victory does not in the American context," Irwin Garfinkel stresses, "set the stage for radical transformations, but rather gradual changes." As in Detroit and Atlanta, El Paso's Anglo elite did not withdraw in discouragement from city affairs after Telles's victory. They knew that Telles's triumph meant only that Mexican Americans would have to be dealt with more seriously in running the city and in distributing municipal resources. This the kingmakers could accept and adapt to what Eisinger terms the "culture of accommodation." Indeed, this adjustment had already been evolving prior to 1957. In this arrangement, the kingmakers retained their dominant class position as bankers and big businessmen. As Eisinger further notes, no internal mechanism exists in American government that could threaten the material interests of the dominant class since the hegemonic political culture is geared to protecting their interests.[72]

Within this context, Telles proved to be a moderately reformist mayor. His reforms included doing away with convict labor and the use of chain gangs, extension of city services to the Lower Valley, a more socially responsible police force, the condemnation of certain slum tenements in south El Paso and the extension of urban renewal including low-cost housing in that area, street and sidewalk improvements in low-income neighborhoods, additional parks and recreation centers in different parts of the city, and airport modernization. Moreover, Telles's administration remained relatively open and responsive to the public. As part of his reform program, Telles in a quiet fashion successfully hired more Mexican Americans to city jobs. A few Mexican Americans had served as policemen, but Telles accelerated their appointments as officers. In the fire department almost no Mexican Americans could be found until the Telles years. In addition, increased numbers of Mexican Americans obtained clerical positions along with their traditional roles as city laborers. Telles further appointed more Mexican Americans to nonpaying city commissions. He insisted, however, that Mexican Americans not be given jobs simply because of their ethnicity.[73] They had to be qualified. Moreover, Telles also administered a financially solvent city government. A prudent individual by nature, Telles regularly balanced the municipal budget while providing more services to an expanding population, but without increasing taxes. Efficient and businesslike, the Telles administration was noted for its honesty. Finally, Telles worked hard to be a good mayor and his success in large part resulted from long hours of labor. "He works 12 hours practically everyday," one reporter observed. "He often works 14 or 16 hours. He usually is at his desk before 8 A.M., works all day, goes home to a quiet dinner with his family, then often returns to City Hall for a solitary night session. Most of the time, he is the last man to leave City Hall at night." [74]

The question of whether Telles might have done more as mayor, especially as the first Mexican-American one, is a debatable issue. Telles supporters insist that he probably was the best mayor El Paso had had for some time. Others, including some Mexican Americans today, believe that he was too cautious and unwilling to offend Anglos, especially businessmen, by moving for greater improvements in the barrios. "He could have done a lot more," one former supporter assessed the Telles years.[75] In the case of slum eradication, for example, Telles did not push for a city code that would have penalized absentee tenement owners for their lack of improvements. Even Pooley at the *Herald-Post*, during Telles's second term, accused the mayor of being too deliberate in handling increased juvenile delinquency and in dismissing incompetent officials. Telles might have gone further on specific Mexican-American problems if one assumes that he was prepared to chance racial-ethnic polarization in the city. However, Telles was neither a gambler nor a social crusader. Conservative in personal and social outlook, Telles in retrospect was a moderate reformer but one liberal for his own historical period. "His careful and cautious approach," a reporter noted, "has surprised those of his opponents who feared he might come into City Hall with a broom, making a clean sweep and appointing his friends to office." [76] The *Herald-Post* called Telles an "instinctive middle-of-the roader." As mayor, he did not interpret his role as an advocate for social causes. He believed, as did many of his Mexican-American contemporaries, that justice was possible through established institutions rather than through direct action in the streets. "As is often the case," D'Antonio and Form conclude in their study of "influentials" in El Paso, "minority groups may outdo Anglo-Americans in living up to ideal beliefs and sentiments of the society." [77] Indeed, Telles viewed the running of city government, as did the kingmakers, as a business operation. "He looks more like a serious-minded junior executive than like the traditional cartoon version of the fat, jovial, cigar-smoking politician," a reporter described Telles.[78]

Moreover, even if Telles had proved more "radical," certain constraints existed that both politically and structurally would have made it difficult—although perhaps not impossible—to achieve greater reforms. For one, the Anglo establishment closely monitored Telles and undoubtedly exerted indirect pressure to prevent him from instituting too populist measures that in their opinion might endanger their privileged status based on access and relationship to Mexican Americans as a source of cheap labor power. Telles, as mentioned, believed that as the first Mexican-American mayor his first duty to himself and the people who had elected him was to prove beyond any doubt that he could capably administer city hall. In this he succeeded, and perhaps his major accomplishment was in proving that a Mexican American rather than plunging the city into economic chaos, as his opponents had warned, instead would help create a relatively prosperous city. Joe Herrera, city clerk under the Telles administration, recalls the skeptical scrutiny under which Telles worked: "The general public they just didn't know what to expect of a Latin being the mayor of this community as to whether he was going to tear things up, or a lot of them would look to him as if we were going to become like a 'presidente municipal' [mayor] of Ciudad Juárez . . . 'la mordida' [bribes] and all that sort of stuff. . . . I even had people ask me: 'Is he going to take any bribes?' . . . People were just expecting him to go down the drain at the beginning." [79] Only in a quiet way did Telles believe he could advance reforms that would aid Mexican Americans. To do more, in his mind, would risk concerted opposition to his reelection bid and lead to possible defeat. Second, even had Telles decided to challenge the establishment, it is questionable how much he could have accomplished through the limited resources of city government to create anything resembling a social revolution. Not even more "progressive" black or Mexican-American mayors in recent years have been able to do this. As Eisinger explains: "City governments can do very little on their own of a systematic nature to create large numbers of jobs, redistribute income, or provide great amounts of good housing." [80]

What local governments can do, Eisinger suggests, is at least to address such problems in an incremental and piecemeal fashion. [81] Hence, incrementalism might best characterize the Telles approach to the relationship between city government and social reform. Moreover, Telles believed that Mexican Americans would advance not so much by what government could do for them, but by increased educational opportunities and by the introduction of new businesses and industries to El Paso that would create more and better jobs. Unfortunately, Telles, tied to administering a city dependent on cheap Mexican labor, failed to appreciate the contradictions between his belief in the remunerative powers of private enterprise and the drive by private enterprise, especially along the border, to secure the cheapest labor possible from the Mexican-American community.

If the Telles years did not produce extraordinary social reforms, his administration nevertheless was a political success story. From a Mexican-

American candidate engaged in one of El Paso's most heated and controversial elections, Telles in four years became the darling of El Paso politics. He accomplished this, on the one hand, by maintaining overwhelming Mexican-American support and, on the other, by astutely building ties to the Anglo establishment. In the 1959 city election no one dared to challenge him. His aldermen faced token opposition and won reelection by wide margins. His political influence as well as his acceptability by the establishment was acknowledged in February 1959, when the El Paso Ministerial Association, some of whose members had questioned Telles's Catholicism two years earlier, endorsed his performance as mayor. Churchmen did not openly admit it, but they essentially praised Telles for not dividing the city along ethnic lines.[82]

In 1961 Telles, after campaigning for John Kennedy, accepted the new president's offer to become ambassador to Costa Rica. Although many of his closest supporters opposed the move, hoping that Telles would instead soon run for Congress, Telles believed that it was important for him to become the first Mexican-American ambassador from the United States. The politics of status had won again. Telles served in Costa Rica until 1967. He then accepted an appointment to the newly formed U.S.-Mexican Border Commission. In 1969 he was removed by President Nixon. He returned to El Paso and challenged incumbent Democratic Congressman Richard White from the Sixteenth Congressional District. Hoping to resurrect the old Telles magic, the former mayor went down to a major defeat. No longer deprived of political status, as more Mexican Americans achieved electoral success, Mexican Americans, including a new and more militant Chicano Generation, did not flock to the poorly financed Telles campaign. Telles thereafter left El Paso and served on the bipartisan Equal Opportunity Commission in Washington and later as a private consultant on Latin American economic affairs until his return to El Paso in 1982 as vice president of a financial concern. Despite Telles's own later political failure, his election as mayor of El Paso in 1957 had assured his place in Mexican-American political history. That election was the pinnacle of the electoral struggles waged by the Mexican-American Generation and opened up new electoral opportunities for the succeeding generation.

PART TWO

Labor and the Left

CHAPTER SIX

The Popular Front: Josefina Fierro de Bright and the Spanish-Speaking Congress

This night will eventually take its place alongside all the other holidays of Mexican people in the celebration of liberty. It is the occasion of the founding of the First National Congress of Spanish Speaking people. For the first time Mexican and Spanish American people have gathered together for unified action against the abuses of discrimination and poverty which have embittered and paralyzed them for so many years.

—JOSEFINA FIERRO DE BRIGHT, April 30, 1939

Middle-class reformers shaped the Mexican-American Generation, but they did not monopolize it. Mexican Americans also gravitated toward leftist politics. They were the inheritors of a radical and militant tendency whose roots can be traced to post-Mexican War social bandits in the Southwest, the Mexican Revolution of 1910, the followers of the anarchosyndicalist Ricardo Flores Magón, and the participation of Mexican immigrant workers in labor struggles, particularly in the mines and fields of the Southwest.[1] These Mexican-American leaders believed in the need to organize around the essentially working-class foundation of Mexican Americans. They were not antagonistic to middle-class leadership but recognized that a broader spectrum of the community had to be organized. Mexican-American working-class leaders disagreed with the middle-class notion, exhibited by LULAC, of separating Mexican Americans from Mexican nationals. Seeing both sectors as objectively part of the working class, these leaders called for ethnic unity transcending citizenship. Moreover, some Mexican Americans became disillusioned with the effects of the Great Depression during the 1930s and like many other Americans sought political alternatives for coping with increased unemployment and poverty. Mexican Americans had to deal with the added problem of the deportation and forced repatriation of thousands of Mexican workers from the United States.[2] Consequently, some Mexican Americans, like other oppressed minorities such as Afro Americans, turned toward a revitalized and militant Communist party. In both the fields and factories of the Southwest, the Communists recruited adherents and admirers because of their willingness to stand up for the rights of Mexican workers. What one historian has said of the relationship during the 1930s between Afro Americans and the Communist party appears to be likewise applicable to Mexican Americans: "Negroes were sometimes attracted to the Party or to the organizations which it controlled, not because they formed a radical ideology or a revolutionary movement; they joined because Communists were frequently the only ones who were attempting to do something immediately about jobs, relief, general welfare." [3]

Yet leftist politics for Mexican Americans during the 1930s and beyond translated into militancy for reform rather than for revolution. The Communist party in both its sectarian period during the early years of the decade and in the later Popular Front era concentrated on reform issues. Working with both Mexican Americans and Mexican nationals, few of whom opted for revolutionary solutions in communities still partly characterized by unstable immigration and migratory conditions, the Mexican-American Left shared with middle-class liberals a reformist character within the boundaries of New Deal welfare capitalism. Reflecting and shaping such sentiments and combining militancy with pragmatism, El Congreso del Pueblo de Habla Española (the Spanish-Speaking Congress), founded in 1938 and led by Josefina Fierro de Bright, represented one of the major efforts by the left-wing of the Mexican-American Generation to form a working-class movement in coalition with progressive liberals and aimed at securing basic rights for all Mexicans and Spanish-speaking people in the United States. [4]

Origins and Founding of El Congreso

The exact details of the origins of El Congreso are obscure, but the initial and main organizer was Luisa Moreno. Born in Guatemala, Moreno emigrated first to Mexico and then to the United States in 1928. Moreno was educated in the United States and graduated from the College of the Holy Names in Oakland. In a 1976 interview with historian Albert Camarillo, Moreno noted that she had worked as a seamstress in a New York city garment factory near Spanish Harlem. Sweatshop conditions plus association with leftist Latino workers led to her radicalization. Moreno first worked as an organizer for the Needles Trades Workers Industrial Union in the early 1930s and then with the AF of L organizing Florida cigar makers. Disenchanted with the conservatism of the AF of L, Moreno joined the new CIO in 1937. She soon found herself working with striking Mexican pecan shellers in San Antonio as an organizer for the militant United Cannery, Agricultural, Packing, and Allied Workers (UCAPAWA). Moreno successfully recruited many Mexican Americans and Mexican nationals into the union movement. Living and working with Spanish-speaking people, Moreno recognized a need for a mass organization of the Spanish-speaking in the United States.[5] More difficult to ascertain in the founding of El Congreso is the specific role of the Communist party (CP). A few years earlier the CP had played the leading role in organizing the National Negro Congress, a Popular Front civil rights group similar to El Congreso. It is possible that Moreno, as a member of the leftist-led UCAPAWA, may have been either a member or close sympathizer of the Communist party. Certainly El Congreso exhibited ideological and political tendencies similar to those of the CP, especially during the Popular Front period characterized by efforts at coalition politics, an emphasis on a reform agenda, and support for the New Deal. Dorothy Healey, a former CP member, recalls that El Congreso was probably the idea of the party. "With the active support of the Party," a CP journal stated in 1949, "a Spanish-speaking Congress of a broad nature was formed."[6]

In 1938 Moreno, after saving $500, took a year's leave of absence from UCAPAWA and traveled throughout the Southwest as well as other parts of the country organizing committees for a National Congress of Spanish-Speaking Peoples (Comités en Pro del Congreso).[7] She also secured support from liberal and progressive Anglo groups and individuals. Looking toward a coalition of such forces, a draft program of El Congreso read in part: "For an alliance between the Spanish speaking people and the progressive, all democratic forces among the Anglo-American and minority groups in the United States on behalf of the preservation and extension of American democratic institutions."[8] Various Mexican-American and mexicano organizations along with CIO unions and liberal-left political associations responded to Moreno's appeal and agreed to sponsor such a National Congress.[9] Moreno's most successful work occurred among the thousands of people of Mexican descent in Los Angeles. There, with the assistance of Mexican-American activists including some earlier supporters of Ricardo Flores Magón, Moreno organized the first barrio conference held by El Congreso. "She was the one that taught us how [to organize]," recalls an early leader of El Congreso. "She [Moreno] was a very educated woman."[10]

On December 4, 1938, the Spanish-Speaking Peoples Congress of California held its first conference in Los Angeles. Founded as a state affiliate of El Congreso, the California body sought through its meeting to mobilize supporters for the First National Congress scheduled for March 1939 in Albuquerque. Eighty-eight delegates representing 73 Mexican-American and mexicano organizations with a total membership of 70,000 attended the Los Angeles convocation. El Congreso as both a state and national organization aimed to improve the economic, social, moral, and cultural conditions of

Spanish-speaking people in the United States in conformity with the U.S. Constitution. This included supporting federal housing projects for the poor, better sanitary and medical care for the Spanish-speaking, elimination of racial discrimination, better education for children, adequate pay for Spanish-speaking workers to allow them to live humanly, support for the unionization of workers, jobs for the unemployed, and the unity of all groups and nationalities who supported the same objectives. Above all, El Congreso would defend any Spanish-speaking person victimized by racial oppression including the threat of deportation.[11]

Besides working in Los Angeles, Moreno organized pro-Congreso committees in other southwestern states. She obtained endorsements for the Albuquerque congress from other bodies, such as the Congreso de Unificación de las Cámaras de Trabajadores held in Dallas, the Convención de Organizaciones Mexicanas del Estado de Texas held in Port Arthur, and the UCAPAWA convention in San Francisco. Determined not to restrict El Congreso only to workers, Moreno acquired support from Anglo and Spanish-speaking legislators in New Mexico, Arizona, and California as well as from Mexican-American professionals. George I. Sánchez of the University of New Mexico, for example, agreed to become provisional president of the National Organizing Committee of the congress. In San Antonio an organizing committee for El Congreso announced a city-wide meeting to prepare a delegation for the Albuquerque meeting. It noted that one of the congresses' main objectives involved unifying Mexican Americans, citizens of Hispanic descent, and Mexican nationals as one Spanish-speaking group of more than two million people. In this effort, it predated the 1980s movement to structure a Hispanic ethnic movement. The San Antonio committee observed that the following general topics would be discussed at its public meeting: jobs, the need for the Spanish-speaking to have access to agricultural lands, housing and health, education, discrimination, and youth. Additional pro-Congreso committees functioned in New Mexico and Colorado.[12]

Having mobilized a variety of Mexican Americans, Hispanics, mexicanos, as well as liberal and progressive Anglo supporters, Moreno and the pro-Congreso committees looked toward the Albuquerque national convention scheduled for March 24–26, 1939. According to one Albuquerque newspaper, the convention would be held on the campus of the University of New Mexico, and delegates would arrive from Colorado, California, Texas, Arizona, Kansas, Illinois, and New Mexico. To put the finishing touches on the convention, Congreso organizers met at the University of New Mexico in mid-February. Arthur L. Campa of the University of New Mexico, as temporary national president, headed the planning committee. The *Albuquerque Journal* remarked on the broad spectrum of sponsors of the national convention. These included Maury Maverick, ex-congressman from San Antonio; Melvyn Douglas of the Screen Actors Guild; J. F. Zimmerman, president of the University of New Mexico; Oliver Wright, organizer for the New Mexico Federation of Labor; Carlos Castañeda of the University of Texas; Donald Henderson, national president of UCAPAWA; George Soule, member of the editorial staff of the *New Republic;* Paul S. Taylor of the University of California; and writer Waldo Frank.[13]

Hoping for a mass turnout of delegates in Albuquerque, the planning committee appealed to labor unions, fraternal and cultural groups, civic and political clubs, religious fraternities, and to Comisiónes Honoríficas of the Mexican consulates. The committee stressed the urgency of such a national convention to deal with the "consequences of increasing economic and cultural poverty." The congress would specifically address itself to the plight of the Spanish-speaking, but it would also address the problems affecting the entire nation. Additional individuals who sponsored the national convention represented a variety of organizations from both the Mexican-American and Anglo communities. These included LULAC, representatives of the New Mexico state legislature, the Liga Obrera of New Mexico, the American League for Peace and Democracy, the Workers Alliance of America, the Women's International League for Peace and Freedom, the Mexican Methodist Church, Fraternal Mexican Union, Amalgamated Clothing Workers of America, the Pecan Workers Union of San Antonio, the International Union of Mine, Mill and Smelter Workers, Federation of Spanish Voters of Los Angeles, and the Mexican American Democratic Progressive Club of Los Angeles. Moreover, several artists and writers, especially from Hollywood, joined in the appeal for the Albuquerque convention. Among these were Upton Sinclair, Herbert Biberman of the Screen Directors Guild, and John Bright of the League of American Writers.[14]

The Albuquerque convention, however, never took place. The reasons are not clear, but it appears that local complaints in Albuquerque about the University of New Mexico hosting a conference of "reds" influenced organizers to cancel the meeting. Bert Corona, a member of the congress from Los Angeles, recalls much red baiting surrounding the Albuquerque convention. As an apparent result of the criticisms, the University of New Mexico pressured both Professors Sánchez and Campa to resign from El Congreso.[15] Unable to meet in Albuquerque, Congreso leaders shifted the convention to Los Angeles and rescheduled it for April. *La Opinión* of Los Angeles acknowledged the transfer and proudly declared that Los Angeles with its large Mexican population was the natural site for the congress. California would stand as a symbol of hope for all the Spanish-speaking.[16] What *La Opinión* failed to mention, and it is a critical distinction in Mexican-American politi-

cal development, is that Los Angeles with its longer history of political pluralism including radicalism could better sustain the presence of what would
prove to be a left-of-center Mexican-American organization. Radicalism, especially a Mexican-American version, was not as easily tolerated in the more
conservative and provincial cultures of the rest of the Southwest.

Hosted by the California Congreso led by Eduardo Quevedo, its president, and Josefina Fierro de Bright, its secretary, the national convention in
Los Angeles would now take place April 28–30. Luisa Moreno arrived from
Texas to assist. Early newspaper accounts noted that the Congreso hoped to
have Eleanor Roosevelt as well as Governor Culbert Olson of California in
attendance. A variety of sessions would be open to the public on topics such
as unemployment, youth, housing, health, "and without forgetting issues
pertinent to women." Two days before the congress opened, *La Opinión* reported that delegations would arrive from Texas, Colorado, New Mexico,
and Arizona. According to Fierro de Bright, the founding convention of the
Spanish-Speaking Congress was also aided by Adolfo de la Huerta, the
Mexican consul-general in Los Angeles. A former president of Mexico, de la
Huerta had been appointed to Los Angeles by President Lázaro Cárdenas, the
most progressive of Mexican heads of state following the Revolution of 1910.
While de la Huerta could not officially intervene in American domestic politics, he possessed deep concerns about conditions affecting both Mexican nationals and Mexican Americans in the United States. He welcomed and unofficially supported the congress by providing information and advice. In
addition, the congress stressed its support for the labor movement in Mexico by inviting Lombardo Toledano of the Confederación de Trabajadores
Mexicanos (CTM). Prohibited from entering the United States, the militant
Toledano instead sent a representative. "The basic objectives pursued by the
Spanish-Speaking Congress," one Congreso member told *La Opinión,* "involve the unification between American citizens of Mexican descent and
Mexican nationals as well as the friendship between the peoples of the United
States and Mexico." [17]

The National Spanish-Speaking Congress formally opened on the eve of
April 29 at the New Mexico and Arizona Social Club at 230-½ South Spring
Street in downtown Los Angeles. Congreso organizers estimated 1,500 in attendance at the opening ceremonies.[18] "A great people's movement," writer
John Bright and husband of Josefina Fierro observed. "That was plain the
initial moment on the first day. The delegates in their physical appearances
and manner, eloquently revealed their representative character. Migratory
workers, teachers, organizers, social workers, housewives, youth leaders." [19]
The meeting hall was filled to capacity. The speakers' platform was decked
with flowers and the walls were decorated with banners and flags of the

United States and Mexico plus slogans of El Congreso. Some of the slogans read: "In the Youth lies the Future," "We Ask for Justice and Equality for La Raza Latina," "Citizens and Non-Citizens Unite Together;" "In Defense of Our Homes We Struggle Against Deportations," and "We Unite for Progress." Official and fraternal delegates came from Texas, New Mexico, Arizona, Colorado, and California. Bert Corona recalls that scattered delegates or guests also arrived from the Midwest and Florida. "Represented by delegates from every conceivable Mexican and Spanish organization," the *People's Daily World,* the arm of the Communist party, reported, "the Congress claims to be the most representative body ever formed among its people." A total of 137 delegates representing mostly southwestern states but including Montana and New York registered from 105 organizations (Mexican American and CIO unions) with over a million members.[20]

In its first full day of work, the congress divided into several panels to discuss major issues facing the Spanish-speaking in the United States. "The convention hall was hot and close," John Bright described the scene. "Yet the several hundred delegates didn't mind, for the issues before them were hot too, and close to their hearts and the bellies of their children."[21] Panelists reflected the congress's efforts to involve a coalition of liberal and left-progressive forces, both working class and middle class. The session on labor, for example, offered Reid Robinson, president of the Mine, Mill and Smelter Workers, plus Donald Henderson, president of UCAPAWA. McWilliams, Juan Fernández of New Mexico, and Oscar Fuss of the Los Angeles Workers' Alliance led the panel on relief and immigration. Floyd Covington of the Urban League and Ramón Welch of the congress chaired a meeting on education and culture. Screenwriter John Bright and Robert Tasker headed a discussion of U.S.-Mexican relations. Other panels concerned civil rights, health and housing, and youth.[22] Despite the varied topics, Bright recorded that all the delegates "were united solidly over discrimination, that curse of an unfulfilled democracy which damns the beet-picker of Colorado, the New Mexico school teacher, the Texas pecan-sheller and the Los Angeles railway worker alike."[23]

On the last day of the convention, each of the panels presented resolutions to the general assembly. Discussion followed predominantly in Spanish. "The resolutions were people's resolutions, dredged out of the pain of everyday existence," one participant later wrote. The congress approved various recommendations for combating discrimination. It suggested the formation of academic departments in colleges and universities to study the history, culture, and society of the Spanish-speaking throughout the Americas. In addition, public schools needed to exercise greater control over textbooks to prevent depicting the Spanish-speaking as inferior people. Schools could

likewise encourage the teaching of Latin American history at a level comparable to European history. The public schools, for example, could organize
"culture schools" to educate the general public about the Spanish-speaking
population. The congress pledged to oppose all pending legislation that "will
tend to do harm to any national minority group or race." The assembled delegates further noted the second-class positions of the Spanish-speaking in
jobs, wages, relief, and cultural opportunities. They called on the U.S. Congress to specifically investigate these discriminatory conditions and propose
federal legislation to correct them. The congress advocated federal, state,
and local laws to meet the housing needs of the Spanish-speaking and to prohibit segregated housing patterns. It supported the passage of a national
health bill as advocated by the Roosevelt administration as well as state
health insurance bills before the California legislature. Considering the funding of the Works Progress Administration (WPA) to be inadequate, "causing
untold misery and suffering to millions of people," El Congreso called on
members to pressure representatives in Washington to endorse legislation
adding $50 million to the WPA. The congress expressed alarm at the level of
illiteracy among Hispanics in the United States and proposed solving this
problem by having schools offer bilingual, bicultural programs to reach
Spanish-speaking children. Like LULAC, the congress favored cultural pluralism. "The cultural heritage of the Spanish-speaking people is part of the
common heritage of the American people as a whole," El Congreso stressed,
"and should be preserved and expanded for the common benefit of all of the
American people." [24]

With its emphasis on organizing working-class people, El Congreso
adopted various resolutions on labor. It called on all Spanish-speaking agricultural and industrial workers to join unions. El Congreso recognized that
only a unified labor movement could best protect the interests of Spanish-
speaking workers. It warned that the existing division between the AF of L
and the CIO weakened all workers, whether organized or not. To educate
and politicize the Spanish-speaking workers, both the AF of L and the CIO
needed to publish Spanish-language newspapers and to translate labor documents into Spanish so that members could understand and participate in
union deliberations. El Congreso also believed in the organic unity between
Mexican-American workers and mexicano workers in the United States and
consequently adopted strong positions on immigration, deportations, and
protection of the foreign born. El Congreso refused to see Mexican nationals
as "aliens" and asserted that many had been enthusiastically welcomed into
the country as workers during prosperous times and had labored for many
years in the United States. It vehemently objected to the deportation of
"aliens" and considered such measures fascistic. Furthermore, El Congreso

abhorred pending legislation at the national, state, and local levels that would deny jobs and relief to noncitizens. Other resolutions covered political action and youth. The congress encouraged delegates and all Spanish speakers to register to vote, to participate in democratic-progressive organizations, and to support only those candidates who combated discrimination. On youth, it favored participation in the National Youth Administration (NYA) and stood for effective and fair probation and delinquency agencies.[25]

Finally, delegates at the Los Angeles convention stressed an internationalist perspective, especially concerning relations with Mexico and other Latin American nations. El Congreso supported, for example, what it called President Roosevelt's "progressive" reaction to the Cárdenas administration's expropriation of foreign oil property in 1938 and warned against reactionary efforts to have the United States intervene militarily in Mexico on behalf of American oil interests. American intervention would destroy Pan Americanism and restore dollar diplomacy and the "imperialistic policies of the anti-New Deal Hoovers." El Congreso praised FDR's Good Neighbor Policy toward Latin America.[26]

The first and only national convention of the Spanish-Speaking Peoples Congress concluded with a fiesta at Olvera Street in the old Mexican quarter of Los Angeles. There, Josefina Fierro de Bright, one of El Congreso's principal leaders, put the convention in perspective to the delegates and the assembled crowd:

> This night will eventually take its place alongside all the other holidays of Mexican people in the celebration of liberty. It is the occasion of the founding of the First National Congress of Spanish Speaking People. For the first time Mexican and Spanish American people have gathered together for unified action against the abuses of discrimination and poverty which have embittered and paralyzed them for so many years.[27]

The Popular Front

Ideologically, El Congreso closely conformed to the Communist party's interpretation of the "Mexican question." The congress may or may not have been controlled by Communists (no documentary evidence exists on this matter), but the CP supported the need for the congress and through members and sympathizers provided ideological and political reinforcement. The general orientation of the congress, for example, paralleled the analysis provided by Emma Tenayuca and Homer Brooks, CP officials and labor organizers in Texas, in their article "The Mexican Question in the Southwest" published in *The Communist* in March 1939. Tenayuca and Brooks regarded all Mexicans north of the border as one people. They endorsed political unity between Mexican Americans and Mexican nationals since the majority of both groups represented predominantly working-class people bound together by a common history, culture, and oppressed condition. Mexican Americans had first become part of the United States as a "conquered population" as a result of the United States' conquest of the Southwest in the nineteenth century. Later Mexican immigrant workers crossed the border and filled roles as exploited cheap manual laborers. Racial, cultural, and political discrimination added to the plight of all Mexicans in the United States. Yet despite this exploitation and oppression, Tenayuca and Brooks were also quick to stress that people of Mexican descent did not constitute a "nation" nor were they simply an extension of the Mexican nation north of the border. Mexicans in the United States did not possess, according to Stalin's classical definition of a nation, either the economic or territorial base for a nation. On the contrary, Mexican Americans and Mexican nationals were inextricably tied to the larger American working class based on the economic and political integration of the Southwest with the rest of the nation plus an expanded Anglo population in the region.[28]

As part of the American people and nation, Mexicans more closely resembled Afro Americans than other American groups. Ironically, the Communist party during the late 1920s had considered Afro Americans in the black belt of the Deep South as a nation. One could make an even more convincing case for Mexican Americans in the Southwest in view of the particular history of the region. However, with the shift to a less radical Popular Front period by the mid-1930s, the CP disregarded this earlier analysis and explained Afro Americans, like Mexican Americans, as part of the more expansive working class and called for their political unification with progressive sectors of both the black and white bourgeoisie.[29] In this revised view, Afro Americans and Mexican Americans formed "oppressed national minorities." This classification more comfortably fitted the CP's stress on a Popular Front with its support for a liberal welfare state. It also helped to downplay political sectarianism in order to better defend against the threat of fascism both at home and abroad and to better rally American support for the Soviet Union as war loomed in Europe.[30]

In the meantime, Mexicans in the United States could alter their conditions. This would involve not only continued struggles but unity among all Spanish-speaking peoples through organizations such as the Spanish-Speaking Congress. Tenayuca and Brooks promoted El Congreso and its objectives. "It is a people's movement, uniting the interests of large and important sections of the population, over two million strong, who, in alliance with the country's democratic forces, in the Southwest and nationally, can free themselves from the special oppression and discrimination in all its phases that have existed for almost a century." Agreeing with the congress's stress on combating discrimination in jobs, wages, education, health, and culture, the Communist party observed that in this movement "the leading role will undoubtedly be played by the proletarian base of the Mexican population, its overwhelming majority." However, the CP warned against the congress's becoming a purely labor organization while insisting that labor had to be in the vanguard of the movement. Calling on the congress to become a part of the Popular Front against antidemocratic forces, Tenayuca and Brooks encouraged it to include progressive Anglos as well as the liberal Mexican-American middle class. In all, the Communist party saw El Congreso and the struggle by Mexican Americans for basic civil rights as part of the CP's strategy for a Popular Front of democratic forces. "The Mexican people's movement in the Southwest will constitute one more important and powerful link in the growing movement for the democratic front in the United States," Tenayuca and Brooks concluded. "The achievement of its objectives will be a decisive step forward toward the national unification of the American people." [31]

Accepting the Popular Front concept, El Congreso's leadership consisted of both left and liberal elements cooperating on basic reform issues and linked by ethnic ties and a belief that the Spanish-speaking deserved a rightful place in American society. "Popular Front culture offered a sentimental, egalitarian, and schematic world view," historian Maurice Isserman has observed of the 1930s, "and provided a bridge by which the children of immigrants could adapt themselves to the culture of the New World without renouncing the ideals that had sustained their parents in the move from the old." [32] Two personalities within El Congreso symbolized this Popular Front relationship. One was Josefina Fierro de Bright. At age 18, Fierro de Bright became one of the main organizers of El Congreso and its executive secretary for most of its short history. She represented the left-wing within the congress but in a nondoctrinaire, pragmatic fashion that suited the reformist character of El Congreso. Josefina's radicalism stemmed from her family history. She was born in 1920 in Mexicali on the Mexican side of the border as her parents fled political persecution from the Revolution of 1910. Her mother, Josefa, had supported Ricardo Flores Magón, the most radical leader during the revolution. Flores Magón gravitated from democratic liberalism to anarchosyndicalism. When Josefina's father returned to Mexico to fight on the side of Pancho Villa and her parents separated, Josefina accompanied her mother to Los Angeles. There, Josefa, as head of the family, opened up a restaurant in the downtown district while the family resided in several neighborhoods from Santa Monica to East Los Angeles. Josefina attended eight different schools because of this urban migration. In time her mother left Los

Angeles and followed the migrant farmworker stream in California with a trailer which served as a temporary home for Mexican farmworkers and as a traveling restaurant. Josefa eventually remarried and settled in Madera in the Central Valley. Josefina recalls her mother's strong hand in shaping her character and consciousness during this period.[33] "For a Mexican woman raised in the old feudal tradition," the *People's Daily World* wrote of Josefina's mother in 1939, "Josie's mother was very modern indeed. Never fall back on your sex, she cautioned her daughter, always rely on yourself, be independent."[34] Josefa Fierro stressed education for her daughter and her younger son and socialized them to the teachings of Flores Magón.

Graduating from high school in Madera and with her mother's permission, Josefina returned to Los Angeles around 1938 to attend UCLA. She hoped to study medicine and become a doctor. Living with an aunt who sang at a Latin nightclub, Josefina often found herself studying in a less than studious environment, "except when the floorshow came I'd stop and then I'd watch it." At the club she met a young Hollywood screenwriter, John Bright, fell in love, and married him. Josefina's marriage to Bright ended her college career but commenced her political-activist one.[35] A man with radical political beliefs, John Bright complemented Josefina's childhood politicization with his own left-leaning ideological views. A concerned writer, Bright belonged to several political organizations and attended many political meetings. He was particularly engaged in the militant Screen Writers Guild. One historian has written of Bright: "Bright was a flamboyant character, with a penchant for booze, big shiny cars, and hanging out in the black section of town near Central Avenue, who had written a novel called *Blood and Beer,* which had been turned by him and his partner, Kubic Glasman, into a picture called *The Public Enemy."* According to Nancy Lynn Schwartz in *The Hollywood Writers' Wars,* Bright was an early member of the Hollywood branch of the Communist party.[36]

Supported by Bright and his political colleagues, Josefina began organizing in the Mexican-American community even before her involvement with El Congreso. Along with other Mexican-American activists, she helped lead a successful consumer's boycott of the Eastside Brewery when it refused to hire workers of Mexican descent even though Mexicans consumed most of its beer. Obtaining money from her new Hollywood friends such as Orson Welles, Anthony Quinn, and Dolores Del Río, Josefina broadcast a news program for the boycott on a local Spanish-language radio station. The boycott proved a success. The brewery agreed to hire Mexicans and even to sponsor Josefina's radio program, which continued informing the barrios about issues and news pertinent to the Spanish-speaking. The beer boycott brought

Josefina to the attention of Luisa Moreno, who saw in the teenage Mexican-American woman someone who could help establish the Spanish-Speaking Congress in Los Angeles.[37] As the *People's Daily World* said of Josefina in 1939, "the currents of her background—Flores Magón, her father who fought with Villa, her mother who understood—finally have joined in the river of the great People's Front." [38]

Whereas Fierro symbolized the Left within El Congreso, Eduardo Quevedo, the congress's first president, represented the liberals or moderates, who were less inclined to sympathize or link themselves with the Communists. Born in New Mexico in 1903 to a copper miner, Quevedo in his youth worked in a variety of jobs including laborer in the mines, truckdriver, and interpreter. He left New Mexico in the 1920s, moved to Los Angeles, and worked in a grocery store while studying nights at UCLA. Fascinated with people and politics, Quevedo gravitated to community and political work. In 1932 he actively supported Franklin Roosevelt's successful bid for the presidency. One year later he campaigned for Upton Sinclair in the novelist's End Poverty in California Movement (EPIC). Quevedo spoke out against the deportation and forced repatriation of Mexican nationals from California. From 1934 to 1937 he worked for the WPA. Helping to reelect FDR in 1936, Quevedo also aided the election of New Dealer Culbert Olson as governor of California in 1938. Well-known in California and Los Angeles political circles, Quevedo became heavily involved in Mexican community organizations such as the New Mexico–Arizona Club, Cultura Pan Americana, and La Beneficencia Mexicana, an important mutual aid society.[39] Besides being an effective political organizer, Quevedo was an eloquent speaker, especially in Spanish. Consequently, in their search for a Popular Front, Moreno, Fierro de Bright, and the Left in El Congreso saw in Quevedo a perfect candidate for the presidency of the congress and one who could attract moderate elements such as social-cultural clubs and church organizations. Quevedo's selection as president, Fierro de Bright recalls, was due to his popularity with the Spanish-speaking community and because he was willing to work with the congress. For his part, Quevedo in a 1943 interview with the FBI contended that he agreed to participate in the congress in order to prevent it from engaging in "any activities inimical to the welfare of this country" and to be able to "observe the development of the organization and the persons who were affiliated with it." Based on this interview, it appears that Quevedo may have been cooperating with the FBI during the time he served as an officer of El Congreso. With apparent good reason, the Left did not completely trust Quevedo and suspected that he was not above taking advantage of the people for his own personal benefit. Quevedo spoke publicly for the congress, but day-to-day activities remained in the hands of the Left. "We were able to control Quevedo pretty good," Fierro de Bright observes. "At least while the Congress was going because he couldn't do anything really by himself." [40]

With this combination of leadership, although effectively under the control of the more militant activists, the Spanish-Speaking Congress hoped to become a national organization or at least a regional one in the Southwest. Unfortunately, this never materialized. With a membership composed of affiliated organizations rather than individuals with the exception of some Los Angeles branches, El Congreso as a specific entity functioned only in California. The congress's inability to operate on a larger scale can be attributed to limited funding, large distances between southwestern communities, lack of skilled organizers, jurisdictional boundaries with other existing organizations, such as LULAC, which might agree with El Congreso's reform objectives but wished to remain independent, and, unlike other southwestern states, the presence of a radical political culture in California that helped sustain the congress. For all practical purposes, El Congreso during its history from 1938 to about 1942 consisted primarily only of the California organization headquartered in Los Angeles. At least ten branches of El Congreso functioned in the greater Los Angeles area. These included branches in central Los Angeles and East Los Angeles, Watts, Lincoln Heights, San Pedro, San Fernando, Norwalk, Wilmington, and Anaheim. Additional branches or Pro-Congreso committees operated in Sacramento, Shafter, San Francisco, and San Diego. It is difficult to determine the exact number of members affiliated with each branch; however, one in 1940 reported a membership of two hundred. [41]

Still, the main organizers and leaders of El Congreso always remained small in numbers. "I used to work so hard it used to kill me," Fierro de Bright remembers. As executive secretary, she became responsible for almost all the Congress's work. "When we had a meeting we'd put Quevedo to speak, open the meeting," she observes, "but the work in the office I'd be there every day." With her contacts in the Hollywood community and her effective bilingualism, Fierro de Bright became invaluable in fund-raising. "I went speaking at least three times a week in English which Quevedo couldn't do to raise money with the League of Women Voters, B'nai B'rith, the Negro places, the Jewish clubs, everywhere I could get in and tell them the position of the Mexican people in California." Movie stars such as Anthony Quinn, Dolores Del Río, and John Wayne contributed money. "Not because they were reds," she explains, "but because they were helping Mexicans help themselves." Working in downtown Los Angeles during the day and then returning to her West Los Angeles home, where she often partied until late at night with her Hollywood friends, Fierro de Bright recalls how exhausting her life was then. "I was always sleepy. God, how I was sleepy. I was the sleepiest lady I know." [42]

El Congreso's Struggles

Between 1939 and the commencement of World War II, El Congreso engaged in a number of activities aimed at protecting the rights of the Spanish-speaking, educating them about the issues of the day, and organizing them around their basic needs. It consistently stressed in these efforts the organic unity between Mexican Americans and Mexican nationals. In one of its initial projects, for example, El Congreso mounted opposition to the Swing bill in the California state legislature. Introduced by Senator Ralph Swing of San Bernardino, this legislation would prohibit the dispensation of relief to noncitizens who had made no effort to become U.S. citizens. The congress correctly interpreted the bill as an anti-Mexican measure and denounced it. Denying Mexican nationals work relief during a period of mass unemployment was an injustice after they had significantly contributed to California's economy in prosperous times. People should not be forced to become citizens under duress. They should become citizens out of their own volition. Quevedo called the bill antidemocratic and one that would deepen racial cleavages. If the bill passed, Quevedo promised to pressure Governor Olson to veto it. [43]

To mobilize opposition, El Congreso urged Mexican Americans and other citizens to write letters of protest to both their state and federal representatives. It circulated a petition demanding that the state legislature defeat the bill. El Congreso also informed Mexican Americans and Mexican nationals about the dangers of the legislation through its Spanish-language radio program and in public information meetings. As a result of the congress's efforts, several officials including U.S. Senators Sheridan Downey and Hiram Johnson, Lieutenant Governor Patterson, and State Senator Robert W. Kenny voiced their concerns over the anticipated effects of the Swing bill. Moreover, El Congreso brought direct pressure to bear on Governor Olson by staging a hunger march to Sacramento after the bill passed the state legislature. "We decided to have a march to Sacramento," Fierro de Bright recounts. "We got a hold of trucks, of cars, of trains, busses, anyway we could to get to Sacramento." The caravan picked up people along the way from Los Angeles to the state capitol, and 20,000 people, by Fierro's estimate, demonstrated in front of the statehouse. At the rally speakers castigated the Swing bill and demanded that the governor veto it. In the meantime, Fierro de

Bright met with Olson concerning the legislation. Sympathizing with the protesters, the governor as a New Deal liberal vetoed the bill in the presence of Fierro de Bright. It would be inhumane, the governor later told the press, to deny assistance to foreign residents in times of crisis. Olson told Fierro de Bright to inform the rally about what he had done and to introduce him to the demonstrators. "It was the biggest hurrah you ever heard in your life— fantastic!" Fierro de Bright notes of the rally's enthusiastic reception of Olson's veto.[44]

The following year El Congreso vehemently opposed state legislation designed to deport noncitizens receiving state welfare. Again, the congress stressed the irony of deporting workers who had earlier produced much wealth for California. The legislation, if passed, would endorse the deportation of thousands of Mexican nationals and lead to the disintegration of family life as parents would be torn from their U.S.-born children. Such deportations would likewise seriously harm Mexican commercial interests in the state. Fortunately, the bill was not enacted.[45]

Besides sponsoring antialien legislation, El Congreso aided Mexican nationals by offering counseling on immigration and naturalization status in its downtown Los Angeles office. "We are here to serve the public and anyone who comes in seeking information we shall provide it without charge," Congreso member F. C. González informed *La Opinión*. Utilizing their bilingual abilities, Congreso members daily handled hundreds of cases primarily by assisting Mexican nationals in filling out forms for resident or citizenship status as well as job applications. El Congreso offered the free services of lawyers, including the Lawyers Guild, for particular cases. To facilitate naturalization for those desiring U.S. citizenship, El Congreso at its third state convention called for a relaxation of language and other prerequisites for citizenship. Ramón Welch of the congress noted that more than a million and a half Mexicans resided in the United States and that many had not become citizens because of their unfamiliarity with English and because they feared losing the protection of the Mexican consulates. If naturalization requirements were less strict, Welch proposed, more Mexican nationals would become citizens.[46]

With millions still unemployed in the late 1930s, El Congreso also supported the continuation and expansion of relief programs. It joined with other groups in the "ham and eggs" campaign to establish an old-age pension system in California. Discrimination in state relief programs constituted a major problem for people of Mexican descent as well as for other minority groups. In early 1940, El Congreso together with blacks in Los Angeles protested against George R. Lane, the head of the State Relief Administration (SRA). Lane had recommended eliminating many Mexicans and blacks from relief rolls as unworthy of assistance. Lane's Los Angeles office served a clientele composed of 40 percent blacks and 35 percent people of Mexican descent. El Congreso lambasted Lane's "un-American" views by picketing the SRA's office in collaboration with the Democratic Luncheon Club, a leading black organization in Los Angeles. "Mexican and Negroes starve," one picket sign read, "while SRA wastes money on Lane's salary." Moreover, at its second state convention, El Congreso advocated the establishment of a federal stamp system in California to "increase the purchasing power of the needy." [47]

Police abuse of both Mexican Americans and Mexican nationals constituted another issue confronted by El Congreso. It protested, for example, the killing of a young Mexican American, Florentino Sánchez, by a Los Angeles policeman, Neal Davison, in the Belvedere section. Davison claimed that Sánchez had resisted arrest. Outraged Congreso members organized more than 2,000 people to participate in the funeral and burial of Sánchez. Quevedo, speaking for El Congreso, delivered the burial oration. Seeing the Sánchez killing as one additional case of police brutality against Mexicans, El Congreso called on Governor Olson to investigate the incident. However, a coroner's inquest ruled that Davison had acted correctly and no subsequent investigation occurred. On another occasion after police killed two Mexican-American boys, El Congreso quickly mobilized several hundred supporters who protested in front of city hall and demanded that the officer be charged with murder. City officials refused to do this but did remove the policeman from the barrio.[48] Other types of police abuse involved Spanish-speaking waitresses often complaining to El Congreso about policemen pressuring them for sexual favors after arresting them on false charges of prostitution. "So when these girls came to complain to us," recalls Fierro de Bright, "we had to go make a citizen's arrest on these cops, follow them, watch them, see what they were doing. We did things like this." [49] Finally, concerned over conditions faced by Mexicans in prisons, El Congreso in 1940 helped secure the right of Spanish-speaking prisoners in San Quentin Penitentiary to exchange correspondence in Spanish with parents and wives.[50] To impress upon law officers its vigilance over police brutality, El Congreso regularly met with the chief of police. "They hated us and we hated them," recalls Fierro de Bright.[51]

El Congreso also concentrated on federally funded low-cost housing projects in the Mexican-American neighborhoods of Los Angeles. It investigated what effect projects such as Maravilla Park and Ramona Gardens would have on the local population, especially on those whose homes the federal government wished to purchase to make room for the new construction. In late November 1939 El Congreso hosted a public meeting attended by several hundred persons where affected homeowners could question state officials. Dissatisfied with the federal government's purchase offer, many Mexican Americans in the Maravilla Park district went to court and obtained a favorable ruling that forced Washington to pay higher prices for their homes. El Congreso assisted in making certain that Mexican Americans obtained access to the new housing projects. It insisted that parents who remained Mexican nationals but whose children were U.S. citizens should receive a certain percentage of the low-cost housing. In all, several thousand Mexican Americans and Mexican nationals obtained new homes.[52]

As part of its multi-issue program El Congreso worked with the Los Angeles schools to ensure a better education for Mexican Americans. "The problem[s] of education among the Mexican people are really vital," the second state convention stressed. El Congreso deplored the segregation of Mexican-American students in inferior Mexicans schools but, like the School Improvement League in San Antonio, realistically called for reforms in such institutions. It succeeded, for example, in obtaining the hiring of more Mexican-American teachers in schools with high percentages of Mexican Americans. It failed, however, in its proposal for the adoption of bilingual instruction "for our children up to the eighth grade so that they may not remain illiterate, and be able to learn both languages." Fierro de Bright remembers Mexican-American children being made to feel embarrassed in the schools because they spoke Spanish. With the assistance of school officials El Congreso organized training sessions for teachers on Mexican-American culture. Furthermore, the congress convinced prominent Anglos to sponsor scholarships for Mexican-American high school and college students. Finally, El Congreso favored accessible education for children of migratory workers as well as improved adult education under Spanish-speaking instructors.[53]

Troubled over the increase in juvenile delinquency among Mexican-American youth, especially the emergence of rival gangs, El Congreso shortly after the first national convention organized a Youth Committee for young people in the barrios. Besides aiding in the general work of the congress, the Youth Committee focused on specific issues of its own. Perhaps its most important work concerned the sponsorship of cultural activities. The committee hoped to generate interest in the establishment of a Centro Artístico Mexicano in the Belvedere barrio by forming art classes for boys and girls and by announcing the organization of a youth art exposition scheduled for October 8, 1939, as part of El Día de La Raza (Columbus Day).[54] Supporting the cultural work of the youth clubs, El Congreso itself sponsored community cultural activities and educational programs. Like middle-class Mexican-American organizations such as LULAC, El Congreso affirmed the importance of a bilingual, bicultural society and of the need to promote and sustain a Mexican-American cultural presence in the United States. El Congreso insisted that Mexicans in this country had made and would continue to make major cultural contributions. In order for this work to be furthered, artists in the barrios had to be encouraged. The congress called for the formation of cooperatives for Spanish-speaking artists and artisans as well as for cultural centers for the general public. El Congreso sponsored community fiestas such as one organized by Lincoln Local No. 7 in the Ramona Gardens barrio in May 1941 where various artists and musicians performed. During the fiesta El Congreso educated the community to its principles and goals through various speakers who took the platform. Dance benefits also became part of El Congreso's cultural and social programs. Every Friday night one could attend free of charge El Congreso's weekly dances. Held in El Congreso's hall on Broadway Street, these dances could not rival the more elaborate ones held at the famous Palladium, yet Fierro de Bright remembers that they were well attended and people donated when the hat came around. Understanding the need for political education, El Congreso initiated a lecture series sponsored by many of the local chapters in which speakers debated issues before Congreso members and the public at large. At one session in San Pedro an official from the district attorney's office addressed the problem of delinquency. Other topics included the learning of English by Mexican-American children, health practices in the barrios, alien registration, and the obtaining of defense-related jobs. To reach even larger numbers of Mexicans, El Congreso utilized access to spots on Spanish-language radio stations in Los Angeles including its own five-minute program "Las Noticias del Congreso." [55]

El Congreso did not directly participate in the labor movement, but it did draw much support from CIO unions. Many delegates at the state conventions of the congress consisted of Mexican-American members of CIO unions. Mexican-American women, as Vicki Ruiz has documented, played leading roles in UCAPAWA unionization in Los Angeles. Luisa Moreno, of course, had founded the congress from her base in UCAPAWA. As a member of El Congreso and UCAPAWA, Moreno aided in the unionization of Mexican women working in Los Angeles canneries. "We . . . need a leadership endeavoring to develop a trade-union consciousness among Spanish-speaking women," Moreno told the *People's Daily World* in 1940. Moreover, Congreso officials on occasion sponsored meetings designed to influence Mexican-American workers to organize in unions. Viewing the Spanish-speaking as an integral part of the labor force, El Congreso advocated a multiethnic working-class movement. "The main problem of labor," El Congreso pointed out, "is creating greater unity and understanding between the Mexican laborer and the American laborer and having Mexican people see the necessity for fighting for the right to collective bargaining, to organize and strike." At its second state convention in 1939, El Congreso outlined a number of actions that could be taken to bring Spanish-speaking workers into the union fold. They included an educational program by El Congreso explaining to Spanish-speaking workers their right to unionize, bargain collectively, strike, and picket, and the need for the extension of social security benefits to include workers on strike or affected by lockouts, the abolition of special police squads used to repress workers, and the liberalization of wages and hour laws as well as increased work projects. The union movement could succeed with Spanish-speaking workers, El Congreso concluded, only if it kept in mind the cultural and language differences between Mexican and Anglo workers. Union meetings had to be conducted in both Spanish and English and information disseminated in Spanish through either the press or radio. Only through all these efforts could Spanish-speaking workers and the U.S. labor movement come together.[56]

Although a less defined issue, the condition of Spanish-speaking women nevertheless formed an integral part of El Congreso's program. Unlike LULAC, which favored separate women's councils, the congress sought to raise gender discrimination to be on a par with racial discrimination and to integrate women within the membership. At the second state convention, El Congreso proclaimed its official position on women:

> Whereas: The Mexican woman, who for centuries has suffered oppression, has the responsibility of raising her children and of caring for the home, and even that of earning a livelihood for herself and her family, and since in this country she suffers double discrimination, as a woman and as a Mexican.
>
> Be It Resolved: That the Congress carry out a program of organization and education of the Mexican women, concerning home problems; that every Pro-Congress Club establish a Women's Committee as soon as possible; that it support and work for women's equality, so that she may receive equal wages, enjoy the same rights as men in social, economic, and civic liberties, and use her vote for the defense of the Mexican and Spanish American people, and of American democracy;
>
> Be It Further Resolved: That the feminine [sic] sex be represented on the State Executive Committee and on the other executive committee of Congress' groups.[57]

To carry out this declaration, the state executive committee included one female officer responsible for recruiting women into the congress. The Comité de Damas del Congreso [Women's Committee] also instructed Spanish-speaking mothers at its weekly and well-attended meetings about certain health problems such as the treatment of tuberculosis for children. The committee welcomed working women who complained about discrimination at their jobs. "A Mexican woman working in a factory," Fierro de Bright observes, "would get less pay than a man for the same job and less pay than the American women doing the same job." El Congreso directed many of these complaints to trade union representatives or to appropriate government officials. El Congreso not only recruited women but integrated them into leadership positions. According to Fierro de Bright, about 30 percent of El Congreso's activists were women. If men resented this participation, she does not recall such sentiments. In addition to Fierro de Bright, other women played leading roles. At the second state convention, for example, delegates elected Cesaria Valdés as vice president of the congress. Still other women served as elected officers in the state executive committee and in the leadership of local councils.[58]

Besides being involved in specific community issues, El Congreso promoted the neutrality movement in the United States by advocating nonintervention in Europe following the Nazi attack on Poland in September 1939. Paralleling the Communist party's position on the European war, El Congreso between 1939 and the German invasion of the Soviet Union in 1941 attacked the European conflict as a war between capitalist nations. Mexicans in the United States, El Congreso asserted, along with other peace-loving people understood that U.S. intervention would benefit only the bankers and the arms merchants. For its part, El Congreso pledged to educate the Spanish-speaking on the importance of maintaining neutrality and peace. Mexican Americans as loyal citizens would defend their country but opposed intervention in a war in which they would only serve as cannon-fodder. "There is today no need of anti-war agitation," Luisa Moreno told the *People's Daily World* in 1940, "but a need of anti-war organization. I have not met a single woman worker or housewife—in homes, fields, trains, that doesn't abhor the idea of sending her sons to war. The anti-war feeling is greatest among the women."[59] Hoping to maintain American neutrality and to protect Mexicans in the United States from right-wing reaction, El Congreso between 1939 and 1941 rededicated its belief in a Popular Front of minorities, labor, women, religious groups, and progressive organizations.

Wartime Unity

Japan's attack on Pearl Harbor on December 7, 1941, and the subsequent American entrance into the war shifted the attention of the Spanish-Speaking Congress. From a Popular Front for civil rights, El Congreso formed a Popular Front in support of the war effort as did most of the Left in the country. In a public statement to all Spanish-speaking communities in the United States, El Congreso attacked the "savage invaders" and "bandits" of

Berlin, Rome, and Tokyo and pledged that they would be beaten back. The war effort, however, would necessitate setting aside differences and divisions among Americans as well as those among the Allied nations. Together the liberty-loving countries of the Americas along with their allies in Britain, the Soviet Union, and China would triumph in the end. In this effort, the Spanish-speaking people of the United States needed to identify with the forces of democracy. "Our liberties, our homes, and our lives directly threatened by Fascism demand our greatest unity." Spanish-speaking Americans would join arm in arm with the Anglo Americans in this struggle to preserve freedom and democracy. El Congreso observed that many Mexican Americans had already heeded the call and patriotically joined the armed forces while others had volunteered for civil defense. Still, the Spanish-speaking could do more. "We as Latinos have had centuries of gloriously fighting for freedom; we shall not abandon this historic tradition in these days of crisis." El Congreso encouraged young Mexican Americans to enlist in the armed forces. It appealed to Spanish-speaking factory workers and farm laborers to work even harder to produce the necessary food and fiber for the war. And it called on every able man, woman, and even children to do their part by cooperating with civil defense, the National Guard, the Red Cross, the Boy Scouts, and the Girl Scouts. "We are also children of the United States," El Congreso concluded. "We will defend her!" Finally, El Congreso prompted all Spanish-speaking organizations to discuss the war effort at their meetings and not to isolate themselves from other Americans in this critical period. "We will march united until finally victory!" [60]

While El Congreso geared its energies for the war effort, it did not totally abandon its civil and human rights reforms. Activist Bert Corona believes that the congress differed from other progressive groups, including the Communist party, because El Congreso did not initially drop its reform efforts during the war. The persistence of antidemocratic conditions was totally incompatible with the basic goals of the United States in the conflict. El Congreso reaffirmed its struggle for reform but now saw it within the context of the war effort. Winning the war in itself would represent a major reform. Hence, the congress declared victory to be its first priority. As part of this movement, El Congreso would fight against fifth-column elements seeking to subvert the loyalties of the Spanish-speaking. Moreover, El Congreso would work to ensure full participation by all Mexicans, citizens or noncitizens, in the war effort. It promised to ensure that defense industries hired workers without discriminating on the basis of race, religion, or national origin. Discrimination in housing, schools, public facilities, and jobs would also have to cease. El Congreso further warned against prejudice against Mexican Americans in the military and hoped that they would be promoted as officers on the basis of ability. [61]

With war production opening a vast array of new jobs for Americans, El Congreso linked its campaign for wartime unity with obtaining access to defense industries for both Mexican Americans and Mexican nationals. Claiming that national security was involved, defense industries refused to hire "aliens." Yet if aliens had to register for the draft and were eligible to provide military service, El Congreso could not understand why they could not obtain jobs in defense industries. This discrimination only contributed to large-scale unemployment in the barrios. El Congreso combated such discrimination by allying progressive groups in forming the Council for the Protection of Minority Rights. The council focused on discrimination in defense industries and the armed forces. It was led by the Jewish People's Committee and consisted of organizations such as CIO and AFL unions, the NAACP, the National Negro Congress, the Japanese Progressive Doho, and the International Workers Order. El Congreso investigated charges of discrimination in particular war-related industries and brought these to the attention of officials, such as the War Manpower Commission. El Congreso further assisted Mexican nationals and Mexican Americans to obtain defense jobs by organizing the Hispanic Committee on Defense Jobs [Comité Hispano de los Empleos de la Defensa], which in cooperation with the War Manpower Commission and California officials organized a census in the Belvedere section in April 1942 to determine the number of Spanish-speaking workers eligible for defense jobs. At the end of the three-day census, *La Opinión* called the effort a success and reported that more than 8,000 people had participated. As a result of the census various job training programs opened in the barrio.[62]

Apprehensive about the effects of the war on Mexicans in the United States, El Congreso strongly opposed the Bracero Program, the contract labor system established in 1942 between the American and Mexican governments. Like LULAC, El Congreso did not reject the principle of contract labor from Mexico, but did protest the exploitative conditions that might result from the program and the dislocating conditions it would impose on domestic labor, especially Mexican-American farmworkers. El Congreso asked for guarantees to protect both braceros and domestic labor. As the program stood, it would aid only U.S. agribusiness, which could hire braceros at lower wages and drive domestic labor out of the fields. El Congreso called for five conditions to be met before farmers could import braceros. These included round-trip transportation from Mexico for the workers, hygienic living conditions, and comparable salaries to domestic labor. El Congreso also suggested that the negotiations between the United States and Mexico be expanded to include representatives of the AF of L, the CIO, and the CTM of Mexico. Finally, El Congreso stressed that no braceros should enter the country until all domestic farmworkers were hired. Unfortunately, while some of the provisions advocated by the congress became part of the bracero agreement, the failure of the U.S. government and the states, such as California, to enforce its provisions led to much exploitation of the workers and the dislocation of Mexican-American farmworkers.[63]

Yet the war effort above all other issues now assumed paramount importance for the congress. Recognizing the value of securing the allegiance of all Mexicans, El Congreso believed it imperative to expose and discredit the work of pro-Fascists within the barrios. The major threat came from the Sinarquistas. Founded in León, Guanajuato, in 1937, the Sinarquista movement in Mexico copied the Spanish Falange. "The Mexican Sinarquismo," one writer in *The Nation* observed, "is the Spanish Phalanx in *guaraches* [sandals]." Claiming half a million supporters in Mexico, the Sinarquistas began to organize in Los Angeles in late 1937. Under the slogan "Patria, Justicia y Libertad" [Country, Justice and Liberty] the Sinarquistas voiced populist slogans defending property, capitalism, and Catholicism. They attacked the Mexican government for implementing "collectivization" at the expense of private ownership and moving Mexico toward atheism. The Sinarquistas called for distribution of property but based on private ownership. Although voicing opposition to both communism and fascism, Sinarquistas attacked communism more vociferously by calling it an anti-Mexican ideology controlled by the Soviet Union. The Sinarquistas claimed that they were the true Mexican nationalists. "El Sinarquismo is a Mexican movement for Mexicans."[64]

In the United States, the Sinarquistas with their irredentist support of returning the Southwest to Mexico when the Nazis triumphed and their exploitation of racism against the Spanish-speaking found a haven among some Mexican immigrants in the barrios. One observer noted that some 50,000 adhered to Sinarquism in California. However, a Department of Justice investigation reported only 2,000 Sinarquistas in Southern California. The Sinarquistas maintained three regional centers: one in northern California based in Bakersfield and with municipal centers in locations such as Fresno, Pismo Beach, Richmond, and San Francisco; a Southern California regional center in Los Angeles with 21 municipal centers in locations such as Azusa, Belvedere, Claremont, La Verne, Oxnard, Pomona, San Bernardino, San Fernando, Santa Ana, Van Nuys, Watts, and Whittier and with an affiliate in San Diego; and, finally, an El Paso regional center with branches in Fabens, Fort Hancock, Laredo, and McAllen. In addition, branches also functioned in New Mexico and in the Midwest (Chicago and Indiana Harbor). The basic purpose of these centers was to raise money among Mexican immigrants for the Sinarquista cause south of the border. The actual composition of the Sinarquistas in the United States is difficult to determine, but they claimed particular strength, as they did in Mexico, among farmworkers because of their support for land allocation to *campesinos* in Mexico. They likewise claimed adherents in urban industries as well as among clerical workers. Jean Meyer in his study of Sinarquismo in Mexico calculates that 85 percent of the Sinarquistas in the United States came from the working class.[65] Yet according to one U.S. investigation in 1941, only in Los Angeles and El Paso did the Sinarquistas seem to have any success in attracting supporters. "They have much hope of obtaining financial assistance in Los Angeles," the U.S. embassy in Mexico City noted. "The Mexican community in that city has made much progress."[66] Indicative of some support in Los Angeles, *La Opinión* defended the Sinarquistas' right to express their views and considered them to be genuine Mexican nationalists.[67] As for the leadership, Fierro de Bright recalls that they were primarily lower-middle-class Mexican nationals. "By using discrimination and langauge difference as a basis," she wrote of the Sinarquista movement in a U.S. magazine, "it attempts to create among these [Mexican] people suspicion and distrust of both the United States and the Mexican Governments."[68]

El Congreso no doubt had the Sinarquistas in mind when at its fourth state convention in 1942 it attacked the "Fifth Columnists who would aid the enemy by crippling our efforts, by planting the seeds of confusion and disunity to reap the harvest of apathy and sabotage." El Congreso worked to expose the identities of the Sinarquistas and in particular charged them with fomenting discontent among Mexican-American youth, especially the "pachucos"—the most alienated sector among the young. One federal official accused the Sinarquistas of trying to influence, although unsuccessfully, young Mexican Americans not to sell war bonds or cooperate with the Red Cross and USO. Fierro de Bright says that the Sinarquistas preached against U.S. involvement in the war. While El Congreso discounted Sinarquista support among Mexican workers in Los Angeles, it nevertheless was concerned because the Catholic Church supported the Mexican Fascists. Some churches in the barrios, for example, allowed the Sinarquistas to sell their newspaper, *El Sinarquista,* after Sunday masses. Not all priests, however, favored the Sinarquistas and some barrio priests affiliated with El Congreso.[69]

The Sinarquistas retaliated against El Congreso by attempting to infiltrate and disrupt Congreso meetings. Yet knowing who the Sinarquistas were and their tactics, El Congreso leaders thwarted these interventions. "We had a big, big meeting in Belvedere Gardens in a big hall," Fierro de Bright explains,

> and they [the Sinarquistas] surrounded us. And we had there Senators from Mexico City that Lázaro Cárdenas had sent us to represent him when we invited him to these things. And they got scared because in Mexico City they [the Sinarquistas] would produce machine guns . . . [and] they were

real rough in Mexico City. . . . They turned off the lights at the meeting. But they weren't able to do anything because our guys surrounded them and kicked them out of there and beat them up. And we restored order to the meeting.[70]

Besides force, Congreso leaders used ridicule on one occasion to prevent Sinarquista disruptions. "I was introducing one of the Mexican workers [CTM] from Mexico City," Fierro de Bright amusingly recounts, "[when] he [the Sinarquista] got up and protested and started talking to them [the audience]." Chairing the meeting, Fierro de Bright told the standing Sinarquista, who happened to be a short man: "Señor, you're interrupting the meeting. . . . At least you could do [us] the courtesy of standing up so we could see you." The short Sinarquista embarrassingly replied: "I am standing up!" Moreover, El Congreso leaders combated the Sinarquistas by performing espionage work against them in cooperation with the Mexican consulate and apparently indirectly with the FBI. For example, Fierro de Bright, posing as a Mexican maid, entered the apartment of Consul Del Amo of Spain, a suspected Sinarquista ally, and took out important documents which she turned over to Consul de la Huerta. The Mexican consul-general in turn reported the information to U.S. authorities.[71] In all, by confrontations and exposure, El Congreso appears to have succeeded, with the help of Mexican and American officials, in denying the Sinarquistas wide popular support.

El Congreso's Demise

El Congreso's decided shift in favor of wartime unity unfortunately also led to its demise. "The thing that stopped the Congress was the war," Fierro de Bright admits. Some in El Congreso argued for continuing the struggle for civil rights while working for wartime unity. However, a majority believed that this was not only impractical but that the two efforts were contradictory. Militant action on civil rights would cause dissension rather than unity. Civil rights struggles only embarrassed the government at a time when unity in fighting fascism took precedence. According to Fierro de Bright, these arguments were voiced most effectively by members of the Communist party and CIO leaders such as Harry Bridges.[72] The CP and the CIO had agreed to cooperate with the war effort and supported, among other things, a moratorium on wage increases and no-strike pledges during the war. The Communist party likewise counseled moderation among Afro Americans. "By the fall of 1941," one historian writes, "the Communists were arguing that a too militant defense of black rights at home would interfere with the war effort."[73] Fierro de Bright and the majority of El Congreso agreed. "You can't have unified effort with the Congress raising hell all the time," she recalls the argument. Congreso leaders also rationalized that a militant civil rights movement would make it difficult to convince young Mexican Americans to join the armed forces and fight for a society that discriminated against them. Militant reformism would only play into the hands of the Sinarquistas, who desired to have the United States embarrassed by discrepancies in how it treated its racial minorities. Congreso leaders, somewhat naively, further believed that the need for wartime unity had already created a more liberal social climate that would eliminate additional racial barriers without continued pressures from civil rights groups.[74] By the middle of 1942 El Congreso lapsed into a limbo stage and effectively ceased to function. Isserman in his study of the Communist party notes that after 1941 other Popular Front organizations such as the American Youth Congress, the American Student Union, and the League of American Writers existed only as paper organizations. Those Congreso members who did not join the armed forces remained and participated in other wartime activities such as selling war bonds. In retrospect, Fierro de Bright concludes that the disbanding of the congress was still the right decision even though more reforms might have been achieved if it had continued to operate.[75]

El Congreso no longer existed by mid-1942, but activists such as Fierro de Bright did not remain dormant when particular cases of racial discrimination surfaced. Ironically, despite El Congreso's belief in a more liberal social climate, racial tensions increased rather than diminished. Los Angeles newspapers practicing yellow journalism began focusing on the alleged threat posed by Mexican-American youth—the pachucos and zoot-suiters. Carey McWilliams believed that the internment of the Japanese and the need for a new social scapegoat during the war were responsible for this dangerous and inflammatory mood. When a gang fight on the outskirts of Los Angeles on August 1, 1942, resulted in the death of a young Mexican American, the police and the media quickly created a sensationalist event dubbed the Sleepy Lagoon Case. Prosecutors never proved the actual cause of death. However, a grand jury indicted twenty-four other young Mexican Americans. During their trial they received limited access to a defense attorney as well as being subjected to cruel treatment including beatings and being unable to bathe and change clothes.[76] Alarmed at the treatment of their sons, many of the parents turned to Josefina Fierro de Bright and the remnants of El Congreso. Fierro de Bright responded by organizing a defense committee that raised money to hire a lawyer for the defendants. "Josefina Fierro . . . was the one who called me up and asked me to help her organize the Sleepy Lagoon Defense Committee," recalls Bert Corona. "Even though I did help her at the initial stages of the work, the credit for organizing the Committee belongs to Josefina." The Sleepy Lagoon Defense Committee consisted of a broad range of members including representatives from church, labor, and Hollywood organizations. Fierro de Bright visited the young men every day in the county jail and attended their entire trial.[77] Despite the committee's work, a local court in a climate of anti-Mexican sentiment built up by the press convicted nine of the defendants on second-degree murder charges and sentenced them to San Quentin. It convicted the others on lesser charges. Following the trial, the Sleepy Lagoon Defense Committee, with Fierro de Bright as one of its principal leaders, continued its activities and helped finance an appeal. Its work in the end succeeded and in 1944 a district court of appeals reversed the conviction of all the defendants for "lack of evidence." The Sleepy Lagoon Defense Committee, chaired by Carey McWilliams, received much criticism, including red baiting but also much praise. "The work of the Sleepy Lagoon Defense Committee received nationwide attention," McWilliams concluded, "and was hailed as an important contribution to the war effort by ex-President Cárdenas of Mexico and by the Mexican consul-general."[78]

Regrettably, the anti-Mexican campaign waged by the Los Angeles press did not abate. It was aided by Captain E. Durán Ayres, chief of the Foreign Relations Bureau of the Los Angeles sheriff's office. In a report Ayres indicted all Mexicans as bloodthirsty potential criminals. "In other words," Ayres wrote, "his [the Mexican's] desire is to kill, or at least let blood. That is why it is difficult for the Anglo-Saxon to understand the psychology of the Indian or even the Latin. . . . When there is added to *this inborn characteristic* that has come down through the ages, the use of liquor, then we certainly have crimes of violence."[79] With such unfounded prejudice a conflict was almost inevitable. It came during the first week of June 1943 in the highly publicized zoot-suit riots. Gangs of servicemen, led by sailors, their nativism fanned by the yellow press, filled the streets of downtown Los Angeles in a week-long tirade against Mexican Americans, especially those dressed in the popular zoot-suits. Many were injured. Fortunately, no death occurred. Fierro de Bright believes that the riots were the work of the Sinarquistas and aimed at embarrassing the United States as well as creating social divisions. She likewise believes that many members of the Los Angeles police, who did little to prevent the beatings, were secretly pro-German. She recalls being shocked by the sight of the assaults. "That was the most horrifying experience of my time. I dreamed about it months afterwards." What remained of El Congreso authorized Fierro de Bright to fly to Washington the week following the worst disturbances and to see personally Vice President Henry Wallace and appeal to the Roosevelt administration to put a stop to the riots. Fierro de Bright took with her letters of protest and copies of Los Angeles newspapers as proof of the hysteria created by the press. As a result of her visit to the nation's capital, according to Fierro de Bright, the Navy Department ordered all its personnel to remain out of the Mexican districts of Los Angeles. With the aid of the federal government, the zoot-suit riots came to an end.[80]

The activists of El Congreso had hoped to reunite after the war. However, this never materialized. A product of the Communist-inspired Popular Front period, El Congreso saw its demise in the shifting fortunes of the Left in the United States. The rise of the cold war and McCarthyism made it difficult to resurrect the earlier coalition of militant leftists and union members. Although no evidence has surfaced from a Freedom of Information request to suggest that El Congreso was heavily investigated by either state or federal officials, still it was listed in 1943 as a "Communist-front" by the House Un-American Activities Committee.[81] In addition, the California State Un-American Activities Committee, better known as the Tenney committee, alleged in 1943 and 1945 that El Congreso was a Communist front.[82] Some ex-Congresistas nevertheless continued to participate in what remained of progressive politics. Fierro de Bright, for example, after a short stay in New York City during the war returned to California and settled in Madera, where she helped organize the Independent Progressive party and campaigns for Henry Wallace in 1948.[83] Unfortunately, ex-Congresistas who remained as activists began to feel the pressure of right-wing reaction during the late 1940s and early 1950s. Some, as Mexican nationals, were deported to Mexico for alleged violation of immigration and naturalization laws. According to historian Vicki Ruiz, Luisa Moreno, a native of Guatemala, was deported to her home country.[84] Fierro de Bright, who had never officially become a U.S. citizen, voluntarily left the United States because she did not want to remain and possibly incriminate friends if subpoenaed. She also believed that she would soon be arrested.[85]

Conclusion

While the Spanish-Speaking Congress functioned for only about three years, it contributed to the evolution of Mexican-American politics. Resurrecting a tradition of militant ethnic protection rooted in the needs of working-class people, El Congreso represented an important effort by one segment of the Mexican-American Generation to develop a mass movement in the United States. Through the struggles of the congress, as with those of more middle-class organizations such as LULAC, Spanish speakers, at least in Los Angeles, achieved a degree of ethnic protection and ethnic representation under still very difficult conditions. Believing more in public protest and direct action than LULAC, El Congreso because of its working-class and leftist ties advanced the Mexican-American struggle by forging links with other oppressed groups. It broadened LULAC's more sectarian vision of Mexican-American politics based on middle-class leadership to include a world view founded on the realization that the Spanish-speaking were predominantly working class and that political alliances had to be forged with not only other oppressed peoples but with middle-class progressives. It further contributed to a political view that argued for common bonds between different Spanish-speaking nationality groups, today's Hispanics, but more specifically between Mexican Americans and Mexican nationals. This legacy of the Popular Front, a product of Communist party politics of the 1930s, would continue to influence the Left in Mexican-American politics in later years (see chapter 8). However, El Congreso's more militant brand of politics did not translate into a revolutionary political position aimed at successfully challenging the dominant reformist tendency in Mexican-American political circles and voiced by groups such as LULAC. Mexican-American left leaders, such as those in El Congreso, although perceived at times as undesirable competitors by their middle-class counterparts, supplemented rather than superseded the reform movements of the period. Here, both liberals and leftists of the Mexican-American Generation came together. In some sense true radicals, El Congreso activists understood with the rest of the Left in the country that both objective and subjective conditions for a revolutionary working class did not yet exist in the 1930s and hence made the most of addressing the immediate needs of working people. Like its Afro-American counterpart, the National Negro Congress, El Congreso arose out of the community rather than from some sinister intrusion by left-wing forces. "In a number of respects . . . the history of the National Negro Congress cannot be understood solely by referral to Communism," one scholar writes, and the same can be said of El Congreso. "Its successes and its internal tensions did not pivot around Communist participation, but around other concerns in the black community." [86] Moreover, the rise of international fascism necessitated a united front of democratic forces. A Mexican-American Left emerged out of the 1930s, but it was one centered on reform not revolution. As a reform movement, the Mexican-American Left rather than being out of step with its time was very much a part of it. For reform and the achievement of the mythical American dream not revolution characterized the most politically active sectors of the Mexican-American communities between the 1930s and the 1960s.

Border Proletariats: Mexican Americans and the International Union of Mine, Mill and Smelter Workers

Here in the southwest the victory of the Phelps Dodge workers under the CIO banner will be a blow in the face of all the fascist-minded employers who utilize racial and national discrimination as a means of paying starvation wages.

—ANTONIO SALCIDO, May 4, 1942

One of the first things we were told when we started to organize [was] that if we weren't U.S. citizens we should not be very outspoken or active, but the rest who were citizens should be very involved.

—J. B. CHÁVEZ, January 18, 1983

If, as a political generation, Mexican Americans sought their place in U.S. society through middle-class civil rights organizations such as LULAC and radical ones such as El Congreso, they likewise did so within the trade union movement of the Southwest. El Congreso, for example, stressed the need to mobilize Mexican-American and mexicano workers but did not itself engage in mass union organizing. Instead, Mexican-American labor leaders such as Luisa Moreno successfully recruited Spanish-speaking workers and helped to develop union if not class consciousness among them.[1] This was no small achievement, since Mexicans had historically not played a major role in southwestern unionization. Shunned by the elitist American Federation of Labor, with its emphasis on skilled craftsmen, and seeing themselves only as temporary sojourners north of the border, most Mexican immigrant workers during the early twentieth century avoided labor confrontations that might lead to loss of jobs or deportation. Mexicano workers, of course, engaged in strikes and work stoppages when faced with particularly overt forms of job and wage discrimination and when organized around objective grievances by progressive unions.

However, such actions were sporadic and failed to lead to permanent unionization. Not until the 1930s did Mexican-American workers, like many other workers, especially of recent immigrant backgrounds, advance union struggles on a larger and more permanent scale. Severe economic dislocation as the result of the Great Depression and the emergence of unionizing vanguards affiliated with the Communist party and the CIO with its stress on organizing the unskilled stimulated the concept of unionization in the 1930s as a viable economic strategy for Mexican-American workers. Furthermore, increased participation in unions symbolized the coming of age of Americans of Mexican descent, who, like their middle-class contemporaries, were now sufficiently acculturated to recognize and demand their rights as U.S. citizens. Rather than leading to conformity, Americanization or acculturation gave rise to protests in pursuit of American principles of democracy. Yet instead of concentrating on struggles over integration of public facilities and education, favored by the middle class, Mexican-American workers interpreted the achievement of civil rights in more economic terms. Hence, they sought integration into the mainstream of American life through the trade union movement. The elimination of job and wage discrimination—the Mexican jobs and Mexican wages of the Southwest—and economic equality with other U.S. workers constituted the major challenges and objectives for Mexican-American labor leaders.

This chapter examines the role of Mexican-American workers, both labor leaders and the rank and file, in the successful organization of the International Union of Mine, Mill and Smelter Workers in El Paso. Mine Mill traced its origins to the old Western Federation of Miners and possessed a history of labor militancy that included attempts to organize Mexican Americans and mexicanos in the mines and smelters of the Southwest. As a founding partner of the progressive CIO alliance in 1936, Mine Mill accelerated its strategy of linking class and racial issues in its effort to unionize unskilled national minorities such as Mexican Americans and Afro Americans. Mine Mill leaders pragmatically understood that without Mexican-American workers, mass unionization in the Southwest and along the U.S.-Mexican border would be a futile enterprise. Consequently, a symbiotic relationship commenced in the late 1930s between Mexican Americans and Mine Mill. Mexican-American workers looked to Mine Mill as a means of ending their second-class economic position and in return Mine Mill accommodated to the particular class, racial, and cultural position of Mexican-American and mexicano workers. Together, against major opposition they waged heroic but little-known struggles for the dignity of working people in the Southwest.[2]

Mexican Jobs and Mexican Wages

El Paso, and indeed the Southwest, proved to be a critical organizing challenge for Mine Mill. Located on the U.S.-Mexican border along the shores of the Rio Grande, El Paso exemplified the organizing problems that Mine Mill confronted. Since the late nineteenth century, the railroads had made this former desert hamlet into a southwestern commercial, mining, and ranching center of almost 100,000 people by 1920. Employers and entrepreneurs flocked to the border to take advantage of the city's location and, as importantly, its cheap labor market. Because of poverty and political revolution, Mexicans commenced the great migration from Mexico to the border between 1900 and the 1920s. As immigrant workers, Mexicans were grateful for available employment in border industries as the Southwest's economy, feeding raw materials to U.S. industries, became integrated with that of the rest of the United States. In El Paso the railroads, retail and wholesale houses, construction firms, urban services, and the expansive smelting plant of the Guggenheim-owned American Smelting and Refining Company (AS & R) employed thousands of Mexican immigrant workers as a nonskilled and low-skilled labor force that came to compose one-half the city's population. Employers profited from the work of Mexicans by paying them the lowest wages in the city. Facing both class and racial exploitation and discrimination—or what some scholars term a segmented or split labor market and what Mario Barrera calls "colonized labor"—Mexican immigrant workers were funneled into a dual occupational structure and a dual wage system. In comparison to Anglo workers, Mexicans were primarily restricted to nonskilled, dead-end manual jobs—the so-called Mexican jobs—and received for their labor what also came to be known as Mexican wages: lower than wages for Anglo workers and lower than for comparable work in areas outside the border district. Early border unionization, principally by the mostly conservative, elitist, and white American Federation of Labor, added to this dichotomy by opposing Mexican immigrant workers and by helping to exclude them from more skilled and better paying positions.[3]

The Great Depression, beginning in 1929, contributed to the burden of Mexican labor and labor in general in the Southwest. As in other regions, unemployment affected thousands of workers, especially the more vulnerable such as those of Mexican descent. Those not holding U.S. citizenship also faced deportation and repatriation pressures as many southwestern communities sought to deal with unemployment and increased job competition by victimizing Mexicans.[4] Yet too dependent on Mexican cheap labor and with its majority Mexican population, El Paso minimized this forced expulsion and continued to survive on the basis of cheap and unorganized Mexican labor. Two key border industries that displayed this reliance were the AS & R plant and the newer Phelps-Dodge refinery that began operations in El Paso in 1930. The largest industries in the city with the biggest payrolls both tapped the mining areas of Arizona, New Mexico, and northern Mexico for supplies of lead, gold, silver, zinc, and copper that were smelted and refined in the border city before being shipped to the industrial sections of the United States as well as Europe. Refining predominantly copper, the Phelps-Dodge plant, for example, contributed to El Paso's boast that it was the copper capital of the Southwest.[5]

Surviving the depression and expanding with the outbreak of World War II, the AS & R smelter and the P-D refinery employed hundreds of Mexican-American and mexicano workers from both sides of the border. Each plant in the late 1930s possessed between 500 and 600 laborers. As with other Mexican workers in the mining and smelting industries of the Southwest, those in El Paso continued to face both class and racial exploitation and oppression. "On the job, Chicanos were restricted to common labor positions," one historian writes, "featuring sub-standard job classifications and pay scales and lacking standard seniority provisions."[6] Of approximately 500 employees at AS & R about 400 were Mexican Americans or Mexican nationals and almost all were common laborers.[7] Humberto Sílex, an early Mine Mill organizer in El Paso, recalls that most employers in the 1930s paid as little as 9 to 10 cents an hour. When Sílex first worked at the AS & R plant in 1937, Mexican common labor received $2.06 for a 10–12-hour day and worked six days a week with no vacation time. By comparison, when Sílex had earlier worked in a Chicago smelter he had received $6–7 a day.[8] "The working conditions were the worst," Sílex further notes. Workers faced dirty, hard, and dangerous labor conditions. Managers employed few safety precautions and workers often faced injuries due to burns or falls.[9]

In addition, AS & R bosses forced their workers to purchase provisions at the company store. "If you didn't owe the store some money you were bound to be laid off pretty soon," Sílex remembers. "Every payday something was docked from your check."[10] Mexican workers further encountered discrimination in job mobility. Sílex, for example, although already an experienced fireman when first hired, began as a helper with an Anglo fireman and an Anglo assistant. Although both Anglos had less experience than Sílex, they received higher wages. Management paid the assistant a dollar more than Sílex and after a few months promoted him to fireman while Sílex remained a helper. When finally upgraded due to a job reclassification, Sílex still did not receive the accompanying wage increase. Indeed, management paid Mexicans with semiskilled jobs only 1 cent more than common laborers. With such low wages, workers found it difficult to provide for their family needs and children often went without necessities such as shoes. Discrimination at the plant further included segregated bathrooms and showers for whites and Mexicans.[11] Finally, many workers at the smelter had to live in depressed and dilapidated housing adjacent to the plant. Since the turn of the century, AS & R had leased the land to its employees, who constructed their own shacks. Smeltertown, as the area came to be called, was further characterized by lack of general sanitation. By the 1930s and 1940s, when the federal government financed new housing projects in the de facto segregated Mexican neighborhoods of south El Paso, most smelter workers could not afford to pay the rents. Those who lived across the border in Juárez possessed no better and probably worse housing.[12]

Unionization at the smelter was not totally nonexistent, but it did very little to increase wages and better working conditions for Mexicans. To circumvent New Deal labor legislation, such as the Wagner Act, and to prevent more progressive CIO organizing, the smelter in 1939 encouraged a company union affiliated with the AF of L. Ostensibly representing both the smaller number of Anglo craft workers and the larger mass of Mexican laborers, the Metal Trades Council and its affiliated federal union, the Smelter Workers Union, were under the control of Anglo leaders including some plant supervisors. The first contract signed by the union provided only a $1\frac{1}{2}$ cent raise for common laborers.[13] Paternalistic in its attitude toward the Mexican workers, the union constituted an additional form of labor control in the plant. "More harmonious relations have been brought about between workers and employers because of the willingness of the management to reach an agreement," a self-deluded Anglo leader of the union stated.[14]

Conditions at the Phelps-Dodge Refinery were no better. J. B. Chávez, who became one of the key Mexican-American leaders of Mine Mill in El Paso and the Southwest, remembered the state of affairs when he first began work at P-D in 1937. Job discrimination and job segregation were the norm at the plant. Chávez, for example, hired on as a furnace laborer while an equally inexperienced Anglo received an initial job as a furnace pipeman, a more skilled position. A dual job system based on race in turn created a dual wage system. Mexicans received less pay than Anglo workers. Chávez obtained about $17\frac{1}{4}$ cents an hour while the Anglo hired at the same time received more. "He was getting a dime more than I was because he was a *gabacho* (Anglo) and I was a Chicano." In Chávez's particular section of the plant, other Mexicans worked predominantly as common laborers. All worked a 40-hour week. Conditions, as at the AS & R plant, were hard and dangerous. Injuries were common, but the workers possessed no health benefits. A Mexican worker laid off due to an injury often was not rehired. Protective equipment such as safety shoes could be purchased only on credit with a downtown store that provided a kickback to a Captain Simpson, the head of security at P-D. Simpson, an ex-Texas Ranger, also forced Mexican workers to buy raffle tickets at a dollar a ticket for used radios he bought. If a worker refused to participate in Simpson's raffles, he would be fired. No Mexican ever won the raffle. Segregated bathrooms and showers also existed. Unlike at the smelter, a company union did not exist at Phelps-Dodge, and one Anglo AF of L union, the Bricklayers, had been crushed after the bricklayers had gone on strike. The company simply promoted and trained other workers to replace them.[15]

The CIO in El Paso

Initial contacts between the CIO and the Mexican smelter and refinery workers took place in late 1939, when a representative for the Packinghouse Workers arrived in El Paso to organize the local meat-packing plant. Nicaraguan-born Humberto Sílex described conditions at the smelter, and the CIO organizer promised to see about having a representative of Mine Mill come to El Paso and organize both the smelter and the refinery. A couple of months later, James Robinson, a long-time activist in Mine Mill and the father of Reid Robinson, the current president of the union, arrived in the border city. The elder Robinson met with Sílex and agreed that Mine Mill would undertake the effort to organize in El Paso. However, a problem that both Robinson and Sílex faced was Robinson's inability to speak Spanish and Sílex's lack of union experience. Both realistically agreed to take advantage of El Paso's border location and the particular nature of labor within a binational context. In a show of international labor solidarity, they asked the progressive Confederación de Trabajadores Mexicanos (CTM) in Juárez to lend one of their organizers to Mine Mill in El Paso. A CTM organizer would be helpful not only in providing Spanish-speaking labor experience but also because of the many smelter and refinery workers living in Juárez. The CTM assigned José Oaxaca to the task. A second CTM organizer later joined Oaxaca in El Paso. Oaxaca, Robinson, and Sílex organized initial small-scale meetings in the barrio. Others gradually agreed to join the union, either in Local 501 of the refinery or Local 509 of the AS & R Smelter. These recruits in turn encouraged their relatives and friends to join the union.[16]

At Phelps-Dodge, J. B. Chávez recalls that he was recruited by Alfonso Molina, who had earlier enrolled in Mine Mill. Chávez did not hesitate to join due to adverse working conditions at the plant and because his own father had been a member of the miners union in Mexico. Chávez notes that the main organizers at P-D were Mexican Americans like himself rather than Mexican nationals. This was a key distinction since, unlike earlier periods when Mexican immigrant workers who led and participated in strikes could be threatened with deportation, Mexican Americans as U.S. citizens had greater legal and constitutional protections. Moreover, Mexican-American workers like Chávez planned permanent residence within the United States as opposed to many immigrant workers who expected to return to Mexico.

"One of the first things we were told when we started to organize," Chávez stresses, "[was] that if we weren't U.S. citizens we should not be very outspoken or active, but the rest who were citizens should be very involved." [17] At the AS & R smelter, Sílex as secretary of Local 509 recruited natural Mexican-American leaders such as Ceferino Anchondo, who as a fireman had belonged to the AF of L company union. His recruitment by Mine Mill convinced still other Mexican-American and mexicano workers to join the union. [18]

Sílex explained to workers the benefits to be acquired from joining a CIO union rather than an AF of L one. A CIO union treated all workers as equals regardless of jobs and organized both craft and unskilled workers together in one union. An AF of L union, such as existed at the AS & R, unfairly divided workers by jobs and discriminated against unskilled labor. Sílex recalls that most Mexican workers preferred the CIO form of union. He and other Mine Mill organizers further informed workers that Mine Mill would be better able to achieve higher wages and more satisfactory working conditions. "We told them how a contract that gave the workers a cent-and-a half wasn't anything." Sílex remembers the main objectives of Mine Mill in El Paso:

> We wanted equal treatment. We demanded that companies such as American Smelting and Phelps Dodge that had plants, mines, and refineries all over the United States and in other parts of the world because they were large monopolies . . . that they pay us the same wages paid in Nebraska, in California. While in the Smelter in San Francisco the workers received five dollars a day, here workers received only two dollars a day. The same company paid the wages, the same work was involved, although perhaps under more difficult conditions. Hence, we asked for equality of wages and of work with other plants in other locations. We also asked for vacation-time and shift differentials. [19]

Still, it was not easy to recruit members to Mine Mill. One of the biggest challenges concerned the presence in the plants of sizable numbers of Mexican nationals living in Juárez. About half the workers commuted from the neighboring border city. Many stayed away from the union for fear of being harassed by U.S. immigration officials. To overcome these hurdles, Mine Mill, besides relying on CTM organizers in El Paso, utilized Spanish-speaking Mexican-American members who together with CTM officials in Juárez visited the homes of AS & R and P-D workers south of the border and encouraged them to join the union. This particular method of border organizing succeeded. Mine Mill also pursued its border strategy by securing the assistance of the Mexican consul in El Paso, who recommended that Mexican nationals become union members. [20] Early Mine Mill leaders understood the practical necessity of organizing Mexican nationals in El Paso including those without documents. "If there were [undocumented workers] we didn't know," Sílex notes. "To us it didn't matter."[21] Besides signing up workers inside the plants, organizers such as J. B. Chávez held union meetings in the numerous cantinas of south and east El Paso, common recreational centers for Mexicans in the city.[22]

Although Mine Mill succeeded in recruiting a good number of workers at both plants by 1940, it faced increased hostility by company officials as well as by local law enforcement authorities. AS & R management, for example, did everything it could to break Mine Mill unionizing efforts, including laying off workers who signed with the union. Bosses singled out leaders such as Sílex, whom they discharged in July 1940. Awaiting a National Labor Relations Board (NLRB) decision on his firing, Sílex found it difficult to obtain another job or to keep one due to what he considered blacklisting by the El Paso Chamber of Commerce. "Everywhere I went to work, they would give me a job and in a few days . . . they would say, 'Well, we don't need you. You're a troublemaker.'"[23] J. B. Chávez recalls that at one meeting of Local 501 Phelps-Dodge managers succeeded in intimidating many workers by waiting outside the assembly hall to record which employees attended.[24] Moreover, management secured the assistance of local immigration officials who harassed Mexican nationals working either at AS & R or P-D by threatening to deport them if they joined Mine Mill.[25] El Paso law enforcement officials led by County Sheriff Chris P. Fox added to the unionizing difficulties of Mine Mill. Discovering where the locals met, Sheriff Fox ordered his men to frighten the workers away. "We couldn't have an open meeting anywhere," Sílex explains.[26]

Mine Mill also faced increased competition from the AF of L, which, with the apparent sanction of both the AS & R and P-D, began drives to sign up Mexican-American workers. As one reporter noted, "El Paso has become the battleground of a jurisdictional struggle between the CIO and AFL for labor supremacy in the Southwest."[27]

Besides these antiunion tactics, red baiting and the linking of communism with the CIO and with Mexican aliens proved another obstacle for Mine Mill. El Paso's red scare was led by Sheriff Fox. Considering the CIO a front for the Communist party, Fox expressed alarm at CIO efforts in the border city. In early March 1940 without formal charges he arrested and held without bond six men whom he claimed were spreading communism in El Paso. Fox alleged that a letter sent by the Communist organizer in the Southwest to the head of the CP in Juárez urged a "hands across the border" policy between Juárez and El Paso Communists. The letter, according to Fox, stated that CIO unions in El Paso should eventually become part of the Communist movement. Fox claimed that U.S. and Mexican Communists had been lecturing to workers on what the sheriff called "cultural orientation." He considered such activity and propaganda to be seditious and noted that he had informed the House Un-American Activities Committee (HUAC) of the possible Communist threat along the border. Fox obtained information on the CIO from his employment of a Mexican-American labor spy, J. G. Escajeda. To corroborate Sheriff Fox's allegations, a special investigator for the HUAC Committee arrived in El Paso to study the growth of communism in the border city.[28]

After making his arrests, Sheriff Fox along with Acting County Attorney W. H. Fryer requested a court of inquiry before a local justice of the peace. The court subpoenaed thirteen persons, including the six arrested by Fox. Two of the arrested, Frank Sener and Domingo López, were both CIO organizers. A third, Alfredo Cásares, was accused of distributing Communist and CIO pamphlets in El Paso urging workers to join both organizations. Miguel Oaxaca, head of the CTM in Juárez, was described as a "writer" of Communist literature. Finally, Guadalupe Pedroza, an El Paso barber living in Juárez, and Joseph Mack Waller, an alleged CP official in El Paso, completed the list of detainees. Denying any link between the local court of inquiry and HUAC, Attorney Fryer engaged not only in red baiting but in what one historian terms the brown scare by attempting to link communism in El Paso with the presence of Mexican aliens:

> The audacity of aliens in coming into El Paso to actively, though secretly, attempt to plow the ground for the planting of the Soviet seed has been surprising. The more surprising fact, however, is that they have been aided and abetted by American Citizens.[29]

In his testimony, Fox implicated various people with alleged Communist subversive activity. He charged that several months earlier Communist leaders in El Paso had borne arms in attending a meeting in a south-side Catholic church hall with the intention of shooting anyone who objected to their distributing Communist literature. Fox also claimed knowledge about the formation of an El Paso unit of the Spanish-Speaking Congress "designed to instill in Mexican aliens living in the United States the principles of the Mexican Communist form of government." He attacked the CIO for authorizing local organizer Maurice Dineen to participate in what the sheriff labeled the "May Day Communist celebration" held in Juárez the previous year and stated that the CIO had instructed Dineen to do so as a Communist and not as a CIO member. Fox further accused Mrs. Katherine Winfrey, the wife of an inspector for the U.S. Bureau of International Revenue in El Paso, of being the "top" Communist in the city. The sheriff added that Waller, one of the men arrested, had admitted to being a Communist and a CIO official and that he had deliberately falsified the time of his joining the union in return for a promise that the CIO would fight his earlier dismissal from the Peyton Packing Company in El Paso. Fox's allegations were strengthened when Waller admitted to the falsification when called to testify before the proceedings. In addition, Fox charged that a large amount of Communist literature had been confiscated by his office. The sheriff concluded his statement by affirming the link between Communists in El Paso and the presence of Mexican aliens: "I began this investigation because I resented, openly and strongly, having Mexican aliens inject their form of government into our country." [30]

Inquisitor Fryer called other subpoenaed witnesses and attempted to draw out implications of ties between the Communist party and CIO organizing in El Paso. Fryer would later say: "To my mind, the hearing in El Paso establishes the fact that when you scratch the hide of a CIO member you find a Communist." The court of inquiry ended its one-day deliberations with the presiding judge concluding that communism needed to be "wiped out" and that criminal proceedings might be brought against one of the six men arrested. The sheriff released three of the men arrested but detained the others. In his column for the *El Paso Herald-Post,* Dr. B. U. L. Conner reiterated the antilabor sentiments voiced by both Fox and Fryer. "Labor unions are okay," he conceded, "but some of the labor leaders are either dumb, or nuts, the way they will get mixed up with Communism." [31]

The CIO responded to the arrests and to the red baiting by attacking Fox's violations of basic constitutional rights. James Robinson castigated Fox's efforts to discredit CIO organizing by suggesting Communist subversion. Robinson pointed out that evidence illegally seized and presented at the inquiry proved the opposite. The only un-American actions involved were those of the sheriff. López and Cásares, both U.S. citizens, had been apprehended without warrants or formal charges. The sheriff had placed them in jail, recorded and fingerprinted them as prisoners, held them incommunicado for two days and three nights, and subjected them to "third degree methods in an attempt to extort information of a connection between the local CIO and the Communist Party." Labor leaders labeled Fox's efforts as nothing more than a "witch hunt" and a "red-scare" deliberately aimed at preventing labor organizing along the border. "The CIO is engaged in the organizing of the unorganized, underpaid, ill-clothed, ill-fed and ill-housed workers," they concluded, "and we know of no place in the United States where a correction of these abuses is more necessary than in El Paso." [32] In support, Homer Brooks, secretary of the Communist party in Texas, noted that of the six arrested only one belonged to the Communist party, a membership not forbidden by law. The issue was not the Communist party and its legal right to exist and assist in the labor movement, Brooks proposed, but the overt violation of civil rights by Fox and his attempt to intimidate workers from their right to unionize.[33] "If they were [Communists] I didn't care," Sílex recalls of his association with Mine Mill organizers. "They were union men; they were officers of a good union and that's it."[34]

To further counter Fox, Mine Mill requested and obtained NLRB hearings concerning antiunion conditions at both AS & R and P-D. Besides utilizing labor spies, Phelps-Dodge, for example, harassed members of the union by firing those who attempted to sign up other workers. Robinson specifically charged at NLRB hearings in El Paso that the company had released seven men in early 1940 for participating in Mine Mill unionizing activity. Not afraid to testify, one Mine Mill member, Aurelio Zacarías, acknowledged that a P-D foreman had warned him that if he continued with the union he "was going to have a lot of trouble with the company." Eduardo Valdívez testified that the same foreman had cautioned him against outside agitators who wanted to raise salaries in El Paso. This, the foreman alleged, would hurt workers rather than helping them. "Mr. Purdy told me that the cost of living would go up if Phelps-Dodge raised wages," Valdívez stated, "because all other companies would also have to pay more and that they would then charge more for commodities." The foreman told Valdívez that such agitators needed to be put in concentration camps. Valdívez concluded his testimony by telling of seeing signs written by one employee that read: "CIO Is No Good." In addition, Mine Mill complained of efforts by P-D to establish an AF of L union and to pressure workers to support it. Another Mine Mill member, Domingo López, testified that officers and supervisors of P-D directed the company union. Finally, Mine Mill charged that the local Farmers and Merchants Association had conspired to block the CIO in El Paso. The association denied this but claimed that its goals consisted of driving out Communists and opposing radicals. Despite these obstacles, the union won its first major victory in El Paso when in February 1941 the NLRB ordered Phelps-Dodge to "cease and desist from discouraging workers at the El Paso plant," to drop recognition of the company union, and to reinstate three discharged employees who had been active in Mine Mill organizing.[35]

Successful in its challenge of Phelps-Dodge before the NLRB, Mine Mill in 1941 filed similar complaints against the AS & R smelter. Various Mexican-American workers courageously testified. Jesús García told an NLRB hearing in El Paso that the manager of the smelter, John D. MacKenzie, had instructed his foreman to pressure Mine Mill members to quit their jobs. Ceferino Anchondo, president of Local 509 and an AS & R employee for fourteen years, concluded that he had been fired for his union activities but that the smelter management had used the false pretext that he had attempted to cheat the company by tampering with an electric meter in the house he rented from the smelter. Anchondo further observed that one smelter foreman had warned him that he would be fired if he continued his affiliation with Mine Mill. Union leader Sílex added that he also had been fired on trumped-up charges. Such firings, Mine Mill asserted, added up to discrimination by AS & R against the union. Instead, the smelter favored the AF of L union in the plant and coerced workers to affiliate with it rather than Mine Mill. Trinidad García testified that an Anglo foreman gave him an AF of L membership application card and threatened: "If you don't join the AF of L, the CIO will close this plant down." The foreman approached other workers. Such company meddling in union affairs violated the National Labor Relations Act. David Díaz, another AS & R employee, told of seeing the head of the AF of L union in the smelter enter the plant and, accompanied by a smelter official, attempt to register recruits to his union. This proved AS & R's bias for the AF of L. "We . . . have several witnesses," James Robinson wrote to a fellow Mine Mill official, "who can prove that the A.F. of L. local at the Smelter is a company union." Unfortunately for the smelter workers, the NLRB in this case ruled in favor of the company and recognized the AF of L affiliate as the bargaining agent for the workers.[36]

Wartime Organizing

World War II, the war to save democracy and the struggle for the Four Freedoms, provided progressive unions such as Mine Mill with additional ideological support and inspiration for achieving union representation and equal justice for racial minorities. At its 1943 national convention, Mine Mill reaffirmed "its efforts in opposition to any and all forms of discrimination as to race, creed, color, nationality, religious or political believe, [*sic*] and pledge itself to work harder than ever before to erase prejudices of this kind wherever they may be found."[37] Mexican-American labor leaders hailed Mine Mill's commitment to achieving equality for Mexican-American workers and called for further assistance from the International board in Denver in securing union recognition.[38] Together with Harry Hafner, field representative of Mine Mill, Sílex and other Mexican-American members of Mine Mill at P-D worked to secure an NLRB-sanctioned election at the plant. Mine Mill understood the significance of a victory at Phelps-Dodge. "Here in the southwest," wrote Antonio Salcido, the president of 501, "the victory of the Phelps Dodge workers under the CIO banner will be a blow in the face of all the fascist-minded employers who utilize racial and national discrimination as a means of paying starvation wages."[39]

However, Mine Mill organizers at P-D found the road to an NLRB election to be rocky. Unable to collect adequate union dues from its El Paso locals, apparently the result of members' unfamiliarity with such contributions, the International dropped Sílex as an organizer at Phelps-Dodge in the midst of the drive to secure additional Mexican-American members of the union. Sílex expressed surprise at his dismissal and worried about the effects of such a change. "I have always thought that when I was put in our International's pay roll last month," he wrote President Robinson, "it was all due to the acknowledgement of the pains taking effort we have gone thru in this community to do what little we have done in behalf of the CIO and our movement in the midst of all these reactionaries [*sic*] enemies in El Paso." His dismissal might hurt morale and damage efforts for an election victory. "The election that is coming is not sure yet," Sílex concluded. "There is lots of work to be done, the boys here will not like this procedure in this delicate hour, we want to win here." [40] Although apparently Sílex did not continue as an organizer, he along with others at the P-D plant had succeeded in enrolling large numbers of workers. These included over a hundred female and black workers who had been brought in to replace Mexican-American employees recruited for service duty during the war. According to J. B. Chávez, the women performed the type of dirty work that the men did and proved to be loyal members of the union. Black workers, at first hired to vote against the union, also joined with their Mexican-American co-workers in endorsing Mine Mill. [41] In late May 1942, Local 501 petitioned the NLRB for an election. "With a majority of P-D workers here signed up with the MMSW," Hafner reported, "members and organizers are sure of winning the poll." Confident of victory, Mine Mill members formed rank-and-file organizing committees in each department of the plant along with grievance committees to formulate complaints to be used in contract talks with the company. [42]

During the last week of June, Mine Mill secured an election at Phelps-Dodge. Out of 385 ballots cast, Mine Mill received 267 while 107 voted for the AF of L union. Ten votes were challenged and one was void. "The victory of El Paso Refinery Workers Union 501," reported the *Mine Mill Union,* "at this important link in the great Phelps-Dodge chain was expected to boost MMSW prestige for other polls, particularly in the southwest, where several important elections are pending." [43] Besides Phelps-Dodge, Mine Mill through Local 509 won union recognition at the much smaller El Paso Brick Company with its predominant Mexican-American labor force. [44]

Mine Mill turned to achieving a similar victory at the larger AS & R smelter. Sílex, who had been rehired at the plant, led the campaign along with Ceferino Anchondo and outside organizers Leo Ortíz and Jess Nichols, the International representative. To prevent Mine Mill from achieving recognition, AS & R bolstered the AF of L company union by providing a 50-cent pay increase in July 1942. Undeterred and undaunted, Sílex and his fellow union leaders organized both inside and outside the plant. "Our work to this time has been under ground just to make these AFLERS think that we are asleep," Sílex wrote to the Denver office, "but we have organized a stewards committee that is active in all departments." This secret work succeeded in signing up over 100 members. Sílex then brought the campaign out into the open. He issued a bulletin notifying the company that Local 509 had enlisted the majority of workers. In addition, Mine Mill organized meetings within the plant. Outside the smelter, the union staged mass meetings at Smeltertown, where workers and families could attend. At one such assembly, 250 people participated. Organizer Nichols, apparently able to speak Spanish, visited the workers in their homes in both El Paso and Juárez and convinced many to sign up with Mine Mill. By late 1942, Local 509 petitioned the NLRB for an election. Nichols reported that out of 600 workers at the smelter, Local 509 had recruited 262. As the new year dawned, the NLRB sanctioned an election at AS & R for the first week in March. "[W]e are confident in winning the election," Anchondo wrote to President Robinson. During the campaign, Mine Mill organizers continued visiting workers in their homes and driving to the polls on election day those who did not have transportation. Mine Mill's patience and hard work paid off and the union scored a second major victory when the majority of workers voted for it.[45]

Part of Mine Mill's successful organizational strategy in El Paso as well as in other southwestern locations consisted of the close links developed by its Mexican-American leadership with the labor movement in Mexico and along the border. Sílex, for example, fostered relations with the Mexican Miners' Union in Chihuahua and, of course, with the CTM in Juárez. Such ties not only helped in organizing but in creating a communications network that helped influence mexicano workers not to scab at either the smelter or the refinery. Mexican-American leaders further understood that labor rallies around Mexican holidays such as the *Dieciséis de Septiembre* (16th of September—Mexican Independence Day) represented good organizing tactics among Mexican-American workers in the Southwest. Ethnicity and culture along with working-class solidarity had to be tapped. In addition, to celebrate Labor Day in 1942 Mine Mill helped organize a highly successful international labor day celebration supported by the CIO and AF of L in El Paso along with Mexican workers in the CTM. Local 509 raised funds for the event by hosting a dance and Sílex traveled to Chihuahua to encourage CTM participation. The celebration expressed international labor unity and provided support for the war effort. "As you know, our Country as well as Mexico has declared war against a common enemy," the chairman of the International Labor Day Celebration Committee told organized labor members in

El Paso. "Many of us are unable to shoulder a gun or fight in the front-line trenches, but we can in various ways make our selves felt in the home front." [46] Mine Mill and the CIO along with CTM leaders in Juárez formed an International Victory Committee. "The workers of North America are united with our working brothers in Mexico in the great fight that humanity wages against its greatest enemy, international fascism," Rodolfo Ingle, president of Local 501, and Sílex, president of Local 509, proclaimed before Mexican workers in Juárez in June 1943. [47] On July 4 of that same year, Mine Mill and the Railroad Brotherhood hosted another international labor day celebration, which featured Lombardo Toledano, the great Mexican labor leader. [48]

Unable to obtain initial contracts with either P-D or AS & R, Locals 501 and 509 appealed to federal regulatory agencies for redress of grievances. Mine Mill understood the need to have union representation on these agencies. It secured the appointment of Leo Ortíz and Ceferino Anchondo to the War Man Power Board. Despite obstacles, Ortíz and Anchondo not only aired grievances but won compensations. Besides the War Man Power Board, Mine Mill appealed grievances to the director of conciliation of the Department of Labor. Protesting through such federal agencies, the union won additional cases for its members. In October 1943, Local 501 received from the War Labor Board a favorable decision granting a wage increase of $11\frac{1}{2}$ cents an hour retroactive to October 1942. Each worker received back pay of almost $200 each. As a show of their loyalty to the war effort, union members purchased several hundred dollars worth of war bonds with some of their wage increase and voted unanimously to donate one day's pay to the community war chest. Throughout the Southwest, Mine Mill won various grievance cases for its majority Mexican-American members during the war years. Sensitive, however, to the charge that Mine Mill was only a Mexican union, the *Union News* of Morenci, Arizona, emphasized that Mine Mill had also won cases for its minority Anglo members. [49]

Patience and continued pressure along with federal support in the end succeeded. After a year and a half of negotiations, Phelps-Dodge agreed to a contract. The following year, despite many of the same obstacles, Local 509 at the AS & R smelter likewise secured a contract. And in June 1945, Mine Mill through Local 509 won an additional election and contract at the smaller Southwestern Portland Cement Company. Under provisions of the Phelps-Dodge contract, similar to the one at AS & R, the company finally recognized Local 501 as the sole bargaining agent for the plant's production and maintenance workers and agreed not to discriminate against union members. The contract provided for a union checkoff to ensure that the union received dues from members. Working hours were set at 40 hours per week and any employee working more than eight hours per day would be paid $1\frac{1}{2}$ times. The company consented to an immediate wage increase of $11\frac{1}{4}$ cents an hour.

Workers would receive one week's vacation at full pay. Seniority would be recognized with regard to advancement, retention, and reemployment. Phelps-Dodge further approved that "there shall be no discrimination against any employee because of race, creed, color or national origin." According to Sílex, the contracts also eliminated the company stores and sanctioned the earlier removals of separate bathroom and shower facilities at both the smelter and the refinery. The contract would be effective for one year. Signed in part by J. B. Chávez, the contract was published in both English and Spanish.[50]

The 1946 Strike

Although Mine Mill in El Paso succeeded in renewing contracts with both Phelps-Dodge and AS & R during the remainder of the war, Mexican-American employees of the plants persisted in condemning the continued dual job and wage system that affected them. These structural inequities plus the International's drive to achieve higher wages for all its members following the war led to the first significant strike carried out by Mexican-American members of Mine Mill in El Paso and proved to be a major test for Mexican-American union leaders.[51]

In February 1946 the International announced that, unless eighteen AS & R plants agreed to increased wages for workers plus acceptance of industry-wide bargaining, the union would proceed with a nationwide strike. Mine Mill called for the equalization of common labor throughout the AS & R plants and the end of regional wage discrimination. In El Paso the union demanded a 30 cent-an-hour increase for laborers, which would raise their pay to $9.90 a day, and insisted on a reduction of work hours, which had once again gone up to 48. It made similar demands on the Phelps-Dodge Corporation. At Phelps-Dodge, Mine Mill demanded a $2-a-day pay increase from the $4.90 minimum being paid. However, both AS & R and Phelps-Dodge rejected the wage increase and industry-wide bargaining. AS & R insisted that it had always negotiated with the union only on the basis of individual plants and that this process had been confirmed by the NLRB. Wages at the smelter, plant manager R. P. Bradford noted, represented the "highest wages or equal to the highest wages in any industrial plant in the area." Bradford discounted the idea of ending regional wage differentials and defended them on the basis of cost-of-living differences. As for work hours, he observed that the current 48-hour week would soon revert to a 40-hour one as more labor became available in the postwar adjustment period. Bradford reiterated that management was prepared to discuss issues, but only at the local level.[52]

Yet AS & R's wage offer in conjunction with a 40-hour work week would actually decrease weekly wages, Mine Mill contested. The union insisted on industry-wide bargaining and through its international headquarters announced that its members, including Local 509 at the El Paso Smelter, would strike nationally on February 25 if no settlement had been reached. With no agreement on that date, Mine Mill, like many other unions in 1946, struck the eighteen AS & R plants throughout the United States. It would be a long strike. In El Paso, 550 workers, almost all Mexican Americans or Mexican nationals, out of 650 employees left their jobs. Only laboratory and technical workers along with plant supervisors and foremen remained on duty. Local 509, avoiding mass picketing, stationed "observers" outside the plant. José Morales, vice president of the local, termed the strike a "peaceful one." Most workers stayed at home or in the union hall at Smeltertown as production at the smelter came to a halt. The *Herald-Post* criticized the strike and attempted to split Local 509 from the International by suggesting that it was not worth it for local members to lose more than $3,000 a day for a nationwide contract that would benefit only union leaders.[53]

A week later, members of Local 501 at the Phelps-Dodge refinery also walked out. Nearly 550 workers, predominantly Mexican Americans and Mexican nationals and almost all union members, refused to report for work. That morning 100 of them picketed outside the plant gates. They carried signs reading Higher Wages or Depression and We're For the Roosevelt Bill of Rights but did not interfere with officials and managers, who were allowed to drive into the plant. D. B. Apodaca, the vice chair of the strike committee, reported that the only thing approaching an incident was when one company official drove by the picket line. "We thought he went too fast," Apodaca told a reporter. He further announced that pickets would be on duty on four-hour shifts throughout the strike. Mine Mill members likewise closed other Phelps-Dodge plants in the country. In New Mexico and Arizona, some 6,000 workers, many Mexican Americans, went on strike. The *Herald-Post* estimated that the El Paso strike cost the workers $2,500 a day.[54]

Prepared for a lengthy strike and led by Mexican-American officers, Locals 501 and 509 aimed to maintain union solidarity and morale. Strikers picketed day and night at both plants as a show of force and to prevent employment of strikebreakers. A joint strike committee linked both locals together with Sílex, representing Local 509, as chairman of the committee along with Ignacio Tovar and J. B. Chávez of 501 as vice chairmen. Each member of the joint strike committee in turn directed a number of picketers. Ignacio Aguirre, for example, a member of the committee from Local 509, supervised 48 men who split round-the-clock duty at the smelter. "We have no need of a picket line now," Aguirre told a reporter in mid-March. "The men watch the Smelter and would report if they tried to bring in strike breakers. I could get a picket line in 30 minutes." Although for the most part peaceful, picketing had its hazardous moments. In late March, Chávez reported that some strikers outside the Phelps-Dodge plant had been attacked four times that day by unidentified persons who drove by the picket line. Chávez complained to local law enforcement officials, who promised to prevent future attacks.[55]

Picketing successfully discouraged strikebreakers and prevented management from using surplus labor along the border to break the strike. Both locals secured the cooperation of the CTM in Juárez, which promised not to allow workers to cross the border and scab at either plant. As a show of border cooperation and international solidarity, more than 500 Mine Mill members from El Paso led by Humberto Sílex marched with 10,000 Mexican workers in the May Day celebration in Juárez. Mine Mill strikers along with CTM members carried signs supporting the strike against AS & R and Phelps-Dodge as well as placards urging United Nations unity and calling for action against Franco in Spain. Other Mine Mill locals along the border, such as Local 470 in Douglas, Arizona, likewise received support from unionists and residents on the Mexican side of the border.[56]

The El Paso locals provided additional support to their striking members in other ways. Strikers received their last paychecks shortly after the strike commenced and hence the union had to meet the material needs of workers and their families. Mine Mill members had few options since the union constitution forbade them from seeking other jobs. Moreover, they were ineligible for state unemployment compensation benefits. Besides receiving some financial support from the International, both locals established a joint CIO Relief Committee to secure funds for the neediest strikers. From March 5 to July 1, the joint committee obtained over $5,000. To help feed its members, the union opened a soup kitchen at CIO headquarters in downtown El Paso for P-D workers and another at Local 509 headquarters in Smeltertown. Each day a kitchen committee from the two locals took sandwiches and hot coffee to pickets on duty. Some strikers were more fortunate than others, especially those who had some savings such as war bonds or those who had sons or brothers recently returned from the war with Army money. Others, of course, knew hardship and were prepared to endure more during the strike.[57]

As part of their strike strategy, the El Paso locals reached out to other CIO unions as well as the larger community for support. Members of the United Bakery Workers, Local 1145, for example, provided boxes of bread and doughnuts for meals prepared at the union halls. The CTM, besides discouraging scabs, donated financial support.[58] The locals organized community rallies where they solicited support and countered hostile publicity by taking their case directly to the public. At one large rally attended by between 1,500 and 2,000 persons, several speakers, including Tovar of Local 509 and Chávez of Local 501, addressed the audience in both English and Spanish.

President Robinson defended the strikers by pointing out that the workers had patriotically stayed on the job throughout the war and that they now deserved better treatment. Addressing the Mexican-American members of Mine Mill, Robinson first praised the efforts of the Southern Conference for Human Welfare, which had representatives at the rally. "You of Spanish speaking origin know you always get the dirtiest, lowest paid jobs in El Paso," he proclaimed. "But slowly democracy is coming to the South, with the aid of such organizations as the CIO and the Southern Conference for Human Welfare." Robinson further observed that the El Paso strikers were part of a national and global struggle against fascism and war. He concluded by recalling that some years earlier his father had been denied the use of Liberty Hall for a CIO meeting largely through the efforts of Sheriff Fox. This time, however, a strong Mine Mill could not be kept out of the hall. "We're back because we workers have organized, because workers have lost their fear of the boss," Robinson stressed. Other speakers included representatives from the CTM, the Locomotive Firemen and Enginemen, and the United Electrical Workers. An orchestra composed of strikers entertained the audience.[59]

Certain community sources responded to Robinson's and the strikers' appeal and provided assistance. One local restaurant patronized by Mexican Americans treated all 68 female members of Local 509 to free lunches. Mexican-American merchants donated food and money. "Business firms have made contributions along with others, and we appreciate them," J. B. Chávez told a reporter. "Our morale is high."[60] Various Anglo liberals formed the Citizens' Committee to Aid CIO Strikers, which raised $500 for food, medical supplies, and other necessities for the strikers. Other El Pasoans mailed contributions directly to the locals.[61] Despite this support, the more than 1,000 strikers and their families still faced much hardship during the prolonged strike. "We have received some local support financially," Ignacio Tovar wrote in early April to a fellow union member, "but funds are getting low, and we fear the reaction on the strikers when their children began [*sic*] to get hungry."[62]

Locals 501 and 509 also printed and distributed thousands of leaflets in both English and Spanish throughout the city and mailed circular letters requesting support from business and professional people.[63] They likewise responded to negative editorials in the local press. In late March, the *Herald-Post* accused Mine Mill of not being able to provide for its members and having to resort to charity. The newspaper reiterated its support for higher wages for the workers but also restated that an industry-wide contract was unrealistic. Hopeful of driving a wedge between the rank-and-file and union officials, the *Herald-Post* red-baited Mine Mill by asserting that its leadership was on the "pink side." It commented that Reid Robinson in his speech at Liberty Hall had criticized Winston Churchill but not Joseph Stalin. In a letter to the editor a few days later, J. B. Chávez countered those verbal assaults. He rejected the idea that Mine Mill was not well managed by observing its discipline during the war and its fulfillment of the pledge not to strike during the conflict. This was evidence of a well-managed union and indicated that "its members and its officers were patriotically devoted to making the implements needed to win the war." Chávez thanked the *Herald-Post* for endorsing higher wages for smelter and refinery workers but disagreed that industry-wide bargaining was unrealistic. If local managers at both AS & R and P-D possessed no power to negotiate on their own, it was ironic for them to insist that the locals do so. If nationwide negotiations suited the industry, so too did they for the union. Chávez also discounted the argument that it was impractical for El Paso workers to receive the same wages for similar work performed in other areas of the country. "We say that to discriminate against El Paso workers on a sectional basis is unrealistic," he wrote. "We believe that the differences in the cost of living between El Paso, and the North, East and Far West, if any is far less than your editorial assumes." Chávez added: "Since you are opposed to freight rate discrimination against the Southwest, why are you in favor of similar discrimination in wages?" He disagreed that an industry-wide contract would benefit only union officials and emphasized the democratic nature of Mine Mill. "Your statement that the leadership of the union is on the pink-side has a familiar ring," he noted in charging the *Herald-Post* of red baiting. Some senators and congressmen had similarly criticized Churchill without doing so to Stalin. "Does that make our congressmen 'pink' too? Communists, maybe?" Chávez concluded by stressing the patriotic character of Mine Mill members as exemplified during the war.[64]

Negotiations between Mine Mill and the companies continued during the course of the strike, but little movement toward settlement of the dispute was made. Early efforts by federal labor mediators likewise proved fruitless. A government fact-finding board recommended a compromise general wage increase of $18\frac{1}{2}$ cents an hour for 37,000 employees in the nonferrous metals industry, including over 1,000 strikers in El Paso. However, management refused a wage hike unless Washington approved an increase in the price of copper. In these unsuccessful efforts, Mexican-American labor leaders received their baptism in nationwide bargaining. For example, J. B. Chávez, representing Local 509 participated in some of the meetings of a federal fact-finding board in Denver. At the local level members of 509 spearheaded discussions on a compromise with AS & R officials in mid-May. They were led by Tovar as president of the local and Sílex as International representative along with Ceferino Anchondo. "We told the company we were willing to accept recommendations given by the Fact Finding Board to be applied on an industry-wide basis." Tovar informed a reporter. He regretted that smelter officials had rejected the compromise. After receiving a report on the meetings with AS & R, members of Local 509 unanimously voted to continue the strike. "Local 509 Special Meeting This Day Reaffirmed Determination on National Negotiations," J. B. Chávez wired Reid Robinson. "Strike Strong as First Day."[65]

A break in the strike finally came in late May, when the Office of Price Administration (OPA) granted a price increase to the companies. Negotiations resumed in Washington, D.C., between management and workers, and on June 11 Mine Mill and AS & R worked out a settlement. However, before being final the agreement would have to be approved by the locals. An elated Sílex and Tovar, as leaders of Local 509, believed that their members would ratify the agreement and end the long strike. In addition to a wage increase of $18\frac{1}{2}$ cents an hour for all smelter workers, 70 percent of them would receive additional pay hikes ranging up to $7\frac{1}{2}$ cents an hour. Tovar pledged that before ratification officials of the locals would make certain that strikers would not face discrimination by management and that retroactive pay granted under the agreement would be distributed in the near future and not several months later "in order to free Smelter employees of indebtedness they have incurred during the three-month strike." One day later, AS & R accepted such terms and 400 members of Local 509 met at CIO headquarters and unanimously approved the new contract. Tovar announced that members would report back to work the following Monday. Four days later, the furnaces of the El Paso smelter blazed again. Tovar, returning to work as a blacksmith, exclaimed to the press: "I am very happy. All of us are glad to be back on the job. It seemed good to have my forge going again." And in a telegram to the International office, Sílex notified it of the resumption of work and the jubilation of Local 509 members over the achieved unprecedented wage scale of $7.00 a day from the previous $4.90. "We are the best paid workers in the Southwest now," Sílex concluded. "Thanks C.I.O."[66]

Within three days, Phelps-Dodge also agreed to a contract. José S. Cordero, acting president of Local 501, cosigned the agreement in El Paso and presented the terms to an approving membership. Almost identical to the AS & R contract, the P-D one gave workers the $18\frac{1}{2}$ cent-an-hour increase with a majority of employees receiving an additional $7\frac{1}{2}$ cents an hour. Members of the local greeted the end of the strike with elation. J. Avena, a shipping department worker, commented to a reporter:

I'll be glad to go back to work. I'm tired of staying home during the day and reading the funny papers to my two kids. My wife has been asking me when I'll start working. Now my kids will be able to go to the picture show again, and get their allowances back.[67]

Francisco G. Villa, general chairman of the local strike committee, responded: "I'm happy the way things have turned out. That's the American way of fighting, when workers and company men can get together and talk things out." And Fred Rodríguez exclaimed: "Now I'll be able to buy my wife some dresses and shoes." [68]

One week later, members of Local 501 returned to work along with other Mine Mill workers throughout the country who ratified agreements with Phelps-Dodge. With satisfactory contracts between the union and other mining and smelting corporations such as Anaconda and Kennecott, the over-four-month strike came to an end. "This is the first strike won against the mighty Phelps Dodge Corp.," Reid Robinson told the *Herald-Post*. "The courageous stand of the workers through their union will bring many benefits not only to the employees themselves but to all of the communities where Phelps Dodge operations are located." J. B. Chávez congratulated his members in Local 509 for achieving the victory. "Credit is due to the fellows on the picket line, rather than union officials," he said. Although Mine Mill did not achieve formal industry-wide bargaining, negotiations with both AS & R and P-D had in fact been conducted at a national as well as local level. Moreover, while the union did not obtain the full range of wage hikes it sought, it did win important increases for workers. In El Paso, the new wage rates, while not completely eliminating the dual wage system affecting Mexican-American workers, did aid in closing the gap between El Paso wages and those paid in other parts of the country. Locally, it made members of Mine Mill among the highest paid industrial workers. "The vicious and discriminating wage differentials of the Southwest were struck a telling blow by additional increases won for workers at the El Paso plant," *The Union* noted of the AS & R contract. [69]

At both AS & R and P-D, common labor now averaged $87\frac{1}{4}$ cents an hour, the highest in the area. Other benefits included shift wage differentials of 4 cents and 8 cents an hour for the workers employed in the afternoon and night shifts, improved vacation schedules, and continuation of the checkoff system. The contract also reinforced seniority rights, which began to see Mexican workers receive promotion to the more skilled jobs such as motormen and mechanics. In return, Mine Mill, under a no-strike, no-lockout clause, agreed to refrain from striking until all grievances procedures outlined in the contract had been exhausted. Adding to the sense of victory, Local 509 led by Humberto Sílex along with a committee composed entirely of Mexican Americans two months later successfully negotiated a new contract with the Southwestern Portland Cement Company similar to the one with AS & R and P-D. "These new high levels of take-home pay have broken all records for this notorious low-wage area of El Paso," *The Union* observed, "where discrimination against Spanish-American workers had previously been the chief weapon of the bosses." [70]

Conclusion

The 1946 strike solidified Mine Mill's position in El Paso. The strike and indeed the entire struggle to bring CIO unionization to the border revealed the collective strength of Mexican-American workers in their efforts to eradicate humiliating class, race, and ethnic discrimination through such forms of labor control as the Mexican job and the Mexican wage. Part of the larger and younger generation of Americans of Mexican descent—the Mexican-American Generation—that came of age during the Depression and World War II, Mine Mill leaders such as Sílex, Anchondo, Chávez, and Tovar, as well as many of the rank and file, recognized as part of their "American heritage" the right to equal job opportunities and equal pay with other U.S. workers. However, their Americanization did not betray their class and ethnic solidarity with Mexican nationals who worked alongside and who also struggled to unionize the plants. Although part of a progressive union considered by some to be leftist, Mexican-American members did not possess a revolutionary class consciousness. But they identified with collective struggles as workers. Reform class solidarity was supported by increased ethnic awareness as Mexican Americans and Mexican nationals revolted against their dual exploitation. Workers of Mexican descent, whether U.S. citizens or Mexican nationals, identified with one another along both job and ethnic lines. A Mexican worker at either AS & R or P-D worked together with other Mexican workers, went home with other Mexican workers, drank in cantinas with other Mexican workers, and lived in the barrio with other Mexican workers. Border conditions which historically had created an expansive Mexican working class on both sides of the border also made it difficult to divide that working class by playing on ethnic prejudices as occurred in more heterogeneous working-class communities in the East and Midwest. The working class in El Paso, with the exception of a distinct minority of skilled Anglo workers, was composed predominantly of Mexicans. The smelter and refinery might have been better able to exploit differences between Mexican Americans and Mexican nationals. However, ethnic and even family ties as well as an international consciousness encouraged by Mine Mill prevented such possible divisions.

Further key variables in Mine Mill's success among Mexican Americans involved the union's ability to adapt to the particular class and ethnic character of the border country and a more favorable climate for unionization in mass industries due to New Deal labor supports. Moreover, multinational corporations such as AS & R and P-D proved in the end more flexible in a period of economic expansion to adjust to unionization. This would be less true for locally owned industries. Although CIO unionization in both the smelter and refinery assisted in beginning to eradicate Mexican jobs and Mexican wages in these two border industries, it did not affect many other Mexican workers in El Paso. Class and race segmentation founded on a cheap labor culture continued to characterize the border city's labor market. In fact, job and wage improvements for some due to unionization in time created a chasm between better-off Mexican-American union members and Mexican immigrant workers, especially the undocumented, who flocked to the border.

Still, the courageous and successful struggle to establish Mine Mill in El Paso as well as elsewhere in the Southwest represented a historical leap forward. Unionization brought relative material gains and economic security as well as constituting another "step," as one Chicano historian puts it, in the evolution of a Mexican-American working class in the United States.[71] Mexican-American workers in Mine Mill were not yet a class totally conscious of itself as a class, but they understood that only as a collective movement and through struggles against employers rather than through individual measures could they gain some of the fruits of their production. Power relationships between workers and bosses may not have been fundamentally altered through these struggles, but workers did gain greater leverage and protection against the most overt forms of labor exploitation. These gains, of course, had been the products of dedicated struggle and in these efforts some became victims of the union's success. Sílex, for example, during the late 1940s was singled out as an alien and barred from participating as an officer in Mine Mill due to the nativist bias of the 1947 Taft–Hartley Act. Unsuccessful but trying deportation proceedings were likewise instituted against him. Sílex never worked with Mine Mill again.[72] Mine Mill as a whole would face more obstacles and challenges because of the cold war and McCarthyism, which led to the union's expulsion in 1950 from an increasingly conservative CIO and subsequent efforts by the U.S. Steelworkers to raid Mine Mill's membership. Yet the majority of Mexican Americans within Mine Mill, led by leaders such as Sílex, Chávez, and Anchondo, remained loyal to a union that had been good for them and that had helped them gain a sense of dignity.[73]

CHAPTER EIGHT

Mexican-American Radicals and the Cold War: The Asociación Nacional México-Americana (ANMA)

> This new generation rejects the old methods and concepts of seeing and doing things. For example, it rejects the pernicious nationalism which argues that we cannot confide in anyone else but Mexicans and that only Mexicans themselves are capable of solving their own problems. Naturally like one of the great Negro leaders of the past has said "Whoever wishes to be free must take the first step." However, we also know that we cannot take the second step without the support and cooperation of the working class movement and the other minority communities of this country. We also reject those anti-Mexican concepts and myths that suggest that we are a weak and inferior people. Instead, armed with more education, the new generation of Mexicans has swept away all of this ideological garbage and marches with firmness and determination to its proper destiny.
>
> ALFREDO MONTOYA,
> *Progreso*, January 1953

Despite the onset of the cold war and the beginnings of McCarthyism by the late 1940s, Mexican-American radicals, like middle-class activists, did not remain dormant. The demise of the militant Spanish-Speaking Congress during the war only temporarily halted the Left tradition in Mexican-American politics. As noted in chapter 7, Mexican-American labor leaders in progressive unions such as Mine Mill successfully continued to organize among Mexican-American workers along the border as well as elsewhere in the Southwest during the 1940s and 1950s. Yet trade-union organization was not sufficient to deal with the varied problems and issues relevant to the majority of Mexican-American working people. A political movement, similar to El Congreso, was likewise needed. Consequently, the late 1940s and early 1950s—a period labeled by historian Rodolfo Acuña as "the decade of defense" for Mexican Americans—witnessed the emergence of a second major Mexican-American left leadership and organization: the Asociación Nacional México-Americana (ANMA).[1] Like its radical predecessor, the Spanish-

199

Speaking Congress, ANMA stressed Popular Front strategies and a multi-issue program on such issues as the peace movement, workers' struggles, the plight of Mexican undocumented workers, housing needs in the Southwest, education, Mexican-American political representation, youth work, the promotion of Mexican-American culture, and police brutality.

The Formation of ANMA

ANMA was mostly organized by Mine Mill through the union's national headquarters in Denver. This militant union, of course, by the late 1940s had organized many of the major mining and smelting regions of the Southwest. Heavily red baited, some of its national officers suffered political persecution, especially during the 1950s, as alleged Communists. The CIO expelled Mine Mill in 1950, along with several other unions, on the charge of being Communist dominated. In New Mexico, Arizona, as well as in El Paso, Mine Mill consisted almost exclusively of Mexican Americans and Mexican nationals. By the early 1950s the three El Paso locals contained more than 2,000 workers, almost all of Mexican descent and led by Mexican-American officers. With such an important Mexican-American membership, the union believed that ANMA could function as its political arm in the Mexican-American communities of the Southwest.

The call for the establishment of ANMA initially originated from Mine Mill members along with other Mexican-American CIO leaders who had participated in the campaign of the Independent Progressive Party (IPP) to elect former Vice President Henry Wallace as president of the United States in 1948. To support the Wallace effort, endorsed by most of the Left including Mine Mill and indirectly by the Communist party, Mexican Americans in the Southwest organized chapters of Amigos de Wallace. At a regional conference of these chapters in El Paso during the fall of 1948, the participating delegates agreed to meet again in a second conference with the intent of forming "a permanent national organization to defend the rights of the Mexican-American people." The delegates further stressed: "The time has come when the Mexican people *must* and *can* form a strong, militant national organization to which the individual can look for protection; and through which the entire Mexican population and its friends and allies can fight for first-class citizenship." [2]

About fifty delegates answered the call and organized ANMA at a two-day meeting in Phoenix on February 12 and 13, 1949. They came, according to an ANMA history, from the sugar-beet fields of Colorado, from the factories of Los Angeles, from the mines of New Mexico, and from the cotton fields of Arizona and Texas. They assembled to establish an organization which would provide a "new voice" for Mexicans north of the border. In fact, most of the delegates, almost all Mexican Americans, came from southwestern locals of Mine Mill although some represented other militant CIO unions such as the furniture workers and the electrical workers. ANMA was to constitute "a national association for the protection of the civil, economic, and political rights of the Mexican people in the United States as well as for the expansion of their education, culture, and progress."[3] Any person or organization interested in the progress of "el pueblo mexicano" could join ANMA regardless of citizenship, nationality, color, religion, or political affiliation. Like the Spanish-Speaking Congress and unlike LULAC, ANMA did not insist on U.S. citizenship for membership. Yet like LULAC, ANMA projected itself as a broad civil rights organization that could be accepted in the barrios as a Mexican-American entity—an identity that Mexican-American labor leaders believed still did not apply to trade unions. The first executive board reflected ANMA's base in the labor-left movement of the Southwest. Alfredo Montoya, ANMA's first and only president, was in 1949 a twenty-seven-year-old Mine Mill organizer from New Mexico. Vice President Isabel Gonzáles, also of New Mexico, had served as national president of Amigos de Wallace and possessed Mine Mill connections. Calling attention to the radical tradition in Mexican-American politics, publicity director Ramón Welch of California had been a founder and leader of the Spanish-Speaking Congress and, according to former Communist party member Dorothy Healey, a member of the CP during the period of the congress.[4]

The objective conditions for the founding of ANMA centered on the particular plight of Mexican Americans and Mexican nationals during the postwar period. Despite certain economic improvements during the war and gains in political and civil rights, Mexicans in the United States still represented, according to ANMA, second-class citizens. ANMA recognized that racial minorities such as Mexicans and blacks received "special treatment" in the form of greater economic insecurities, lower wages, inferior education, and suffered more than whites from recent rollbacks of New Deal welfare services. "What is even worse," ANMA proclaimed, "the Mexican people are objects of an accelerated program of discrimination, deportations, physical assaults, police brutality, and, at times, murder." In addition, Mexicans in the United States continued to suffer cultural discrimination and the stereotyping of Mexicans as lazy, passive, and inferior people. With such conditions plus the ascendance of political right-wing reaction in the country, ANMA concluded that the time was ripe for organizing all Mexicans into a national organization for ethnic self-defense. This was no time for distinctions among the 4 to 5 million people of Mexican descent. ANMA believed that earlier attempts by others to unite Mexicans had been characterized by false leaders and by betrayals, but it emphasized that Mexicans, despite standard stereotypes, could in fact be organized. ANMA hoped to be the vehicle for such unity especially among workers, intellectuals, youth, and professionals.[5]

From Phoenix, ANMA state conventions were held in Colorado, New Mexico, Arizona, and California. At the California founding convention in Los Angeles in October 1949, more than 115 delegates assembled in the Centro Aliancista Hall. Like its radical predecessor the Spanish-Speaking Congress, ANMA stressed Popular Front tactics, and hence the listed sponsors of the convention represented a diverse group of liberals and radicals. These included writer-civil rights activist Carey McWilliams; former state attorney general Robert W. Kenny; the Reverend Oscar Lizárraga; state CIO president James Daugherty; Aaron Heist of the American Civil Liberties Union; Charlotta Bass, publisher of the *California Eagle,* an Afro-American newspaper; and William Elkonin of the United Electrical Workers. Other organizations supporting the convention were the Alianza Hispano-Americana, the International Workers Order, the IPP, the Hidalgo Society, the Carmenita Women's Club, and the New Mexico–Arizona Social Club.[6] Rafael Cuarón of the furniture workers union and the national executive secretary of ANMA observed that the Los Angeles meeting marked one additional step in the formation of a viable Mexican-American national organization.[7]

Local chapters of ANMA sprang up throughout the Southwest. These included Phoenix, Tucson, Denver, Albuquerque, El Paso, San Antonio, San Jose, Santa Clara, Grant County in New Mexico, Miami and Morenci in southern Arizona, Santa Fe, Taos, Carlsbad in New Mexico, Oakland, Contra Costa County in California, Berkeley, San Francisco, Hollister, and Watsonville in California. In Southern California, ANMA chapters in Los Angeles and surrounding communities formed in Boyle Heights, Maravilla, San Fernando, Downey, Estrada Courts, Lincoln Heights, Stanton, Hicksville, Van Nuys, and Hollywood. Outside the Southwest, an ANMA chapter operated in Chicago. ANMA further claimed contacts in Utah, New York, San Diego, and Dallas. Total membership in ANMA is difficult to gauge. In 1950 it reported a membership of 4,000 with more than thirty locals. However, in another report that same year ANMA recorded a membership of 50,000 with thirty-five locals. The truth is probably closer to a few thousand even though active members are also difficult to estimate since in some locals an overlap existed between ANMA membership and Mine Mill union membership. Montoya remembers that no more than 2,000 paid members, mostly Mexican-American CIO trade unionists, belonged to ANMA.[8]

Having organized at the state and local levels, the first national convention of ANMA took place on October 14 and 15, 1950, in Los Angeles with eighty delegates and observers representing thirty-five locals in six states.

The delegates approved a far-ranging constitution that stressed ANMA's basic objective as being "to struggle for the recognition, protection and full development of the human, civil, economic, educational, cultural, civic and social rights of the Mexican people, and the Mexican-American, in the United States." In its General Principles, ANMA committed itself to five basic goals: (1) the political unification of Mexicans in the United States, (2) the achievement of basic democratic rights for all Americans, (3) the development of ethnic and political awareness, (4) the renewal of familiar ties with Mexicans south of the border, and (5) the operation of ANMA on the basis of democratic practices. Resolutions adopted at the national convention reflected the persistent problems facing Mexican Americans and outlined the praxis ANMA would follow. They included those on public housing, civil rights, mass deportations, constitutional rights, women, and cooperation with trade unions.[9]

Finally, a word should be said about the role of the Communist party in the formation of ANMA. Although the FBI claimed that ANMA was controlled by the CP, no direct evidence is provided through the Freedom of Information Act to substantiate such a charge nor were any ANMA members ever indicted or convicted of illegal or "subversive" acts. On the other hand, as in the case of the Spanish-Speaking Congress and Mine Mill, it appears that Mexican-American members or sympathizers of the CP or those who had gravitated to a more radical position did play a role in the organization and guidance of ANMA. These individuals were not, despite FBI insistence, subversives or dupes of the Soviet Union. Instead, they were Mexican Americans who had inherited an organic Mexican-American radical tradition and who, owing to their involvement in CIO organizing efforts, had found in the Communist party a militant and supportive ally in the struggle to achieve democratic rights. As revisionist historians have documented, the CP played an important reform role within both the labor movement and the campaigns of oppressed minorities. The CP can be seen as a product of a distinct U.S. experience rather than as a foreign intrusion into American politics.[10] Committed to a Popular Front strategy arising from the absence of objective revolutionary conditions in the United States, the CP since the 1930s had essentially represented an advanced reformist albeit militant political organization. It downplayed its role during the war but surfaced again in the postwar period and despite initial cold war pressures played an active part in labor and minority affairs. At its 1948 convention, for example, the CP took strong positions on Afro Americans, Puerto Ricans, and Mexican Americans. In its "Resolution on Party Work Among the Mexican-American People," written by the Mexican-American Commission of the CP in Los Angeles County, the party stressed building the CP among "this oppressed section of the working class." To do so, the party accepted various tasks. They included increased internal discussion of the Mexican question in the United States in order to arrive at a scientific analysis; the distribution of Spanish-language political literature on Mexican Americans as well as on Mexico and Latin America; the sponsorship of schools in the Southwest for the "training of Mexican cadres"; support of the Mexican-American electoral movement through the organization of Amigos de Wallace clubs; and intensification of the struggle within the unions for the integration of Mexican-American workers and the end to job discrimination against Mexican Americans.[11] Moreover, the CP provided ANMA with media coverage through the party's West Coast newspaper, the *People's Daily World.*

Class, Race, and Culture

Ideologically, ANMA, while forging a reform program, voiced radical views within the context of Mexican-American politics. Its interpretation of Mexican-American history, for example, had a different emphasis from that of LULAC. Whereas LULAC through the influence of historians like Carlos Castañeda concentrated on the Hispanic foundation of the Southwest to convince Anglos of the integral role played by people of Spanish-Mexican descent in U.S. history, ANMA instead focused on the conquest of northern Mexico by the United States in the mid-nineteenth century. For ANMA, Mexican-American history had commenced in violence, conquest, and the subjugation of the resident Mexican population. While not advancing what in the 1960s and 1970s would be referred to as "internal colonialism," ANMA did urge the role of conquest. Because Mexicans had been annexed through force rather than voluntarily entering the United States, in the Southwest they possessed a culture and tradition quite different from the rest of the country. These differences had been recognized by the Treaty of Guadalupe Hidalgo, which ended the Mexican War in 1848 and had promised to protect the Mexican's distinct culture and heritage. These guarantees, however, had not been fulfilled and arriving Anglos had abused the Mexican's culture, language, political rights, and economic holdings. Consequently, since 1848 Mexican Americans or what ANMA called "el pueblo olvidado"—the forgotten people—had been treated as an underclass of American citizens. Such a legacy, moreover, continued into the twentieth century, when southwestern economic concerns imported and exploited thousands of Mexican immigrant workers. Important as cheap labor during boom times, Mexicans also served as surplus labor and hence in the depressed 1930s faced unemployment, deportations, and forced repatriations. This historical experience, according to ANMA, had created much adversity for Mexicans in the United States.[12]

Unlike other Mexican-American civil rights organizations which stressed only unity through citizenship as well as ethnic ties, ANMA also emphasized

unity through the fundamental working class nature of the Mexican population in the United States. Ninety-five percent of Mexicans north of the border
were workers, and ANMA believed this condition to be not only objective
grounds for organization but proof of the inescapable bonds between Mexican Americans and the union movement. Alfredo Montoya observed that
what progress Mexican workers had achieved during the past fifteen years
had been due to the gains made possible by southwestern industrial unions
which had organized Mexican workers. If the unions had recognized that unorganized Mexicans only weakened the labor movement, so too had Mexican
workers come to realize that if the unions were destroyed they would also
suffer and lose their hard-fought gains.[13] Noting that the aspirations and
needs of Mexicans in the United States were fundamentally identical with
those of the trade unions and stressing the basic working-class character of
Mexican Americans, the first ANMA national convention resolved: "That
. . . all members and leaders of ANMA not . . . lose a single opportunity to
cement relations with the trade unions on the basis of mutual respect and solidarity."[14] ANMA did not proclaim what can be considered a revolutionary
class position calling on Mexican workers to overthrow capitalism and erect a
socialist society. One could have been indicted and sent to prison for holding
such views during the McCarthy period. Yet ANMA did bring attention to
the working-class condition of most Mexicans, their class interests with other
workers, and the exploitative nature of the class system in the Southwest. An
economic elite exploited Mexicans as cheap labor and in turn amassed great
profits.[15]

If ANMA recognized class in the formulation of its ideology, it also
paid attention to the realities of race and culture. Mexicans were exploited as
cheap labor, but they were also oppressed as a distinct ethnic racial community. ANMA in its short existence did not produce a sophisticated theory on
race and class, but it did make it clear that Mexicans along with blacks faced
double oppression. In a 1952 editorial, *Progreso,* ANMA's newspaper, commented that the Mexicans' participation in the class struggle had to directly
contend with ethnic/racial segregation and discrimination. Such conditions
aided in reducing the Mexicans' standard of living and forced them to accept
hard, dirty, and cheap jobs. Besides suffering abuse in employment, Mexicans likewise faced discrimination in housing, education, political representation, public services, and other areas. Racism, according to ANMA, had
become so pervasive and destructive that some Mexican Americans believed
themselves inferior to Anglos and attempted to pass as "Spanish Americans"
or "nice Mexicans," as ANMA referred to them. These types of Mexican
Americans either blamed other Mexicans for the existence of discrimination
or else pretended it did not exist. However, ANMA observed that few Mexicans, regardless of skin pigmentation and class background, successfully es-

caped prejudice. It recalled that recently even Edward Roybal, Los Angeles's only Mexican-American city councilman, had been refused the sale of a home because he was of Mexican descent. ANMA further noted how the postwar housing boom permitted poor whites, but not Mexicans, to purchase homes. An exploitative class structure fueled racial/ethnic prejudice and discrimination. ANMA saw racism directly linked to a white ruling class and did not associate all whites, especially workers, with the perpetuation of such a system. ANMA would struggle alongside Anglo workers who also desired to eliminate racism. All workers would benefit from the elimination of an underclass of cheap labor. To ANMA both class and race had to be considered in developing a strategy for the liberation of Mexicans in the United States.[16]

ANMA complemented its views on race and class by its discussion of culture. Although Mexicans in the Southwest had been deprived of an autonomous cultural development, they still possessed a distinct culture which needed protection and encouragement and could also be an objective basis for political organization. "In the Southwest there are between four and five million Hispanos and Mexican Americans," an ANMA report stated. "Some have been here a few generations. Others several centuries. We are all united in a common bond of language, culture and way of life."[17] Employing a popular approach to culture, ANMA promoted a form of cultural nationalism. It acknowledged the Mexicans' distinct cultural heritage in the Southwest and praised efforts at cultural resistance. "This struggle is a cultural struggle," read a resolution on cultural freedom adopted by ANMA's second national convention in El Paso in 1952, "not only on behalf of Mexican-American people but on behalf of building a cultural democracy, our culture and our customs."[18] Yet Mexican-American culture had come under a more aggressive attack in the early 1950s. The cold war, McCarthyism, and the "Great Fear" had resulted not only in violations of civil liberties and constitutional protections, unjust arrests, and deportations of so-called subversives, but also in an irrational apprehension over anything considered un-American. Consequently, Mexican Americans and Mexican nationals faced heightened cultural prejudice.[19]

ANMA countered this cultural attack on Mexicans in the United States by calling on Mexican Americans to rediscover their cultural roots both in the Southwest and in Mexico. "Therefore, in the ANMA we insist that the Mexican people never completely integrate themselves in all aspects of the national life of this country," Montoya declared concerning cultural nationalism, "at least that they be permitted to develop their cultural forms toward their flourishing, including the use of their language."[20] Only by being proud of their culture and by promoting it could Mexican Americans enrich the cultural life of the United States and achieve mutual respect with other ethnic groups. Cultural revitalization or cultural nationalism, however, necessitated replacing false consciousness regarding identity, which rejected one's Mexican heritage, with a new cultural and ethnic awareness.[21]

Although ANMA encouraged cultural nationalism, it did not advance a theory of nationhood for Mexican Americans similar to that developed, if only briefly, by the Communist party for Mexicans in the United States. "I always rejected the concept of a separate nation," Montoya recalls of this issue.[22] On the other hand, the CP, in supporting ANMA's analysis of Mexican Americans as a "conquered people" and by comparing their oppression with that of blacks in the South, flirted for a time with the concept of nationhood for Mexicans in the United States. Regarding Mexican Americans as an extension of Mexico and hence possessing all the attributes of a nation including an economic base, the CP called for some type of possible reunification of Mexican Americans in the Southwest with Mexico.[23] ANMA did not go so far and instead stressed the political integration of Mexican Americans through the acquisition of civil rights and the acceptance of cultural pluralism whereby Mexican culture would be given due recognition in the United States. While ANMA endorsed ethnic and cultural nationalism, it insisted, as had the Spanish-Speaking Congress, that its basic aims were reformist in nature and consisted of the full attainment by Mexican Americans of democratic rights as provided in the U.S. Constitution. The goal was integration, although along pluralist rather than melting pot lines, or as Montoya put it, "what we used to call in those days first-class citizenship."[24] ANMA brought attention to the ethnic and cultural ties of Mexican Americans with Mexico but emphasized that they represented an American or U.S. movement. ANMA saw in its own militancy a new generation of Mexican Americans who no longer asked but demanded their rights as U.S. citizens.[25] Unlike its predecessors, this new generation—the Mexican-American Generation—had been educated and socialized in the United States and they knew their rights and expected them. *Progreso* noted in 1953:

> But this is a new era. The Mexicans of today are not the Mexicans of yesterday. We cannot be as easily deceived as before. We may still be slandered and attacked, but we will not be allowed to be deviated from our goals. The new Mexican generation has removed from its eyes the veil of ignorance, of disunity, and of the old and erroneous concepts. We are conscious of our constitutional rights and we intend to achieve them through legal and effective means.[26]

In fighting for the rights of Mexican Americans, ANMA also believed it important to encourage an internationalist consciousness. This was of particularly keen concern with respect to Mexico and the rest of Latin America.

It claimed, for example, that Mexicans in the United States represented mirrors reflecting U.S. attitudes and policies toward Latin America. If the United States treated Mexican Americans as second-class citizens, so too did it deal with Latin America as an inferior entity. Discounting specific differences, ANMA proposed the interrelationship between Mexican Americans and Latin Americans to be crucial and that the struggle for Mexican-American liberation was linked with that of Latin America. "[A]s long as this country takes unjust advantage of those people south of the Rio Bravo [Grande]," Alfredo Montoya concluded, "we shall never achieve what we are struggling for—first class citizenship." [27] Calling on Mexican Americans to shun the idea of a frontier between themselves and Mexico, ANMA proclaimed its defense of the rights of Mexican nationals in the United States and promised to maintain and develop ties of solidarity with Mexicans south of the Rio Grande in their struggles and in adherence to a common history, culture, and tradition. At its first national convention, ANMA pledged itself to this "Mexican connection." [28]

ANMA advocated a domestic united front in addition to international solidarity. It opposed sectarianism and called for alliances with other Mexican-American organizations subscribing to similar general principles and goals. A divided people would never alter their conditions, but united Mexican Americans could. "The situation and the times does not allow us the luxury of jealousies, distrusts, and suspicions amongst us," Montoya appealed. "Such characteristics are almost semi-feudal vestiges which in the past have fatally damaged our cause. For this reason, our organization is ready to cooperate with others whose aim is to improve the lot of the Mexican people, and who believe in cooperation based on mutual respect and benefit." [29] ANMA, unlike most middle-class-oriented Mexican-American groups, aspired to a united front with other oppressed peoples within the country, in particular blacks and Jews. Mexican Americans represented only one of several minorities, who in some cases were worse off than Mexicans. The struggle and gains of one aided those of the rest. [30] "We should unite with Blacks who suffer similar conditions as our own, and in this way reinforce both groups," an ANMA official exhorted. [31] ANMA believed such a coalition, including progressive labor unions, indispensable to the Mexican-American cause.

Political Praxis: The Peace Movement

Linking ideology to praxis, ANMA developed a varied political program between 1949 and 1953. Responding to the cold war and U.S. military intervention in Korea, ANMA placed a high priority on supporting the peace movement in the country and throughout the world. This was no easy task due to the hostile and accusatory attitude of McCarthyism, which questioned the patriotism and loyalty of any American who protested the cold war and the U.S. role in Korea. Despite these intimidations, ANMA encouraged other Mexican Americans to stand up for peace in Korea and for the easing of tensions between the United States and the Soviet Union. In 1950, for example, ANMA along with other organizations in Los Angeles participated in a two-day weekend mobilization to circulate the Stockholm Peace Appeal calling for an end to the cold war. "The biggest danger which exists today is the danger of another war," Alfredo Montoya warned. "We, the Mexicans, recognize the sacrifices and horror of war. During the last war our people sacrificed more lives in proportion than any other group in the country. This is the reason why the Mexican people want peace." [32]

Shunning a provincial political outlook, ANMA tied domestic reforms for Mexican Americans with the issue of world peace. "Progress cannot be made in a state of war," it declared. "For the well-being and progress of the people we must have peace." Encouraged by the community's response to the peace movement, Virginia Ruiz, ANMA's executive secretary, announced in 1950 that more than 20,000 Mexican Americans had signed the Stockholm petition. In addition, various ANMA locals invited peace advocates to address the membership. One speaker who had participated in the 1951 Warsaw Peace Conference further encouraged ANMA's involvement in the peace movement. "The sentiment for peace is there among the people," she observed. "It is up to such organizations as ANMA and the unions to give them the answers and leadership on the road to peace." Peace also included disarmament and an end to the production of atomic bombs. "They forget to tell you that an Atomic Bomb is not a national catastrophe like an earthquake," Professor Philip Morrison told an ANMA sponsored meeting on the nuclear threat. "Its fall can be predicted. It can be stopped, and furtherance of the peace movement is the rational system for defense of the A-Bomb." And in San Francisco the ANMA local held a fund-raiser to assist one of its members, Abagail Álvarez, to attend the Hemispheric Peace Conference in Mexico City. [33]

The U.S. intervention in the Korean conflict in 1950 only accelerated ANMA's commitment to the peace process. Like the later Chicano Generation of the 1960s and 1970s with respect to the Vietnam War, ANMA members questioned the necessity for U.S. involvement in Korea and protested the loss of Mexican-American lives. "Well everywhere in our organization the people ask 'What are we doing in Korea?'" Montoya stated in 1951: "From Brigham Canyon, Utah, where we set up a new chapter, down through Boulder, Colorado, and back into Arizona the different questions about Korea and war in general reveal strong anti-war sentiments and peace hopes. . . . The people are concerned at the preponderance of Spanish sounding names on the casualty lists." [34] In Denver, "La Voz de ANMA" [The Voice of ANMA], the local's newsletter, proclaimed: "We Mexican-American people of the Southwest are speaking up for peace. We stand together with millions of other Americans who find that this is an unjust and unnecessary war." [35] At the second national convention in El Paso, the delegates approved a resolution urging the United Nations and President Truman to exert their influence for a quick settlement of the Korean conflict and for the calling of a conference of the major world powers "for the purpose of settling their basic differences through negotiations and reconciliations, thus laying the foundations for a lasting peace throughout the world." [36] ANMA's Denver local also organized a Peace Committee led by Mrs. Dolores Gonzáles. Besides attending national peace conferences such as the Chicago Peace Congress in 1951, the Peace Committee publicized the human losses being sustained by the Mexican-American communities in Korea. "ANMA proves that Mexican-American boys are being used as cannon fodder in the Korean War," the Peace Committee stressed. It observed that in Colorado Mexican Americans represented 10% of the state's population but 28% of the casualties in Korea from that state. In Arizona Mexican Americans were 20% of the population and 44% of the casualties. In New Mexico the ratio of population to casualties was 49 to 56% and in Texas it was 17 to 30%. The Peace Committee urged Mexican Americans to protest such an unfair burden carried by Mexican Americans in the war by writing to President Truman. "Tell him that the Mexican-American people of the United States want peace. We want our boys home." [37]

Not only was the war costing the lives of hundreds of Mexican Americans, but it was also affecting the well-being and rights of the Mexican-American community. Montoya noted that attacks on Mexicans had increased since the commencement of the war in the form of police brutality, racial discrimination, the victimization of Mexicans through the application of the so-called anti-subversive Smith and McCarran acts, the loss of economic benefits through the use of the antilabor Taft–Hartley Act, and the loss of social services for the poor, the aged, and the young. Moreover, minority groups such as Mexican Americans had to unjustly bear the costs of the war through excessive taxes, prices, and decreased wages. [38] "Many Mexican people are saying," added a sixteen-year-old woman in "La Voz," "we're good enough to fight and die in Korea for nothing, but not good enough to get jobs at home without discrimination and to be treated equal with respect and dignity." [39] Consequently, ANMA believed that the war had to receive priority attention since it affected and magnified so many other issues. ANMA urged nations to resolve their problems through negotiations. "This is more sensible and civilized than killing millions of lives including those of our youth." As part of the struggle for basic rights, ANMA included the right to peace.[40]

Labor, Undocumented Workers, and McCarthyism

With its emphasis on working-class solidarity, ANMA supported the particular struggles of Mexican-American workers in the Southwest. It endorsed and publicized the gallant efforts of Local 890 of the Mine Mill workers at Bayard, New Mexico, in its fifteen-month strike for improved wages and working conditions. The Bayard strike, of course, would be immortalized in the classic film *Salt of the Earth*. The ANMA local in Denver provided money and donations of clothes to the strikers and their families and especially lauded the courageous role of the Mexican-American women who walked the picket lines after their husbands had been barred from doing so. "The importance of the Bayard strike to the three and a half million Mexican-Americans cannot be overemphasized," Montoya asserted.[41]

ANMA also brought attention to the plight of migrant workers in southwestern fields and supported a $1 an hour minimum wage for agricultural workers as well as a guaranteed annual wage. At the El Paso national convention ANMA endorsed support for migrant agricultural workers and their right to join unions. ANMA observed the magnitude of the migrant labor problem by declaring that it affected millions of workers on both sides of the border.[42] Alfonso Sena, writing in "La Voz de ANMA," in particular called attention to the plight of Mexican beetworkers in Colorado, especially the low wages, poor working conditions, and the hardship of seasonal employment: "The beet workers go home empty handed but we are always sure of what will be waiting for them next year—the old barns and chicken coop without windows or screens where they are forced to live and the ditches where they get their drinking water."[43] As part of its reaction to migrant labor, ANMA protested the Bracero Program under which Mexico supplied field hands to U.S. agriculture. ANMA considered the program to be a boom to agribusiness at the expense of both braceros and domestic farm workers. Braceros were worked as "peons," while Mexican-American workers were forced to leave their homes in search of employment because they could not compete with cheaper bracero labor. ANMA advocated a suspension of the program and the involvement of both Mexican and U.S. labor unions in the drafting of an alternative solution to the need for agricultural labor in the Southwest.[44] In addition, ANMA worked to secure better jobs and wages for other Mexican-American workers to protect them from employment discrimination and to secure assistance for them in time of need. ANMA locals in Albuquerque, San Jose, and Los Angeles advocated better welfare treatment for Mexican Americans and for individual communities and states to adopt Fair Employment Practice Codes.[45] Finally, as part of its labor program, ANMA through its association with CIO unions encouraged unionism among Mexican Americans.[46]

Working class oriented and internationalist in consciousness, ANMA protested the mass deportation of Mexican immigrant workers, especially the undocumented, that climaxed in Operation Wetback in 1954, when over a million were deported. Between 1951 and 1954 more than 3 million Mexicans were expelled from the United States.[47] Moreover, with the passage of new and harsher antialien and antisubversive laws such as McCarran–Walter all Mexicans, whether Mexican national or U.S. citizen, became subject to harassment by the FBI or Immigration Service for their political views and activities. In its critique of mass deportations, ANMA correctly observed that such periodic drives of Mexican workers across the border, which had also occurred dramatically during the Great Depression, were inextricably tied to the historic role played by Mexican immigrant workers in the Southwest. Welcomed as cheap labor, Mexicans had formed the labor base for the economic development of the Southwest since the turn of the century. Yet, owing to the proximity of Mexico and because immigrant workers were viewed as cheap and surplus labor, their dismissal at times of depression could easily be justified on the grounds that U.S. workers deserved available jobs. Hence, immigrant workers from Mexico had always been useful to southwestern capitalists for four main reasons: (1) they represented cheap labor, (2) they were perceived to be more manageable than U.S. workers, (3) they could be used to divide the working class in the region, and (4) they could easily be deported back to Mexico. "We are the only people in the United States who have been used constantly as a beast of burden brought by enlistment from the Mexican countryside to work in the American fields and once completed they are again expelled to the other side of the border to the Mexican country," an ANMA statement on deportations emphasized.[48] Praising migrant labor from Mexico for extracting the wealth of the Southwest, ANMA contrasted their contribution with the continued poverty, irregular employment, and discrimination faced by these workers. Moreover, mass deportations further served as a weapon for agribusiness to consolidate a system of "peonage and even semi-slavery."[49] To bring attention to the maltreatment of Mexican immigrant workers, ANMA in 1951 unsuccessfully appealed to the United Nations Commission on Human Rights to investigate the status of Mexican agricultural workers in the United States. ANMA hoped that the United Nations would reaffirm "the traditional and historical rights of the

Mexican people to migrate to the borderlands without being persecuted." It charged that mass deportation violated the Treaty of Guadalupe Hidalgo (1848), which had concluded the Mexican War and which assured Mexicans remaining within the conquered territories full constitutional protections.[50]

At the local level, ANMA chapters carried out actions designed to protect individual Mexican nationals apprehended for deportation. In Los Angeles in 1951 ANMA opposed deportation orders pending against certain Mexican nationals. In San Jose, ANMA Local 25 collected contributions for Mexican nationals ordered deported from California, and in San Francisco the ANMA chapter committed its program of action to protesting mass deportations. ANMA locals likewise organized mass meetings such as one attended by over two hundred people on March 13, 1952, in Los Angeles that featured Abner Green of the American Committee for the Protection of the Foreign Born and at which ANMA hosted as guests of honor sixteen Mexican nationals threatened with deportation.[51]

ANMA linked its protest against mass deportations with its denunciation of intimidating antialien and antisubversive laws passed during the hysteria of the cold war and McCarthyism. Such legislation under the guise of controlling "subversives" in fact aimed to destroy legitimate organizations such as labor unions working for people's rights. Anyone who protested discrimination, police brutality, or injustice on the part of governmental agencies could now be accused of being a Communist and prosecuted and even deported under the McCarran Act, passed by Congress in 1950, and the 1952 McCarran–Walter Act. ANMA declared both laws to be direct violations of the Bill of Rights.[52] It further objected to the enactment of local red-baiting legislation that violated constitutional rights. In 1950 Virginia Ruiz, ANMA's executive secretary, pledged to fight against a Los Angeles city and county Little Mundt–Nixon ordinance that required members of the Communist party to register with the Los Angeles County sheriff's office.[53] ANMA applauded the courageous stand of Mexican-American councilman Edward Roybal, who alone that year voted against the ordinance which was later declared unconstitutional.[54]

ANMA's vehement reaction to McCarthyism also resulted from the political harassment experienced by its own members or supporters. FBI agents in their infiltration and investigation of ANMA reported on its relationship to Mexican nationals and how this might affect the application of antialien and antisubversive laws to the organization. In early 1952 J. Edgar Hoover requested his special agent in charge in Los Angeles to determine whether ANMA members were native-born U.S. citizens, naturalized citizens, resident aliens, or undocumented aliens.[55] At the same time, the Immigration and Naturalization Service requested from Hoover information that the FBI might possess on ANMA "concerning subversive resident aliens or naturalized United States citizens who are expected to attend the convention of the organization in El Paso, Texas in May 1952."[56] Investigation at times led to arrests. Immigration officials apprehended and held for deportation Adolfo Hernández, an ANMA member in San Jose, and accused him of belonging to a Communist organization through his membership in ANMA. Only swift action by ANMA along with the Mexican consul and other Mexican groups prevented immediate deportation by posting the $1,000 bail. ANMA warned that if Hernández could be deported, no one in the association was safe. A few months later ANMA again protested, this time in Chicago the arrest and deportation of Refugio Ramón Martínez, an ANMA supporter and leader in the United Packinghouse Workers. Forced to leave his wife and family in Chicago after twenty-nine years of residence there, Martínez boarded a train bound for Mexico but died of a heart attack en route. He had suffered a stroke the previous year and was in ill health when ordered to leave the country. ANMA accused the Immigration Service of deporting Martínez because he had joined the Communist party for a brief period in the 1930s and more important because he had helped organize other Mexican workers.[57]

What all this meant—the deportations and harassment of Mexican Americans—ANMA concluded, was that both employers and their government supporters would not tolerate efforts by Mexicans in the United States to improve their conditions. Various excuses might be cited to justify deportations but the bottom line was to prevent the unification of the Mexican communities, which in turn might jeopardize the value of those communities as pools of cheap and surplus labor. Employers feared such organization more than the plague and hence supported the efforts by immigration officials to deport community leaders. ANMA believed that such attempts were a testimony to the fear that ANMA might succeed in its work. Moreover, threats to deport leaders like Adolfo Hernández aimed at intimidating other Mexicans from joining ANMA or from struggling against injustices. ANMA indirectly criticized more moderate Mexican-American organizations by stating that those who hoped to escape political persecution by pleading their unadulterated patriotism were fooling only themselves. "These appeals on one's knees do not prevent attacks," ANMA claimed. "The only thing that is respected is unity . . . the only defense is Unity." No one was immune and ANMA held up as proof several Mexicans in Los Angeles who had been arrested for having engaged in unemployment struggles back in the 1930s but who had not participated in any political activism since. Only unity could prevent such injustices and ANMA proposed itself as the basis for that unity and protection.[58]

Cultural Politics

Culturally, ANMA pursued a twofold strategy. On the one hand, it attacked prevalent stereotypes of Mexicans especially in the mass media. In the call for its national convention in El Paso in 1952, ANMA noted that "there is a subtle and sometimes open campaign designed to discredit our true historical heritage, our culture and our native language." [59] In its 1952 platform, ANMA specifically announced a national campaign against the perversions of Mexican culture through the press, literature, radio, and television and called particular attention to the Judy Canova radio show, which depicted Mexicans through the character of "Pedro" as lazy and stupid. [60] "The accent with which he speaks," "La Voz de ANMA" in Denver observed, "tries to show that the Mexican people cannot speak English correctly. He uses these words constantly, 'Pardon me, Señorita, for speaking in your face.'" [61] Mexican Americans possessed a sense of humor, it being one of the few things enjoyed by poor people, and appreciated humor done in good taste, one ANMA official stated. However, the "humor" in the Canova show Mexican Americans could easily do without. "Behind the image of a stupid, lazy, and ignorant clown that is Pedro," Alfonso Sena of Colorado charged, "there is a century of persecution and deprivation of our people." [62] It was not funny, Sena added, that more than 80 percent of Mexicans in Denver labored in unskilled jobs and that the average family income of Mexican Americans in 1949 came to only $1,840 compared to $1,930 for a black family and $3,020 for an Anglo family. Nor was it funny that the average family income of a migrant family in Colorado amounted to only $1,424. [63]

To protest comedy at the expense of Mexicans, ANMA along with certain allied labor unions initiated a national economic boycott of the Colgate Palmolive Peet Company, the sponsor of Canova. They asked the public to protest radio stations airing the show and to boycott such products as Palmolive soap, Cashmere Bouquet soap, Colgate shaving cream, Super Suds, and Fab. To ensure a successful boycott, ANMA pledged several additional steps. A nationwide petition addressed to the Colgate Palmolive Peet Company would demand the immediate removal of all slanderous references to Mexicans on the Canova show. Boycott materials such as leaflets, posters, and letters, would be prepared and distributed. Special material would be published stressing the real and rich culture of Mexican Americans. Appeals for assistance on the boycott would be made to unions, black organizations, and any other groups which would provide financial and moral support. ANMA chapters would be in charge of local boycott activities. Two months later, *Progreso* reported that owing to the boycott and protests, the Colgate Company had dropped its sponsorship of the Canova show and that NBC had canceled the program. Undoubtedly, ratings and other factors proved decisive as well in the termination of the Canova show. However, the Mexican-American protests and boycott reinforced doubts about the show and, more important, exhibited ANMA's leadership on the sensitive issue of racial and ethnic defamation. To prevent such future stereotyping in the media, ANMA adopted a resolution urging the employment of Mexican Americans in motion pictures, radio, and television.[64]

Besides the character of "Pedro" in the Canova show, ANMA objected to other media stereotypes and demanded that they be replaced by positive ones. It criticized, for example, the hit song "Mañana" by Peggy Lee for its stereotypic imitation of how Mexicans or Latin Americans spoke English and for suggesting that Mexicans were inherently lazy by always wishing to put off actions until the next day. Another distorted media image was the Mexican sleeping under a cactus with his sombrero over his face. ANMA discredited such an image by pointing out that few Mexicans possessed the luxury of not working. "This is a false picture," "La Voz de ANMA" stated, "because the Mexican people must work doubly hard to make a living."[65] In Los Angeles ANMA condemned Weber's Bread Company for its stereotypic caricature of Mexicans by the use of actor Leo Carrillo, who publicized the company's product by saying on the air: "I am a leetle hongry por Weber's Bread."[66] Stereotyping of Mexicans, of course, had always been prevalent in Hollywood films. In his review of the movie *The Ring* in *Progreso,* critic Carlos Vicente Sánchez commended Hollywood for beginning to provide Mexican and Latin-American actors such as Lalo Ríos and Rita Moreno with starring roles and for beginning to treat some of the social problems faced by Mexicans in the United States. Unfortunately, *The Ring,* which dealt with a Mexican-American boxer, still projected negative images of Mexican Americans. The film admitted that Mexican Americans encountered discrimination but at the same time suggested that Mexican Americans themselves were the causes of this prejudice because they always carried a "chip on their shoulders." Moreover, the film reinforced the image of Mexicans as lazy and socially parasitic people. It even went so far as to claim that Mexican food was unhealthy. In one scene, for example, the Anglo manager of Mexican-American boxer Tommy Kansas tells him before a bout: "Don't forget don't eat heavy and greasy Mexican food like tacos, tortillas, instead go to a restaurant and order a good steak." Even worse, Vicente Sánchez noted, the film left the viewer with a sense that it was useless to struggle against injustice and that Mexican Americans should instead resign themselves to their conditions. Sánchez rejected such a proposition and observed that a solution lay in the organization and unity provided by groups such as ANMA.[67]

In addition to an antidefamation cultural strategy, ANMA actively promoted Mexican-American cultural traditions. Regarding Mexican Americans as historically a conquered population, ANMA stressed the importance of culture in building a political movement for the liberation of Mexican Americans. Yet like others of the Mexican-American Generation, ANMA leaders favored cultural and ethnic pluralism within the United States. "ANMA works to keep our rich Mexican culture and language and history and seeks to bring before other American groups a knowledge of our heritage," ANMA proclaimed in its constitution. "By bringing a knowledge of each other's culture and problems we build a mutual respect so essential for building a strong democratic America." [68] The flowering of Mexican-American culture would enrich the cultural life of the country. To reflect its commitment to the cultural heritage of Mexican Americans, ANMA emphasized that its national emblem would be an Aztec pyramid and not a slumbering Mexican under a cactus. [69]

And to present a more positive image of Mexicans and to promote ethnic pride, ANMA sponsored a variety of cultural programs. Through its national director of culture it encouraged locals to organize functions which would tap the talents of Mexican Americans. According to ANMA, music represented the art form which engaged most people and should therefore be concentrated on by the locals. "More than art, dance, and even literature," *Progreso* informed, "music occupies first place in our communities." Despite a variety of music in the barrios such as *corridos, huapangos, jarabes,* as well as the influences of Anglo-American music, ANMA recommended that local directors of culture identify the most populist forms of music in their communities as well as those who performed them. Having done this, the locals should stage community concerts which would involve not only performances, but education through teaching the audiences the music and words of songs so that they could directly participate. [70]

As part of its program of cultural presentation and cultural revitalization, ANMA stressed the maintenance of the Spanish language. Spanish expressed the culture of Mexican Americans and ANMA believed that no Mexican should be denied the use of his or her native language whether in school, on the job, or in any public institution. When the Los Angeles Board of Education proposed that ANMA members speak only English when holding meetings in Los Angeles public schools, Alfredo Montoya rejected the notion as "merely another excuse to wipe out all vestiges of Mexican culture in Los Angeles." [71] ANMA also encouraged more Spanish-language newspapers in the United States. [72] At the same time, ANMA acknowledged that bilingualism and biculturalism should also be fostered to accommodate the heterogeneity of the Mexican population in the United States, which resulted from cultural erosion and language discrimination faced by Mexican Americans. Although written predominantly in Spanish in order to reach most Mexican nationals and Mexican Americans and to promote Spanish, *Progreso,* ANMA's newspaper, did publish some articles in English.[73] Accepting English as a fact of life and not dogmatic in its cultural nationalism, ANMA incorporated the values and benefits of bilingualism and biculturalism. "We are in favor of bi-lingual education in schools and areas where the majority attending are of Hispanic and Mexican-American origin," ANMA advanced in New Mexico. "And that schools attended by a majority of our peoples give courses in our history."[74] ANMA in New Mexico further insisted that all legal notices, as well as all legislation and court proceedings, be printed in both Spanish and English. In addition, certain ANMA locals provided language classes in both languages, as did the ANMA-operated Lázaro Cárdenas School in Chicago.[75]

Women in ANMA

Like its predecessor on the Left, the Spanish-Speaking Congress, ANMA as part of its reform program supported leadership roles for women. At the founding convention of the Southern California regional of ANMA in 1949 the delegates accepted a resolution on women which stressed that because women had proved to be loyal and steadfast partners, because they were natural and courageous organizers, because history had proved that no "righteous causes can be won without full support of women," and because women had played a tremendous role already in the Mexican-American struggle for full democracy, ANMA resolved to integrate women at all levels in addition to establishing a specific women's committee.[76] In New Mexico, ANMA adopted a 1949 program "Equality and Fraternity of Mexican-American Women," submitted by the Ladies Auxiliary of Local 209 of Mine Mill in Grant County. The resolution read:

> Women of our nationality have long had many obstacles to fight, low wages, indescribable living conditions, the unnecessary deaths of our beloved children through malnutrition and lack of doctors, the age-old custom that women should remain at home and be secondary citizens . . . all these hurdles we must overcome as Mexican-American women. Slowly, but very surely we are crossing these wide rivers. ANMA is an organization that will help our women to grow and learn, and to work for themselves through organization.[77]

Although it is difficult to assess the proportion of women to men within ANMA, Mauricio Terrazas recalls that about one-third of ANMA's membership in Southern California were women. At the level of leadership, despite some opposition, women visibly exerted themselves. Isabel Gonzáles, for example, was elected the first vice president. When she unfortunately died a few months later in 1949 at a still young age, the New Mexico chapter of ANMA eulogized her by noting that this former leader among the unemployed and migrant workers had been one of the initial proponents of forming ANMA. Other women in national offices included Xochitl Ruiz, selected as first secretary-general of ANMA, and Florencia Luna as the first secretary treasurer, and Celia Rodríguez elected as vice president of ANMA in 1952. At the local level, women served in a variety of positions. In 1951 the Los Angeles board of directors of ANMA included Grace Montañez as vice president, Mary Jasso as building committee chair, Amelia Camacho as public relations chair, and Virginia Montoya as social chair. Julia Luna Mount, in addition, contributed as secretary-treasurer of the Southern California regional. Finally, at least two women served as presidents of local ANMA chapters: Carmen Contreras, an officer in the Longshoremen's Union in San Francisco, and Dolores Heredia in Chicago.[78]

An insight into who some of these ANMA women were can be captured by examining the background of Julia Luna Mount. Raised in Los Angeles, she recalls that as a teenager during the 1930s she was heavily influenced by her very political uncle. As an organizer for the Worker's Alliance, which struggled for the unemployed, her uncle often took Julia to alliance meetings. Julia soon joined the alliance and even represented the Los Angeles branch at a national convention in the East. Her work in the alliance introduced her to other political issues and movements. She protested the U.S. embargo against the Republican government in Spain. When the Spanish-Speaking Congress organized, Julia joined it. By the late 1930s she worked in the Los Angeles canneries and helped unionize her co-workers, mostly other Mexican-American women, for UCAPAWA. Following Pearl Harbor, Julia, like many other women, entered the industrial work force. She found a job with the Douglas airplane factory, where she further helped organize for the United Auto Workers. By the end of the war, she shifted jobs to the county hospital, where she assisted in the formation of the United Public Workers of America. During this time Luna Mount likewise went to the support of the young Mexican-American men arrested in the Sleepy Lagoon Case. In the postwar period, she enlisted in the efforts of the Committee for the Protection of the Foreign Born. Disdainful of McCarthyism, Luna Mount refused to sign a Los Angeles County loyalty oath stipulating that she was not a Communist even though FBI and employer harassment followed. When ANMA organized in Los Angeles, Julia Mount once more joined.[79]

Police Brutality

A final but critical aspect of ANMA's reform-oriented program concerned the sensitive issue of police brutality against Mexican Americans. The dislocating pressures of the postwar period only exacerbated a history of poor police-community relations in the Southwest. At the founding convention of the Los Angeles chapter of ANMA, delegates called attention to this problem. One resolution that was adopted pledged ANMA "to seek discipline of police responsible for acts of brutality." And at the formation of ANMA in Colorado delegates placed particular stress on police brutality "weaving a nation-wide pattern of indignities, court injustices and senseless killings suffered by the Mexican American people." Some ANMA locals originated as a reaction to cases of police brutality. In the mining community of Sonora, Arizona, for example, Mexican-American miners organized a branch of ANMA after the killing of a Mexican national by sheriff's deputies during a dance hall dispute. Although no fatality occurred, a similar case in Fierro, New Mexico, led to the organization of the Grant County chapter of ANMA after deputy sheriffs beat up, arrested, and held without bail for as long as ten days several members of the local Mine Mill union. In the Rock Hill community of Los Angeles County, a group of youths established an ANMA youth club as a result of police threats. And in nearby Downey, ANMA originated after an Anglo bartender shot and killed a Mexican-American teenager who had demanded to be served. ANMA's protests led to the bartender's arrest and conviction.[80]

In a number of cases, ANMA objected to police overreaction in dealing with Mexican Americans. This seemed to be particularly true in the Los Angeles area. In October 1949, ANMA supported nine Mexican-American youngsters arrested for first degree murder in Santa Ana. Three sixteen-year-olds were eventually sentenced to San Quentin although ANMA claimed that if the teenagers had been Anglos no arrests would have occurred in the first place. ANMA further accused the police of brutality in making the arrests and charged officials including the presiding judge with denying the suspects their civil rights.[81] One month later an ANMA delegation visited the sheriff of Los Angeles County and protested the "brutal and contemptuous treatment of the Mexican Americans by Deputy Sheriffs in the Downey area."[82] The most celebrated case of police brutality in which ANMA intervened, however, concerned the Maravilla incident. On February 4, 1950, Los Angeles County sheriffs along with the county riot squad arrested fifty Mexican Americans, including pregnant women and children attending a baby shower in the Maravilla section of East Los Angeles. The sheriffs justified their actions as a reaction to disturbance of the peace and the possible presence of narcotics. The Maravilla local of ANMA called the arrests unwarranted and noted that no search warrants had been issued by officers in entering the house nor had a formal complaint been made by neighbors. Moreover, ANMA charged the sheriffs with utilizing brutal tactics and abusive language in making the arrests. In a pamphlet entitled "Facts on the Mass Arrest of Maravilla," ANMA further called the apprehensions illegal and a violation of civil rights. Assisting along with the Civil Rights Congress in providing lawyers, ANMA unsuccessfully appealed to the County Board of Supervisors, which refused to grant ANMA a hearing. Rebuffed by the board, ANMA issued a public letter of protest addressed to the supervisors.[83]

In addition, ANMA members protested at the district attorney's office to "demand an end to acts of brutality and intimidation against the Mexican-American population particularly." Mauricio Terrazas, executive director of ANMA in Los Angeles, along with other ANMA members further called on Chief of Police William Parker and insisted on an "end to police attacks on eastside Mexican-Americans under the guise of controlling 'wolf packs.'" Charges against all the defendants were eventually dropped, only to be replaced by new ones filed against nine of them for rioting and disturbing the peace. Officials later released some of them but convicted the others on lesser charges. Successful in bringing attention to such cases and in providing assistance against police brutality, ANMA concluded that the best defense consisted of Mexican Americans joining ANMA and helping to build a mass movement to achieve first-class citizenship.[84]

Building a United Front

To better achieve the goals of this movement, ANMA favored a united front not only with labor unions but with other liberal and left forces as well. Both Alfredo Montoya as president of ANMA along with Mauricio Terrazas representing Southern California participated in the short-lived American Council of Spanish-Speaking People headed by Dr. George I. Sánchez of the University of Texas. ANMA also had some ties with the Community Service Organization (CSO) in the Los Angeles area, which concentrated on voter registration and civil rights. However, no evidence exists of direct association with prominent but middle-class-oriented Mexican-American organizations such as LULAC or the American G.I. Forum. It is not unlikely that these staunchly anti-Communist groups shied away from the red-baited ANMA. Bert Corona insists that the CSO was formed in order to prevent "radicals" and "Communists" from organizing the Mexican communities. On the other hand, Montoya praised middle-class groups as reflecting along with ANMA the aspirations of Mexican Americans and of providing effective leadership. While ANMA's united front with such Mexican-American civic organizations was limited, its contacts with left-oriented non-Mexican-American groups was not. Progressive but red-baited associations supporting ANMA included the Independent Progressive Party, the Los Angeles Committee for the Protection of the Foreign Born, the Civil Rights Congress, and the Jewish Fraternal Order of the International Workers Order.[85] Finally, ANMA in its bid for a united front placed major emphasis on unity with progressive Afro Americans. "The Mexican People in their struggles for first-class citizenship," ANMA officer Virginia Ruiz observed in 1951, "are becoming more and more aware that the only way to win this fight is to have the closest unity with our strongest ally, the Negro people." Ruiz pledged that ANMA would jointly struggle with Afro Americans against job discrimination as well as segregation in housing and education.[86] Political unity with blacks, however, could be fostered by cultural relations as well. Hence in Los Angeles ANMA sponsored the first Mexican-American observance of Negro History Week in February 1950. One year later, *Progreso* affirmed that it was important for Mexican Americans to participate in Negro History Week "because it affords an opportunity to become more conscious of the contributions that the Negro people have made in the fight against oppression of all minorities throughout our history." Yet ANMA further recognized that race alone did not constitute the key foundation for a progressive united front. That foundation had to be based on a full commitment to democracy and social justice regardless of one's racial or ethnic background. To ANMA, one's politics in the end was more important than one's race.[87]

The Cold War and Political Persecution

Because of its progressive ideology and reform program in a period of conservative reaction, plus its affiliation with left organizations such as Mine Mill and its contacts with the Communist party, ANMA faced much harassment and political persecution as a so-called red-front group. At its 1952 national convention in El Paso, for example, one local newspaper announced the gathering with a headline reading: Red Front Leaders Gather for Meeting. Interviewed by the *El Paso Herald-Post*, President Montoya denied that ANMA was allied with only Communist organizations, but he was repeatedly questioned on whether ANMA supported the Korean War. In a biased statement intended to discredit ANMA, the *Herald-Post* wrote: "Montoya refused to give a 'yes' or 'no' answer as to whether or not he or his organization favors action against Red aggression in Korea." The newspaper also attempted to link ANMA with potential violence by reporting that the chief of police was "keeping his eye" on the convention. The *Herald-Post*

further attacked ANMA for its criticism of Mexicans in the media, especially
the comic strip characters "Little Pedro" and "Gordo." In an editorial entitled "Spreading Poison," the *Herald-Post* dismissed ANMA's position as
pure propaganda intended to breed hate and distrust in American institutions.
"There's nothing harmful in roly-poly, good-natured Gordo, who brings ad-
miring smiles to his readers. And Little Pedro is a smart chap who has a way
of doing the unexpected." The newspaper concluded that ANMA's aim was
simple: "Create class hatred, stir up trouble that can be used to enlist more
fellow travelers—that's the object of such speeches." [88]

More seriously, ANMA faced investigation and harassment by the FBI.
Documents from the agency reveal that it believed ANMA to be linked with
if not controlled by the Communist party. In acknowledging the information
that an organization called the Asociación Latino-Hispano Americana had recently been formed in the San Francisco area and had chosen to affiliate with
ANMA, FBI Director J. Edgar Hoover instructed his agent in charge in San
Francisco: "In view of the reported Communist domination of this organization, it is desired that an investigation be made of the organization and a report should be submitted to the Bureau as soon as possible in compliance
with existing Bureau instructions pertaining to the newly found Communist
front groups." [89] Carrying out Hoover's directives, the FBI relied first and
foremost on either its own designated agents or those informants recruited
from within ANMA. Available FBI documents reveal a number of agency
informants within ANMA. [90] Informants appear to have been either dis-
gruntled or disillusioned members. "I have joined an organization called the
ANMA," one Mexican American wrote to the FBI in 1949, "which is taking
a very strong hold in New Mexico, Colorado, California and Texas, and all it
is, is a Communist organization, which is operating out of Mexico. It might
be a good idea for you to investigate. I will be more than glad to help you in
any way that I can." [91] Another ANMA member appeared at the FBI office in
San Francisco and agreed to become an informant because ANMA had
gained the reputation of being Communist controlled. Besides reporting on
ANMA activities, the informants provided the FBI with membership lists
and background information on officers and members. [92]

The FBI carried out an extensive surveillance of ANMA with the intent
of making a case that ANMA possessed a direct link to the Communist party
and hence should be declared a subversive organization. FBI agents charged,
for example, that many of ANMA's members had either been recruited to the
CP or were Communist sympathizers. An FBI survey of ANMA in 1952 contained seven pages of members "identified" as belonging to the CP (names
now deleted) and two pages of ANMA national committee members and executive board members also "identified" as Communists (names likewise now

deleted).[93] Three years earlier one agent reported to Director Hoover that Cresencio Ruiz, the editor of *Progreso,* was "known in Communist and pro-Communist circles as 'Chris'!"[94] In Chicago one FBI agent noted that certain ANMA members there "were known in the Mexican colony in Chicago to be Communists."[95] Still another dispatch had some ANMA members being hosted at a New Mexico dude ranch that allegedly catered to Communists. If not card-carrying Communists, some ANMA members were tagged as "fellow-travellers." One agent claimed that Antonio Montoya, chief organizer of ANMA in San Jose and a member of the Marine Cooks and Stewards Union, while not a CP member was "sympathetic to Communist Party aims and principles and associates with Communist Party members."[96] Other ANMA members were charged with being Communist sympathizers if they spoke at rallies that included CP participants or were sponsored by the Communist Party or if they associated with other groups declared to be "subversive" by the attorney general.[97]

Not content with implicating ANMA with the CP in personal and institutional connections, the FBI additionally claimed that ideologically ANMA and the CP were one. After the founding of ANMA in 1949, the FBI reported: "Formation of this organization and its activities implement the Communist Party line as set forth in resolutions adopted at the National Convention of the CP 8-3-48 concerning work among the Mexican people." In particular, the FBI compared the CP resolutions on Mexicans in the United States with those of ANMA and concluded that owing to similarities ANMA had to be a Communist organization. The fact that other groups, including some in the Democratic and Republican parties as well as among churches, might support the same issues did not seem to deter the FBI from its conclusions. In a 1952 FBI survey of ANMA one section entitled "Extent to Which Policy and Position Taken by ANMA Does Not Divide From the CP Line," the FBI quoted from CP resolutions or publications and then compared them to ANMA's position. Hence it examined the two organizations' policies on police brutality and because both advocated greater community protection and an end to police violence against Mexicans, the FBI suggested a direct tie between the CP and ANMA. Guilt by ideological association was likewise extracted from comparison of stands on other issues such as racial discrimination, mass deportations, Mexican culture, the peace movement, the labor movement, the history of the Southwest, and black-Mexican unity. In Colorado the FBI compared CP statements on Mexicans in the United States with the proceedings of the first Colorado state convention of ANMA and reported a marriage between the two because both supported a $1 minimum wage for migrant workers.[98] On these as well as other issues the FBI in its extensive surveillance defined ANMA as a Communist front.

Convinced of this relationship, J. Edgar Hoover in 1952 instructed his agents in the Southwest to prepare evidence to list ANMA as a security threat under the Internal Security Act (McCarran Act) of 1950. ANMA would join other organizations also declared subversive, such as the American Committee for the Protection of the Foreign Born, the Civil Rights Congress, the Veterans of the Abraham Lincoln Brigade, the American Slav Congress, the American Peace Crusade, the California Labor School, and the National Lawyers Guild, among others. One year later Warren Olney, the assistant attorney general, notified ANMA headquarters that the U.S. attorney general had decided to designate ANMA as a subversive organization due to its ties with the Communist party.[99]

Upon receiving this news, Montoya alerted the membership and announced that ANMA disputed the designation and would appeal it. He remarked that "this unjust and unconstitutional action" was not unexpected. Since its formation ANMA had been the victim of efforts to destroy it by southwestern economic interests who were anti-Mexican and antilabor along with their allies in the FBI and Immigration Service. Montoya insisted that the issue behind the assault on ANMA was not communism "but the eminent danger (to the profits of the enterprises which exploit Mexicans) that the Mexicans may succeed in unification." Moreover, the attorney general aimed to intimidate ANMA members and potential members from political action. The attorney general, however, underestimated ANMA's determination. "It seems that these types will never understand," Montoya observed. "They do not reckon with the untamable courage and determination of our members and of every Mexican in the defense and extension of his constitutional rights and protection of the organizations throughout which these rights are attained." Montoya did not deceive himself. ANMA was not yet a powerful mass organization, but the FBI wished to destroy it because of ANMA's potential, "which represents a seed capable of growing enormously if they do not crush and destroy it as quickly as possible." The political persecution of ANMA also intended to divorce it from the labor movement and the black community. But rather than divide ANMA from other movements, the FBI harassment would actually strengthen these contacts. In persecution lay unity. Montoya declared it an honor to be mentioned on the attorney general's list along with other progressive organizations. Montoya reminded the membership that the FBI offensive against ANMA had to be seen as part of the larger one against Mexicans during the cold war that had resulted in mass deportations, efforts to destroy unions such as Mine Mill, which organized Mexican workers, and the increased cases of police brutality, especially against Mexican-American youth. Yet ANMA was not un-American. It struggled for democratic and constitutional rights and it would not be deterred from this goal.[100]

Despite ANMA's appeal, the attorney general listed it as a subversive organization in 1954. Prior to the listing, ANMA had been further accused without evidence of representing a front for the Communist party during the El Paso trial of Mine Mill organizer Clint Jencks. At the Jencks trial, Alfredo Montoya had also been charged with being a member of the Communist party. Convicted of filing false non-Communist affidavits, Jencks was later acquitted, partly on the grounds that witnesses who had testified against him had lied as paid FBI informers. Investigated in 1956 and 1957 by the House Un-American Activities Committee and the Senate Subversive Activities Board, Montoya himself was never convicted of the CP charge.[101]

FBI harassment plus the political effects of the Immigration Service's deportation drives and local police intimidation tactics unfortunately and eventually took their toll on ANMA. Although it pursued essentially a reformist program and declared its loyalty to the democratic principles of the U.S. Constitution, ANMA along with other radical and even liberal groups including the NAACP posed a perceived threat to a paranoid ruling circle during the cold war and could not be allowed to function peacefully. "They began to realize that we were a threat," Mauricio Terrazas recalls of the FBI. "They came out to destroy us."[102] In addition, ANMA's demise has to be seen in light of the political attacks on Mine Mill, ANMA's chief patron. Although the union survived, its own efforts to protect itself appear to have detracted from the attention and support it could provide ANMA. "In truth we have to confess that the tactics of the 'red-scare' has impeded our progress," Montoya noted in early 1953.[103] The FBI reported later that year that the ANMA chapter in San Francisco had withdrawn from the national organization due to the listing of ANMA as a subversive organization.[104]

Conclusion

ANMA did not survive the cold war. By 1954 the FBI reported no ANMA activity in cities such as Albuquerque, Los Angeles, Phoenix, and San Francisco. Yet despite its demise, ANMA represents, along with the Spanish-Speaking Congress, one of the most important manifestations of a Mexican-American radical tradition in the United States. Concerned over the problems of working-class Mexican Americans and their communities, ANMA, more so than the congress, articulated a particular Mexican-American radical or left political perspective. Yet although apparently influenced by the Communist party, ANMA, like the American CP, concentrated more on activism than on ideology, and like other radical forces in the United States, it was strongly shaped by its belief and commitment to the democratic principles of the Declaration of Independence and the U.S. Constitution— principles themselves forged out of revolution. ANMA members could more accurately be labeled "radical democrats." Out of conviction and restrained by the political temper and culture of its time, ANMA developed a program and a praxis centered on democratic reformism. Nevertheless, ANMA correctly stressed the working-class conditions of most Mexicans in the United States and the exploitative class character of the American system in the mid-twentieth century. Moreover, ANMA's efforts to link class, race, and culture in integrating the Mexican-American experience constitutes one of the first significant intellectual efforts by Mexican Americans to explore these themes.

The location of ANMA within a Mexican-American radical tradition was not necessarily a conscious part of the day-to-day ideological baggage of the activists. "I didn't consider myself a radical," Mauricio Terrazas recalls. "I just considered myself an activist—a person really interested in making changes in the community." [105] Alfredo Montoya confesses that he never conceived of ANMA as the Mexican-American Left. At the same time, however, he agrees that ANMA represented a left-of-center or progressive position within Mexican-American politics. "It's also true to say that we were a product of our time," he concludes of ANMA, "and I'm sure that we must have been affected by the Left in the country." [106] Montoya denies that he was a Communist and asserts that he was not aware of Communists in ANMA. Yet Montoya and Terrazas acknowledge that the CP constituted an ally of ANMA and that it played a positive role in Mexican-American struggles. "They were right with us and we worked together," Terrazas recalls of the Communist party. [107] Moreover, if we put aside the political propaganda of the time, the CP, as other revisionist studies have concluded, while supportive of the Soviet Union, emerged out of the Great Depression and World War II as the inheritor of a U.S. radical tradition and was a product of its American environment. [108] Within this context, the history of ANMA is a testimony to the courage and dedication of those Mexican Americans who, standing up for their rights as U.S. citizens and refusing to be intimidated by the reactionary climate of the cold war and McCarthyism, dared to challenge the contradictions of American society. "It did take a lot of courage to speak out in those days and maybe a lot of foolhardiness," Montoya remembers. [109] ANMA became a victim of its time, but it continued the legacy of the Mexican-American Left and challenged others who would follow. As Montoya indicates, "it is our conviction that the Mexican organization which discovers the 'key' to the Mexican question, is that organization which effectively reflects, defends, and fights for the genuine aspirations of the Mexican people, that is, the organization which has the support of the Mexican people." [110]

PART THREE

Mexican-American Intellectuals

CHAPTER NINE

Carlos E. Castañeda and the Search for History

This tendency on the part of American scholars to refer to the United States as North America and to take no cognizance of that section of the continent settled by Spain more than a hundred years before the founding of Plymouth is not only misleading but historically unfounded.

—CARLOS E. CASTAÑEDA, January 1932

Our people in Texas today are largely American born; many are descended from pioneers who tilled the soil and made their homes in Texas more than a hundred years before Austin and his seekers set foot upon the land. . . . Yet they are still considered today to be Mexicans and nothing more, made to feel they are being tolerated, suffered to stay, and expected to show abject gratitude for not being put out.

—CARLOS E. CASTAÑEDA, undated speech

Although minuscule in numbers, intellectuals, in addition to middle-class and working-class leaders, formed part of the Mexican-American Generation. Mexicans of letters were certainly not strangers to previous generations, but their interests were either consumed by the consequences of the U.S. conquest in the nineteenth century or as political refugees during and after the Mexican Revolution of 1910 by their passion for their native country, Mexico. By contrast, Mexican-American intellectuals as American ethnics confronted critical issues affecting the permanent position of Mexican Americans north of the border and their integration with other Americans. Of this handful of professional intellectuals the triumvirate of historian Carlos E. Castañeda, educational sociologist George I. Sánchez, and folklorist Arthur L. Campa stand out. Other Mexican Americans, of course, can be said to represent intellectuals or semi-intellectuals, such as Dr. Ernesto Galarza, but they did not function as university-based professionals. Galarza, for example, although a Ph.D. from Columbia University in the 1930s, worked most of this period with the Pan-American Union and with efforts to organize farmworkers. Indeed, his major intellectual contributions came in the 1960s and 1970s with *Merchants of Labor* (1964), *Spiders in the House and Workers in the Field* (1970), and *Barrio Boy* (1971). Still others, such as Américo Paredes and Julian Samora, became Ph.D.s in the 1950s but their major work was begun toward the end of the Mexican-American Era. Mexican-American fiction writers such as Cleo Jaramillo, Josefina Niggli, Luis Pérez, and Mario Suárez published during this era, but their work appears to have only marginally contributed to the making of what historian Richard García calls the "Mexican-American mind."

As intellectuals and as activists in their own right, Castañeda, Sánchez, and Campa helped shape a Mexican-American intellectual culture and scholarship that played a role in the academic world while providing some direction in the realm of ideas to the struggles of the Mexican-American Generation. As such, Castañeda, Sánchez, and Campa predated the efforts by the larger number of Chicano intellectuals a generation later to link the world of scholarship to the social realities of the Mexican-American community.

Carlos E. Castañeda

A son of the border country, Carlos E. Castañeda was born in Camargo, Tamaulipas, in 1896 but raised and educated in the Texas border town of Brownsville. The son of a schoolteacher, Castañeda very early displayed a love of learning and graduated as valedictorian of his senior high school class besides being the only Mexican American to graduate that year. He won a scholarship to attend the University of Texas, where he initially hoped to study engineering. However, a student job with the noted Texas historian Eugene C. Barker brought out Castañeda's deep attraction to history, especially Texas and Mexican history. "I learned much that is not taught in classrooms about honest scholarship and the painstaking accuracy required of a historian," Castañeda later recalled of his initial contact with Professor Barker:

> I learned how to handle manuscripts and I experienced the sheer joy of reconstructing the past from stray scraps, notes, letters, documents, those bits of men's minds and hearts that are traced in black and white on paper made frail by age. Handling old manuscripts as I did in my initiation to history was as printer's ink [is] to the printer, as the smell of powder [is] to the soldier. It was fascinating and exciting; it got under my skin and into my blood.[1]

Soon, Castañeda forgot engineering altogether and turned wholeheartedly to history. He graduated Phi Beta Kappa from Austin in 1921 with a bachelor of arts in history. While teaching in high school, he worked on an M.A. in history, which he completed in 1923. Attracted to the Spanish colonial period of Texas, Castañeda for his thesis wrote a study of the Spanish-

Mexican archival holdings at the San Antonio County Courthouse. He desired to be a college professor, but to be one meant having to leave Texas and
go to Virginia, where for four years he served as an instructor of Spanish at
William and Mary College. Castañeda enjoyed his years in the East but
longed to return to Texas. That opportunity presented itself in 1927, when he
accepted the position of librarian of the newly established Latin American
Collection at the University of Texas. Once again in Austin, Castañeda also
enrolled in a Ph.D. program in history under his earlier mentor, Professor
Barker, and the Mexicanist Charles W. Hackett. Employed full-time as a librarian but diligently working on his doctorate, Castañeda completed and received his Ph.D. in 1932 after writing an annotated translation of Fray Juan
Agustín Morfi's *History of Texas*. Castañeda remained as librarian at Austin
but soon accepted an invitation to join the history faculty, where he remained
until his death in 1958.[2] This chapter, like those concerning Sánchez and
Campa, concentrates on Castañeda's intellectual contributions to the making
of the Mexican-American mind.

Castañeda's Philosophy of History

In over thirty years of teaching and writing, Castañeda produced a
wide variety of books, translations, articles, and reviews. "No Mexican-
American historian in this century," writes his biographer Félix Almaraz,
"has approximated his solid publishing record of twelve books and seventy-
eight articles."[3] Devoting his inexhaustible energies to the history of Texas,
Castañeda produced his most noted studies: the seven-volume *Our Catholic
Heritage of Texas, 1519–1936* (1936–1950), *The Mexican Side of the Texas
Revolution* (1928), and his published dissertation on Morfi's *History of Texas*
(1935). In these as well as in other works, Castañeda projected an optimistic
and positivist view of history. Progress for Castañeda involved the evolution
of European-Christian civilization. Accepting a Eurocentric and Catholic
view of history, Castañeda considered the expansion of Europe as an advancement in human history. He particularly glorified the deeds of Spain in
the Americas. In a series of essays on historiography, Castañeda put forth his
philosophical conceptions of history. Besides seeing Western history as stages
of progress, Castañeda interpreted history in moral terms: good versus evil.
World War II with its theme of democracy against fascism especially influenced Castañeda's moralistic interpretation of history. All of history including that of his beloved Texas was a constant struggle by Christianity against
the forces of evil. If Christianity advanced, humanity did also. "[I]f we are to
win a peace that will be lasting," he wrote during the war, "because of its
foundation on political, economic, and social justice to all men and all races,

we need to study history, to analyze objectively the experience of mankind in the past in order to avoid its pitfalls and insure the uninterrupted progress of Christian civilization."[4] And in a 1949 article entitled "The Rhythm of History," Castañeda added:

> The rise and fall of states, emperors, and peoples through the ages teaches us the inexorable rhythm of history. Each recurrent wave has advanced mankind. It may stop temporarily for a longer or shorter period of time, but on the firm basis of the past, it rears its new foundations to rise again and carry man to new heights.[5]

Optimistic in his views of history and in the ability of Western Christianity to overcome adversity, Castañeda in his treatment of Texas and the Southwest argued not for a history of conflict between the Spanish-Mexican past and the Anglo-American past, but rather for a complementary history. Despite certain conflicts in the dual heritage of the Southwest, in general both traditions complemented each other. This was due to three essential facts: (1) both peoples were of European descent; (2) both held to a common religious faith, Christianity; and (3) both upheld Western and European values and standards. A middle-class member of the Mexican-American Generation, Castañeda saw history as providing more grounds for cooperation between Mexican Americans and Anglos than for conflict. Reinforcing the common attitude of many Mexican-American leaders, such as those in LULAC, Castañeda stressed similarities more than differences. Moreover, southwestern history that included both Mexican Americans and Anglos had to be seen in a broad context. "This tendency on the part of American scholars to refer to the United States as North America," Castañeda wrote in 1932, "and to take no cognizance of that section of the continent settled by Spain more than a hundred years before the founding of Plymouth is not only misleading but historically unfounded."[6] Influenced by the work of Herbert Eugene Bolton, Castañeda shared a Boltonian perspective by accepting the concept of "Greater America." American history was not just nationalistic history but one that transcended national boundaries and made the interconnections that linked regions such as the Southwest with the history of Spain, Mexico, as well as the rest of the United States. "A new conception of what has rightly been called 'Greater America' is spreading," he observed, "and an explanation is being demanded of those differences which characterize the two predominant civilizations in the New World, which but yesterday aroused either contempt or idle wonder."[7] What was needed was an internationalist historical consciousness. "America must strive more than ever for a sane, rational presentation of facts on which future generations may build a broader outlook based on justice, fairness, and mutual respect," Castañeda advanced in the midst of World War II. "A continued emphasis on nationalism can lead only to disaster." [8]

The Spanish-Mexican Foundation of Texas History

To support this Boltonian view, Castañeda attacked the myopic interpretation that considered the history of Texas as commencing with the appearance of Anglo-Americans. "There are some who until very recently," he noted, "still maintained that little or nothing transpired in Texas worthy of record before the coming of the first settlers from the United States." [9] One had to understand that the real foundations of Texas history and of the Southwest were to be found in the Spanish-Mexican past. The early explorations of the Spaniards, for example, years before even the first English people settled along the Atlantic coast constituted the initial European presence in what later came to be the American Southwest. Castañeda consistently pointed out that locations, cities, rivers, and other well-known geographic landmarks had first been observed and discovered not by Anglo-Americans but by Spaniards. The Piñeda expedition, for example, first explored the coastline of Texas and navigated some of the rivers that cut through Texas, such as the one that came to be called the Río Grande. The explorer Garcy in his efforts to found the town of Garcy along the banks of the Río de las Palmas (the Río Grande) represented the first European effort to constitute a city council "within the present limits of the United States." Spanish soldiers as part of the vanguard of European civilization in Texas and the Southwest produced the first play ever performed in the region. Such facts needed to be brought out in order to counter the traditional and provincial view of Texas history that discounted the Spanish-Mexican contributions and heritage. Fortunately, some historians such as Bolton and Barker had begun such a revision and Castañeda saw himself as continuing and advancing this new and broader interpretation and scholarship. [10]

In stressing that the Spanish-Mexican legacy complemented rather than competed with the Anglo-American one, Castañeda urged what he interpreted to be the positive contributions of the Spanish-Mexican heritage to the history of Texas. He strove to revise that history and by extension that of Latin America by including the Spanish-Mexican foundation. He praised studies such as those by Arthur Whitaker, who in his *Latin America and the Enlightenment* "prove[s] a powerful corrective to the erroneous but tenaciously held idea that there was no intellectual or cultural development in the vast dominions of Spain in America, that the colonial period in the history of our southern neighbors was an abysmal void in which their minds were consistently starved and deadened." [11] On the contrary, the Spaniards were the vanguard of European civilization in the New World. They were led in this venture by the Church and its missionaries. Not only as a Mexican-American but as a devout Catholic, Castañeda sought to further revise the popular perception of the history of Texas and the Southwest by an appreciation of the Church's role. To achieve this, however, he had to combat historical and contemporary prejudices against Catholicism, especially the view of the colonial church as a participant in a ruthless conquest. "The tradition has persisted to our day," Castañeda observed, "and even Catholics in the United States are sometimes prone to condemn the church in Spanish America through ignorance of the facts." [12] The facts were that the Church represented the main civilizing force in the conquest of the Americas. To Castañeda, the colonial history of the Southwest and of Latin America was dominated by the moral force of the Church. Anglo America needed to recognize this contribution and appreciate the "civilizing" work carried out by the Church for three hundred years before Anglos set foot in Texas. Without such prior roots, Anglo Americans would have entered a wilderness. [13]

Perhaps no better example of the Church's contribution to the advance of Euro-Christian culture existed than in its work among the Indians. Unlike later Chicano scholars who upheld the Indian way of life over the Spanish, Castañeda refused to accept an exploitation theme in Spanish-Indian relations, a modern version of the colonial anti-Spanish "black legend" sponsored by rival England. He further did not subscribe to the thesis of advanced Indian civilizations in Mexico. Unwilling to romanticize the Indian past, Castañeda believed that incorporation into the Spanish-American empire constituted a forward historical step for the Indians. The English, as the Spanish, had faced three choices when they confronted the Indians: (1) to exterminate them, (2) to place them in reservations, or (3) to respect their rights and attempt to socialize them into European culture. The English chose the first two, while the Spanish proved to be more "civilized" and through the Church Christianized and Europeanized the Indians while respecting their communities and certain of their traditions. [14] In the specific case of Texas history, Castañeda regarded the Indians of the area as having been simple, cruel, and child-like. The friars had consequently assumed the main responsibility of Christianizing and civilizing the indigenous population. "For them," Castañeda wrote of the missionaries, "it was a question of saving the souls of the untutored children of the forests, of instructing them in the tenets of our Catholic faith, and of teaching them the arts and habits of civilized life." [15] The friars accomplished this and the result was a new era of progress for the

Indians. "The bloody sacrifices of old were replaced by the bloodless holocaust of the Mass, their rude instruments of labor were exchanged in the mission for the hoe and the plow, the spindle, the lathe, the brush and the chisel; their picture writing gave place to modern writing, the native dialects were reduced to grammar, and dictionaries were prepared; Spanish was taught and Latin was studied." [16] This was the Church at work and Casteñeda believed that it proved the civilized legacy of the Spanish past in Texas, which Anglo-Americans should accept as part of their total heritage. In so doing, they would likewise accept Mexican Americans, for they were the outgrowth of Spain in Texas.

Civilization and Spain's role in spreading it included other contributions worthy of acceptance by Anglo Americans. The Spaniards, for example, produced the first "American play" shortly after the occupation of Mexico. "Thus almost two hundred years before the first play was given in Williamsburg, Virginia, dramatic representations were common in Mexico City," Casteñeda wrote in 1932. [17] Utilizing religious themes, these theatrical presentations throughout the empire including the Southwest furthered the Christianization of the Indians. Indian actors even performed in some plays. "[T]hese plays can with more reason be called American than the one presented in Williamsburg," Casteñeda boasted, "in as much as both those presented by the Spaniards and those presented by the Indians were in many instances written by residents or settlers of America." [18] The Spaniards also contributed to civilization in the Americas by introducing the first printing press. A literate people, the Spanish also established the first American universities. Casteñeda contradicted what he considered to be the general misimpression that the English led in founding formal education while the Spaniards only lusted over material acquisitions. In fact, the Spaniards had opened the University of Mexico almost a century before Harvard was established. In 1776 the Royal and Pontifical University of Mexico had been operating for 223 years, and fourteen other colleges serviced Mexican students. In the English Colonies only nine colleges existed at the commencement of the American Revolution. Finally, Casteñeda noted in other studies that the Spaniards had operated the first hospitals in Texas and introduced the first doctors and dentists. Civilization in the colonies may have been less splendid than in Spain, but the Spaniards had penetrated the wilderness and brought the initial rudiments of civilized life well before other Europeans. To honor such contributions, Casteñeda in 1952 called upon the Texas state government to do more in preserving the existing Spanish missions, as California had done since at least the turn of the century. The missions and the Spaniards had contributed to the history of Texas by standing guard over European civilization until the arrival of Anglo Americans. [19]

Castañeda further implied that no basis existed for conflict between Mexican Americans and Anglo Americans because both groups derived from freedom-loving peoples. In the case of Mexican Americans, the Spaniards had contributed not only to the dissemination and establishment of European civilization in the New World but to the Western concepts of government and liberty. Spanish America and Anglo America shared a history of struggling for freedom. Castañeda reminded his readers that Spain and its colonies had supported the American Revolution. "The great liberator of Spanish America, the father of the movement of independence of all the countries south of the Rio Grande, the immortal Francisco de Mirande struck his first blow for liberty in the cause of the independence of the Thirteen American Colonies." [20] In turn, when the Spanish-American colonies struggled for their independence, the United States aided in this effort. Linked by their rebellion against European colonialism, all the new independent nations of the Americas held to the same principles and all respected their sovereignties. Moreover, Latin Americans upheld the Monroe Doctrine of 1823, which warned against further European intervention. "President Monroe served notice to the old monarchies of Europe that the New World was closed to the extension of their arbitrary system," Castañeda wrote in 1943, "and that here in the virgin soil of the continent discovered by the great Columbus mankind was to find always a refuge from oppression, where men might start life anew, inspired by the vast freedom of a land conceived in liberty and dedicated to democracy." [21]

Pioneers of Christian Culture and Democracy

If Mexican Americans and Anglos shared complementary histories and cultures, they also shared a common character and personality. Both Anglos and Mexican Americans, for example, derived from a pioneer culture. Like the English, Spanish colonists had tamed a wilderness in Texas and introduced civilization. These were the "Pioneers of Christian Culture" as Castañeda referred to them. Like Jefferson's self-sufficient farmers—the backbone of American democracy—the Spaniards had taught the Indians to become settled farmers by instructing them in the techniques of agriculture. "The missionaries themselves set them an example," Castañeda observed. "With plow or hoe in hand they showed the Indian how to till the soil, how to plant the seed, how to raise the crop." [22] Together, missionaries and Indians cultivated the soil as the Almighty intended and laid the foundation for an agrarian democracy. The Spanish-American frontier, like the American frontier, proved to be more democratic than the older settled communities. Like Frederick Jackson Turner, Castañeda stressed the flourishing of self-government on the Texas frontier. The missionaries not only Christianized the Indians but in the process taught them local self-government. A mission settlement contained its own governing council, its own military, and its own judicial system. "Each mission," Castañeda added, "was a self-governing Indian community under the wise guidance of the missionaries."[23] In addition to citing joint agrarian and democratic traditions, Castañeda proposed that both Mexican Americans and Anglo Americans inherited a respect for education. The Spaniards had not only established the first schools and universities in the Americas, but after independence the Latin American nations had produced great educators such as Domingo Faustino Sarmiento of Argentina, who with Horace Mann stood out as one of the greatest educators in the Western Hemisphere during the nineteenth century.[24] Sharing such similar pasts and character, Mexican Americans and Anglo Americans could also share a present and a future in Texas.

Yet to convincingly advance the idea of a complementary rather than a conflictive history, Castañeda had to confront the Texas Revolution of 1836, which had torn Texas from Mexico and laid the groundwork for its later annexation in 1845 to the United States. Long seen as the root of Anglo-Mexican antipathies, the Texas Revolution was popularly and even academically perceived as a major Anglo triumph. "Such accounts," Castañeda noted of the Anglo view of the revolution, "repeated and impressed upon the sensitive minds of young students are largely responsible for the superiority complex that underlies the attitude towards the Mexican in Texas today."[25] Castañeda, however, did not see the revolution in these terms and called for a revision that would place Mexican Americans on the side of victory. Castañeda argued that Mexican Americans and Anglo Americans should be just as proud of the Mexican participation in the revolution. In 1943 to celebrate the 107th anniversary of the Battle of San Jacinto, where Texan forces had decisively beaten the Mexican army under Santa Anna, Castañeda delivered an address entitled "The Fight for Democracy." In it he honored both Anglos and Mexicans who fought in the Texan armies and who "made the supreme sacrifice and paid their last measure of devotion to the cause of democracy and freedom." Castañeda observed that at San Jacinto one army—the Texan—stood for freedom and democracy while the other—the Mexican—stood for tyranny and dictatorship. Yet the Texans were a cosmopolitan group of freedom-loving fighters from all over the world including Mexican Americans. Castañeda equated this allied force to the Allied cause against fascism in World War II. "From the four corners of the world the dauntless warriors of liberty had come to take their place," he told his audience, "all against might and despotism, even as today the lovers of liberty have flocked from the four corners of the world to defend the democratic way of life, to defend the dignity of man threatened by the despotic theories of the so-called modern totalitarian state, in order that free institutions might not perish from this earth." [26]

Even before the Texas Revolution, Mexico and Anglos in Texas had cooperated and worked together to build a reliable society out of frontier conditions. The frontier, as Turner had written of nineteenth-century America, had made both Mexican and Anglo settlers into the pioneers of democracy. It was not race against race, nationality against nationality, that had brought on the Texas Revolution but rather the efforts of the despot Santa Anna to enforce his edict and stamp out democracy in Texas that moved all citizens of that province—both Anglo and Mexican—to opt for revolution. Texas Mexicans like Juan Nepomocino Seguín had heard the call of battle and hastened to defend their homeland, Texas. Almost one hundred years later the descendants of Seguín and those Mexicans who had supported the Texas Revolution and fought at San Jacinto once again were rallying to the side of freedom and democracy, this time against the worldwide fascist threat. "Mexicans from Texas and New Mexico and from the entire Southwest are fighting today in all the battle fronts of democracy," Castañeda proclaimed. "Thousands upon thousands have answered the call of duty, thousands upon thousands have gone forth with their fellow-citizens, animated by the same determination as their forefathers who fell upon this battlefield, to fight for democracy, to put an end to despotism, to redeem the enslaved peoples of Europe and the world." United in revolution and in the struggle for democracy, Mexican Americans and Anglo Americans in Texas had displayed a common bond and a common history. Texas equally belonged to them and its history extolled both peoples. In Castañeda's revisionist view of the Texas Revolution, divisions were replaced by unities. All were Texans and all were Americans. [27]

A Syncretic History

What can be concluded from a review of Castañeda's historical work is that this Mexican-American historian, raised in the border country of Texas and educated at the University of Texas, possessed a holistic view of the history of his state and of what Bolton had called "Greater America." Castañeda regarded history as a moral instrument for the advancement of good and strove to revise Texas history from being Anglo centered and anti-Mexican to one that accepted Anglos and Mexicans as cocontributors to the state's heritage. [28] Texas was not just everything since the Texas Revolution but everything since the initial entrance of Spanish explorers and friars who were the authentic pioneers of the state. Believing that better ethnic and race relations began with human understanding, Castañeda consciously and unconsciously steered his study of history to stress what Anglos and Mexicans held in common rather than what divided them. Castañeda could make such a revision because of his own biases, which placed a premium on Spanish civilization and which credited the expansion of Spain in the Americas with the advance of Christianity. Refusing to confront the paradoxes of Spanish expansionist ideology rooted in the humanistic Laws of the Indies and the actual reality of conquest and subjugation of the Indians, Castañeda rather than seeing contradictions saw progressive synthesis. Syncretic in his treatment of colonial Spanish history, Castañeda projected this synthesis to the Anglo-American conquest of Texas and the Southwest. Hence the nineteenth-century expansion of the United States symbolized not conflict but the further spread of Western civilization and democracy, from which both Anglos and Mexicans benefited. Castañeda was not blind to conflict, especially racism toward Mexican Americans in Texas, but as we shall see in his writing on contemporary social issues, he believed, like most of the middle class of the Mexican-American Generation, that such problems resulted from ignorance and misunderstandings. If Anglos could be enlightened to the cooperative and complementary history of both ethnic groups, then that history would once again become a reality.

Race and Ethnicity

Besides his historical studies, Castañeda through his participation in community organizations such as LULAC and in his role as chairman of the Fair Employment Practices Commission in the Southwest during World War II wrote various essays on the contemporary condition of Mexican Americans. In them, Castañeda analyzed the causes for the particular plight of Mexicans in the United States. Not unlike later Chicano writers who have attempted to understand race, class, and cultural questions affecting Mexican Americans, Castañeda in his own and more elementary way also established a framework for such an analysis. However, Castañeda, unlike many Chicanos who favored a radical interpretation, did not begin with a questioning of the American system. True to the general Mexican-American temper of his times, affecting both the Right and the Left, Castañeda believed the system to be essentially sound but that parts of it needed corrective surgery. From a reformist perspective, Castañeda developed his analysis.

Like other critical Mexican-American activists and intellectuals, Castañeda had to confront the most overt condition affecting Mexican Americans: racial/ethnic discrimination. No conscientious Mexican-American leader, irrespective of how much faith he/she possessed in American democracy, could avoid dealing with the racial/ethnic issue. Castañeda regretfully accepted the fact of discrimination against Mexican Americans and tried to understand it by suggesting the existence of a stratified southwestern society based on race and ethnicity. Within such a society Mexicans faced discrimination justified on both ideological and material grounds. While noting the heterogeneity of Mexicans in the country due to generational, language, and cultural differences, Castañeda observed that despite such internal diversity Mexicans were still stereotyped by Anglos as being essentially all the same. Most Anglos considered the Mexican to be "non-American" and foreign. "In other words," Castañeda wrote in an essay entitled "The Problem of the Mexican," "it makes little or no difference in the Southwest whether a member of this group is or is not an American citizen. He is still a 'Mexican.'" Such imposed identification was compounded by Anglos viewing Mexicans as non-white although officially classified as white. "Because of the predominance of the darker shades of brown in pigmentation," Castañeda observed of Mexican Americans, "the tendency to class them as 'non-white' had become general." He noted that in practice most people accepted three component parts of the population: white, colored, and Mexican or white, colored, and non-white. Most whites in Texas and the Southwest rather than seeing race in dualistic terms—that is, white and black—made an adjustment for Mexicans. Not considering Mexicans to be white and yet reserving the category of colored for blacks, the race-conscious southwestern system devised the concept of "non-white" for Mexicans. "Thus the Mexican may not be considered 'colored,'" he stated, "but he certainly is not 'white' either in the opinion of the man on the street." [29] Such discrimination particularly mortified Castañeda and other Mexican-American leaders because Mexican Americans in fact were more native to Texas than were Anglos.

Although Castañeda like most other Mexican-American leaders supported the official census classification of Mexican Americans as white, he did not personally blind himself to the racial nuances of people of Mexican descent. He recognized *mestizaje*—the historic mixture of Spanish and Indian—and disliked those Mexican Americans who worked to pass as Spaniards in order to be accepted by Anglo society when in fact most Mexican Americans were mestizos. "There are some who would prefer using the term 'Spanish' in the Southwest," he countered, "but historically speaking, they are 'Mexican' rather than Spanish, for they came to the Southwest not directly from Spain, exception being made of isolated cases, but from Mexico, and most of the early settlers in the area were in fact *mestizos* by the time they moved into the area." [30] Spanish was a historic term implying a culture and a civilization but not exactly a race in the Southwest. Castañeda also attacked patronizing Anglos who accepted some Mexican Americans as "white Mexicans," thereby implying that all others were to be considered non-white and less acceptable.[31] Anglos needed to appreciate not only the correct racial characteristics of Mexican Americans but also the fact that they were not foreign to Texas or to the United States. With the longer history of Spain in America, Mexicans were more "American" than Anglos. "In the Southwest," Castañeda wrote in 1951, "and more particularly in Texas, our public schools have to deal each year with the children of the oldest Americans, except for the Indian, our citizens of Latin-American extraction. They are in no sense new Americans, rather they are old Americans who because of a series of circumstances have been allowed to drift from the mainstream of American life to form eddies."[32]

Castañeda, however, went beyond treating racial discrimination as only an ideological problem. Although hardly a Marxist, Castañeda, the political liberal, concluded that economic factors were inextricably linked to the discrimination faced by Mexican Americans. "Basically the problem is an economic one," he insisted. "The dominant group tolerates, encourages, and perpetuates the pattern of an inferiority complex in this group in order to exploit it."[33] A group declared to be inferior could not claim or be allowed to be remunerated at the same value as whites. In this way employers could justify low wages. "As long as the community brands him as inferior by the treatment accorded him," Castañeda added, "the employer can continue to exploit him with a clear conscience."[34] Economic exploitation in turn kept the Mexican in an impoverished and isolated state that only reinforced the impression that he could not be assimilated with Anglos. Although not systematic in analyzing the exact relationship of material exploitation to ideological domination, Castañeda nevertheless correctly connected racism with economic exploitation and indirectly with class exploitation. He understood that such conditions maintained the large majority of Mexicans as pools of cheap labor.[35]

Economic exploitation translated into second-class citizenship. Castañeda equated the treatment of Mexican Americans and Mexican nationals in the Southwest with that of blacks in the south. "Socially this group," he noted of Mexican Americans, "is subjected to humiliation and slights almost as great as the Negro."[36] Although not subject to de jure segregation and discrimination like blacks, Mexican Americans still faced de facto segregation and discrimination in restaurants, hotels, movie houses, and schools. Mexican Americans were not deprived of the right to vote like blacks through devices such as grandfather clauses but nevertheless remained restricted in their franchise through poll taxes and faced obstacles to involvement in electoral politics. Cities such as San Antonio and Los Angeles with large Mexican-American populations did not have a single Mexican-American on their

city councils. Combined with cultural and language discrimination, the whole
added up to second-class citizenship and a society rigidly stratified racially
and ethnically. Paradoxically, while Castañeda ideologically opposed segregation for both Mexican-Americans and blacks, he could not transcend at
times his own socialized biases—if indeed not racism—toward blacks. In
writing to Judge G. C. Hardman in Freeport, Texas, in 1934, Castañeda com-
plimented the judge on the apprehension and conviction of two blacks for
certain crimes. "I am glad also to hear that you have gotten rid of that entire
lot of rotten niggers," he wrote. "There is no question but that Freeport is
better off with them away." [37]

Yet although Castañeda indirectly acceded to a structural interpretation
of racism he was not prepared to indict the American capitalist system or to
recommend an alternative one. This was surely not in his own class or ideological baggage. Instead, like most other Mexican-American leaders of his
time, Castañeda protested against discrimination as a reformer, not a revolutionary. He called for basic reforms that would lead to better racial/ethnic
relations and that would lift the Mexican American from his position as a
source of cheap labor. To accomplish this, Castañeda advocated a continuation of the federal surveillance of southwestern industries as carried out during the war by the Fair Employment Practices Commission, which prohibited
employers from discriminating in jobs against Mexican-American workers.
Increased educational opportunities, of course, would ultimately in Castañeda's view be the key to greater Mexican-American mobility. [38] "Given a
decent wage and equal opportunities with all others to advance and improve
himself," he proposed, "the Mexican American, as well as the members of
every other minority group, will raise his standard of living, and in proportion as he gains in welfare and education he will become a better American
citizen and a stauncher defender of a democracy that is a reality." [39] Castañeda further suggested that racism and discrimination could be combated by
an exposure to knowledge and truth. Anglo Americans first had to acknowledge the existence of prejudice that went against the tenets of American democracy and, through understanding the Mexican-American condition, had
to begin to rectify these deviations from the basic principles of the nation.
Prejudice and discrimination were "radical ailments" that required "radical
cures." If no remedies surfaced, Castañeda warned that the only victor would
be the enemies of democracy. A staunch anti-Communist, like other middle-
class Mexican Americans and most Americans, Castañeda feared Communist subversion but instead of repression called for liberal reforms on such
issues as race and economic discrimination in order to eliminate the grounds
for Communist influence. [40]

American Pluralism

In his call for cooperation and understanding between Anglo Americans and Mexican Americans, Castañeda likewise forwarded his vision of America as a pluralistic society. Like the members of LULAC, Castañeda indirectly rejected the assimilationist melting-pot model and instead suggested diversity within unity. In dealing with the cultural question confronting Mexican Americans, Castañeda opted for plurality and appealed in his popular writings and speeches for Anglos to be broad-minded and tolerant of cultural differences. He believed that this was possible and noted that the United States as a result of the Good Neighbor Policy during the 1930s toward Latin America and more important owing to its participation in the United Nations during World War II had already broken out of its isolationism and begun to embrace internationalism. This augured well for the acceptance of diversity at home and abroad. Not to do so, however, would be to run the risk of greater worldwide holocausts, especially with the dawning of the atomic age. "Unless man comes to love his neighbor as himself, to understand his fellowmen through intellectual cooperation," Castañeda cautioned, "ruthless rivalry and the hate it engenders will destroy us all."[41]

In a 1932 piece entitled "Modern Language Study and World Peace," Castañeda expanded his view of the United States as a pluralistic society by advocating multilingualism and indirectly, certainly in the case of Texas, bilingualism for Anglos and Mexican Americans. In no case, however, did he ever propose an official dual-language arrangement or a separatist movement. Worldwide conflicts had been very much the result of cultural and linguistic misunderstandings. "What the world needs today is mutual understanding," Castañeda stressed:

> More effective in shutting off communications between nations than the high tariff walls in keeping nations apart erected since the World War, more powerful than the strongest fortification built on the national boundaries; more costly than national armaments because it is their cause, is the ignorance of our neighbors' language. Not until the people of the world can understand each other through the only medium provided by nature for mutual communication will national prejudices disappear, misunderstanding cease, and a true and sympathetic understanding of each other be reached.[42]

Such understanding could be achieved only through the study of different languages. "The man who speaks only one language," Castañeda stated, "is like the man that lives in a large house with but one window." Americans had to forgo this "careless and indifferent attitude" toward languages and instead become "foreign language conscious." The United States could no longer afford to interpret the world through a translator.[43] Although Castañeda did not treat the relationship between Mexican Americans and Anglos in this article he must have had this relationship partly in mind. Indeed in a 1934 letter to the president of the Congress of Parents and Teachers, Castañeda concluded that PTAs in the state needed to become involved in promoting language studies that would help to foster international understanding "by removing unfounded prejudices which are the result of misunderstandings."[44] One year later Castañeda further called for the establishment of bilingual library services for the Spanish-speaking in Texas. This was practical due to the large number of Spanish-speaking citizens, especially along the border, but also because such a service would allow both Mexican Americans and Anglos to "become acquainted with the highest ideals of the two races."[45] Rejecting total assimilation for Mexican Americans, Castañeda accepted plurality and the need for Anglos to appreciate Mexican culture and the Spanish language. Castañeda, however, believed in effective bilingualism and, while advocating Spanish and other non-English languages, he also supported the learning of English by the Spanish-speaking and Americanization programs for them that would be tempered by a pluralistic conception of American society.[46]

In a 1953 address to a Catholic War Veterans banquet in San Antonio, Castañeda extended his views on pluralism by equating the American way of life with diversity. Such tolerance for differences, however, was under attack because of the cold war. "There is apparently in our midst an increasing number of individuals who feel that to meet the threat of totalitarianism abroad," Castañeda warned, "we must give up some of our time-honored freedoms and suppress the diversities we have long considered minority group rights in our society." He deplored such a fear while not denying what he regarded to be the Communist threat. Yet conformity was not the American way. Instead of one American way of life there were many. This seeming paradox in fact strengthened the United States. This was no accident of history but what the Founding Fathers had intended and what had been nourished by successive waves of immigration. "We constantly need to remind ourselves, it seems to me," Castañeda wrote, "that the first settlers of this country were people of different languages, divergent religious beliefs, and varying socio-economic backgrounds." Upholding cultural diversity, Castañeda attempted to make it more palatable to Americans by comparing pluralism with free enterprise. Just as the economic marketplace tolerated divergent competitive interests so too could the cultural and intellectual marketplace accommodate and prosper through the interaction of different cultures and ideas.[47]

Castañeda contrasted the heterogeneity of American society with what he considered the uniformity of culture under Communist dictatorships. To resist such mass control of thought and culture, Castañeda supported diversity in American higher education. Young Americans in universities and colleges should be exposed to a variety of ideas that would support diversity without being divisive. Yet unable to completely resolve the paradox of freedom of thought and national unity, Castañeda exposed his own staunch anticommunism by acceding to the need to suppress Marxist ideas within the academy. "I believe that we educators," he told his audience, "have a duty to see that this is so and that we also have an obligation to cooperate with all other patriotic Americans in keeping communists and communist doctrines out of our schools, colleges, and universities." Castañeda could comfortably advocate diversity within unity because he self-censored his views of diversity to include only those ideas and cultural manifestations that in themselves posed no serious challenges to, and did not call into serious question, the American capitalist system. At the same time, Castañeda in 1953, unlike other "cold warriors," was not necessarily obsessed with communism. He considered communism a minor rather than a major problem and instead advocated a positive revival of pluralism within the university. Diversity and pluralism had made America great and Castañeda called on other Americans not to abandon this foundation that distinguished in his view the United States from the Soviet Union. Indirectly interpreting Mexican Americans for an Anglo audience, Castañeda suggested that diversity, such as that sustained by the Mexican-American presence in the Southwest, should not be feared because Mexican Americans subscribed to the basic principles of the country. They posed no threat. "Despite our diversities," he concluded, "we are held together by certain basic spiritual, moral, political, and other beliefs which we freely share in common because we believe them to be right." [48]

The Latin American Connection

As a Latin Americanist by training, Castañeda in his popular writings also utilized the opportunity to further extend his concept of American pluralism to include the peoples and cultures of Latin America. A true Boltonian, Castañeda believed that just as Mexican-American and Anglo-American histories in the Southwest were complementary, so too were the larger histories of the United States and Latin America. Although an American of Mexican descent, Castañeda, like most others of his generation, still possessed strong ethnic and cultural affinity with Mexico and by extension with Latin America. As a young instructor of Spanish at William and Mary College, Castañeda first attempted to explain Latin America to the United States. In a 1924 essay entitled "The Educational Revolution in Mexico," he extolled the great strides in public education that Mexico had undertaken since the conclusion of the Revolution of 1910. He saw the expansion of education as Mexico's real revolution. New educational opportunities that prepared Mexicans to be better trained and more dedicated citizens constituted a phenomenon that Castañeda believed that Americans could relate to and sympathize with. It showed that rather than being an inferior society, Mexico was on its way to emulating the United States in its commitment to an enlightened citizenry.[49] And in an essay two years later in 1926, "Is Mexico Turning Bolshevik?" Castañeda came to the defense of the Mexican Revolution by explaining that despite the friction between church and state in Mexico owing to the revolution's secularization of schools and the removal of the Church from politics, the Mexican government was not antireligious and was not converting Mexico into a Bolshevik bastion in the Western Hemisphere despite such criticism within the United States.[50] That same year Castañeda initially expressed his commitment to Pan-Americanism in a short essay in *The North American Review* in which he celebrated the 100th anniversary of the First Pan-American Congress, sponsored by the liberator Simón Bolívar in Panama. "Today, after one hundred years of varying success and slow but certain progress," Castañeda wrote of Bolívar's aspirations, "his dream has at last become a reality, and the union of the American republics is the greatest guarantee of peace and good will in the New World."[51]

Castañeda's most important efforts in supporting Pan-Americanism, however, came in the 1930s and 1940s—the period of the Good Neighbor Policy. He saw in President Roosevelt's New Deal for Latin America a major break with a past replete with U.S. military intervention in Latin America and a disdain for the people and their culture. Castañeda noted that Roosevelt had announced the Good Neighbor Policy at the same time as Hitler's declaration of Aryan race superiority. Whereas Hitler's policies produced hatred and destruction, FDR's promoted democracy and peaceful relations among neighbors in the Americas. Moreover, the Good Neighbor Policy represented more than just a foreign policy. For Castañeda it symbolized the common ties that bound the United States to Latin America. As in his other writings, Castañeda returned to the theme of a shared tradition. "Latin America is today as much of the American way of life as the United States," he wrote. The American way of life included a commitment, shared by all of Latin America, to a democratic spirit of independence and individualism. Latin Americans might express such a commitment in a different style, but they believed in democracy no less than the people of the United States. The Good Neighbor Policy had succeeded in making Americans aware that perceived differences in Latin American values, culture, and politics were not signs of inferiority. All the countries of the Western Hemisphere shared common origins in Western Christian culture and civilization. This was Pan-Americanism. Latin America and the United States likewise shared a common future. Castañeda believed that they were the future, for they represented the "New World."[52]

Yet the Good Neighbor Policy went beyond values and tradition. It expressed an interdependence that Castañeda believed could not be avoided and that laid the foundation for future cooperation and joint development. He observed that Latin America's population had caught up with that of the United States and would soon exceed it. Latin America and the United States were also economically linked. Latin America served as a major market for U.S. exporters, importers, and investors. In turn, Latin Americans relied on U.S. imports and technological skills for their own development. Relating economic development based on industrialization to a consumer society with culture, Castañeda wrote: "It is becoming increasingly evident every day to the peoples of the two Americas that they are more and more dependent on each other in the preservation of what we proudly call the American way of life."[53] Moreover, Castañeda hailed the growing cultural ties between Latin America and the United States that had become more evident and important during the war. To further such cultural understanding, Castañeda advocated in 1935 that Latin American history be taught in every Texas high school alongside U.S. history.[54] And at the university level Castañeda proposed to the Rockefeller Foundation the formation of an Institute of Spanish American Studies at the University of Texas. Such an institute would aid in the diffusion of Latin American culture in the United States and legitimize its study by U.S. scholars. This would be Latin American Studies, however, and not the study of Spain. "You know as well as I do," he wrote in 1938 to Irving A. Leonard at the Rockefeller Foundation, "that in the mind of many reputable scholars who are broad in their outlook, there is still a feeling that Spanish American literature does not compare with Spanish literature and is, therefore, unworthy of serious study; that Spanish American history is only a brand of American history and a very secondary brand unworthy of being raised to a position of equality; that Spanish American education has no place in the general study of educational movements in other parts of the world. The establishing of an Institution as outlined here would have a tremendous psychological effect in correcting these aberrations."[55]

Finally, Castañeda like many other Mexican-American leaders gravitated toward the Good Neighbor Policy and to Pan-Americanism because he saw in them the ideal relationship between Mexican Americans and Anglos in the Southwest. The Good Neighbor and Pan-Americanism had to begin at home first. The Good Neighbor's stress on cooperation, consultation, arbitration of differences, peace, and goodwill comprised the exact ingredients that Mexican Americans such as Castañeda were looking for in the Southwest to determine racial/ethnic relations. The Good Neighbor and Pan Americanism articulated exactly what Mexican Americans wished to express to other Americans. By linking themselves with FDR's declarations, Mexican Americans helped advance Pan-Americanism at home and at the same time expanded the concept to include "Latin America within the United States."

A Mexican-American Historian

Carlos Castañeda's major contributions as a Mexican-American historian lie in his efforts to revise Texas and southwestern history to include the early colonial legacy implanted by Spain. Castañeda was committed to such a revision due to his own intellectual biases, but it also reflected the great need by Mexican Americans to explain themselves to Anglo Americans. Moreover, Mexican Americans needed a past, a history, to understand themselves and their position in American society. Deprived of historical independence by the U.S. conquest of the nineteenth century and by racist educational practices that sought to Americanize them, Mexican Americans had lost their own historical memory. Castañeda hoped to recapture that memory for himself, for other Mexican Americans, and for Anglo society. This "hunger of memory" was important in order to allow Mexican Americans to prove their assimilability with other Americans. Mexican Americans derived from a history and tradition that was just as viable as that of Anglo Americans. Products of a history and a culture complementary to the Anglo-Saxon heritage, Mexican Americans could and should be accepted within a pluralistic American society. Castañeda through his scholarship and other writings called for an America with a pluralistic face.

Yet to advance such a revisionist but complementary view of history, Castañeda unfortunately also had to unconsciously distort history. In his need to show the positive contributions of Spain to the advancement of Euro-Christian cultures in Texas and throughout the Americas and to link that enterprise with Anglo-America, Castañeda failed to examine the full complexity of the Spanish-American past. He saw only advancement, progress, and civilization where in fact there was also conquest, destruction, and exploitation. His view of Spain's colonial heritage was unidimensional rather than dialectical. He saw coexistence rather than what Miguel León-Portilla refers to as the "encounter" of two worlds.[56] This was especially the case in his treatment of the Indians under Spanish rule and of Mexican-Anglo relations in Texas. Instead of understanding the subordinate and exploitive position of the Indian, Castañeda, owing to his own Hispanophile inclinations, saw only historical progression. In striving to prove that the Texas Revolution had little to do with ethnic and racial conflict, Castañeda avoided the historical roots of the racism that he sought to eradicate during his own lifetime. Consequently, despite his contribution to revealing that Mexican Americans possessed a rich history that ought to be validated by Anglo America, Castañeda in the process abdicated his role as a critical historian by refusing to expose the other side of the Spanish-American past. Castañeda shares a legacy with later Chicano historians who also sought to highlight and even romanticize the early Spanish contributions to prove historical parity if not superiority to Anglo-Saxon culture, but that shared legacy ends where Castañeda used this history to establish the basis for a Mexican-American complementary culture rather than the Chicano counterculture of the 1960s. In the end, Castañeda surfaces as a less than critical historian but one who in his various writings reflected and helped shape the intellectual temper of his historical period and of his political generation.

CHAPTER TEN

George I. Sánchez and the Forgotten People

In the march of imperialism a people were forgotten, cast aside as the byproduct of territorial aggrandizement.

—GEORGE I. SÁNCHEZ, 1940

Uncritical evaluations might lead to the conclusion that at least 50 percent of the Spanish-speaking children represented by their large sample was unfitted to participate in any but the simplest tasks of life. Such a wholesale indictment of a people would be indefensible—yet such are the results of test *application*.

—GEORGE I. SÁNCHEZ, 1934

I sometimes wonder if the problem of bilingualism is not as much due to the language handicap of the educator as it is to that of the child.

—GEORGE I. SÁNCHEZ, 1954

George I. Sánchez was born in Albuquerque, New Mexico, in 1906. Unlike Castañeda, whose views and experiences were shaped by border culture, Sánchez descended from colonial Spanish-Mexican settlers. He received his elementary and secondary education in New Mexico and partially in Arizona, where his father worked for a time as a hard-rock miner. Wanting to teach, Sánchez in 1923 at the age of 16 became a rural schoolteacher and principal in Bernalillo County, New Mexico, an experience that would help shape his research interests in later years as well as provide him with insights concerning the relationship of Mexican-American children to the public schools. During the summers he worked toward his college degree at the University of New Mexico, where he received his B.A. in 1930. Upon graduation from college, Sánchez was promoted to superintendent of his poor school district. Desirous of advancing educationally, Sánchez soon left for the University of Texas at Austin, where with the aid of a fellowship he obtained his M.A. in educational psychology and Spanish in 1931. He continued to the University of California, Berkeley, where in 1934 he obtained his Ph.D. in educational administration. He maintained his contact with New Mexico during this time by also serving as director of the Division of Information of Statistics in the New Mexico State Department of Education from

1930 to 1935. Returning from Berkeley, Sánchez accepted an appointment as associate professor of education at the University of New Mexico. In 1940 he left his home state for what would become his second home—the University of Texas, where he taught as a professor in the Department of History and Philosophy of Education until his death in 1972. Like Castañeda, Sánchez combined his life as an intellectual with that of an activist. A member of LULAC, he served as director general of education from 1940 to 1943 and as president of the organization from 1941 to 1942. In the 1950s, he helped organize and lead the American Council of Spanish-Speaking People. During the 1960s and the rise of the militant Chicano Movement, Sánchez continued to teach, write, and to work forcefully for the advancement of Mexican Americans, especially on the issue most dear to him: the education of Mexican-American children.[1]

As a schoolteacher and a student of education, George Sánchez was primarily concerned with the effects of American education, principally through the public schools, on Mexican-American children. Like most others of the Mexican-American Generation, Sánchez saw education as the key variable in the potential integration and acculturation of Mexican-Americans into U.S. society. In over four decades of research, Sánchez produced close to fifty books, monographs, and reports as well as some eighty articles. He is best known for *Forgotten People,* a study of Mexican Americans in New Mexico published in 1940. Throughout his writings Sánchez sought to revise and correct certain misinterpretations surrounding the performance and capacities of Mexican-American schoolchildren. He was concerned about the causes that led to their high dropout rate. In 1934, for example, he noted that in New Mexico during the 1932–33 school year there was a total of 24,810 Spanish-speaking children enrolled in the first two years of elementary school of the state public school system. Yet at the same time only 546 were enrolled in the twelfth grade.[2] He further questioned the ability of standard I.Q. tests as applied to Mexican-American children to effectively determine intelligence. He pioneered in examining the role of bilingualism in the schools and questioned whether it should be seen as a liability as it pertained to Mexican-American children. Finally, Sánchez critically studied the effects of de facto school segregation on Mexican Americans. Whereas Castañeda used history to interpret American society and the Mexican American's place in it, Sánchez used his studies of the schools and of educational techniques likewise to understand the same relationship.

History and Second-Class Citizenship

In his research, Sánchez attempted to get at the root of the educational problems that affected the poor school performance of Mexican Americans and their lack of educational mobility. The standard response by educators suggested that the problem lay in the Mexican Americans themselves. They were less intelligent according to I.Q. tests; they came from backgrounds that did not encourage education; and they were culturally handicapped by their reliance on Spanish rather than English. Sánchez criticized these unproved assumptions. He rejected the false judgment of American society that indicted ethnic minorities such as Mexican Americans as being the source of their worst problems. Relying on a historical approach, Sánchez saw the roots of the educational problem in the particular history of the Southwest and of Anglo-Mexican ethnic relations. Unlike Castañeda, who dwelt little on the post-Mexican War history of Mexican Americans in his efforts to stress ethnic harmony rather than conflict, Sánchez in a more militant and bolder fashion, reminiscent of later Chicano writers, countered that the post-Mexican War period was the key to the plight of Mexican Americans and of their second-class position in the United States. In an interpretation similar to that of radical Mexican Americans of his time and of later Chicano historians, Sánchez referred to Mexican Americans as a "colonial people" following their annexation to the United States.[3] As a colonized people, Mexican Americans from the very beginning were subjected to discrimination of various sorts. In a 1941 piece entitled "New Mexicans and Acculturation," Sánchez observed that in the case of educational backwardness this condition had nothing to do with the Mexican American's mental or physical condition but everything to do with the history of Mexican Americans under U.S. rule.[4]

Sánchez conceded that during the Spanish colonial period in New Mexico education was limited and retarded, but that this was the norm not only throughout the Americas but in the Western world. Consequently, the real roots of the educational dilemma that still faced Mexican Americans lay not in the Spanish colonial period but in the nineteenth and twentieth centuries and in particular during the period of U.S. control over New Mexico and the rest of the Southwest. "The last hundred years," he stressed, "have set the stage for the scenes enacted today. By commission or omission during those hundred years, the agencies of public welfare and education have brought about the educational situation confronting the state at present."[5] Even if one argued that educational underdevelopment for Mexican Americans resulted from their backwardness under Spain and Mexico, one would still expect that under more "progressive and intelligent" U.S. rule Mexican Americans would have experienced educational improvement and mobility. Yet this had hardly been the case. The federal government apparatus that administered New Mexico as a territory until 1912 neglected the educational needs of the native New Mexican population. In Sánchez's interpretation of Mexican-American history, and in what later under Chicano writers would be considered a radical interpretation, the U.S. conquest was not a blessing. While other sections of the country experienced an expansion and improvement in public school education, New Mexico was left devoid for the most part of public schools, as education remained in the limited hands of the Church and of private schools. "The Spanish-American of New Mexico was left to the mercy of waves of exploiters: merchants, cattle barons, land grabbers, venal politicians—merciless all," Sánchez wrote in 1940. "We were not given schools, so we remained ignorant of the new way of life that had been ruthlessly thrust upon us."[6] Mexican-American leaders did not accept this neglect, but their protests fell on deaf ears. Moreover, statehood did not produce significant improvements and in education the New Mexican continued, in Sánchez's term, to be the "stepchild" of the state.[7]

Yet educational neglect on the part of the state represented only one aspect of a larger condition that relegated Mexican Americans in the post-Mexican War period to second-class citizenship or to being what Sánchez referred to as the "Forgotten People." "In the march of imperialism a people were forgotten," Sánchez stressed, "cast aside as the byproduct of territorial aggrandizement."[8] In describing what later Chicano writers such as Acuña and Barrera would term "internal colonialism," Sánchez pointed out that economic and political factors including land use and management, taxation, health, and institutions of local and state government were also involved in a general inability of the new Anglo system to relate to the particular circumstances and culture of native New Mexicans. Sánchez indicted the Anglo period of New Mexico's history: "All of these conditions—products of much the same cause—have produced the situation which today we descriptively summarize in the phrase 'the educational backwardness of the New Mexican.'"[9]

The neglect and second-class treatment of Mexican Americans in New Mexico, however, was not an isolated phenomenon. The U.S. conquest and the subsequent history of the Southwest affected all Mexicans in the region in a similar fashion. One year after the 1943 zoot-suit riots in Los Angeles, Sánchez commented that the existence of Mexican-American youth alienation in Los Angeles as well as elsewhere, especially that symbolized by the "pachuco," had its foundation in the historic discrimination faced by Mexicans in the United States. "Today we reap the whirlwind in youth whose greatest crime was to be born into an environment which, through various kinds and degrees of racial ostracism and prejudicial economic subjugation, made them a caste apart, fair prey to the cancer of gangsterism," he wrote in 1944. "The crimes of these youths should be appropriately punished, yes. But what of the society which is an accessory before and after the fact?" To Sánchez the segregation and economic exploitation of Mexicans in California since 1848 had laid the grounds for contemporary youth problems, including the pachuco. He observed that this second-class treatment involved humiliating discrimination in public facilities and services such as restaurants, barbershops, stores, parks, swimming pools, churches, courthouses, public hospitals, and, of course, in the schools. The Mexican American whether in California or New Mexico was not the problem but the victim of historical changes in the Southwest. Quoting another Mexican American from California, Sánchez insisted that the "Mexican problem," whether in regard to the schools or in other areas, had to be regarded in another light. "The so-called 'Mexican problem,' is not in fact a Mexican problem," he wrote. "It is a problem foisted by American mercenary-interests upon the public. It is an American problem made in the U.S.A." [10]

The Mexican problem, moreover, related to what Sánchez further termed the "cultural indigestion" experienced by the American body politic as it concerned Mexican Americans. Anglo society, ethnocentric in character, refused to recognize and validate the existence of a significant number of culturally different groups such as Mexican Americans. Consequently, unable or unwilling to fully integrate the culturally different, Anglo Americans suffered cultural indigestion. Yet the cause of this digestion problem was not the Mexican American but the Anglo system. Sánchez asserted that in the post-Mexican War era the new American establishment did not possess the social institutions or "cultural know-how" to effectively acculturate the Mexican population. "So the Spanish-speaking peoples of the Southwest remained Spanish-speaking," he noted in 1953, "and culturally isolated-unassimilated citizens, subject to the ever-increasing dominance of a foreign culture, of the 'American Way.'" The increase in Mexican immigration during the twentieth century only added to the inability of Anglo Americans to confront the possibilities of a pluralistic society. Refusing to accept Mexican Americans as equals, Anglos relegated them to segregated and menial conditions. "What for brevity I choose to call 'cultural indigestion,'" Sánchez proposed, "can be documented by health and educational statistics, by pictures of the slums of San Antonio, and by all sorts of depressing socio-economic data from all over the Southwest." [11]

Intelligence Tests and Mexican Americans

If Anglo society in general and the history of the U.S. conquest of the Southwest laid the foundation for second-class conditions, the schools reflected and helped maintain them. Second-class citizenship as transmitted by the schools involved the indictment of the low mental capabilities of Mexican Americans through the use of I.Q. tests. Since at least the 1910s such tests had been used in the so-called Mexican schools of the Southwest and the conclusion had been nearly unanimous: the Mexican child rated extremely low and his/her intelligence was linked to race and culture.[12] Having worked as a young schoolteacher in New Mexico, Sánchez found it impossible to accept such biased conclusions. One of his main research topics centered on I.Q. tests and Mexican-American pupils. Sánchez first of all discounted the "objectivity" and scientific accuracy of such tests. Under the guise of scientific measurement, these tests had led to abuses and errors. "This is especially true," Sánchez cautioned, "of those who, blindly accepting the doctrine of individual differences, fail to recognize the importance of the fundamental personal, social, and cultural differences of the pupils and of the extremely important question of differences in milieu."[13] Intelligence tests did not take into consideration a vast array of differences among schoolchildren, especially those such as Mexican Americans. In their effort to be objective I.Q. tests falsely assumed a "universality in community of experience." Yet this was a distorted view of reality. Sánchez held that I.Q. tests could be valid, or what he termed of "relative validity," only if all children experienced the same norm upon which the tests were based.[14] This was not the case in a heterogeneous society such as the United States. Unfortunately, because test examiners refused to take this into account they committed some of the worst abuses when dealing with bilingual students, or what Sánchez called "environmentally handicapped children." An even greater abuse, however, concerned the charge of racial superiority for some and inferiority for others based on test results. Sánchez dismissed such conclusions as ridiculous and in the 1930s and 1940s especially criticized the claim of Nordic or Aryan superiority supported by fascists, including some in the United States.[15] "The educational backwardness of a people is not an inherent or biological characteristic," he wrote in 1944.[16] Yet racial assertions did not bypass Mexican Americans, and Sánchez noted that a test by a Dr. T. R. Garth in Colorado among some 1,000 Spanish-speaking children had found a median I.Q. of 78, with a suggestion that most Mexican Americans were "morons."[17]

In the particular case of Spanish-speaking children, Sánchez argued that "group differences" had to be taken into account rather than "racial differences" in accurately measuring performance in I.Q. tests. Group differences resulted from historical and environmental circumstances. History, culture, and language represented key variables in analyzing the particular problems of Mexican-American children.[18] "Isolation, economic differences, a foreign language, and similar conditions have presented obstacles to the education of Spanish-speaking children that have not operated among the majority of children in the United States," Sánchez observed.[19] By no means, however, were Mexican-American children plagued by some inherent genetic inferiority. The value of I.Q. tests did not lie in what they revealed about intelligence, but in how they could be used as tools by the schools to estimate the special problems faced by Mexican-American children as they entered and progressed through grades and in determining what were the effective remedies to integrate these children into the "norm." [20]

In his own research, Sánchez discovered that rather than being static I.Q.s underwent considerable change due to various conditions. In his 1931 M.A. thesis at the University of Texas and in subsequent publications based on this research, Sánchez substantiated this hypothesis. Entitled "A Study of the Scores of Spanish-speaking Children on Repeated Tests," Sánchez's thesis tested a second-grade group of Mexican-American children in the Griegor-Candelaria School in Bernalillo County, New Mexico, where he had served as superintendent from 1927 to 1930. Sánchez first noted that in their tests of Spanish-speaking children various scholars had revealed consistently lower scores on standard mental and educational tests than for "normal American children." Sánchez proposed that based on other findings the causes of low performance on I.Q. tests by Spanish-speaking students might be accounted for by one or a combination of the following factors: (1) hereditary limitations, (2) inferior home environment, (3) language limitations, (4) unsuitability of tests, and (5) "lack of parallelism of conditions under which tests [were] given." Sánchez, as he would in later studies, first rejected hereditary explanations for performance in I.Q. tests. Race in fact was not an issue in the case of the Spanish-speaking in New Mexico since most were essentially of European-Spanish descent and because a minimal amount of Spanish-Indian mixing had occurred during the colonial period, unlike in the rest of Mexico. "The Spanish-speaking people of New Mexico," he contended, "are representative descendants of the Golden Age of Spanish Life." Moreover, even the mixing that had taken place had still produced a highly cultured people since the Indians involved, the Pueblos or Aztecas, represented a high state of Indian civilization. Although Sánchez appears to have accepted the idea of some Indian inferiority, his purpose here was to discount any assumption of racial inferiority based on test scores since he considered the Spanish-speaking of New Mexico mostly of European stock. [21] Sánchez later modified his position on the race question by acknowledging that throughout the Southwest most Mexican Americans were of mixed racial background, the product of mestizaje. [22]

Other factors besides race were more relevant in explaining low I.Q. scores among Mexican-American children. They included what Sánchez termed an "inferior home environment." Here he utilized the pathbreaking work of his mentor, Professor H. T. Manuel at Austin, who stressed environmental and cultural variables in the educational performance of Mexican Americans. Manuel had written in 1930: "Nearly half of the Mexican children in the schools have parents classified as unskilled laborers, and among these the wages are often pitiably low and employment distressingly unsteady." Sánchez observed that similar conditions applied among the Spanish-speaking in New Mexico. "These conditions . . . impel us to believe firmly that differences noted in test results of Spanish-speaking children in New Mexico may in large degree be explained by the low socio-economic status of the people," Sánchez proposed. "In interpreting test results, then, due considerations must be given to the environmental influences which surround these children and to the extent to which these influences are responsible for inferior test results." In addition, Sánchez cited the question of language differences in explaining poor performance by Mexican Americans in I.Q. tests. Spanish continued to be the language of Mexican Americans in New Mexico and this factor had to be seriously weighed in measuring performance in tests. Sánchez agreed with another scholar who suggested that perhaps I.Q. tests in Spanish should be administered to Spanish-speaking students. Culture posed still another variable. Mexican anthropologist Manuel Gamio in his study of Mexicans in the United States during the late 1920s asserted that literacy and cultural differences were important in evaluating I.Q. tests for Mexican Americans. "He contends further," Sánchez added of Gamio's conclusion, "that Mexican children have a background of culture vastly different from that of American children, and that the performance of the Mexican to [*sic*] intelligence tests is not merely the response of an inherent intelligence but also the response of a different cultural experience." [23]

Finally, Sánchez in his own experiment with New Mexico schoolchildren sought to prove that I.Q. tests results would change, indeed improve, as children received remedial assistance and as they took the tests at different intervals. Sánchez administered the Standard Achievement Test and the Haggerty Intelligence Test to a group of 45 Spanish-speaking students in grades 3 to 8 at intervals of 4, 5, and 7 months. He found the median I.Q. to be 72. The tests were then repeated twice the following year. Over the two-year cycle the children's average I.Q. increased with each succeeding test. By this time, the median I.Q. had risen to almost 100 or normal. [24] Sánchez later wrote: "Thus the tests served a very useful purpose as tools—though their value as yardsticks of 'intelligence' was questionable throughout the entire procedure." [25] Sánchez concluded that test results improved relevant to school training and to increased facility in English. I.Q.s were not static or biologically determined. Sánchez argued that what in fact had taken place in his experiment was that the children underwent an improved quality school environment that compensated for economically underprivileged conditions in their homes. The higher "quality of life" in the schools aided in the ability to learn and hence to increase I.Q. scores. This was especially important for children as they first entered school. "It is quite possible, therefore," Sán-chez suggested, "that school experience is an important factor in producing improvements in the abilities (or in revealing native abilities) of children of inferior home environment."[26] In this as well as in other studies on intelligence tests, Sánchez consistently advocated that intelligence tests should be used with caution, that they should focus on a variety of conditions affecting the children, especially those like Mexican Americans who possessed different historical and cultural environments, and that tests not be regarded as sacred testimony about intelligence.[27]

Yet I.Q. formulators needed more than sensitivity to the Spanish-speaking child. The schools themselves had to assume a much larger responsibility and role in creating a conducive climate for the culturally different child to learn and to acculturate the standard norms and experiences of other American children. The failures of the Spanish-speaking students, including their low I.Q. scores and their high dropout rate, were less an indictment of their background and culture and more of the schools themselves. "[I]t is possible that the low standard of scholarship observed among bilinguals reflects a function of the school," Sánchez wrote.[28] The problem of the I.Q. tests was only a symptom of the school system's failure with bilingual children, which included a reliance on de facto school segregation in so-called Mexican schools. "In other words," Sánchez stressed, "and in spite of any and all excuses that might be offered, *the Spanish-speaking group is not receiving a comparable education.*" He found it difficult to believe, for example, that so few Mexican-American students were capable of high school education. "Then, who has failed," he asked, "—the child or the school? What of compulsory education? What of the duty and responsibility of the State? What of the democratic theory of education?" Only if the school provided the Spanish-speaking child with the necessary and required education and experience to succeed and then the child still failed could the student be properly faulted. This, however, was not yet the case and Sánchez urged the schools and the state—especially those of the Southwest—to fulfill their duties and to provide Mexican Americans with equal and adequate education.[29]

Language, Culture, and Education

Along with I.Q. tests and with general performance in the schools, Sánchez likewise focused on language and more specifically the role of bilingualism among Mexican-American children. "At what point should formal reading enter into the education of these children," Sánchez asked in his 1931 thesis, "and should instruction be in English or in the home language of the children? If bilingualism is an intellectual advantage how may it best be cultivated? If it is a handicap, what measures should be taken to overcome it?"[30] Although in his early years Sánchez displayed an ambivalence about the exact role that bilingualism might play in the education of Mexican-American children, he did concede that one of the causes for the high dropout rate for Mexican Americans was their inability to speak English. Sánchez as president of the New Mexico Educational Association in 1934 reported that more than half the school population spoke Spanish and that the schools and teachers failed to adopt their techniques to the bilingual child.[31] At the same time, he agreed with scholars such as Professor Manuel that children from foreign-language homes in the beginning of their educational careers possessed a serious language handicap because they needed to learn more. They possessed what could be termed a "dual language handicap."[32] However, Sánchez questioned some suggestions that a foreign-home language caused "mental confusion which hinders the expression of possible innate ability."[33] Instead he concluded in the 1930s that Spanish-speaking children upon entering schools did have a language handicap in their lack of English, yet he believed that this handicap was not the fault of the children but that of the schools which failed to address this issue.[34] "The language problem illustrates the inadequacy of current instructional practices," Sánchez wrote in 1940:

> Imagine the Spanish-speaking child's introduction to American education! He comes to school, not only without a word of English but without the environmental experience upon which school life is based. He cannot speak to the teacher and is unable to understand what goes on about him in the classroom. He finally submits to rote learning, parroting words and processes in self-defense. To him, school life is artificial. He submits to it during class hours, only partially digesting the information which the teacher has tried to impart. Of course he learns English and the school subjects imperfectly! The school program is based on [the] fallacious assumption that the children come from English-speaking homes—homes that reflect American cultural standards and traditions.[35]

Sánchez called particular attention to the "basal vocabulary" that affected Spanish-speaking children in New Mexico upon entering schools. He observed that as most Mexican-American children entered the first grade they knew almost no English. At the end of one year the objective might be for them to have picked up a basal vocabulary of 500 words, but most would not have achieved this. This was not their fault but that of the inferior conditions of the Mexican schools. "In fact," he declared, "with the observed inferiority of educational opportunity illustrated by short school terms, lack of equipment, inefficient teachers, etc., it is even doubtful that many of the children have the opportunity to become exposed to the basal vocabulary—much less instructed to the point of mastery!"[36] Hence the schools had to assume the major burden of providing the remedial assistance needed by Mexican-American children. The lack of English preparation increased the importance of public kindergarten's providing minimum English training so that the children could succeed in the first grade. Resembling what later became LULAC's Little School of 400 and the Headstart Program of the 1960s, Sánchez's proposal for increased English-training proficiency in kindergarten held the school system rather than the children responsible for success or failure.

Over the years Sánchez placed even greater responsibility on the schools and on teachers in dealing with the dual language handicap that affected Mexican-American children. In one of his most significant articles, "The Crux of the Dual Language Handicap" (1954), Sánchez stated: "I sometimes wonder if the problem of bilingualism is not as much due to the language handicap of the educator as it is to that of the child." Spanish as a language used by Mexican-American children as they entered school was not the problem. The knowledge and proper use of other languages such as Spanish were not a handicap. "If the child were truly bilingual he would present no special problem," Sánchez proposed. The problem was not language, but preschool experiences that would allow the child to conceptualize language, whether it be in Spanish or English. Did the child undergo experiences that helped in thinking, in developing their mental processes? If not, then the child would be less able to adequately manipulate languages which depended on conceptualization. Consequently a child who experienced poverty and illiteracy in the home might enter school with a conceptual handicap that would translate into a language handicap in both Spanish and English. Sánchez noted:

> The child with a dual language handicap has been retarded in conceptualization—he has fewer concepts and he knows what he knows less clearly than does the child with a well-developed vernacular (whether the vernacular be English or some other language). He does not *think* well, because his tools for thought (concepts) are comparatively few and blunt. If he is to overcome his retardedness he must acquire the *meanings,* and the facility in manipulating those meanings, that are normal for one of his age and intellectual potential. This process is more one of remedial work in conceptualization rather than simply one of "teaching English." To ignore this is to put the cart before a nonexistent horse.[37]

Sánchez stressed that if the particular handicap of these children was to be adequately treated, it would be the further responsibility of teachers to understand the backgrounds and cultures of their Spanish-speaking students. The teachers would not only have to be sensitive to the culturally different child but they would have to become to some extent bilingual and bicultural themselves. Teachers and pupils needed to communicate with one another by using similar concepts as well as language. If this could occur, then learning could take place.[38]

Although Sánchez in his various writings before 1960 never proposed a detailed model for bilingual education, he did advocate the incorporation of Spanish not just as a foreign language but as part of the language of learning in general. As he stressed conceptual development rather than just the learning of English, Sánchez also suggested the importance of schools' acknowledging that the use of Spanish was not the problem and that, on the contrary, an effective bilingual child represented an asset to society.[39] In a 1935 paper entitled "The Elementary School and the Challenge of Bilingualism," Sánchez pointed out that Spanish and the culture of the Spanish-speaking needed to be utilized as a viable instructional tool. He suggested, for example, that instruction in health, citizenship, and other primary subjects could be more effectively offered first in Spanish to predominantly Spanish-speaking children in New Mexico. Spanish would bridge the gap between the home and the school and help to reduce learning barriers based on language differences. He likewise urged the complementary inclusion of Mexican and Mexican-American history into the curriculum. In turn, Anglo children would profit by a bilingual and bicultural education by developing an awareness of cultural differences. "Sánchez believed that if Mexican culture became part of the total curriculum in New Mexico," one writer noted, "the schools would then be meeting the needs of bilingualism."[40] Although Sánchez conceded that owing to poverty and ethnic segregation, the Spanish-speaking child entered school under a certain "language handicap," he at the same time proposed that the Spanish-speaking child likewise represented a significant cultural asset. He especially urged the recognition of this asset during World War II, when the United States needed to cultivate allies south of the border. "The Spanish language needs no 'sales talk' in the United States," he wrote in 1942. "It has long been accepted as a part of our secondary and higher education curricula. Furthermore, recent international events give added importance to the study of this language and augurs that Spanish may soon become the second language of the United States."[41]

The Mexican Schools

If I.Q. tests and the inability of schools to comprehend the relationship of language to education had proved harmful to Mexican-American children, then segregation had added insult to injury. "Side by side with indifference to the educational need of the Spanish-speaking children," Sánchez commented in 1934, "is the vexing and questionable practice of segregation." [42] While Mexican Americans had historically not been segregated by law, they had faced the humiliation of having to attend de facto segregated Mexican schools in the barrios. Sánchez believed that whether by law or by fact segregation in any form was both unconstitutional and inimical to the best educational interests of the children. In a 1948 article, "Spanish Name Spells Discrimination," he made it very clear that segregation in southwestern schools was based on race and ethnicity and not on any other factor. [43] Sánchez praised the legal challenges based on the Fourteenth Amendment by Mexican-American parents and organizations such as LULAC concerning the constitutionality of segregating Mexican-American children. He hailed the Westminster and Delgado decisions (1946 and 1948). In both cases, attorney Carlos Cadena credited Sánchez with providing major research and arguments. [44] Analyzing the implications of the Westminster and Delgado cases, Sánchez stressed the following legal consequences. First and foremost, as the courts had ruled, the segregation of Mexican-American children was illegal irrespective of whether the school board or district had specifically intended to segregate. It was likewise illegal regardless of the wishes of the Mexican-American community. Sánchez argued:

> Oftentimes the segregation is simply a product of long standing custom—a custom sometimes approved and encouraged by the Spanish-speaking people themselves. Nonetheless, whether by 'custom, usages, and practices' or regulations, segregation is illegal. The current or past acquiescence of the Spanish-speaking people is irrelevant. People cannot choose to give up their constitutional rights! [45]

The court cases also aided in undermining the argument that de facto segregation existed not on any ethnic basis but as a result of grouping children who possessed similar abilities or lack of abilities. Sánchez conceded that such a condition might have a pedagogical role, except that he found it difficult to believe that in almost all cases Mexican-American children would be represented in an inferior bottom grouping. This spelled discrimination rather than education. As for the argument that owing to irregular attendance Mexican-American children had to be placed in separate classrooms, Sánchez concurred with the courts' interpretation that this practice was likewise illegal. Separation could not be legally carried out simply on the basis of irregular attendance due to economic circumstances. Children for the sake of class placement had to be judged not as a group but on individual merit, and the same criteria had to be equally applied to all, whether Mexican American or Anglo. "There is no place in American educational theory or law," Sánchez pointed out, "which tolerates a 'special education' for children simply because they engage in farm labor and enter school late." [46]

The same criteria held for separation on the basis of language difference. Schools could legally justify language separation at the first grade level only if each child were individually administered a scientific and standard test to determine language proficiency. If this were done, Sánchez concluded that it probably would be found that some Anglo children would score below the dividing line for special classes while some Mexican-American children would score above the line and be placed in "normal" classes. Special classes for language purposes could legally be defended only if within these classrooms the schools provided special procedures and instruction to teach English. If these were not available, as in fact was the case in most southwestern schools, then it could only be reasoned that segregation existed on the basis of race and ethnicity. Sánchez further attacked school segregation founded on tactics such as gerrymandering, neighborhood schools, and the idea of allowing children a "free choice" of which schools they wished to attend. These cases, as in the others, aimed to maintain separate schools for Mexican Americans and were in fact illegal. Finally, Sánchez emphasized that local school districts and individual state governments could not support school segregation by insisting that education was a state and local responsibility with no role for the federal government. Public schools were state schools and individual states could not deprive individuals or groups of the protection of the U.S. Constitution. "In sum," Sánchez concluded, "the segregation of these children is a matter of national concern, is subject to the provisions of the national Constitution and may be adjudicated through the federal courts." [47]

In his critique of school segregation, Sánchez went one step further and discredited the actual pedagogical rationalizations that school boards and officials over the years had offered to justify the separation of Mexican Americans and Anglo children. These rationalizations included the following: segregation would facilitate the learning of English and other subjects without the competitive conditions involved if Anglo children were present; segregation would allow special attention to the language difficulties of Mexican-American children; segregation would provide more individual time and help to Mexican-American children; Mexican-American children needed time to undergo Americanization; and, of course, Mexican-American children entered school speaking only Spanish. [48] Sánchez noted that pedagogical segregation of Mexican Americans was based on a confusion of what constituted learning, which in turn was based on illogical assumptions. Many of these revolved around equating the mastery of English with education. "The first error which such school authorities make," he asserted, "is to confuse 'English' with 'education'—that is, it is evident that they assume that the entire school policy or program should revolve around the question of whether or not a given child or group of children know English."[49] Teachers believed that success in all phases of the curriculum depended on knowing English. Sánchez believed otherwise. He observed that many school activities at the elementary level did not require a proficiency in English. These included playground activities, drawing, music, arithmetic, "participation in auditorium activities and in cafeteria or lunchroom experiences." Activities of this kind formed an integral part of education, but success in them did not depend on mastery of English. Consequently, the learning of English could be coupled with other such school activities in an integrated atmosphere. "Furthermore," Sánchez added, "even if English could be learned best under segregation, there is no doubt but that the rest of education would suffer under segregation. Therefore, in the interest of those other highly important phases of primary education, separation would be deemed undesirable."[50]

Teachers who believed that Mexican-American children would best learn English under segregated conditions were absolutely wrong. They incorrectly assumed that children learned English only from the teacher. Children learned as much from their English-speaking classmates under real everyday conditions both on and off the school grounds. Not adhering to this pedagogical principle created a vicious circle. Mexican-American children remained segregated because they did not know English and they did not know English because they were segregated. Another false assumption was the idea that all the English-speaking children in a given grade in a regular nonsegregated school knew more English than the "supposedly Spanish-speaking" children in the same grade but in a segregated class or school. Sánchez countered that this simply was not the case. In any event, school authorities in no case had applied a scientific test to prove this assumption. Sánchez suggested that even if they did they would undoubtedly discover that the correct mastery of English was uneven among both Anglo and Mexican-American children. He reemphasized that it was more important to first discern the level of conceptualization among students and then whether they could translate these thoughts into either English or Spanish.[51]

Instead of segregated schools Sánchez proposed integrated ones where Mexican-American and Anglo children could learn together. He recognized that certain children, especially Mexican-American ones, would need some initial specialized English instruction. However, this could best be done within a mixed classroom. Other ethnic children such as Germans and Czechs had not faced school segregation in Texas and under mixed classroom instruction had quickly learned English. Only through integrated education did Sánchez believe that Mexican-American children would acquire the educational experience to succeed in American society. He lamented the great harm that segregated schools had already inflicted on Mexican Americans.

The majority of such students knew less English; they were more inclined to drop out of schools; they felt inferior to Anglos; and in general, they were discouraged from proceeding in their school careers. School segregation was not only pedagogically incorrect, but it was un-American.[52] Segregation negated those principles and ideals rooted in American democracy. Segregated schools could not make good Americans out of Mexican-American children. Sánchez held the public schools, which he called a melting pot and training ground for democracy, responsible for the Americanization of Mexican-American children. "The social and economic problems of a democracy," he concluded in 1942, "are not solved by the application of the concentration camp idea—and the segregation of 'Mexican' children in some schools of the Southwest cannot be regarded as other than the infusion of an undemocratic 'ism' to educational policy."[53]

Pluralism and Pan-Americanism

Yet Sánchez, like his colleague Castañeda, interpreted integration through a pluralistic prism. Integration did not mean for Mexican Americans to give up all their distinct differences as an ethnic group. "America has borrowed not only peoples but also cultural elements from all over the world," Sánchez wrote in 1939, "and fused them into a cultural mosaic within which characteristic aspects of the various groups are still distinguishable."[54] And on another occasion he wrote: "It is also from this lack of sameness—from cultural pluralism—that the American democracy receives its basic inspiration. The very essence of Americanism is observed in the right and duty of heterogeneous social and economic groups, as well as of individuals, to contribute from their respective cultural wealth to the welfare of the masses."[55] In concert with Castañeda, he stressed that because of their ties to the Spanish colonial settlers in the Southwest, Mexican Americans were more authentically native to the region than Anglos. Moreover, the U.S. conquest of the region in the nineteenth century had made Mexican Americans into a "subject people" who had not invited incorporation into the United States. This particular history convinced Sánchez that Mexican Americans deserved a special position and should not be seen as simply one more immigrant group. "He [the Mexican American] is not impelled by the driving motive to become an 'American' that drive[s] the immigrants who fled Italy, or Germany, or Greece in comparatively recent years. He is at home and at ease about his culture, his language, his belongingness here."[56]

Sánchez recognized the continuous large wave of Mexican immigrants during the twentieth century but did not consider them to be "true immigrants." He observed that Mexican Americans did not possess the same drive to learn English or to make money as did other immigrants. "They are not '150 per cent Americans,' but just people who are in this land of long standing and who belong with that land and its government."[57] Sánchez appears to have been suggesting, as did Carey McWilliams in his classic *North From Mexico* (1949), that Mexicans coming north to the Southwest were in fact returning home to a region that historically was part of what might be considered "Greater Mexico." Such an interpretation can be questioned, but by linking all Mexican Americans with the earlier Indian-Spanish inhabitants, Sánchez made a case that if historical precedence had any bearing, the rights and needs of Mexican Americans had priority over those of other ethnic groups. Moreover, unlike other Mexican-American leaders, Sánchez did not shy away from accepting minority status for Mexican Americans and proposed that the federal government had a "very special moral obligation" toward Mexican Americans due to their status as a "subject people." He regrettably noted that while Indians, blacks, Filipinos, and Puerto Ricans received such attention from the federal government, Mexican Americans did not. "He has been, and he continues to be," Sánchez wrote of the Mexican American, "the most neglected, the least sponsored, the most orphaned major minority group in the United States."[58] The federal government owed a responsibility to Mexican Americans and in turn Mexican Americans possessed various cultural qualities that while setting them apart from other Americans at the same time could prove potential assets to a pluralistic America.[59]

Sánchez strengthened his pluralistic world view by joining with Castañeda and other Mexican-American leaders in their support of the Good Neighbor Policy and Pan-Americanism. Sánchez's interest in inter-American relations also derived from his research in Mexico and Venezuela during the 1930s. From 1935 to 1937 he worked for the Julius Rosenwald Fund in a study of education in Mexico that resulted in the publication of *Mexico: Revolution By Education* (1936). Sánchez then traveled to Venezuela, where he served as chief technical consultant to the Ministry of Education between 1937 and 1938. He later showed his concern with Latin America by participating as a member of the Institute of Latin-American Studies at the University of Texas and as chair of the Statewide Committee on Inter-American Education.[60] In a 1940 article "Latin America and the Curriculum," Sánchez counseled U.S. public schools to integrate the history, language, and culture of Latin America into their curriculum as a contribution to Pan-Americanism. Latin Americans were not strangers to the people of the United States. Sánchez observed that a substantial number of people of Latin American descent resided within the country. These included Mexican Americans. Here lay the foundation of Pan-Americanism.[61]

Besides promoting curriculum enrichment in Latin American studies, Sánchez advocated that teachers themselves take courses in Latin American history, government, economics, and the arts. Finally, the Spanish and Portuguese languages had to be given greater attention and had to be better integrated into the curriculum of southwestern schools. Such changes, Sánchez concluded, would allow students to see Latin Americans as people, and this would advance not only Pan-Americanism but improve the relationship between Anglos and Mexican Americans in the United States, or what he referred to as "cultural rapprochement."[62] Pan-Americanism and the Good Neighbor Policy had to begin at home. Sánchez added in a 1942 article, "Cultural Relations Within the Americas":

> If school children, their teachers and their parents cannot learn to appreciate those Latin Americans in their midst, there is grave doubt that the study of the peoples of the other American republics will lead to more than superficial impressions and skin-deep appreciations. Successful cultural relations within the Americas involve more then [*sic*] the study of academic facts. They call for collaboration among people, for mutual tolerance, and for a truly neighborly social interaction. We in the United States are very fortunate in having as fellow citizens large numbers of Latin Americans with whom we can practice the good neighbor policy which we profess toward Latin American nations.[63]

Sánchez's Pan-Americanism, however, did not go so far as to suggest that Mexican Americans were somehow hoping to reincorporate themselves into Mexico or to strike out for an independent national existence, the *Aztlán* advocated by some later Chicano radicals of the 1960s. For Sánchez as for Castañeda and the Mexican-American Generation as a whole, Pan-Americanism maintained national boundaries and loyalties but, as did Roosevelt's Good Neighbor Policy, stressed common recognition that all the countries of the Americas shared a common past, present, and future and that for that reason should treat one another fairly and equitably. Mexican Americans contributed to Pan-Americanism by insisting that for it to be convincing to Latin Americans south of the border it had to begin at home. Anglo America had to first prove that it could get along with Latin Americans within the United States before applying the policy outside its borders. At the same time, Sánchez as a loyal U.S. citizen accepted differences between himself and Latin Americans from other countries including Mexico. In a controversial and somewhat contradictory position in view of his earlier views on the uniqueness of Mexican immigration, Sánchez in the 1950s supported immigration restrictions, especially against "illegal aliens" or wetbacks, even if it meant deporting other persons of Mexican descent. In 1952, for example,

Sánchez warned that the gains Mexican Americans had made in their struggle to integrate into American society and to achieve acculturation were being threatened by uncontrolled mass migration from Mexico. Like other Mexican Americans, Sánchez regretted having to take such a position but in his efforts to reach a compromise position with Anglo America accepted a proposed curtailment of mass Mexican immigration. As American ethnics, moreover, Mexican Americans believed that such migration in fact harmed their economic interests by maintaining the Southwest as a low-level wage market. They further convinced themselves that the infusion of Mexican immigrant culture with its orientation toward Mexico restricted the advance toward a truly bicultural society in the United States that entailed cultural compromises by both Mexican Americans and Anglo Americans.[64]

Conclusion

Unlike Castañeda, whose views on southwestern history were indirectly challenged by Chicano historians of a later generation who saw more conflict than harmony as proposed by Castañeda, Sánchez displays more contemporary resonance in his writings. In the corpus of his works on educational sociology, Sánchez's major contribution was to transcend the ideological hegemony of many contemporary scholars who held racial minorities such as Mexican Americans to be the producers of their own problems and who in a racist fashion argued for the inferiority of Mexican Americans as evidenced by low I.Q. scores. While Sánchez came of academic age at a time when some of the more racist assumptions of educators writing in the 1920s were being challenged, still it took much courage on his part, as a Mexican-American intellectual, to confront what had been a standard interpretation. According to one analysis of Sánchez's writings, the standard I.Q. test administered in the 1930s was still not much questioned since the 1910s.[65] By contrast Sánchez placed the American system, especially its earlier treatment of Mexican Americans as a conquered population and the role of the schools in maintaining that subjugation, at the center of the educational problems facing Mexican Americans. For Sánchez, as for Octavio Romano in his seminal writings in *El Grito* during the late 1960s, the Mexican American was not and had never been the problem. On the contrary he was the victim of a governmental and educational system that chose not to understand or sympathize with the particular history and condition of Mexican Americans. Hence Sánchez, unlike Castañeda, saw conflict and disharmony in southwestern history. Through his writings on I.Q. tests, on language acquisition, and on educational segregation, Sánchez challenged the system to live up to its stated advocacy of democracy for all.

Yet despite what might be considered Sánchez's "radicalism," his analysis, like Castañeda's, was limited and contradicted by its steadfast acceptance of the American system. The system had its faults but it could be reformed. Sánchez strongly believed that when Anglo Americans learned about and appreciated the history and culture of Mexican Americans, they would support needed reforms. "Jim Crowism—is a mass mental aberration, a disease of which we must be cured for our own sakes, if only because of enlightened self-interest," he wrote in 1951.[66] And like Castañeda, Sánchez acknowledged a type of class-racial segmented society but did not believe it to be inherent to American capitalism. For Sánchez as for Castañeda the American class-racial structure, while rigid, was not totally inflexible. It could change and be changed. "Sánchez was concerned about the concept of democracy that was inadvertently fostered by the American public schools," one writer notes. "Sánchez spoke out for a broader interpretation of democracy, one that defined it as a whole system of social relationships growing out of a common human value and working to the mutual benefit of all individuals and groups in society."[67] Consequently, Sánchez, like most others of his political generation, challenged the system but never seriously doubted it. As one writer notes of Sánchez, he was an American first and second a member of an American ethnic minority group.[68]

In *Forgotten People*, Sánchez concluded that the issue for the Spanish-speaking in New Mexico—and indirectly for other Mexican Americans—concerned a compromise—or what he termed "cultural balance." While accepting that Mexican Americans represented a "conquered population," Sánchez also accepted that they had to be fully integrated into American society. Unlike Chicano writers of the 1960s who proposed an "internal colonial" model and suggested separation from American society, Sánchez argued the reverse. He believed that Mexican Americans needed to undergo a type of "modernization" that would equip them to compete with other Americans at all levels: economic, political, and cultural. "Their struggle is, in reality, not one against material factors," Sánchez contended:

> They battle their own cultural inadequacy. They are unprepared to act in their new environment—unprepared because of centuries of isolation. They have no tradition of competition, of education, or of Western civilization beyond the sixteenth century. The New Mexican is not yet an American culturally, the Treaty of Guadalupe notwithstanding.[69]

Modernization, however, would involve the American system through institutions such as the schools in the task of understanding the particular history and culture of Mexican Americans. Moreover, Sánchez did not foresee that in this modernization-integration process Mexican Americans would have to forsake all of their "cultural baggage." Mexican Americans needed to accept modernization but in turn American society had to be sensitive to the cultural position of Mexican Americans and utilize their resources. Only in such a relationship could American democracy work for the "Forgotten People." [70]

CHAPTER ELEVEN

Arthur L. Campa and the Cultural Question

And, who are the common people? It is the group of people who, due to its spontaneous and simple way of life, has not abandoned the realities of life. It is this group which has given us our distinctiveness as a race. . . . It is the common people who determine all civilization and that remaining culture is rather universal.

Essentially, we cannot lose time in foolishness and preoccupations which make us the mockery of everyone else. By being New Mexican we will be Mexicans because of our undeniable culture and Spanish for never having denied ourselves.

—ARTHUR L. CAMPA, 1939

With Castañeda in history and Sánchez in educational sociology, Arthur L. Campa completes the triumvirate of major Mexican-American intellectuals between the 1930s and the 1960s. Campa studied popular culture and bridged folklore, literature, history, and cultural anthropology. He focused on the richness and durability of Mexican-American culture in the Southwest. Born in Guaymas, Sonora, in 1905, Campa spent his early childhood in Mexico, where his father labored as a Methodist missionary. With the outbreak of the Mexican Revolution of 1910, Campa's father was commissioned as an officer in Porfirio Díaz's army and served until killed by the forces of Pancho Villa. Campa's mother fled with her family to El Paso and later moved to Albuquerque, where the young Arthur Campa attended the Harwood Methodist School. Campa enrolled at the University of New Mexico and graduated in 1928 with a degree in languages. Two years later he received his M.A. in languages. Arthur taught high school for a short period but soon left to begin what would be a distinguished university career by teaching Spanish at the University of New Mexico. He realized, however, that to remain in higher education he needed a doctorate. In the midst of the Great Depression he left the Southwest when accepted into a Ph.D program at Columbia University. In 1940 he completed the requirements and obtained the degree in languages. Campa, as prodigal son, returned to the University of New Mexico, where he taught until 1943, when he enlisted in the armed forces and served for two years in Europe as a combat intelligence officer during World War II. He resumed his academic life following the war by accepting an offer from the University of Denver, where he taught from 1946 to 1973 besides chairing the Division of Languages and Literature as well as directing the Center of Latin American Studies. Although not as politically active as Castañeda and Sánchez, Campa nevertheless supported efforts through LULAC and other organizations to improve the status of Mexican-Americans. Campa died in 1978.[1]

In his career encompassing numerous articles and monographs, Campa probed the deep-rooted nature of Mexican-American culture. In concert with both Castañeda and Sánchez, Campa noted that the Spanish-Mexican tradition within the borders of the United States antedated the Anglo-American presence in the New World and, as important, had persisted over the centuries. Mexican-American culture was not only authentically native, but its historic foundations in locations such as New Mexico, Campa's main cultural laboratory, meant that it could not easily be dissolved. It would change, and indeed it had, but it would not wither away or be swept away by Americanization. Like Sánchez, Campa insisted that Mexican Americans should not be seen as just another ethnic-immigrant population that in time would be melted with the rest. Campa, along with Castañeda and Sánchez, helped frame the ideological argument for a Mexican-American pluralist world view. He agreed with Castañeda and Sánchez that Mexican Americans were not strangers in the United States although unfortunately treated as such. To underline cultural authenticity and persistence, Campa devoted his research to the study of popular culture or the culture that emanated from the Spanish-speaking common people of the Southwest. This involved folk poetry, folktales, folksongs, folk theater, as well as sayings and riddles. The true culture of Mexican Americans had its origins in the oral tradition. While other scholars, including the New Mexican Aurelio M. Espinosa, had preceded Campa in the exploration of Hispanic popular culture, Campa, unlike the others, placed his studies within the context of Mexican-American life in the United States. Not a native New Mexican by birth, Campa transcended the false consciousness of many Mexican Americans in New Mexico who considered themselves unique. Instead Campa connected the culture of the Spanish-speaking in New Mexico with that of other Mexican Americans in the Southwest as well as with Mexico. In so doing he confronted the cultural questions facing the Mexican-American Generation.[2]

Folk Culture and the Common People

Akin to later Chicano scholars, Campa believed that the true essence and culture of the Spanish-speaking could best be discovered through folk culture. He saw his work as linking history and folklore and in later years he reflected that in truth both disciplines were very similar. Both used different methodologies, but they aimed to rediscover a human past and the meaning of that past. Campa admitted that folklore could never be as objectively accurate with respect to facts as history, but that through its more subjective approach folklore could perhaps better understand human emotions from the past.³ Moreover, Campa believed that for a people such as the Spanish-speaking in the Southwest folklore or popular culture represented the best evidence for uncovering history and cultural evolution. Songs, for example, revealed the "unadulterated rhythm of the masses."⁴ Besides being a very old form of communication, proverbs or *refranes* likewise conveyed the "fundamental elements of history, literature, science, and the common arts." In addition, the philosophy, reasoning, customs, and practices of a people could be better gauged through an understanding of popular culture and the oral tradition.⁵ Above all, Campa, as would later Chicano scholars, insisted that the history and culture of Mexican Americans were steeped in ordinary men and women who possessed a rich oral tradition.⁶ More than Castañeda and Sánchez, Campa displayed a populist research emphasis on "la gente"—the people. "And, who are the common people?" he asked in 1939:

> It is the group of people who, due to its spontaneous and simple way of life, has not abandoned the realities of life. It is this group which has given us our distinctiveness as a race. It has provided us with ballads, folktales, popular art—that art from which we all benefit and which in the most polished form is found in the best homes. It is the common people who determine all civilization and that remaining culture is rather universal—the same holding true for France, England and Spain.⁷

In his own view of southwestern history, Campa stressed its popular foundation through the initial Spanish settlements. He saw settlers and missionaries—the common folk—rather than conquistadores as the true pioneers in the settlement of New Mexico. Characterized by smaller holdings of land or communal properties rather than the larger *haciendas* of central Mexico, a New Mexican populist economy in turn led to a popular culture. "The assimilation of Indian captives, *genizaros,* and slaves was greatly facilitated by the absence of social distinction of consequences," Campa pointed out. "There was no titled nobility, nor great wealth that would create class distinction; the majority of the settlers were small landholders who farmed their holdings and raised a few sheep."⁸ A culture Spanish in form adapted to the New Mexican environment and mixed with the indigenous peoples and culture. A frontier society, New Mexico also remained isolated from the mainstream cultural currents, more in contact with Europe and the rest of New Spain (Mexico). Cultural adaptation together with relative isolation resulted in an archaic quality to Spanish culture in New Mexico. Campa noted, however, that this did not imply that somehow an exact replica of Spain could be found in New Mexico. Rather, a Spanish-Mexican culture cut off from that of central Mexico in itself was changing and evolving into a synthesis of Spanish, mestizo, and Indian traditions. "If New Mexico shows more archaic elements in its popular lore it is because of an arrested stage and not because New Mexico is any more Spanish than the other regions of America." [9] A popular culture syncretic in nature and deeply rooted in the lives and customs of ordinary people possessed an enduring quality. [10]

In his research and writing, Campa concentrated on varied aspects of popular culture. One of these involved the collection of folklore and folk poetry passed down through the centuries by oral tradition. Campa spent years interviewing old *trovadores* (troubadors) and recording their repertoire of oral literature. "The older generation is fast disappearing," Campa wrote in 1930, "and it behooves all who are interested in the Spanish folk-lore of the Southwest to lend their efforts to the continuation of this program of research." [11] Folk poetry had been transmitted through the songs and verses commemorating heroes, important events, and everyday occurrences spontaneously composed by the local trovadores or *cantadores*. Campa observed:

> The Spanish folksong in New Mexico owes its existence today to the relatively small group of troubadours and singers who, for centuries, have composed and sung the traditional songs of Spain, Mexico, and New Mexico. Had it not been for their efforts and their continued interest, the Spanish folksong in the Southwest would have perished long ago. The *cantadores* of New Mexico were not the only ones who sang, but it was they who kept alive the tradition and perpetuated a heritage that otherwise would have been lost. We acknowledge today the debt that we owe the New Mexican troubadour for having enriched the repertoire of folk singing during its three and a half centuries of existence north of the Rio Grande. [12]

Through musical compositions such as the *décima, cuando, corrido, romance, indita,* and *canción* as well as other forms of folk songs, Campa collected numerous examples of folk poetry dating back to the Spanish colonial period. These folk songs and folk poetry were not exclusive to New Mexico. Many of the same types of songs or variations could be found in central Mexico, other parts of Latin America, and, of course, Spain. Some such as the *indita,* however, arose in New Mexico as Spanish and Mexican culture adapted to the region. "To see it written," Campa observed of the *indita,* "one would take it for a ballad, and to hear it sung one would think it was an Indian chant. It is this combination that makes the *indita* a truly New Mexican product." [13] In addition to the village singer, trovadores had composed folk songs and folk poetry as they accompanied trading parties during the Spanish colonial period as well as during the nineteenth century which traveled between New Mexico and Chihuahua City. "Every caravan, so tradition tells us," Campa explained, "boasted a good bard who not only sang for the traders but who composed all sorts of humorous verse based on anecdotes of happenings along the road." [14] Still other songs expressed emotions of love, happiness, devotion, sorrow, and of particular life occurrences.

Besides folk poetry transmitted through songs, Campa discovered oral literature in the folktales of New Mexico and the Southwest. "In the villages as in larger cities," Campa noted of the passing of folktales from one generation to another, "there was always an old man who sat in the neighborhood grocery, surrounded by children eager to listen to his unending repertoire of *cuentos.*" These tales had their cultural roots in Spain and Mexico and variations of them could be found throughout Latin American. Yet Campa observed that as with folk songs and folk poetry the tales of the Southwest conformed to the environment and customs of the region as well as being inherited by succeeding generations. "There was hardly a boy who did not know the stories of *Juan el Oso* (John the Bear), *El Caballito de Troya, Los llanos de Berlín y las cuevas de Qui qui ri qui,* as well as whole series of stories of kings, princesses in distress, and giants," Campa added. [15]

Folk theater represented a third form of popular culture researched by Campa. Introduced by the Spaniards as they settled New Mexico, the drama especially in its religious format became synonymous with the origin of Spanish-Mexican culture in the Southwest. The Oñate expedition of 1598 that led to the first permanent Spanish enclave in New Mexico also performed the first play, "The Moors and the Christians," in what would become the later confines of the United States. [16] "The religious drama dates back to the Spanish stage," Campa explained. "Most folklorists agree that the New Mexican religious drama came directly from Spain and that some of it was probably written by Spanish Friars in New Mexico." [17] The Church utilized the religious drama in its conversion of the Indians. Unable at first to communicate with the Indians, Spanish missionaries resorted to pantomime and miming through the *auto,* the religious drama, to convey a message of conversion. [18] "Two facts may be firmly established, in regard to the Spanish folkdrama of the Southwest," Campa declared. "First, that the missionaries wrote most, if not all, of the compositions, and second, that the plays were intended principally for purposes of instruction." [19] Such plays as "Adán and Eva," "Cain and Abel," "La Pasión," and the Christmas plays "Las Posadas" became standard repertoire not only for missionaries but for parishes in villages and towns which performed many of these plays on a yearly basis. [20] "The religious drama as a means of popular entertainment is one that has persisted more uniformly throughout New Mexico," Campa observed. "Es-

pecially is this true of the Christmas plays which are very laboriously produced even in the most humble hamlet."[21] Although most of the plays were
adaptations of those transferred from Spain, a few originated in New Mexico, such as the secular drama "Los Comanches." "The most significant
thing about the Spanish religious theater in the Southwest is its almost un-
altered persistence," Campa concluded.[22]

A final form of oral tradition that Campa studied consisted of the thousands of riddles, proverbs, and sayings (refranes) that together composed the
folk wisdom of the Spanish-speaking. "I venture to say," Campa wrote,
"that it would be almost impossible to find half a dozen New Mexicans of
Spanish descent who would not be unable to recite a score of riddles." Based
on folk culture, these additional genres of oral literature were adapted over
the centuries by the common folk of the Southwest. They likewise composed
new ones by combining some of the old ones. Many were of regional and
local origins. "A large number of universal proverbs are expressed in language that is purely New Mexican or at least Southwestern." As with the rest
of the oral tradition, Campa maintained that proverbs, sayings, and riddles
symbolized an evolving American culture.[23]

Cultural Retention and Adaptation

Besides calling attention to the populist nature of Mexican-
American culture, Campa emphasized cultural retention and cultural adaptation. Mexican Americans possessed an inherited but living tradition. Cultural
traditions successfully passed from one generation to another. By word of
mouth the oral tradition in folk poetry and folk songs continued to be practiced, especially in the rural areas of New Mexico and the Southwest. "From
father to son these tales have come down to the present time," Campa wrote
in 1930, "and in this transmission they have been somewhat altered."[24] Yet
culture was not static. Folk stories in contemporary New Mexico, for example, involved not only old popular tales but new ones, as twentieth-century
bards spun out tales of "political intrigue and strife, important happenings,
births, etc.; and write funeral dirges at the death of some well known citizen."[25] Folk theater likewise survived.[26] Integral to the continuation and retention of popular culture was, of course, the Spanish language. Spanish
served as the communication link for the passing of the oral tradition. "There
is hardly a single spot in the entire state where the language introduced four
centuries ago is not spoken alongside of English," Campa noted of New
Mexico, "and there are entire counties where English is still a foreign tongue.
New Mexico is the only state in the Union where a law must be written in two
languages."[27]

The "Mexican connection," moreover, reinforced and refurbished Spanish-Mexican culture and assured that it would not die. "The songs composed in Mexico," Campa wrote of the tie between Mexico and the Mexican Southwest, "found their way into New Mexico through the natural channels of trade, and through the influx of Mexicans who settled in this state." [28] Campa further recorded that it remained very difficult to distinguish in most cases between New Mexican and Mexican songs, although Mexican songs were adapted to New Mexican culture. "A number of Mexican airs have been brought over and new words written to the same tune." [29] The Mexican connection also held for folk theater. He observed:

> "In the case of the creation play called *Adán y Eva*, we have a definite date for its first presentation in Mexico City. It is difficult to ascertain if the New Mexican play is the same, since in matters of origin hardly any distinction can be made between Mexico and New Mexico. Culturally, these two regions are seldom separated by the Rio Grande, and much less in the seventeenth century. Even today the folksong of Mexico is unmindful of international boundaries, and the New Mexican peasant sings obliviously, "Qué lejos estoy del suelo donde he nacido" [How far I am from the land of my birth] although for several generations his kin has lived north of the river. [30]

If the Mexican connection historically had refreshed New Mexican popular culture, it was no less true in the twentieth century, although with some different adaptations. "Today the same contact is increasing with improved means of communications," Campa explained in 1946. "The radio and the Mexican motion pictures have introduced a repertoire of songs hitherto unknown in the state." [31] Mexico's proximity to the Southwest not only influenced Mexican culture throughout the region but helped to create a particular Mexican-American border culture that exhibited even closer ties to Mexico. Campa observed that this was certainly the case for southern New Mexico:

> For this reason it can be said that this portion of the state is more alive, more actively Spanish then the north. The language itself is more expressive, far more extensive and less corrupted by Anglicisms or by deterioration from lack of instruction. Books, newspapers, and literature in general have helped to keep the language from falling into disuse. Spanish is more than a domestic language here, appearing in prose, in poetry, and in business announcements. In short, Spanish in Southern New Mexico has the vitality of a language that is living and active. The Mexican-American border is a place in the Southwest where one may find large numbers of individuals who are truly bilingual, that is, able to speak both languages without noticeable accent in either. In the far north, English is spoken with a great deal of Spanish accent and in the central region of the state, Spanish is spoken *a la* English. [32]

Mexico's propinquity to the Southwest also made possible another source of cultural contact: the mass movement of Mexican immigrants who entered the United States during the early twentieth century. Their presence along with their cultural baggage revitalized Mexican-American culture. For example, Spanish-language radio stations on both sides of the border followed the migrant trail north and by the 1920s and 1930s broadcast a wide variety of music popular in Mexico. In addition, as phonograph players became more widely available, Mexican Americans along with Mexican immigrants purchased and played the records produced in Mexico. Campa noted that these sources of mass culture strongly influenced older New Mexican song forms. Community trovadores picked up the Mexican songs and added them to their repertoire. Consequently Campa feared that in some areas the older indigenous ballads would soon disappear and be completely replaced by the newer Mexican tunes. Campa feared cultural erosion but also recognized a dialectic at work. Cultural connections with Mexico, even in mass cultural forms, expanded the musical horizons of Mexican Americans and reawakened their interest in Latin American culture. "The *rumbas, congas, tangos, boleros, pasodobles,* and *flamencos* comes [*sic*] by way of Mexico," he wrote in 1946, "[and] along with other traditional airs familiar to New Mexicans, have become well known to the audiences of the state. In time, this will mean an enriched 'songology' that will equal any in Spanish America." [33] This cultural revitalization tied to Mexican immigration meant that Mexican culture north of the border in a variety of forms would constantly be reinforced and hence not easily lost to Americanization. Almost thirty years later, Campa found that in Denver the older Spanish folk songs of New Mexico brought into the urban area by migrants from small rural communities and mountain villages still coexisted with the newer musical tastes more closely identified with Mexican immigrants who came either during the Mexican Revolution or after World War II. Together, Mexican Americans and Mexican nationals maintained a visible and audible Mexican cultural presence:

> These three Spanish speaking groups have the language in common, albeit the fact that there are many dialectical and morphological differences among the colonials and thé Mexicans. They also have in common the desire to sing and hear Spanish folksongs whether it be in public or in the home, through the radio, the phonograph or in gatherings and wedding fiestas where a guitar is passed around with other forms of social enjoyment. There are professional singers who perform in public, either in night clubs or over the radio, but there are also traditional *cantadores* who sing in small friendly neighborhood gatherings. The former lean more toward the current Mexican folksong, while the older *cantadores* prefer the traditional songs they learned in their youth. [34]

The Spanish Fantasy

Like Castañeda and Sánchez, Campa also concerned himself with the question of identity: Who was the Mexican American? Campa was particularly sensitive to this issue because of his New Mexican upbringing and his long professional association with that state. Owing to its distinction as the first permanent Spanish settlement in the Southwest and its relative isolation from central Mexico, New Mexico had become characterized by many of its Spanish-speaking inhabitants referring to themselves as Spanish with the implication that racially and culturally they had more to do with Spain than with Mexico. Campa, however, rejected the "Spanish Fantasy," as Carey McWilliams termed it, and through his understanding of New Mexican popular culture attempted in his writing to paint a more complex racial and cultural portrait. Campa understood the importance of self-identification and the problem of terminology. At the same time, he regretted that self-identification by the Spanish-speaking, whether they called themselves natives, Spanish, Spanish Americans, or even Mexicans, was based on misconceptions and reflected more a state of mind than a clear concept of race or culture. Self-identification, moreover, was confused due to the additional ingredient of Anglo-American racism that in equally naive terms labeled all Spanish-speaking people as "Mexicans" with a pejorative emphasis and considered them to be "nonwhite." Campa expressed the complexity of self-identification for the Spanish-speaking in New Mexico in these words:

> Obviously they are not Mexicans, and they have not been since 1848; neither are they natives exclusively. Few can prove conclusively to be of Spanish descent, and none of them are Spanish-Americans, considering that such an adjective applies to people in Spanish-America. On the other hand, there are valid reasons why New Mexicans may claim in part any or all the foregoing appellations. Legally and nationally they are Americans; linguistically, Spanish; Spanish-American, geographically; culturally, Mexican; native by birth, and New Mexican by state boundaries. What are they racially, since that seems to be of so great concern? The answer to that question may be found in the history of the conquest.[35]

Campa confronted certain issues regarding identity. First, the Spanish-speaking of New Mexico were not racially pure Spaniards. The conquest of New Mexico and the centuries of settlement had produced a racially mixed population—mestizos—who were no different from other Spanish-speaking people in the Southwest or in Mexico. The Spanish-speaking in New Mexico used the term "Spanish" in describing themselves because they mistakenly identified "Mexican" as a race and because they wished to avoid Anglo racism by claiming Spanish lineage and hence membership in the white race. Yet the Spanish-speaking in New Mexico represented a mixed people and they did not deceive Anglos by their recourse to Spanish pretensions. "The difficulty with 'Spanish-American' is that while it suits the New Mexican in the abstract," Campa concluded, "there is little in his appearance and origin that upholds the distinction he is trying so hard to make." [36] He later added more boldly: "Today there are people who claim pure [Spanish] blood lines—nonsense before the facts which history presents." [37] A second consideration was that the term "Mexican" had to be disassociated from race and even nationality and understood in cultural terms. The historical acculturation, or what the anthropologist Fernando Ortiz called "transculturation," of Spanish and Indian cultural ingredients had evolved into a syncretic Mexican or mestizo culture. The Spanish-speaking in New Mexico shared in this culture and it tied them to other Spanish-speaking people on both sides of the U.S.-Mexican border. They were culturally Mexican in addition to sharing common racial characteristics. Moreover, cultural differences between the New Mexican and the Mexican south of the border added up to only regional variations of a similar culture, although Campa did not discount the fact that because of Americanization Mexican Americans north of the border had made further cultural adaptations. "The substitution of the name 'Spanish' for everything in New Mexico does not change the substance of traits that are undisputedly Mexican," he insisted. "The 'Spanish' suppers given by clubs and church societies are in reality Mexican dishes to which no truly Spanish palate is accustomed. The 'Spanish' songs sung by school children and by radio performers in New Mexico are as Mexican as *tortillas de maíz, chicharrones de puerco, chile con carne,* and the *sopapillas* at Christmas time." [38] To suggest that the Spanish-speaking in New Mexico were culturally Mexican did not mean, however, that no significant Spanish cultural traits existed. What it did suggest was that these traits had "become identified with the soil" and by so doing had been culturally transformed into a new culture: a mexicano culture. Campa observed that not all the Spanish-speaking in New Mexico denied their cultural and racial realities and that if one went to the common people one would find that they were not so obsessed with racial distinctions as were the more middle class:

> They [common people] conceive of their own kin in realistic terms such as *nosotros, nuestra gente, la raza,* and *nosotros los mexicanos.* By *mexicanos* they do not mean Mexicans, neither can it be translated as such. In fact the term must remain in the language in which it was conceived. *Mexicanos,* the culture that still nurtures them when out of school. Mexican art, dress, music, and food are still the rule among these *mexicanos* north of the

river. *Mexicanos de México,* is the phrase that distinguishes the Mexican national. By inference it admits of a *mexicano* on either side of the river.[39]

If race and culture consciousness shaped self-identification, regionalism did likewise. Campa called on the Spanish-speaking in New Mexico to identify with the land of their birth—New Mexico. He noted that in other regions where the Spanish settled they soon came to identify with that land. They saw themselves as Argentineans, Chileans, and Mexicans. "Precisely, had it not been for this manner of thinking and feeling, the independence of the Americans would have never occurred," Campa pointed out. "Simón Bolívar, Hidalgo, and many of the heroes of Independence were actually Spanish. Nevertheless, for having been born in their respective New World countries, they no longer considered themselves Spaniards, but rather, natives of their birth place." Yet in recognizing and validating the term "New Mexican," one still had to stress the Mexican connection. "[W]here did he get the name 'New Mexican'?" Campa asked. "The name says it all. To become New Mexicans he first had to be Mexican. And what is denigrating about this?" Recognizing that many Americans as well as Europeans during the 1930s had become enchanted with Mexico and Mexican culture, Campa appealed to his fellow Mexican Americans in New Mexico to stop being ashamed of considering themselves Mexicans. "What does exist is a Mexican culture," Campa reiterated concerning the interconnection between New Mexican and Mexican cultures:

> That is to say, the men who are products of this culture speak Castilian, sing traditional ballads and compose their own songs, such as "El Rancho Grande," "Cielito Lindo," etc., etc. Now let us observe to what extent New Mexicans are "Mexican" in culture and to what point they are "Spanish." Here, we enjoy a good life of frijoles and tamales, not to mention *mole* made in Santa Fe. We sing all the latest Mexican songs and we have the same tradition. The "Varsoviana" came to us through Mexico's Second Empire, and we like brown-skinned maidens with dark eyes. Essentially, we cannot lose time in foolishness and preoccupations which make us the mockery of everyone else. By being New Mexican we will be Mexicans because of our undeniable culture and Spanish for never having denied ourselves.[40]

Finally, Campa in a newspaper essay in *El Nuevo Mexicano* in 1939 entitled "La Nueva Generación" [The New Generation] observed that although ethnic identity was important, ultimately more important would be whether Mexican Americans could obtain the education, knowledge, and abilities to make substantive changes for their communities. This would be the "New

Generation" or new "aristocracy" and Campa suggested that he saw such a generation, obviously including himself, on the rise. This generation would put aside the "Spanish Fantasy" and, possessing a realistic and secure conception of themselves, would become the new leaders of their people. Through their skills as college-trained professionals they would bring not only honor to their communities but, more important, concrete improvements:

> [A] new generation has arisen—a generation without the stupid preoccupation of whether one is or is not a true Spaniard. Persons who promoted aristocratic ideas and other absurdities now see themselves succeeded by a younger generation who will take over shortly and lead the Hispanic people through more favorable and advantageous parts. While the "Spanish people" have been boasting of their race and wasting their energy trying to convince everyone, including themselves, of their grand ancestry, the more humble have attended universities throughout the country, searching for something which will give them a true meaning in society. This new generation is aware that in the world of action the only aristocracy that exists is that of men with KNOWLEDGE AND ABILITY.[41]

Southwestern Paradox

Cultural retention and self-identification as mexicanos, however, did not preclude degrees of acculturation with Anglo-American life. Campa understood that a paradox operated in the Southwest. A double form of acculturation characterized Mexican-American life. The older Mexican-American culture of the region was acculturating at the same time to both Mexican immigrant culture and to Anglo-American culture. Yet such acculturation had not always occurred in a balanced fashion. Following the Mexican War, the Spanish-Mexican culture of the Southwest found itself in a disadvantaged position with the new American one. In the case of New Mexico, Campa observed that the penetration by the railroads into the central plateau and the arrival of Anglo settlers had forced Mexican-American culture on the defensive. "Eventually, through an overwhelming majority of Anglo settlers, and through the efforts of educational institutions," Campa added, "the American tempo of life became the rule, and Spanish ways became interesting exceptions, quaint modes of life to be studied rather than lived."[42] English became the dominant language and Spanish in time began to incorporate various Anglicisms so that Mexican Americans would now say "watchear unrato, parkear un carro, and flunkear una examinacion with the naive conviction that they are speaking Spanish!"[43] Regretting such cultural changes not only in New Mexico but in other areas of the Southwest such as California, some New Mexican trovadores composed *canciones* (songs) poking jest at "Anglocized" Mexican Americans, referred to as "pochos." One such canción entitled "Los Pochis de California" stated:

Los pochis de California
No saben comer tortillas
Porque sólo en la mesa
Usan pan con mantequilla.

Me casé con una pochi
Para aprender inglés
Y a los tres días de casado
Yo ya le decía *yes*.[44]

[The pochis of California
No longer know how to eat tortillas
Because now only on their tables
They use bread and butter.

I married a *pochi*
In order to learn English
And after three days of marriage
I had learned to say yes.]

Cultural defensiveness, however, gave way to cultural revitalization with the mass migration of Mexican immigrants in the twentieth century, which helped to slow Americanization and bring about a renaissance in Mexican-American culture. It now became more assertive. "One begins to hear Castilian in the classrooms; teachers mention Spanish literature; Don Quixote is read; the history of the conquest is studied; and following Coronado, one by one Juan de Oñate, Diego de Vargas, de Anza, Hidalgo, Santa Ana and Chávez are praised," Campa reported of this cultural revival in New Mexico.[45] Campa regarded it as fortunate that the resurgence of Mexican culture was occurring at a time when Mexico itself was undergoing a cultural rebirth due to the nationalism of the Mexican Revolution of 1910.[46] Spanish-Mexican culture in the Southwest survived the Anglo-American conquest and hence the issue for Mexican Americans in the twentieth century was not cultural capitulation but cultural coexistence.

Recognizing and validating a distinct Mexican-American cultural presence in the United States, Campa more than both Castañeda and Sánchez believed that Mexican and Anglo cultures remained competitive rather than complementary. Campa shared a cultural pluralist world view with Castañeda and Sánchez but gave greater emphasis to cultural differences than cultural similarities. He asserted, for example, that the U.S. conquest of the Southwest had produced not only political and economic dislocations but also cultural ones. Mexicano culture had been challenged and threatened by a new

Anglo social order. Cultural conflict or divergence between Anglos and Mexican Americans found its roots in the particular histories of Anglo-Saxons and Hispanic peoples. Campa reflected years later in 1973:

> English culture was basically insular, geographically and ideologically; was more integrated on the whole, except for some strong theological differences; and was particularly zealous of its racial purity. Spanish culture was peninsular, a geographical circumstance that made it a catchall of Mediterranean, central European and north African peoples. The composite nature of the population produced a marked regionalism that prevented close integration, except for religion, and led to a strong sense of individualism. These differences were reflected in the colonizing enterprise of the two cultures.[47]

Historical differences produced a clash in values. Hispanics and Anglos valued life in different terms. Campa in his 1973 article "Anglos vs. Chicanos" contended that in general Anglo culture was absolutist whereas Mexican culture was relativistic. Anglos believed that dominant values such as justice, charity, and honesty formed universal values that all other cultures shared or should share. Campa believed, however, that such a view was in fact self-centered rather than being universalist. It imposed one's own culturally biased values on another who possessed different historical and cultural experiences. Mexican Americans, on the other hand, derived from Hispanic peoples, who placed less of a moral value on one's actions and whose values were based more on concrete social and economic conditions than on "universal" abstract notions. Campa further observed differences with respect to individualism. Anglo individualism was calculating and bound to a set of rules and collective standards, whereas Mexican individualism was more emotional and subject to momentary change.[48] Campa noted that status in the Anglo tradition was more contradictory and hypocritical than in the Hispanic. Whether they were peasants or landowners, mexicanos under Spanish and Mexican rule understood their particular status in society through the prevailing ideology that supported stratification. They knew their place and what they could or could not do, given their class status. Yet under U.S. rule, Mexican Americans were told that all men were equal while in fact that clearly was not the case. Status did not conform to ideology. "Once this region was established as part of the North American nation, there arose the right for all to *do* the same things—that is to say, the concept of American democracy," Campa wrote in 1939. "But what was strange was that on one hand he was told in a loud voice that now he had equal rights to *do* what he wanted within the law, and on the other hand he was frowned upon because he was of Mexican or Spanish origin."[49] Campa did not, of course, support feudalism over bourgeois democracy, but he did believe that democratic ideology had to be lived up to not just in the abstract but in fact. Finally, Campa asserted that a basic value differentiation between Anglos and Mexican Americans concerned their view of money and business. Anglos placed business relationships above human relationships while Mexican Americans due to their particular heritage did not. "Cervantes himself never kept track of the money which he lent his friends, not because he wanted to steal what was not his, but because his friends came first and then came business," Campa explained. "After so many years, the Mexican continues placing great importance on the individual and the human being because for him, nothing stands above humanity." [50] Mexican Americans did not tie self-worth to material status but rather to one's humanity.

Anglos and Mexicans also possessed contradictory conceptions of time. In a 1939 article entitled "Mañana Is Today," Campa noted that the Spanish-speaking of New Mexico saw the past, present, and future in different terms than Anglos. Whereas Anglos were obsessed with the future, Mexican Americans derived from a tradition that validated the past and the present and that regarded the future as too abstract. However, the present was real, and when the present reverted to the past, that also was real; it was part of one's memory and tradition. For Mexican Americans the past was more than just utilitarian; it was one's heritage. [51] "It could be said that the Hispano lives twice," Campa observed in another 1939 essay, "once when he passes through the present, and the next time when he remembers it." [52] Being past and present oriented, Mexican Americans could define the future only by using the indefinite term, *mañana*. "The translation of this word has led to a misinterpretation of purpose on the part of those who view the New Mexican with the degree of objective criticism characteristic of so many Hispanists," Campa wrote. "*Mañana,* like the shrug of the shoulders, expresses a remoteness that the word 'tomorrow' does not convey. It does not mean tomorrow." [53] Campa repudiated the idea that the Mexican-American view of the future meant putting off certain actions. Instead, it meant doing those actions now and not later. "The New Mexican never puts off until tomorrow what can be done *only* today," he added. "Life must be lived today, else one finds, too late, that the calendar does not turn backward." [54] Mexican-American philosophy was that of the realist. "Mañana stems from the Spanish concept of reality which gives prominence to the present, that is, to reality," he further concluded in 1951. "He calls the present 'actualidad' that which really exists." [55] Campa likewise challenged the view held by many Anglos that Mexican Americans because of their view of time were lazy. This was not the case and the difference here was not one of industry, but of the worth of that industry. "We characterize the Mexican peasant as a lazy indifferent fellow, yet the market is filled with millions of craft products made tediously by hand, and with superb craftsmanship."[56]

Such cultural differences, which related to history, values, and conception of time, Campa also believed to be based on a rural-urban dichotomy. He argued that one of the causes of cultural tensions between the two major ethnic groups in the Southwest was that one was still rooted more in a rural folk culture while the other, the Anglo, represented an essentially urban culture. Folk culture produced different values and world views that did not easily coexist with a more materialistic urban society. "In a further consideration of a cultural amalgamation in New Mexico," Campa stressed, "one must take into account that American civilization is, for the most part, dependent upon industrialization, while New Mexico is composed of rural communities where the folk element is still a vital force."[57] Nevertheless, Campa believed that some levels of accommodation could be reached and that Mexican Americans could undergo urbanization identified as material and educational development without surrendering their "truly Hispanic nature." Urbanization did not necessarily mean assimilation, but rather acculturation. In 1971 he wrote:

> When we recommend that the Spanish-speaking community acquire more technical competence, that they accept or adapt to the change instituted by progress, that they develop more acquisitiveness, that they base their behavior on principle rather than on custom, and that they manifest a greater faith in the educational process, we are speaking of urbanization pure and simple. To the degree that Hispanics move in the direction pointed out by these objectives, they became more urbanized but not necessarily dishispanized as it is feared by some and expected by others.[58]

In the end, although Campa stressed cultural differences and even cultural conflict between Mexican Americans and Anglos, he did believe that cultural coexistence was possible in the Southwest. Mexican Americans through urbanization were already making their cultural compromises. They could afford to do so because, as Campa saw it, their historical culture refreshed by contact with Mexico could sustain acculturation with Anglo America without being seriously damaged. Mexican-American culture would endure although in an adaptive rather than static form. To achieve cultural coexistence, however, Anglos would have to begin to respect and accept Mexican-American culture. They would have to accept it not just as a curious archaic culture but as one which continued to live and flourish. "The language of New Mexico, the song of the troubadours, the folk theater, and other forms of folklore constitute a fundamental basis of his existence," Campa said of Mexicans to an Anglo audience. "Take each one of these elements in its native state and deal with it as a living force rather than as so

much material to be catalogued according to some preconceived index."[59]
Cultural differences did not have to be irreconcilable, Campa argued just before his death, if approached with mutual respect and understanding.[60] Indeed
cultural compromise over the years had already taken place as Anglos and
Mexican Americans borrowed various aspects of one another's cultures.[61]
"Both groups," he wrote, "have crossed each other's borders, so to speak,
with unintentional success."[62] Campa observed the mixing of English and
Spanish in the Southwest as one manifestation of cultural adaptation. He reflected in 1971 that the current "Chicano Renaissance" was important and
that Anglos had to realize there could be no "instant acculturation" for Mexican Americans, given their unique history and traditions. Acculturation could
take place only in stages, and one involved the need by Mexican Americans
to be proud of their culture and their identity as Mexican Americans at the
same time that they perceived the need to accommodate to urban American
life.[63] If these adjustments could be made, Campa believed that the Southwest and in particular his favorite state of New Mexico could stand out as a
model of true cultural pluralism and form the foundation for what Campa
referred to in 1939 as a "new civilization":

> If the future of the North American nation rests spreading southward in its
> economic and moral development, the most strategic and important place is
> where two civilizations meet. The Rio Grande will be the place where both
> civilizations shall join hands and form the culture of the New World—an
> American culture in the fullest sense of the word.
>
> The Rio Grande will see the development of a new civilization: gifted
> with the serenity of the Indian, guided by the zealous spirit of the Yankee,
> and tempered by the spirituality and love of life of the Mexican heir of
> Spain who cultivates his inheritance in the land of Anahuac![64]

Conclusion

While Campa failed to understand Mexican-American culture
within a more definite socioeconomic context, and hence risked romanticizing
or "folklorizing" that culture, still Campa predated the Chicano Movement's
stress on popular culture. By his studies of New Mexican and Southwestern
folk culture, Campa drew attention to the organic character of Mexican-
American culture and to its authenticity in the Southwest. Yet disdaining
provincialism, Campa reflected his own Mexican-Americanism by making
connections between New Mexican cultural traditions and those of other
Mexican Americans in the Southwest as well as with Mexico. For Campa,
Mexican-American culture was an evolving phenomenon, although rooted in

southwestern history. In his studies, Campa sought answers to the prevailing questions of identity and cultural presence that affected a new Mexican-American Generation which sought the border, or what Juan Bruce-Novoa has called the *space,* between their Mexican and American roots.[65] The quest for identity and culture did not begin with the Chicano Movement of the 1960s, and in Campa one finds many of the same questions, although perhaps not the same answers, that the later generation would also ask.

Conclusion

CHAPTER TWELVE

The Chicano in American History

Historically, Mexican-Americans have been, and continue to be, a pluralistic people.

—OCTAVIO ROMANO, 1968

Chicanos view themselves as participants in the historical process, for they are inseparable from history.

—OCTAVIO ROMANO, 1970

Chicano or Mexican-American history as a particular field has been explored only during the past twenty years. Although a traditional literature has existed for some time on the Spanish Borderlands, it has been too concentrated on the Spanish colonial period of the Southwest. Until recently, historians have mostly been oblivious to the presence of Mexicans in American history of the nineteenth and twentieth centuries. Mexicans have served only as footnotes to the United States expansion into Mexico's northern territory during the nineteenth century, the clash with Mexico during the Mexican War of the 1840s, and the U.S. response to the Mexican Revolution of 1910. In general, Mexicans, Chicanos, and Mexican Americans have remained invisible, or "forgotten people," as George Sánchez termed them. Early anthropological and sociological studies by scholars such as Bogardus, Gamio, and Taylor appeared during the 1920s and 1930s, but they contained only passing historical perspectives.[1] Not until Carey McWilliams's 1949 monograph, *North From Mexico: The Spanish-Speaking People of the United States,* did a more complete text appear on what later would be called Chicano history.[2] Fortunately, the social convulsions and accompanying ethnic movements of the 1960s, including the Chicano Movement, generated a new awareness in the history of those ethnic groups, such as Mexican Americans, who for the most part had been as isolated or segregated in U.S. history as they were in real life. The movements of the 1960s penetrated American universities and provided for the first time significant opportunities for the training of young minority scholars. By the mid-1970s a cohort of historians, many of Mexican descent, had completed their Ph.D.s—what I call the Generation of '75, since many received their degrees in 1975—and began researching and teaching in major southwestern universities. The result has been what Camarillo has called the "florescence" of Chicano history.[3] This manifestation is part of a larger revisionist movement in the historiography of the United States since the 1960s which has fundamentally changed our historical perspectives. Afro-American history, women's history, the "new ethnic history," the "new immigrant history," the "new labor history," and the "new social history" have all come to represent the most dynamic new developments in U.S. historiography and have broadened the meaning of the American experience. At least at the level of higher education (for no satisfactory trickle-down process into the high schools and grade schools has been achieved), it is difficult to view the history of the United States as we did before.

The Integration of Chicano History

Chicano history in its short period of development has contributed to this revised history of the United States and, in particular, to the history of the Southwest. Now it is almost impossible to ignore the Mexican in southwestern history. To the extent that Chicano history likewise has a close affinity to events in Mexico, it has further added to that neighboring republic's historiography. Yet it is important to stress continually the integration of Chicano history within the mainstream of U.S. history. Historians outside ethnic history need to confront at different levels the presence of the Mexican in American life. At the same time, Chicano historians also need to integrate Chicano history within U.S. history. Still too closely tied to the political spirit of the Chicano Movement, which stressed alienation from American life and distance from traditional American values, Chicano historians have added to the search for alternatives to the question of who and what is an American. Yet the danger of an overemphasis on alienation and separation is that we isolate the history of the Mexican from its proper U.S. context. We misread the complexity of that history by overstressing what can be called either the victimization approach to history, which portrays Mexicans essentially as victims rather than as makers of history, or the resistance approach to history, which pictures all Mexicans in history as prototypes of the Chicano militants of the 1960s and 1970s.

How can we more realistically treat Chicano history as U.S. history, and how does the present book fit into this effort? The Spanish colonial experience in what came to be the southwestern portion of the United States, for example, can be interpreted, as Bolton years ago suggested in his discussion of "Greater America," as part of the colonial history of the United States.[4]

The founding of Santa Fe in 1609 and the establishment of missions, presidios, and towns from Texas to California is no less the history of what came to be the United States than the settlements at Plymouth and Jamestown. The history of the United States is not just an east-to-west affair, but a south-to-north one as well. In studying the nineteenth century, we need to incorporate the meaning of the rise of Manifest Destiny, the Texas Revolution of 1836, and the Mexican War (1846–48) in light of what these events signify about the attitudes of Anglo Americans toward other peoples on this continent and how they add to the ethnic history of the United States. While the Mexican War is often treated as an additional step in the coming of the Civil War, it is in fact a watershed for those who became Mexican Americans as the result of that conflict. The incorporation of Mexican Americans through conquest further revises our meaning of the process of becoming an American.

The Mexican War transferred to the United States not only a massive amount of territory but a historical space with a previous past, a people (both Indian and Mexican), and varied cultural traditions. For Mexicans, the end of the conflict began what can more correctly be called the Mexican-American experience. Hence to discuss origins—roots—it is not sufficient to consider only ethnic and cultural distinctions; one must confront history and, in particular, the history of the United States. Chicano history begins in conflict, conquest, and subordination. That subordination is part of what can be considered the extension of the Reconstruction and post-Reconstruction period in the South to the Southwest. Territorial aggrandizement, the lure of new wealth, and the commencement of the integration of this previously Mexican territory into the larger political economy of the United States led in time to the economic displacement of Mexicans, especially those who held important land concessions coveted by the new "gringo" settlers and entrepreneurs. It also meant the introduction of American racism and the construction of an informal and de facto system of Jim Crowism in the Southwest toward another people of color: Mexican Americans. Consequently, by the end of the nineteenth century, Mexican Americans, although granted U.S. citizenship, were in fact second-class citizens and part of the dispossessed in American history.

By the turn of the century, Chicano history represents even more the history of the United States. Seemingly relegated to an isolated or relatively insignificant status, with the exception of northern New Mexico, Mexican Americans underwent a major revitalization and reinforcement during the early twentieth century due to the first great migration from Mexico to the United States. It is in this historical moment that the complexity of the Mexican in American history is revealed. As nineteenth-century subjects of the United States who in many cases could trace their ancestry to the Spanish explorations and settlements of the seventeenth and eighteenth centuries, Mexican Americans on the one hand are an old ethnic group. Yet with the arrival of millions of immigrants from Mexico during the twentieth century, they are also a new ethnic group. This latter migration—what McWilliams referred to as coming "North from Mexico"—resulted from the full absorption of the Southwest into a national economic system. The triumph of industrial capitalism, with its need for new sources of industrial raw materials as well as foodstuffs to feed the growing industrial armies being assembled in the East and Midwest, meant turning to virgin areas such as the Southwest for a complementary extractive economy. The development of a railroad infrastructure, mining, smelting, agriculture, and ranching all necessitated a vast and continuing supply of cheap and manageable labor. Mexico and Mexican immigrant workers served that purpose. Consequently, between 1900 and 1930 more than a million Mexicans—mostly poor immigrant workers—crossed the border and became Mexican Americans. Here the history of the Mexican in the United States coincides with the history of millions of other immigrants in the process of becoming Americans. This is a history rooted in the relationship between the labor needs of industrial capitalism and the displacement of millions of people in Eastern and Southern Europe, Mexico, and to a lesser extent Asia, owing to changes in the world economy and their need to migrate in order to survive. Consequently, Mexican Americans in the twentieth century form part of an expansive new addition to the American national experience: the incorporation of millions of new immigrants as sources of cheap labor.

While grateful for a haven in the United States, despite much hardship and labor exploitation, the new immigrants and their children, as part of their Americanization, in time experienced a process of rising expectations. By the 1930s, as children of the new immigrants began to come of age, they introduced a new historical period. First becoming Americans as sources of cheap labor, the new ethnic Americans aspired now to a new position where they could become Americans in the fullest meaning of the term, as expressed in the Declaration of Independence and the U.S. Constitution. They desired to become "Americans All." The Mexican American is no different. What *Mexican Americans* has attempted to define is that new phase in Chicano history which is part of a wider one in the history of ethnic America. It is the political, economic, social, and cultural movement by the new immigrants and their children, born in the teeming slums, ghettos, and barrios of an industrializing America, to achieve the fruits of their labor and to be accepted as first-class U.S. citizens. If the Great Depression momentarily stymied this effort, it did not destroy the aspirations associated with it, which received further stimulation by the populism and pluralism of the New Deal.

The outbreak of World War II and the U.S. entrance into the conflict literally collapsed many of the barriers to greater assimilation, at least for European ethnics. The War for the Four Freedoms, to save democracy, and a war for all Americans proved to be the major advancement in the immigrant pursuit of the American dream.

The Mexican-American Generation

If Mexican Americans, like Afro Americans, Asian Americans, and Native Americans, still faced obstacles to what Gordon calls structural assimilation in comparison to eastern and southern Europeans, they did not lose faith.[5] What I have sought to relate are the struggles by Mexican Americans, led by a new ethnic leadership—the Mexican-American Generation— to achieve equal status with other Americans. This was a generation, certainly in its manifestation as a political generation, which sought its place in American history. Mexican Americans, like other descendants of the new immigrants, came of political age by the Great Depression and World War II. Unlike the nineteenth-century Mexican Americans or the previous generation of immigrants from Mexico, Mexican Americans by the 1930s and 1940s recognized themselves as U.S. citizens, knew that their country was the United States and not Mexico, had become increasingly socialized to U.S. norms, ideologies, and mass culture, and expected to be treated like other Americans. At the same time, they were not as a whole ashamed of their ethnic and cultural backgrounds. Like other ethnics, they were sensitive and insecure as to what their identity represented, but they hoped for some balance between respect for their parents' culture and their own consciousness that they were different—they were Americans. Yet for Mexican Americans, perhaps even more than for European and Asian ethnics, the meaning of being an American was translated and interpreted in continuing ethnic terms due to greater obstacles to structural assimilation and acculturation, plus the continuing flow of new immigrants from Mexico and the adjacency of Mexico to the Southwest. Faced with dualities and paradoxes as Mexican Americans, this generation actively sought the meaning of being American and its place in U.S. society. Consequently, the making of the Mexican American was not only predicated on their ethnic-class position, which was based on this country's valuation of Mexicans as cheap labor, but also the result of the struggles by Mexican Americans themselves to achieve first-class citizenship and a secure identity.

The history of the Mexican-American Generation, like that of their counterparts among Afro Americans and other racial-ethnic minorities, is one of mixed success. As noted in the case studies of this generation, some achievements were accomplished by breaking down legal and de facto barriers to first-class citizenship. The Mexican-American middle class, especially in the areas of education, political representation, and public facilities and led by groups such as LULAC, the School Improvement League in San Antonio, the Unity Leagues in Southern California, the Community Service Organization (CSO), the American G.I. Forum, as well as other Mexican-American veterans' associations, successfully asserted the rights of Mexican Americans. Mexican-American radicals in organizations such as the Spanish-Speaking Congress and ANMA, although directing their efforts more toward working-class issues and to the plight of immigrants, supplemented the general civil rights movement led by the middle class. Clearly, reform and not revolution characterized the Mexican-American Generation. Mexican-American labor leaders in the new, aggressive CIO unions such as Mine Mill advanced the integration of Mexican-American workers into the mainstream of the U.S. working class and extended organization and protection that was lacking in earlier periods. Finally, a new but still infinitesimal Mexican-American professional intelligentsia surfaced in the likes of Castañeda, Sánchez, and Campa. These intellectuals, in concert with community activists, forged a new meaning and definition of what it meant to be an American of Mexican descent.

Yet although the Mexican-American Generation represented a complex and dynamic leadership and achieved a number of breakthroughs, it, unlike European ethnic groups, failed to capture first-class citizenship for its people. Mexican-American reforms and a new consciousness did not, in the end, affect the structurally deep-seated class and racial limitations on mobility imposed on people of color. Initially deprived of their resources in the post-Mexican War era of the nineteenth century, invited and transported in by the millions in the twentieth century as cheap labor for the railroads, mines, smelters, fields, and industries of the country, Mexican Americans have historically served as a source of cheap labor. Their struggles to remove themselves from their oppressed ethnic class and social position strike at the very heart of the particular socioeconomic system of the Southwest and to a larger extent of the United States. The Mexican-American Generation influenced and pressured this stratified system but could not fundamentally dent it. This failure, of course, also resulted from internal Mexican-American conditions and consciousness. Middle-class Mexican Americans, despite their commitment to an unrelenting struggle for first-class citizenship, possessed a "false consciousness." That is, they incorrectly believed in the ability of the system to reform itself. Problems, they contended, could be dealt with by moral persuasion, appeals to democratic principles, and through peaceful protest. In their own personal success, a growing, although still small, Mexican-

American middle class deceived itself into believing that their progress meant progress for all other Mexican Americans.

Radicals and working-class leaders of the Mexican-American Generation faced their own dilemmas and frustrations. Correctly recognizing that a more militant class movement was not yet possible, radicals such as those in El Congreso, and like the U.S. Left in general, placed too much value on the Popular Front strategy and its critical support for the New Deal to win reforms and to advance the class struggle. Consequently, critical support gave way during World War II to unconditional support for the New Deal and the ultimate abandonment of Popular Front groups such as El Congreso. ANMA attempted to resurrect the left tradition in Mexican-American politics after the war, but despite certain successes in organization faced the even greater problem of the cold war and McCarthy era, which in time led to ANMA's demise. Working-class leaders such as those in Mine Mill organized and achieved new and better economic status and security for their members but, like other U.S. workers, went no further than bread and butter reforms. Moreover, by the 1950s, despite a militant reform tradition, Mexican-American unionists, like the rest of the Mexican-American Generation, confronted the oppressive political culture of the time, which stymied additional reforms.

The Chicano Generation

Not until the easing of McCarthyism and the cold war in the early 1960s would a new political generation—the Chicano Generation—arise and lead another and perhaps more profound struggle. Yet the Chicano Generation, despite the efforts of some scholars to isolate it from history, built on both the successes and failures of the Mexican-American Generation. There was no quantum leap, as suggested by the rhetoric and symbols of the Chicano Movement, from the rebels of the Mexican Revolution of 1910 to the Chicano militants of the 1960s. The Mexican-American Generation and era mediated the historical development of the Chicano Movement. The success of the Mexican-American Generation, for example, in education, jobs, political representation, and public accommodations allowed their children— the Chicanos—or at least a portion of them to achieve more education and better opportunities for social mobility. The Mexican-American Generation laid the foundation for a new era of the politics of rising expectations. That foundation would help create a leading vanguard of the Chicano Movement of the 1960s and 1970s: the Chicano student movement. At the same time, the failures of the Mexican-American Generation meant that the paradox of progress and poverty, of progress for some but poverty for many, continued to characterize the Mexican-American experience. Coming of age in a new period of reform and rising expectations embodied by John Kennedy's New Frontier and later Lyndon Johnson's Great Society, affected by a greater awareness of other struggles such as the black civil rights movement, the Black Power Movement, the youth movement, the efforts for national liberation in the Third World, and faced with the tragic consequences of the Vietnam War, including the loss of thousands of Chicano lives, the Chicano Generation moved to rectify the failures of the past and to break through the ideological handicaps of the Mexican-American Generation.

For the Chicano Generation, reforms were not enough. National liberation—Chicano Power—or some form of it was now demanded. Similarities with other Americans were of no importance. Differences were now valued. Rather than just being a minority, Chicanos were now to be regarded as a conquered people suffering "internal colonialism" but struggling to achieve their national independence. To address that liberation and to find historical support, Chicanos turned not to the American Revolution but to the Mexican Revolution of 1910. For a new sense of identity, Chicanos turned away from cultural pluralism and a sense of being "Americans All" and looked toward the pre-Columbian past and to the indigenous roots of the mestizo. The mythical state of Aztlán—the alleged Aztec name for the Southwest—was now the homeland, not the United States. Cultural and ideological liberation would in turn lead to political liberation and a new people—a new nation. In its obsession for a new history and a new culture, the Chicano Generation created its own myths and "false consciousness." Nevertheless, for the first time, on a larger scale than ever before, Americans of Mexican descent challenged the very basic ideological foundations of the United States. If the Mexican-American Generation had hopes of achieving the American dream, the Chicano Generation despaired of it. If the Mexican-American Generation was an optimistic one, the Chicano Generation was at once a skeptical, pessimistic, and romantic one. Yet like the Mexican-American Generation, the Chicano Generation was a product of its historical time. Despite its rejection of the American experience, it was born out of that experience. It marched in step with other Americans. Instead of being marginal to U.S. history, it was part of the central forces shaping that history in the 1960s and early 1970s. If the Mexican-American Generation was part of the movement of the new immigrants to capture first-class citizenship, the Chicano Generation was part of a wider youth alienation and rebellion that sought alternative models of social change in post-industrialized America.

If the Chicano Generation was more radical in its aspirations, nevertheless it did not completely break with its own past. As part of a history of a people dispossessed in a war of conquest in the nineteenth century and recruited as cheap immigrant labor in the twentieth century, the Chicanos of the

1960s and 1970s advanced the struggles by Mexicans in the United States to achieve a better and more secure life. The efforts to achieve first-class citizenship so central to the Mexican-American Generation, although clothed in a different style and rhetoric, were still visible among the Chicano Generation. The militant politics of the Spanish-Speaking Congress and of ANMA, together with the stress on the role of workers advanced by Mexican-American trade unionists, was likewise further manifested in the Chicano Movement. The reinterpretation of history, society, and culture in the works of Mexican-American intellectuals such as Castañeda, Sánchez, and Campa also finds a place in the evolution of the Chicano mind. The history of both the Mexican-American Generation and the Chicano Generation is testimony that for certain members of ethnic America, rooted in the transport of millions of new immigrant workers into an industrializing America at the turn of the century, the road to first-class citizenship has been a very long one, owing to the greater deviations of racial and class discrimination as they have affected Americans of color.

Both the Mexican-American Generation and the Chicano Generation—as expressions of leadership—attempted in their own distinct styles to confront and challenge the historically exploited positions of Mexicans in the United States. Neither generation fully succeeded. Yet each advanced the struggle. Each passed on and added to a legacy of Mexicans as historical actors struggling to achieve self-determination. Unfortunately, this tradition has found a less receptive audience in the post-Chicano Movement era of the late 1970s and the 1980s. Rigid conservatism and political reaction, as epitomized by the Reagan–Bush administration and a cautious Democratic party, have more forcefully opposed the legitimate demands of racial minorities such as Mexican Americans. Harder political times in turn have weakened Mexican-American leadership and its resolve to wage concerted campaigns for equal rights, equal rewards, and ethnic integrity. While some pockets of progressive Mexican-American leadership remain, primarily in the labor movement and on university campuses, Mexican-American leadership on the whole has seemed more disposed to conform to the conservative temper of the times. Mexican-American leaders, besides pursuing a reduced agenda on the civil rights front, have allowed government and the mass media to define them as "Hispanics" and thus obliterate or disguise the historically based effort by Mexican Americans at self-definition. These displays of powerlessness have instead helped to create a nebulous and weak "Hispanic Generation." The self-proclaimed Decade of the Hispanic in the 1980s has only resulted in a growing alienation of Mexican Americans and the withholding of the just fruits of their labor. Educational reform, for example, one of the centerpieces of both the Mexican-American Generation and the Chicano Generation, has been a disastrous experience in the 1980s. Today, more Chicano children than in the last three decades find themselves in segregated and inferior schools.

The challenge of the 1990s and beyond will be whether a new generation of community-oriented activists can give new meaning and life to the Mexican-American legacy of struggle. A revitalization of the effort to combat a permanent minority status for Mexicans in the United States seems to be in order. However, to regain such momentum this new political generation will need to discard the historical amnesia of the 1980s, so well revealed in Richard Rodríguez's classic statement of the decade, *Hunger of Memory,* and instead recapture a "memory of history"—a history of uncompromising dedication and struggle for full equality with other Americans.

Conclusion

Although Chicano or Mexican-American history possesses its particular characteristics and should be appreciated for them, it should also be interpreted as part of the larger history of the United States. The history of this country is a complex and heterogeneous one, composed of many and varied experiences, and Mexican Americans form one aspect of it. Segmented by history, class, race, ethnicity, gender, and culture, this country is a vast panorama of people. The Mexican-American experience is one aspect of this panorama and increasingly a greater portion of it. In the twenty-first century Hispanics/Latinos will compose the largest minority population in the United States. Within this group, Mexican Americans now represent well over half of these numbers. In the Southwest, states such as Texas and California with their burgeoning Hispanic/Latino populations are already faced with Latin Americanization. We must understand these profound ethnic and demographic changes and seek to learn from history what they will mean in a new ethnic era of the country. Yet to benefit from these lessons we must approach this history—as I hope I have in *Mexican Americans*—with an understanding of its complexity and with the perspective that rather than being a foreign and alien experience, the history of Mexican Americans as well as that of other Hispanic/Latino groups is in fact an authentic American experience.

Note on Sources

As mentioned in the acknowledgments, this study is dependent on archival sources. Hence much of my task in conceptualizing the Mexican-American Generation was to locate primary materials. Fortunately, particular libraries and archives contained sufficient documents to provide the nexus for this study.

MANUSCRIPT COLLECTIONS

Any study of LULAC must consult the expanding LULAC Collection in the Benson Latin American Library of the University of Texas at Austin. The LULAC Collection consists of a number of individual collections of former LULAC leaders. Those of special value to me were the William Flores Collection, the Ben Garza Collection, the Oliver Douglas Weeks Collection, the M. C. González Collection, the Andrés de Luna Collection, and the Jake Rodríguez Collection.

The LULAC Collection also contains the most complete repository of the *LULAC News*. Other important LULAC sources are privately held collections such as the Henry Martínez Collection in El Paso, the Belén Robles Collection in El Paso, the E. B. León Collection in El Paso, and the M. C. González Collection in San Antonio. There is a small FBI file on LULAC available through the Freedom of Information Act. Additional material on LULAC can be found in the Mexican-American Collection at the Houston Public Library.

Other key archival collections at the Benson Library include the Eleuterio Escobar Collection, which contains the correspondence, records, and related documents of Escobar and the School Improvement League in San Antonio. In addition, the Carlos E. Castañeda Collection represents a vast array of documents concerning Castañeda's career as a librarian/historian at the University of Texas at Austin.

My chapter on Ignacio L. López relied on the Ignacio L. López Collection in Special Collections of the Cecil H. Green Library at Stanford University. The López Collection consists exclusively of an original as well as microfilm copy of *El Espectador*. Material on López was supplemented by the private collection of Leonor Varela López in Pomona, California, and the FBI file on López. Other key archival holdings at Stanford University on the Mexican-American Generation consist of the Manuel Ruiz Jr. Collection, which documents civil rights activities in Los Angeles from the late 1930s to the 1960s; the Ernesto Galarza Collection, which, for my purposes, contains important documents on the Spanish-Speaking Congress; the Eduardo Quevedo Collection, which also provides information on the Congress. Additional sources on the Mexican-American Generation in Southern California were located in the Carey McWilliams Collection in Special Collections at the UCLA Research Library.

Key archival sources for the involvement of Mexican Americans in the International Union of Mine, Mill and Smelter Workers are the expansive archives of Mine Mill in the Western History Collection at the University of Colorado, Boulder. The collection is divided into particular union locals as well as chief union leaders. The Mine Mill archives further contain original copies of the union's newspaper, *The Union*. Primary sources on Mine Mill in El Paso were also available through the U.S. Steelworkers Local in El Paso.

On the Asociación Nacional México-Americana (ANMA), the key sources proved to be the extensive file on ANMA collected by the FBI and obtained through the Freedom of Information Act. Additional material on ANMA was located in the Natalie Gross Collection in the Southwest Collection of the El Paso Public Library and in the Mine Mill archives in the Western History Collection.

The Cleofas Calleros Collections, both at the El Paso Public Library and in Special Collections at the University of Texas at El Paso Library, contained further material on the Mexican-American Generation.

NEWSPAPERS AND PERIODICALS

Besides archival documents, newspapers and periodicals of the time provided a second major source of information for my study. In addition to the *LULAC News, El Espectador,* and *The Union,* already mentioned, various other southwestern publications shed light on particular topics. The *El*

Paso Times and the *El Paso Herald-Post,* for example, were indispensable for my study of the election of Raymond Telles as mayor of El Paso in 1957. *El Continental* of El Paso provided additional data on the Telles election. The *Times* and the *Herald-Post* also contained important material on local LULAC activities and Mine Mill in the border city, as did the *Labor Advocate,* published in El Paso. *La Opinión* (Los Angeles) contained valuable coverage of the work of the Spanish-Speaking Congress. The Communist party's West Coast newspaper, the *People's Daily World,* also proved useful for the congress as well as for ANMA. Copies of *Progresso,* ANMA's newspaper, were located both in the Mine Mill archives and in the Natalie Gross Collection. The *Eastside Sun* (Los Angeles) likewise provided some coverage of ANMA's activities. Finally, *La Prensa* (San Antonio) provided general coverage of Mexican-American activities in Texas.

ORAL HISTORY

Without oral history, my study of the Mexican-American Generation would contain significant gaps. The manuscript collections and newspapers do not tell the entire story. Hence, oral history is vital. I was fortunate to have been able to locate influential members of the Mexican-American Generation who shared with me their experiences, as well as providing me, in some cases, with documents and photographs. In addition to the oral histories listed in the footnotes, additional oral histories were consulted at the Institute of Oral History at the University of Texas at El Paso, the finest repository of oral histories in Chicano and border history.

GENERATIONAL THEORY

Utilizing the concept of political generation, I found the literature on generational theory to be of great value. The following sources are of particular importance: Karl Mannheim, "The Problem of Generations," in *Essays on the Sociology of Knowledge* (New York: Oxford University Press, 1952); Marvin Rintala, *The Constitution of Silence: Essays in Generational Themes* (Westport, Conn.: Greenwood Press, 1979); Rintala, "A Generation in Politics: A Definition," *Review of Politics* 25 (Jan. 1963): 509–522; Richard Samuels, ed., *Political Generation and Political Development* (Lexington, Mass.: Lexington Books, 1977); Julián Marías, *Generations: A Historical Method* (Tuscaloosa: Univ. of Alabama Press, 1970); Samuel Ramos, "The Conflict of Generations," in Ramos, *Profile of Man and Culture in Mexico* (Austin: Univ. of Texas Press, 1972, 2d ed.); Graham Murdoch and Robin McCran, "Consciousness of Class and Consciousness of Generation," in *Working Papers in Cultural Studies* 7–9 (1975–76): 192–207; Alan Spitzer, *The French Generation of 1820* (Princeton, N.J.: Princeton University Press, 1987); Spitzer, "The Historical Problem of Generations," *American Historical Review*, 78 (Dec. 1973), 1353–1386; Robert Wohl, *The Generation of 1914* (Cambridge: Harvard University Press, 1979); S. M. Eisenstadt, *From Generation to Generation: Age Groups and Social Structure* (New York: The Free Press of Glencoe, 1956); Lewis S. Feuer, *The Conflict of Generations: The Character and Significance of Student Movements* (New York: Basic Books, 1969); José Ortega y Gasset, *The Modern Theme* (New York: Harper Torchbooks, 1961); Maurice Zeitlin, "Political Generations in the Cuban Working Class," *American Journal of Sociology*, 71 (March 1966): 493–508; Anthony Esler, ed., *The Youth Revolution: The Conflict of Generations in Modern History* (Lexington, Mass.: D. C. Heath, 1974); special issue on "Generations," *Daedalus*, 107 (Fall 1978); Robert Tyler, "Of Generations, Generation Gaps, and History," in *Connecticut Review*, 5 (Oct. 1971): 5–12; Norman B. Ryder, "The Cohort as a Concept in the Study of Social Change," *American Sociological Review*, 30 (Dec. 1965): 843–861; Hans Jaeger, "Generations in History: Reflections on a Controversial Concept," *History and Theory*, 24 (1985): 273–292; Wilbur J. Scott and Harold G. Grosmick, "Generations and Group Consciousness: A Quantification of Mannheim's Analogy," *Youth & Society*, 11 (Dec. 1979): 191–214.

THE MEXICAN-AMERICAN GENERATION IN CHICANO HISTORY

Although the Mexican-American Generation, as I have conceptualized it, has received only minimal attention in Chicano historiography, nevertheless some sources do concern themselves with it. They include Richard A. García, "The Making of the Mexican-American Mind, San Antonio, Texas, 1929–1941," Ph.D. diss., University of California, Irvine, 1980; Richard A. García, "The Mexican-American Mind: A Product of the 1930s," in Mario T. Garciá and Francisco Lomelí, eds., *History, Culture, and Society: Chicano Studies in the 1980s* (Ypsilanti: Bilingual Review Press, 1983) 67–93; Richard A. García, "Class, Consciousness, and Ideology—The Mexican Community of San Antonio, Texas: 1930–1940," *Aztlán* 9 (Fall 1978): 23–70; Guadalupe San Miguel, "The Struggle Against Separate and Unequal Schools: Middle Class Mexican Americans, and the Desegregation Campaign in Texas, 1929–1957," *History of Education Quarterly* 23 (Fall 1983): 343–359; Guadalupe San Miguel, "Mexican American Organizations and the Changing Politics of School Desegregation in Texas, 1945–1980," *Social Science Quarterly* 63 (Dec. 1982): 701–715; Guadalupe San Miguel, *Let All of Them Take Heed: Mexican-Americans and the Quest for Educational Equality in Texas, 1918–1981* (Austin: University of Texas Press, 1987); Mario T. García, "Mexican Americans and the Politics of Citizenship: The Case of El Paso, 1936," *New Mexico Historical Quarterly* 59 (April 1984): 187–204; Mario T. García, "Americans All: The Mexican-American Generation and the Politics of Wartime Los Angeles, 1941–1945." *Social Science Quarterly* 68 (June 1987): 278–289; Mario T. García, "Mexican-American Labor and the Left: The Asociación Nacional México-Americana, 1949–1954," in John S. García et al., eds., *The Chicano Struggle: Analysis of Past and Present Efforts* (Binghamton, N.Y.: Bilingual Review Press, 1984): 65–86; and Mario T. García, "La Frontera: The Border as Symbol and Reality in Mexican-American Thought," *Mexican Studies/Estudios Mexicanos* 2 (Summer 1985): 195–225.

Notes

CHAPTER ONE: *The Mexican-American Generation*

1. The term "Mexican-American Generation" is not an original term. It was first used by sociologist Rodolfo Álvarez in a 1973 article. Álvarez, however, uses the term more to refer to a biological generation than to a political generation, as this study does. See Álvarez, "The Psycho-Historical and Socioeconomic Development of the Chicano Community in the United States," *Social Science Quarterly* (March 1973), 920–942.

2. Octavio Ignacio Romano V, "Minorities, History, and the Cultural Mystique," *El Grito* (Fall 1967), 5–11; "The Anthropology and Sociology of the Mexican-Americans: The Distortion of Mexican-American History," *El Grito* (Fall 1968), 13–26; "The Historical and Intellectual Presence of Mexican Americans," *ibid.* (Winter 1969), 32–46; "Social Science, Objectivity and the Chicanos," *ibid.* (Fall 1970), 4–16.

3. See Oscar Martínez, "On the Size of the Chicano Population: New Estimates, 1850–1900," *Aztlán* (Spring 1975), 43–67.

4. See U.S. Department of Commerce, *Abstract of the Fifteenth Census of the United States* (Washington, D.C., 1933), p. 81; also see Frances Jerome Brown and Joseph S. Roucek, eds., *One America: The History, Contributions, and Present Problems of Our Racial and National Minorities* (New York, 1952, 3d ed.; 1st ed., 1937), pp. 663–679; Emory Bogardus in a 1929 study of second-generation Mexicans estimated that about 70 percent of Mexican children in the United States had been born in this country ("Second Generation Mexicans," *Sociology and Social Research* 12 [1929], 276–283).

5. See, for example, Mario T. García, *Desert Immigrants: The Mexicans of El Paso, 1880–1920* (New Haven, 1981), pp. 65–84.

6. Vicki L. Ruiz, *Cannery Women, Cannery Lives: Mexican Women, Unionization, and the California Food Processing Industry, 1930–1950* (Albuquerque, 1987).

7. Marvin Rintala, *The Constitution of Silence: Essays in Generational Themes* (Westport, Conn., 1979), p. 8.

8. Karl Mannheim, "The Problem of Generations" in *Essays on the Sociology of Knowledge* (New York, 1952), p. 292.

9. Rintala, *Constitution of Silence*, p. 6.

10. Samuel P. Huntington, "Generations, Cycles, and Their Role in American Development," in Richard J. Samuels, ed., *Political Generation and Political Development* (Lexington, Mass., 1977), p. 12.

11. Julián Marías, *Generations: A Historical Method* (Tuscaloosa, 1970), pp. 43–44.

12. *Ibid.*, p. 13.

13. Mannheim, "Problem of Generations," p. 303.

14. Alan B. Spitzer, *The French Generation of 1820* (Princeton, 1987), pp. 3–34; Samuel Ramos, "The Conflict of Generations," in Ramos, *Profile of Man and Culture in Mexico* (Austin, 1972), p. 146.

15. Ramos, *Profile of Man*, pp. 146–147. Also see Graham Murdock and Robin McCran, "Consciousness of Class and Consciousness of Generation," in *Working Papers in Cultural Studies* (1975–76), pp. 192–207.

16. William Quandt, "Generational Change in the Arab World," in Samuels, ed., *Political Generation*, p. 84.

17. Alfred C. Stepan, "The Concept of Generations in Military Institutions: Brazil and Peru Compared," in Samuels, ed., *Political Generation*, p. 57.

18. See Samuels, ed., *Political Generation*, p. 18.

19. Quandt, "Generational Change," p. 84.

20. Mannheim, "Problem of Generations," p. 304.

21. Marvin Rintala, "A Generation in Politics: A Definition," *Review of Politics* (Jan. 1963), 521.

22. Spitzer, *French Generation;* Robert Wohl, *The Generation of 1914* (Cambridge, 1979).

23. Mannheim, "Problem of Generations," p. 313; Spitzer, "The Historical Problem of Generations," *American Historical Review*, 78 (Dec. 1973), 1360.

24. Marías, *Generations*, p. 187.

25. Quandt, "Generational Change," p. 84.

26. Marías, *Generations*, p. 105.

27. Wohl, *Generation of 1914*, p. 17. For more on political generations see S. N. Eisenstadt, *From Generation to Generation: Age Groups and Social Structure* (New York, 1956); Lewis S. Feuer, *The Conflict of Generations: The Character and Significance of Student Movements* (New York, 1969); José Ortega y Gasset, *The Modern Theme* (New York, 1961); Maurice Zeitlin, "Political Generations in the Cuban Working Class," *American Journal of Sociology* (March 1966), 493–508; Anthony Esler, ed., *The Youth Revolution: The Conflict of Generations in Modern History* (Lexington, Mass., 1974). Also see Annie Kriegal, "Generational Difference: The History of an Idea," *Daedalus*, 107 (Fall 1978), 23–38, plus other contributions in a special issue on "Generations" in *ibid.;* Robert Tyler, "Of Generations, Generation Gaps, and History," in *Connecticut Review*, 5 (Oct. 1971), 5–12; Norman B. Ryder, "The Cohort as a Concept in the Study of Social Change," *American Sociological Review*, 30 (Dec. 1965), 843–861; Hans Jaeger, "Generations in History: Reflections on a Controversial Concept," *History and Theory*, 24 (1985), 273–292; Wilbur J. Scott and Harold G. Grosmick, "Generations and Group Consciousness: A Quantification of Mannheim's Analogy," *Youth & Society*, 11 (Dec. 1979), 191–214.

28. For a class and racial analysis of the Chicano experience see Mario Barrera, *Race and Class in the Southwest: A Theory of Racial Inequality* (Notre Dame, 1979); also Robert Blauner, *Racial Oppression in America* (New York, 1972).

29. John Higham, "Current Trends in the Study of Ethnicity in the United States,"

Journal of American Ethnic History (Fall 1982), 8–9; also see Rudolph J. Vecoli, "Return to the Melting Pot: Ethnicity in the United States in the Eighties," in *ibid.* (Fall 1985), 7–20.

30. Vecoli, "Ethnicity: A Neglected Dimension of American History," in Herbert J. Bass, ed., *The State of American History* (Chicago, 1970), p. 80; also see Oscar Handlin, *The Uprooted: The Epic Story of the Great Migrations that Made the American People* (Boston, 1951); David M. Potter, *People of Plenty* (Chicago, 1954); Daniel Boorstein, *The Americans: The National Experience* (New York, 1965); Richard Hofstadter, *The American Political Tradition and the Men Who Made It* (New York, 1948); and Marcus Lee Hansen, *The Immigrant in American History* (New York, 1940).

31. Higham, "Current Trends," pp. 5–15. Also see Higham, "Integrating America: The Problem of Assimilation in the Nineteenth Century," *Journal of American Ethnic History* (Fall 1981), 7–25. For views on the "new" ethnic history, see, for example, Stephan Thernstrom and Ann Orlov, eds., *Harvard Encyclopedia of American Ethnic Groups* (Cambridge, 1980).

32. García, *Desert Immigrants.*

33. Deborah Dash Moore, *At Home in America: Second Generation New York Jews* (New York, 1981), p. 11. On the contemporary ethnic debate see Samuel Koenig, "Second and Third Generation Americans," in Brown and Roucek, eds., *One America,* pp. 505–522; Nathan Glazer and Daniel P. Moynihan, *Beyond the Melting Pot: The Negroes, Puerto Ricans, Jews, Italians and Irish of New York City* (Cambridge, 1973); Stephen Steinberg, *The Ethnic Myth: Race, Ethnicity, and Class in America* (Boston, 1981); Milton Gordon, *Assimilation in American Life* (New York, 1964); Michael Novak, *The Rise of the Unmeltable Ethnics* (New York, 1971). Also see Vecoli, "European Americans: From Immigrants to Ethnics," in William H. Cartwright and Richard L. Watson, eds., *The Reinterpretation of American History and Culture* (Washington, D.C., 1973).

34. Olivier Zunz, "American History and the Changing Meaning of Assimilation," *Journal of American Ethnic History* (Spring 1985), 57.

35. Lawrence Stone, "The Revival of Narrative: Reflections on a New Old History," *Past and Present* (Nov. 1979), 3. For a discourse on Stone's essay, see E. J. Hobsbawm, "The Revival of Narrative: Some Comments," *ibid.* (Feb. 1980), 3–8, and Philip Abrams, "History, Sociology, Historical Sociology," *ibid.* (May 1980), 3–16.

36. Stone, "Revival of Narrative," p. 4.

37. John Higham, ed., *Ethnic Leadership in America* (Baltimore and London, 1978), p. 14.

38. *Ibid.,* p. 1.

39. *Ibid.*

40. *Ibid.,* p. 12.

41. Mannheim, "Problem of Generations," p. 313.

42. Higham, *Ethnic Leadership,* p. 2.

43. *Ibid.*

44. See Rodolfo Acuña, *Occupied America: The Chicano's Struggle Toward Liberation* (San Francisco, 1972); Barrera, *Race and Class;* Tomás Almaguer, "Class, Race, and Chicano Oppression," *Socialist Revolution* (July–Sept. 1975), 71–99; Edna Bonavich, "A Theory of Ethnic Antagonism: The Split Labor Market," *American Sociological Review* (Oct. 1972), 542–559; Richard Edwards, Michael Reich, and Daniel M. Gordon, eds., *Labor Market Segmentation* (Lexington, Mass., 1975); Mario T. García, "Racial Dualism in the El Paso Labor Market, 1880–1920," *Aztlán* (Summer 1975), 192–218;

Robert Staples, "Race and Colonialism: The Domestic Case in Theory and Practice," *Black Scholar* (June 1976), 37–48; David Montejano, "A Journey through Mexican Texas, 1900–1930: The Making of a Segregated Society" (Ph.D. dissertation, Yale University, 1982), and Montejano, *Anglos and Mexicans in the Making of Texas, 1836–1986* (Austin, 1987).

45. For literature on the Conquest Era and the Conquered Generation, see Albert Camarillo, *Chicanos in a Changing Society: From Mexican Pueblos to American Barrios in Santa Barbara and Southern California, 1848–1930* (Cambridge, 1979); Arnoldo De León, *The Tejano Community, 1836–1900* (Albuquerque, 1982), and *They Called Them Greasers: Anglo Attitudes Toward Mexicans in Texas, 1821–1900* (Albuquerque, 1983); Richard Griswold del Castillo, *The Los Angeles Barrio, 1850–1890—A Social History* (Berkeley, 1979); Leonard Pitt, *The Decline of the Californios: A Social History of the Spanish-Speaking Californians, 1846–1890* (Berkeley, 1966); Robert J. Rosenbaum, *Mexicano Resistance in the Southwest: The Sacred Right of Self-Preservation* (Austin, 1981); David Weber, ed., *Foreigners in Their Native Land* (Albuquerque, 1973); Armando Navarro, "The Evolution of Chicano Politics," *Aztlán* (Spring and Fall 1974), 57–84; and Antonio Ríos-Bustamante and Pedro Castillo, *An Illustrated History of Mexican Los Angeles, 1781–1985* (Los Angeles, 1986).

46. Álvarez, "Psycho-Historical Development," p. 926.

47. For the Immigrant Era and the Immigrant Generation see García, *Desert Immigrants;* Camarillo, *Chicanos in a Changing Society;* Lawrence Cardoso, *Mexican Emigration to the United States, 1897–1931* (Tucson, 1980); Mark Reisler, *By the Sweat of Their Brow: Mexican Immigrant Labor in the United States* (Westport, Conn., 1976); Ricardo Romo, *East Los Angeles: History of a Barrio* (Austin, 1983); Francisco E. Balderrama, *In Defense of La Raza, the Los Angeles Mexican Consulate and the Mexican Community, 1929 to 1936* (Tucson, 1982); Pedro Castillo, "The Making of a Mexican Barrio: Los Angeles, 1890–1920" (Ph.D. dissertation, University of California, Santa Barbara, 1979); Julie Pycior, "La Raza Organizes: Mexican American Life in San Antonio, 1915–1930 As Reflected in Mutualista Activities" (Ph.D. dissertation, University of Notre Dame, 1979).

48. Dept. of Commerce, *Abstract*, p. 81.

49. See Joan Moore, *Mexican Americans* (Englewood Cliffs, N.J., 1970), pp. 100–102.

50. Mario Barrera, "The Historical Evolution of Chicano Ethnic Goals: A Bibliographic Essay," *Sage Race Relations Abstracts* (Feb. 1985), 18–19. For studies which clearly distinguish the Mexican-American Generation, see Richard A. García, "The Making of the Mexican-American Mind, San Antonio, Texas, 1929–1941" (Ph.D. dissertation, University of California, Irvine, 1980); Richard A. García, "The Mexican American Mind: A Product of the 1930s," in Mario T. García and Francisco Lomelí, eds., *History, Culture, and Society: Chicano Studies in the 1980s* (Ypsilanti, 1983); Richard A. García, "Class, Consciousness, and Ideology—The Mexican Community of San Antonio, Texas: 1930–1940," *Aztlán* (Fall 1978), 23–70; Guadalupe San Miguel, "The Struggle Against Separate and Unequal Schools: Middle Class Mexican Americans, and the Desegregation Campaign in Texas, 1929–1957," *History of Education Quarterly* (Fall 1983), 343–359; San Miguel, "Mexican American Organizations and the Changing Politics of School Desegregation in Texas, 1945–1980," *Social Science Quarterly* (Dec. 1982), 701–715; and San Miguel, *Let All of Them Take Heed: Mexican Americans and the Quest for Educational Equality in Texas, 1918–1981* (Austin, 1987); Mario T. García, "Mexican Americans and the Politics of Citizenship: The Case of El Paso, 1936," *New*

Mexico Historical Quarterly (April 1984), 187–204; Mario T. García, "Americans All: The Mexican-American Generation and the Politics of Wartime Los Angeles, 1941–1945," *Social Science Quarterly* (June 1984), 278–289; Mario T. García, "Mexican American Labor and the Left: The Asociación Nacional México-Americana, 1949–1954," in John A. García et al., eds., *The Chicano Struggle: Analysis of Past and Present Efforts* (Binghamton, N.Y., 1984), pp. 65–86. For other studies which touch on the Mexican-American Generation see Carl Allsup, *The American G.I. Forum: Origins and Evolution* (Austin, 1982); Luis Arroyo, "Chicano Participation in Organized Labor: The CIO in Los Angeles, 1938–1950, An Extended Research Note," *Aztlán* (Summer 1975), 277–303; Albert Camarillo, "Research Note on Chicano Community Leaders: The G.I. Generation," *Aztlán* (Fall 1971), 145–150; Edward Garza, "L.U.L.A.C." (M.A. thesis, Southwest State Teachers College, 1951); Ralph Guzmán, *The Political Socialization of the Mexican American People* (New York, 1976); Beatrice Griffith, *American Me* (Boston, 1948); Pauline K. Kibbe, *Latin Americans in Texas* (Albuquerque, 1946); Raúl Marín, *Among the Valiant: Mexican Americans in World War II and Korea* (Los Angeles, 1963); Frances Jerome Woods, *Mexican Ethnic Leadership in San Antonio, Texas* (Washington, D.C., 1949); Douglas Guy Monroy, "Mexicans in Los Angeles, 1930–1941: An Ethnic Group in Relation to Class Forces" (Ph.D. dissertation, UCLA, 1978); Victor B. Nelson-Cisneros, "UCAPAWA Organizing Activities in Texas, 1935–50," *Aztlán* (Fall 1978), 71–84; Ruiz, *Cannery Women;* Cletas Daniel, *Bitter Harvest: A History of California Farmworkers, 1840–1941* (Ithaca, 1981); Luis Arroyo, "Industrial Unionism and the Los Angeles Furniture Industry, 1918–1954" (Ph.D. dissertation, UCLA, 1979); and Ramón D. Chacón, "Labor Threat and Industrialized Agriculture in California: The Case of the 1933 San Joaquin Valley Cotton Strike," *Social Science Quarterly* (June 1984), 336–353. Also see forthcoming study by Arnoldo De Leon, "Sunbelt Hispanics: A History of Mexican Americans in Houston;" Alex M. Saragoza, "The Significance of Recent Chicano-related Historical Writings: An Appraisal," in *Ethnic Affairs*, 1 (Fall 1987), 24–63; and Philip Gonzales, "A Perfect Furor of Indignation: The Racial Attitude Confrontation of 1933" (Ph.D dissertation, UC Berkeley, 1985); and F. Arturo Rosales, "Shifting Self Perceptions and Ethnic Consciousness Among Mexicans in Houston, 1908–1946," *Aztlán*, 16 (1985), 71–94.

51. Álvarez, "Psycho-Historical Development"; F. Chris García and Rudolph O. de la-Garza, *The Chicano Political Experience: Three Perspectives* (North Scituate, Mass., 1977); Alfredo Cuellar, "Perspectives on Politics: Part I," in F. Chris García, ed., *La Causa Política: A Chicano Politics Reader* (Notre Dame, 1974), pp. 34–46; Guzmán, *Political Socialization;* Navarro, "Chicano Politics." Also see Christine M. Sierra, "Chicano Political Development: Historical Considerations," in Eugene García et al., eds., *Chicano Studies: A Multidisciplinary Approach* (New York, 1984), pp. 79–98.

52. Álvarez, "Psycho-Historical Development," p. 933.

53. Barrera, "Historical Evolution," pp. 10–18; John Chávez, *The Lost Land: The Chicano Image of the Southwest* (Albuquerque, 1984), p. 109.

54. Cuellar, "Perspective on Politics," p. 43. Navarro distinguishes between what he calls the "politics of accommodation" between 1915 and 1945 and the "politics of racial change" between 1945 and 1965 ("Chicano Politics," pp. 61–71).

55. Guzmán, *Political Socialization*, p. 128.

56. See Feuer, *Conflict of Generations*, p. 318.

57. *Ibid.*, p. 12.

58. Álvarez, "Psycho-Historical Development," p. 936. Also see Aileen S. Kraditor, "American Radical Historians on Their Heritage," 56 *Past and Present* (Aug. 1972), 136.

59. Chávez, *Lost Land*, p. 109.

60. See Vecoli, "Ethnicity," p. 81, and Joshua A. Fishman, *Language Loyalty in the United States* (The Hague, 1966). Also see John Higham, *Send These to Me: Jews and Other Immigrants in Urban America* (New York, 1975), pp. 240–243, and Kathleen Neils Conzen, "German-Americans and the Invention of Ethnicity," in Frank Trommler and Joseph McVeigh, eds., *America and the Germans: An Assessment of a Three-Hundred-Year History* (Philadelphia, 1985), pp. 131–147. For contrasting strategies on assimilation with black and Jewish leaders, see David Levering Lewis, "Parallels and Divergencies: Assimilationist Strategies of Afro-American and Jewish Elites from 1910 to the Early 1930s," *Journal of American History* (Dec. 1984), 543–564, and E. Franklin Frazier, *Black Bourgeoisie: The Rise of a New Middle Class* (New York, 1957).

61. Feuer, *Conflict of Generations*, p. 26.

62. Camarillo, "G.I. Generation."

63. Michael Parenti, "Ethnic Politics and the Persistence of Ethnic Identification," *American Political Science Review*, 61 (Sept. 1967), 717–726.

64. Edward Corsi, "Italian Immigrants and Their Children," in Thorsten Sellin and Donald Young, eds., "Minority Peoples in a Nation at War," special issue of *The Annals* of the American Academy of Political and Social Science, 223 (Sept, 1942), 103.

65. Wohl, *Generation of 1914*, p. 4.

66. See Allsop, *American G.I. Forum*.

67. García, "Making of the Mexican-American Mind."

CHAPTER TWO: *In Search of America*

1. See Paul S. Taylor, *An American-Mexican Frontier, Nueces County Texas* (Chapel Hill, 1934); Douglas E. Foley, *From Peones to Politicos: Ethnic Relations in a South Texas Town, 1900–1977* (Austin, 1977); David Montejano, *Race, Labor Repression, and Capitalist Agriculture: Notes from South Texas, 1920–1930* (Berkeley, 1977). Also see Montejano, "Journey Through Mexican Texas."

2. O. Douglas Weeks, "The League of United Latin American Citizens: A Texas-Mexican Civic Organization," *Southwestern Political and Social Science Quarterly* (Dec. 1929), 3. Also see Unsigned to State Commission of Immigration and Housing of California, Feb. 24, 1926, in Oliver Douglas Weeks Archives, box 1, fld. 18, Rare Books and Manuscript Collection, Mexican American Archives, Benson Latin American Library, University of Texas at Austin. Hereinafter, all archival documents, unless otherwise cited, are from the Benson Latin American Library.

3. See J. C. Machuca statement (no date) in William Flores Collection, box 3, fld. 11.

4. M. C. González Private Archives. Also see statement (no date) in M. C. González Collection, box 1, fld. 3, Benson Library.

5. As quoted in Moisés Sandoval, *The First Fifty Years* (Washington, D.C., 1979), p. 4. A copy of this publication was made available courtesy of Larry Trejo of El Paso.

6. Weeks, "League of United Latin-American Citizens," p. 4.

7. Richard A. García, "Making of the Mexican-American Mind," p. 9.

8. González, "Social Evolution," p. 1.

9. Weeks, "League of United Latin-American Citizens," p. 4.

10. See J. Luz Saenz's statement in *El Paladín* (Corpus Christi), May 17, 1929, and as quoted in Weeks, "League of United Latin-American Citizens," p. 15.

11. M. C. González, "To My Fellow-Workers," *La Verdad*, Feb. 8, 1930, in Weeks Collection, map folder, fld. 3.

12. See Sandoval, *First Fifty Years,* pp. 7–8; see Weeks, "League of United Latin-American Citizens," p. 5; Minute Book, Order of Sons of America, Council No. 4, in Weeks Col. Council No. 4 in 1924 listed 46 members. Also see George J. Garza, "Founding and History of LULAC," in *LULAC News,* silver anniversary issue, 1954, p. 4. Also see various newspaper clippings in Ben Garza Col., box 1, scrapbooks 1926–27 and 1929–30; *OKA News,* Dec. 1, 1927, and Jan. 1928 in Weeks Col., box 1, fld. 2.

13. Perales's League organized councils in various south Texas towns including Brownsville, Laredo, and McAllen; see Garza, "History of LULAC," p. 4; Eduardo Idar to Tafolla, Laredo, Dec. 14, 1927, in Andrés de Luna Col., box 1, fld. 1; Perales to James Tafolla, McAllen, Sept. 23, 1927, in de Luna Col., box 1, fld. 1; Tafolla to Eduardo Idar, San Antonio, Dec. 16, 1927, in de Luna Col., box 1, fld. 1. Also see Tafolla to C. E. Castañeda, San Antonio, Feb. 7, 1929, in Weeks Col., box 1, fld. 3; Perales to Garza, Managua, June 22, 1928, in de Luna Col., box 1, fld. 1; and Garza, "History of LULAC," p. 6.

14. Garza, "History of LULAC," p. 21; see typed transcript of *El Paladín,* Feb. 22, 1929, pp. 1–2, Weeks Col., box 1, fld. 9. Professor Weeks of the University of Texas attended the founding LULAC convention as a delegate.

15. Weeks, "League of United Latin-American Citizens," p. 7; Garza, "History of LULAC," p. 22.

16. Typed transcript of *El Paladín,* Feb. 22, 1929, p. 13.

17. Garza, "History of LULAC," p. 22. For additional information on the LULAC founding convention see Sandoval, "First Fifty Years," pp. 11–13, in Andrés de Luna Col., box 1, fld. 1; and newspaper clippings in Ben Garza Col., box 1, scrapbooks, 1926–27 and 1929–30.

18. See LULAC Constitution in Weeks Col., box 1, fld. 7. Also see Garza, "History of LULAC," p. 22.

19. See foreword to LULAC Constitution in Weeks Col., box 1, fld. 7.

20. LULAC Constitution in Weeks Col.

21. Interview with M. C. González, San Antonio, March 18, 1983, by Mario T. García; Conzen, "German-Americans"; Weeks, "League of United Latin-American Citizens," p. 13. Also see Alonso S. Perales, "La Unificación de los México-Americanos," *La Prensa* (San Antonio), Sept. 4, 5, 1929, in Weeks Col., map fld. 2.

22. *La Verdad* (no date), in Ben Garza Col., box 1, scrapbooks, 1926–27 and 1929–30; see undesignated newspaper clipping in Garza Scrapbooks.

23. LULAC Constitution.

24. Weeks, "League of United Latin-American Citizens," p. 10. For a case study of LULAC's history in San Antonio during the 1930s that stresses more a cultural than a political and economic interpretation, see Richard A. García, "Mexican-American Mind: A Product of the 1930s," pp. 67–93. García sees LULAC as principally representing a cultural and ideological challenge to the older mexicano society of San Antonio led by an elitist class of wealthy refugees from the Mexican Revolution of 1910—Los Ricos. Their challenge coalesced in the development of a Mexican-American cultural and ideological synthesis.

25. *LULAC News,* Sept. 1, 1949, n.p. Besides expansion, LULAC was also proud of its successful revolving leadership that represented additional proof of Mexican-American socialization to American democratic principles and structures. See *LULAC News,* May 1932, p. 5. In 1942 an FBI report from San Antonio noted that about 2,000 members belonged to LULAC; see FBI report SA 64–272, San Antonio, Sept. 4, 1942, obtained from Freedom of Information request.

26. García, "Mexican-American Mind."

27. *LULAC News*, Dec. 1931, p. 1.

28. *Ibid.*, Dec. 1955, p. 4; Oct. 1937, p. 21.

29. *Ibid.*, Sept. 1947, and Nov. 1932, p. 7.

30. *Ibid.*, Sept. 1954, in Jake Rodríquez Col., box 4, fld. 1.

31. Andrés de Luna to J. T. Canales, Corpus Christi, June 4, 1940, in Andrés de Luna Col., box 1, fld. 3.

32. See article by Alfredo R. González in *LULAC News*, Dec. 1953, p. 3, in William Flores Col.

33. See typewritten essay to Corpus Christi *Caller Times*, n.d., but appears to be during early 1940s in de Luna Col., box 1, fld. 3.

34. *LULAC News*, Feb. 1949, n.p. See also "On the Question of the Hyphen," in *ibid.*, April 1940, n.p.; resolution by Council No. 132 in Flores Col., box 3, fld. 9; and Jacob L. Rodríguez, "What LULAC Means to Me," *LULAC News*, Feb. 1937, p. 7. To further stress the Americanism of Mexican Americans, LULAC encouraged its members to participate in community-wide civic affairs in addition to their work among Mexican Americans. Americanization also meant learning the basic customs and traditions of the United States. LULAC's own logo consisted of a shield with the title LULAC bordered on one side by the American stars and on the other by the American stripes.

35. *LULAC News*, April 1940, n.p.; also see Sept. 1953, pp. 1–2.

36. *Ibid.*, Feb. 1932, p. 5.

37. *Ibid.*, Oct. 1954, p. 7.

38. *Ibid.*, Dec. 1938, n.p.; May 1955, p. 15.

39. *Ibid.*, March 1933, p. 1.

40. Clipping from *El Paso Times*, June 6, 1938, p. 1, in El Paso Vertical File, "LULAC," Southwest Collection, El Paso Public Library; see "Special Resolution," *LULAC News*, July 1939, p. 28, and "Our Americanism," *ibid.*, p. 13.

41. *LULAC News*, Dec. 1940, n.p. See also E. A. Sheridan, Office of Civilian Defense, to A. Álvarez, Washington, D.C., Oct. 2, 1942; James M. Landis, director of Civilian Defense, to A. Álvarez, Washington, D.C., July 26, 1943, in Flores Col., box 2, fld. 9; and Minutes of Council No. 132, El Paso, Aug. 21, 1942, and Nov. 1, 1944, in Flores Col., box 3, fld. 8.

42. *LULAC News*, July 1945, p. 6.

43. *Ibid.*, July 1953, n.p.; July 1949, n.p. During the Korean War, LULAC sponsored its own "LULAC Marine Platoon"; see *El Paso Times*, Sept. 27, 1953, p. 12–A. Despite its strong anticommunist pronouncements, LULAC was investigated by the FBI, beginning in the late 1930s, as to its possible communist connections. Although some FBI agents reported that communists had infiltrated the organization, the FBI concluded that LULAC did not pose a subversive threat either from the left or the right. See LULAC file obtained from the FBI through the Freedom of Information Act. This material has been summarized in José Angel Gutiérrez, "Chicanos and Mexicans Under Surveillance: 1940–1980," in *Renato Rosaldo Feature Series Monograph*, 2 (Spring 1986), 29–58.

44. *LULAC News*, April 1954, p. 1.

45. In his study of Mexican Americans in San Antonio during the 1930s, Richard García described the middle class in these terms: "The middle class Mexicans constituted a relatively small percentage of the Mexican population. The class of Mexicans who made up the clerks (government employees, public store employees, truck drivers, etc.) and skilled laborers (tinners, bricklayers, barbers, plasterers, shoemakers, plumbers, tailors,

painters, mechanics, cement workers, carpenters, etc.) had, for the most part, steady jobs and early earnings that brought a relatively 'modest standard of living . . . a permanency of residence and a possible interest in citizenship.' In addition, there was a small layer of upper middle class Mexicans: doctors, lawyers, businessmen, etc. In absolute numbers (approximately 5,000 individuals) this middle class was small, but their influence went beyond their numbers due to their income, status, business holdings, and their ability to articulate their ideas." See García, "Making of the Mexican-American Mind," pp. 203–204.

46. *LULAC News*, Dec. 1932, p. 5; Nov. 1932, p. 17. Also see Special Agent in Charge to Director, FBI, Houston, Aug. 23, 1944.

47. *Ibid.*, Jan. 1949, n.p.; Aug. 1953, p. 14.

48. *Ibid.*, July 1956, p. 8.

49. *Ibid.*, Sept. 1932, p. 1.

50. *Ibid.*, Dec. 1932, p. 6.

51. *Ibid.*, Dec. 1937, pp. 28–30.

52. *Ibid.*, March 1938, pp. 11–13.

53. *Ibid.*, May 1939, p. 12; Dec. 1937, p. 21; May 1938, p. 31; May 1939, pp. 29–60.

54. González interview.

55. *LULAC News*, March 1932, n.p.

56. *Ibid.*, March 1933, pp. 9, 16.

57. See "What Price Good Citizenship," in *ibid.*, Jan. 1956, n.p.

58. *Ibid.*, March 1938, n.p.

59. *Ibid.*, Oct. 1932, p. 1; Dec. 1938, n.p. Also see newspaper clippings in Henry Martínez Scrapbook, Henry Martínez Private Col.

60. *Ibid.*, Aug. 1938, n.p.

61. See newspaper clipping dated June 6, 1930, in M. C. González Col., box 1, fld. 2.

62. *LULAC News*, Dec. 1932, n.p.

63. *Ibid.*, Oct. 1956, n.p. Also see April 1940, n.p.; Nov. 1954, p. 3; June 1939, n.p.; and Henry Martínez Scrapbook.

64. *Ibid.*, July 1937, n.p.; March 1933, n.p.; Feb. 1940, n.p.

65. Historian Richard García is too strict in defining the boundaries of LULAC's pluralism but nevertheless notes of Lulacers: "They sought a duality: Mexican in culture and social activity, but American in philosophy and politics" (García, "Mexican-American Mind: A Product of the 1930s," p. 88). On "political ethnicity," see Félix M. Padilla, *Latino Ethnic Consciousness: The Case of Mexican Americans and Puerto Ricans in Chicago* (Notre Dame, 1985).

66. *LULAC News*, Feb. 1932, n.p.; Oct. 1932, n.p.; *ibid.*, Oct. 1932, p. 10. Also see April 1940, n.p.; June 1939, n.p.; March 1934, n.p.

67. *Ibid.*, Feb. 1932, p. 13.

68. See address to Daughters of American Revolution, no date, but appears to have been around late 1930s or early 1940s, in de Luna, box 1, fld. 6, and *LULAC News*, Aug. 1939, n.p. Upholding a rich ethnic-racial heritage, LULAC viewed the history of the Southwest in pluralistic terms and/or as compatible with Afro-American history. Historical pluralism stressed that the history of the Southwest was as much Mexican as it was Anglo.

69. *Ibid.*, Oct. 1932, n.p.; Dec. 1940, n.p. Also see Sept. 1940; Dec. 1931; June 1939, p. 29; Dec. 1932; and Oct. 1937.

70. "Inglés y Español," in *ibid.*, Feb. 1932, n.p.

71. González interview.

72. *LULAC News*, Dec. 1940, n.p.; Nov. 1932, n.p.; *El Paso Herald-Post*, Feb. 4, 1941; *LULAC News*, Feb. 1954, p. 3; "Por Qué Debemos Estudiar Español," in Nov. 1932, n.p.

73. *LULAC News*, Dec. 1938, n.p.; "American Cowpokes Corral Roles as Folk Heroes," in Sept. 1954, n.p.; Dec. 1931, p. 11; Nov. 1932, n.p.

74. Interview with Mrs. Amadita C. Valdez, El Paso, Jan. 13, 1983, by Mario T. García.

75. See *LULAC News*, Jan. 1955, pp. 5, 8, 9, and Oct. 1954, n.p. LULAC's attraction to ethnic and cultural pluralism can also be understood within the context of the international political climate of the 1930s and the war years, specifically FDR's Good Neighbor Policy and the renaissance of Pan-Americanism.

76. *Ibid.*, Oct. 1937, p. 6.

77. *Ibid.*, April 1960, n.p.

78. *Ibid.*, Feb. 1932, p. 1. See also "Are Texas-Mexicans 'Americans'?" in *ibid.*, April 30, 1932, p. 7; Philip J. Montalbo, "Our Rights," in Feb. 1938, p. 3; Montejano, "Journey through Mexican Texas," pp. 264–265; and Andrés Hernández, Jr., "In Relation to Our Civil Liberties," *ibid.*, Aug. 1938, p. 12.

79. William Flores to Members of Council No. 132, El Paso, Sept. 28, 1945, in Flores Col., box 2, fld. 9.

80. *LULAC News*, Feb. 1938, p. 20. See Daniel C. Thompson, *The Negro Leadership Class* (Englewood Cliffs, N.J., 1963), pp. 70–79.

81. *Ibid.*, March 1937, n.p.

82. *Ibid.*, Dec. 1940, n.p.; Oct. 1932, p. 18; Dec. 1939; Jan. 1949; July 1953, p. 3; Nov. 1954; also see newspaper clippings in M. C. González Col., box 1, fld. 2, and *El Paso Herald-Post*, Oct. 11, 1952, p. 1, and July 2, 1953, pp. 1, 8. Also see letter and ordinance, Corpus Christi, Dec. 1942, in de Luna Col., box 1, fld. 3, and Mexican Chamber of Commerce et al., to Honorable Mayor and City Commissioners, Corpus Christi, Jan. 9, 1943, in de Luna Col., box 1, fld. 3.

83. *LULAC News*, March 1937, n.p.; *ibid.*, Feb. 1940; Minutes, Council No. 132, El Paso, Dec. 8, 1945, in Flores Col., box 3, fld. 8; *LULAC News*, Sept. 1954, p. 1; July 1957. LULAC also objected to the continued use of the word "Mexican" in a derogatory fashion or the use of the word "Greaser" in reference to Mexicans; see May 1934 and *El Paso Herald-Post*, July 28, 1953. Also see García, "Politics of Citizenship," and Rosales, "Self Perceptions."

84. See Gustavo C. García, "An Informal Report to the People," in Ruben Munguía, ed., "A Cotton Picker Finds Justice! The Saga of the Hernández Case," in Rare Book Col., Benson Library.

85. See Carlos C. Cadena, "Legal Ramifications of the Hernández Case: A Thumbnail Sketch," in Mungía, ed., "Hernández Case."

86. García, "Informal Report."

87. See Herrera to Luciano Santoscoy in *LULAC News*, June 1954, pp. 4, 19–20. See Chief Justice Warren's opinion in Mungía, ed., "Hernández Case"; also García, "Informal Report," and Cadena, "Legal Ramifications," in *ibid.*

88. Cadena, "Legal Ramifications." Not all Lulacers agreed on working with blacks as Cadena proposed. "We fought our battles by ourselves," M. C. González recalls. According to González, Mexican Americans in LULAC had attempted to place some cultural distance between themselves and lower-class Mexicans, who were perceived as being partly responsible for causing prejudice against all Mexicans. Consequently, Lulacers did

not want to then turn around and establish links with blacks, who suffered even more prejudice. See González interview.

89. *LULAC News,* June 1939, p. 31; Minutes, Council No. 132, Feb. 21, 1941, and March 14, 1941, in Flores Col., box 3, fld. 3; *LULAC News,* May 1950; July 1945, p. 28; March 1938; Dec. 1954; and *El Paso Herald-Post,* Sept. 18, 1954, pp. 1–5. During the 1930s, LULAC in San Antonio strongly opposed strikes by Mexican-American pecan shellers because they had been organized by the communist-led Workers Alliance and later by the CIO (see Richard García, "Making of the Mexican-American Mind," pp. 145–152).

90. See resolution, LULAC National Convention, June 10–12, 1949, in *LULAC News,* July 1949, n.p.; July 1956, p. 10; July 1945, pp. 13, 15–16; Jan. 1955, p. 3; Oct. 1954, pp. 1–2.

91. See clippings in Garza Col., box 1, Scrapbook, 1926–27, 1929–30; see also LULAC resolution, June 24, 1944, in Flores Col., box 1, fld. 4; *El Paso Times,* Nov. 9, 1949, p. 3; June 23, 1956, p. 1; and *LULAC News,* July 1958, p. 8; July 1949; July 1954, pp. 2, 4; July 1956. On the Bracero Program, see Ernesto Galarza, *Merchants of Labor* (Santa Barbara, 1964), and Juan Ramón García, *Operation Wetback: The Mass Deportation of Mexican Undocumented Workers in 1954* (Westport, Conn., 1980). Also see Otey M. Scruggs, "The United States, Mexico, and the Wetbacks, 1942–1947," *Pacific Historical Review,* 30 (May 1961), 149–164, and Scruggs, "Texas and the Bracero Program, 1942–1947," *ibid.,* 32 (Aug. 1963), 251–264; and N. Ray Gilmore and Gladys W. Gilmore, "The Bracero in California," *ibid.,* pp. 265–282. Also see Hart Stilwell, "The Wetback Tide," in "The Mexican American: A National Concern," *Common Ground* (Summer 1949), 3–14, and Carey McWilliams, "California and the Wetback," *ibid.,* pp. 15–20.

92. *Lulac News.,* Aug. 1955, p. 2; March 1954, p. 8; H. T. Manuel, "The Latin-American Child in the Public Schools" [typescript], in H. T. Manuel to Andrés de Luna, Austin, May 9, 1931, in de Luna Col., box 1, fld. 2. Also see Alonso S. Perales, "Our League and the Education of our People," *LULAC News,* March 1937, and H. T. Manuel, "Education: The Guardian of Democracy and the Hope of Youth," Nov. 1940, p. 3.

93. Clipping from *LULAC News* appears to be early 1930s.

94. Manuel, "Latin American Child." On Mexican schools, see García, *Desert Immigrants,* pp. 110–126. Also see San Miguel, *Let All of Them Take Heed,* pp. 32–58; unsigned to the Monday Club, n.d., in de Luna Col., box 1, fld. 6; "Our Public Schools, Their Needs," in *LULAC News,* Dec. 1936, pp. 3–6; and George J. Garza, "Status of the Education of Latin American Children in Texas," Aug. 1946, pp. 12–13.

95. Manuel, "Latin American Child" and "Should Mexican School Children be Segregated?" in *ibid.,* Dec. 1940.

96. See President, LULAC, to W. B. Ray, Corpus Christi, May 4, 1938; R. B. Fisher to A. de Luna, Corpus Christi, May 17, 1938; de Luna to Fisher, Corpus Christi, May 13, 1938: all in de Luna Col., box 1, fld. 2. Also see *LULAC News,* March 1939; March 1954, p. 4; Feb. 1937, p. 12; July 1937, p. 18; May 1934, p. 20; March 1939, n.p.; Dec. 1938, p. 16; Oct. 1939, p. 32; Aug. 1953, n.p.; and Feb. 1955, p. 13.

97. See *Independent School District et al. v. Salvatierra et al.,* Court of Civil Appeals of Texas, San Antonio, Oct. 29, 1930, in M. C. González, box 1, fld. 3.

98. *Ibid.; LULAC News,* May 1932, p. 14; also see clipping on Del Rio case in Weeks, box 1, fld. 6; *LULAC News,* Oct. 1931 and Feb. 1932.

99. See *Méndez et al. v. Westminster School Dist. of Orange County et al.,* Civil Action No. 4292. District Court, San Diego, Calif., Central Division, Feb. 18, 1946, in *Federal Supplement,* vol. 64 (1946). Also see Charles Wollenberg, *All Deliberate Speed:*

Segregation and Exclusion in California Schools, 1855–1975 (Berkeley, 1976), and Gilbert G. González, "Segregation of Mexican Children in a Southern California City: The Legacy of Expansionism and the American Southwest," *Western Historical Quarterly* (Jan. 1985), 55–76.

100. *Ibid.*

101. "LULAC 50 Years." Also see W. Henry Cooke, "The Segregation of Mexican-American School Children in Southern California," *School and Society* (June 5, 1948), 417–421.

102. See *Minerva Delgado v. Bastrop Independent School District of Bastrop County, Texas, et al.*, Civil Action No. 388, United States District of Texas, Western District of Texas, Austin, Texas, June 15, 1948. LULAC raised over $10,000 to support the Delgado litigation (see George I. Sánchez, "Special School Fund Report," *LULAC News*, Jan. 1949). Also see *Herminia Hernández et al. v. Driscoll Consolidated Independent School District*, U.S. District Court for the Southern District of Texas, Corpus Christi Division, No. 1384, Jan. 11, 1957. For a survey of Mexican-American legal challenges to the schools see Guadalupe Salinas, "Mexican Americans and the Desegregation of Schools in the Southwest," *Houston Law Review*, 8 (1971), 929–951. Also see San Miguel, "Mexican American Organizations," pp. 701–715.

103. *LULAC News*, Dec. 1954, p. 10.

104. *Ibid.*, Feb. 1957; July 1957; Aug. 1958; Aug. 1955, p. 2. Besides its educational litigation, LULAC through its councils sponsored college scholarships for Mexican Americans. For more on Mexican-American efforts against school segregation, especially in Texas, see San Miguel, *Let All of Them Take Heed*, pp. 113–138.

105. On the "Little School" see *LULAC News*, Jan. 1954, p. 2; April 1962, p. 3; and *El Paso Herald-Post*, April 9, 1958; May 16, 1959; and April 13, 1964. Also see *El Paso Times*, July 25, 1959, p. 5; May 19, 1957, pp. 1, 10; July 26, 1959, p. 8; "A Report on the 'Little School of the 400'" (1960), in E. B. León Private Collection, El Paso; and San Miguel, *Let All of Them Take Heed*, pp. 139–163.

106. Albert Armendáriz interview, Jan. 12, 1983, by Mario T. García.

107. *Herald-Post*, July 27, 1959.

108. *Times*, Sept. 26, 1965; Aug. 15, 1965; Feb. 5, 1965; *Herald-Post*, April 4, 1964; Sept. 25, 1965; *LULAC News*, Aug.–Sept. 1968, p. 1. See LULAC Resolution by Albuquerque Council No. 8002 in Flores Col., box 1, fld. 7.

CHAPTER THREE: *Education and the Mexican American*

1. Frances Fox Piven and Richard A. Cloward, *Poor People's Movements: Why They Succeed, How They Fail* (New York, 1977), p. 20.

2. Eleuterio Escobar Final Autobiography, 1894–1958 (typescript) in Eleuterio Escobar Collection, box 1, fld. 1e, Rare Books and Manuscript Collection, Mexican American Archives, Benson Latin American Library, University of Texas at Austin. Both his parents' families had lost land to the incoming Anglos by the turn of the century. Hereinafter, all documents cited are from Escobar Collection.

3. *Ibid.*

4. *Ibid.*

5. Taylor, *An American-Mexican Frontier*. Also see Montejano, *Anglos and Mexicanos*.

6. Escobar Autobiography.

7. *Ibid.*

8. The casino lasted until 1931; see *La Prensa* (San Antonio), Oct. 30, 1927, Miscellaneous Newspapers folder.

9. Escobar Autobiography. In the early 1930s, Escobar and other Mexican-American businessmen and professionals also sponsored the Hispano American League for amateur baseball players.

10. See clipping from *San Antonio Evening Express,* July 25, 1930, in Miscellaneous Newspapers.

11. Escobar Autobiography.

12. See correspondence and documents of Association of Independent Voters in box 1; hereinafter referred to as Association. See flyer "A Los Ciudadanos México-Americanos, Jan. 22, 1932," Miscellaneous Newspapers. See unsigned to Escobar, San Antonio, June 11, 1932; Walter Tynan to Escobar, Aug. 23, 1932; Hart McCormick to Association, July 28, 1932; flyer: "Mensaje Del. Lic. Alonso S. Perales"; and see sample ballot: "Ejemplo de la Boleta," in Association, box 1.

13. Escobar Autobiography.

14. Alonso S. Perales to Escobar, Managua, Nicaragua, Nov. 22, 1932, in Miscellaneous Incoming Mail & Telegrams, 1929–1969 and undated in box 1.

15. Escobar Autobiography.

16. See "Preliminary Notes to Autobiography," box 1. On the Depression in San Antonio see García, "The Making of the Mexican-American Mind," and Julia Kirk Blackwelder, *Women of the Depression: Caste and Culture in San Antonio, 1929–1939* (College Station, Tex., 1984).

17. See fld. 1d, "A Revised Autobiographical Draft."

18. Escobar Autobiography.

19. See Escobar to A. B. Stevens, San Antonio, May 4, 1934, in folder "Escobar Archives," box 1; see pamphlet "More and Better Schools for the Western Section," in "Escobar Archives," box 1.

20. See incomplete document dated 1934 in fld. 3, box 2, and "More and Better Schools."

21. Undated document but apparently written in 1934 in "Escobar Archives," box 1.

22. See Board of Education documents, Oct. 23, 1934, in fld. 3, box 2, and undated document apparently written in 1934 in "Escobar Archives," box 1. Conditions in the Mexican schools in other parts of Texas were no better. In El Paso, for example, 41 percent of the Mexican children only attended half-day school in 1934. In one school there existed an average of 61.4 pupils per room. See *LULAC News,* Dec. 1936, pp. 3–6.

23. "More and Better Schools."

24. Undated document apparently written in 1934 in fld. 3, box 2; see Escobar to Honorable Board of Trustees, San Antonio Independent School District, April 9, 1934, in "Escobar Archives," box 1, and "More and Better Schools."

25. Undated document apparently written in 1934 in fld. 3, box 2; also undated documents, "Escobar Archives," box 1. See "La Verdadera Situación Escolar," in "Escobar Archives," box 1; "More and Better Schools"; undated document apparently written in 1934 in "Escobar Archives," box 1; and president, LULAC Council 16, and Escobar to the Honorable Board of Trustees, San Antonio Independent School District, n.d., 1934, in "Escobar Archives," box 1.

26. See Escobar to R. S. Menefee, president, San Antonio Board of Education, April

9, 1934; Gregory Salinas to Menefee, April 12, 1934; same to same, April 30, 1934; president, LULAC Council 16, to Menefee, May 1, 1934; same to Honorable Board of Trustees, May 5, 1934; unsigned to same, May 5, 1934; president, LULAC Council, to Menefee, May 24, 1934, all in "Escobar Archives," box 1.

27. Escobar to Board, San Antonio, May 17, 1934, in "Escobar Archives," box 1.

28. See Perales statement, San Antonio, May 15, 1934, in "Escobar Archives," box 1.

29. "More and Better Schools."

30. Perales statement, May 15, 1934, in "Escobar Archives," box 1.

31. Escobar to Dr. B. F. Pittinger, San Antonio, Nov. 17, 1934, and Escobar to Dr. Marberry, San Antonio, Nov. 17, 1934, in "Escobar Archives," box 1.

32. Escobar to W. O. W. Juárez, San Antonio, Sept. 4, 1934, in "Escobar Archives," box 1; see form letter in both Spanish and English written by Escobar, San Antonio, Sept. 28, 1934, "Escobar Archives," box 1.

33. See Escobar form letter, San Antonio, Oct. 19, 1934, "Escobar Archives," box 1.

34. See list of contacts in *ibid.*; form letter, Sept. 28, 1934, and Escobar to H. C. Bell, San Antonio, Oct. 13, 1934; also see Escobar to James Tafolla Jr., San Antonio, Nov. 1, 1934, in "Escobar Archives," box 1. For a list of sponsoring organizations see clipping from *La Prensa*, Oct. 21, 1934, in Miscellaneous Newspapers.

35. Eugenio Salinas to R. S. Menefee, San Antonio, Aug. 15, 1934, "Escobar Archives," box 1.

36. L. A. Woods to Escobar, Austin, Sept. 17, 1934, "Escobar Archives," box 1.

37. Escobar form letter, Oct. 18, 19, 1934, "Escobar Archives," box 1; see program, Oct. 21, 1934, in fld. 3, box 2.

38. Escobar Autobiography; Escobar to José Rendón, San Antonio, Nov. 7, 1934, "Escobar Archives," box 1; *La Prensa*, Oct. 24, 1934, Miscellaneous Newspapers.

39. Escobar Autobiography.

40. Escobar to Reverend Pedro Reyna, San Antonio, Nov. 10, 1934, "Escobar Archives," box 1.

41. Same to Respetable Auditorio, San Antonio, Dec. 14, 1934, "Escobar Archives," box 1.

42. Same to Dr. O. Gerodetti, San Antonio, April 4, 1934, "Escobar Archives," box 1, and same to C. E. Castañeda, San Antonio, Sept. 4, 1934, in fld. 1, box 3.

43. See Escobar Autobiography; "Minutes & List of Founding Members & Organizations of the School Improvement League, 1934," in fld. 1, box 2; "Liga Pro-Defensa Escolar Acto Primordial," in fld. 2, box 2; and Pedro Hernández to Dr. Orlando Gerodetti, San Antonio, Dec. 5, 1934, and "Refutación a un Informe Dado Por El Concilio No. 16 de los LULACS," in "Escobar Archives," box 1. Escobar officially resigned from being president of the LULAC Committee and from Council 16 on March 16, 1935; see Escobar to Gerodetti, San Antonio, March 16, 1935, "Escobar Archives," box 1.

44. See R. L. Reoder to Escobar, Austin, Jan. 28, 1935, fld. 2, box 3, and *La Prensa*, Jan. 7, 1935, Miscellaneous Newspapers; see *The Defender of the Youth*, Feb. 16, 1935, Miscellaneous Newspapers.

45. A. Barrera to Ernest Fellbaum, San Antonio, Feb. 4, 1935, fld. 2, box 3; see additional telegrams in fld. 2, box 3.

46. *El Defensor de la Juventud*, Feb. 16, 1935, pp. 1, 6, in Miscellaneous Newspapers.

47. *Ibid.*, p. 1.

48. *El Defensor*, March 9, 1935, p. 1; Escobar to Agustín Lara, San Antonio, March 5,

1935, fld. 3, box 3; same to same, April 16, 1935, fld. 2, box 3; same to same, May 6, 1935, fld. 3, box 3; Fiesta program, fld. 13, box 4; Carlos E. Castañeda to Escobar, Del Rio, March 27, 1935, fld. 2, box 3; J. Tafolla, Sr. to Santos S. López, San Antonio, June 8, 1935, fld. 2, box 3; and *San Antonio Evening News,* June 11, 1935, Miscellaneous Newspapers.

49. *La Prensa,* July 21, 1935, in Miscellaneous Newspapers.

50. Escobar Autobiography; Escobar radio transcript, undated, fld. 9, box 5; "Informe del Presidente Escobar—Jan. 27, 1948," fld. 6, box 5; *ABC,* Sept. 1948, p. 3, fld. 12, box 4; Escobar radio transcript KIWW, Jan. 11, 1950, fld. 8, box 5; Articles of Incorporation of School Improvement League, Oct. 7, 1947, fld. 1, box 4. During the war, Escobar invested in wholesale silver craft manufacturing through his own company, the EECO Silver Craft Factory. He also represented certain Mexican oil interests that required manufactured equipment from Texas.

51. *ABC,* Sept. 1947, pp. 3, 14, fld. 2, box 4.

52. *San Antonio Evening News,* Sept. 2, 1947, p. 1, in Escobar Scrapbook, 1947–50.

53. *Ibid.,* Sept. 3, 1947, p. 1; Escobar radio transcript, KIWW, Feb. 15, 1950, fld. 8, box 5.

54. *San Antonio Light,* Aug. 20, 1947, in Scrapbook.

55. See affiliation cards, 1947–48, in box 2; *ABC,* Sept. 1947; Escobar to Dwight Allison, San Antonio, Dec. 29, 1947, fld. 4, box 3.

56. Escobar speech to General Assembly of League, Aug. 27, 1947, fld. 3, box 5.

57. League radio transcript, undated, fld. 5, box 5.

58. Elpidio Barrera radio transcript, Oct. 1947, KCOR, fld. 5, box 5; League radio transcript, undated, fld. 9, box 5; transcript of Escobar speech at San Fernando School, Nov. 26, 1947, fld. 3, box 5; Escobar radio transcript, KMAC, undated, fld. 9, box 5.

59. Transcript of Escobar address to League, Aug. 22, 1947, fld. 3, box 5; and Escobar to Honorable C. Ray Davis, San Antonio, Sept. 10, 1947; same to Arthur Fenster-Maker, San Antonio, Sept. 10, 1947; Thomas B. Portwood to Escobar, San Antonio, Oct. 13, 1947; James T. Shea to Escobar, San Antonio, Oct. 15, 1947, all in fld. 4, box 3.

60. See undated report, appears to be 1947, in fld. 8, box 6; *San Antonio Evening News,* Aug. 25, 1947, in Scrapbook; Escobar–Henry B. González report, undated appears to be 1947, fld. 4, box 6; Manuel Castañeda radio transcript, KIWW, Sept. 11, 1947, fld. 5, box 5; transcript of Escobar address to League, Dec. 8, 1947, fld. 5, box 5; and *ABC,* Sept. 1947, p. 2.

61. See report of Fire Prevention Bureau, Nov. 1, 1947, fld. 3, box 4.

62. League radio transcript, KMAC, undated, appears to be 1947, fld. 9, box 5.

63. As quoted in *San Antonio Express,* Nov. 13, 1947, in Scrapbook.

64. *Ibid.;* also see "Comité de Delegados de la Liga Pro-Defensa Escolar en la presentación de su Petición Oficial ante el Consejo Escolar," Nov. 12, 1947, fld. 2, box 4; Escobar radio transcript, KCOR, Nov. 17, 1947, fld. 5, box 5; transcript of Escobar speech, San Fernando School, Nov. 26, 1947, fld. 3, box 5; transcript Escobar speech, Jan. 27, 1948, fld. 6, box 5; and Escobar radio transcript, KCOR, Nov. 25, 1947, fld. 5, box 5.

65. *Express,* Nov. 13, 15, 1947, in Scrapbook.

66. Transcript of Escobar speech, undated, appears to be 1947, fld. 7, box 5; Escobar to School Board Committee, San Antonio, Dec. 1, 1947, fld. 5, box 5; *Evening News,* Nov. 26, 1947; *Light,* Dec. 10, 1947; *Express,* Dec. 17, 1947, in Scrapbook and transcript of Escobar speech, undated, fld. 9, box 5; Escobar radio transcript, KCOR, Dec. 15, 1947, fld. 5, box 5.

67. Escobar to Board of Trustees, San Antonio, Nov. 28, 1947, fld. 4. box 3; Escobar to Board, undated, but appears to be Dec. 1947, fld. 8, box 4.

68. League radio transcript, KIWW, Jan. 18, 1950, fld. 8, box 5; *Evening News,* Nov. 22, 1949, p. 102, Miscellaneous Newspapers; Escobar radio transcript, KIWW, April 26, 1950, fld. 8, box 5; undated report, fld. 5, box 6; undated report, fld. 14, box 4; *Light,* March 29, 1948, Miscellaneous Newspapers; undated document in "Escobar Archives," box 1; *Light,* March 29, 1948, Miscellaneous Newspapers; Escobar speech, undated but appears to be 1948, fld. 14, box 4.

69. League radio transcript, KIWW, Feb. 15, 1950, fld. 8, box 5; "Growth and Development of Sidney Lanier School According to Enrollment, Buildings and Grounds Since 1923–1950," Feb. 13, 1950, fld. 2, box 6.

70. "Growth and Development at Sidney Lanier."

71. Undated document, fld. 5, box 6; *Express,* Jan. 8, 1950; *La Prensa,* Jan. 8, 1950; Jan. 10, 1950, in Miscellaneous Newspapers.

72. See undated clipping from *Express,* Miscellaneous Newspapers; *ibid.,* Jan. 15, 1948, Miscellaneous Newspapers.

73. Manuel Castañeda radio transcript, KCOR, April 5, 1948, fld. 6, box 5; Escobar radio transcript, KCOR, April 5, 1948, fld. 6, box 5; newspaper clipping, Miscellaneous Newspapers.

74. League flyer, fld. 14, box 4.

75. Escobar to Woods, San Antonio, Aug. 12, 1948, fld. 5, box 3.

76. As quoted in Escobar to Elpido Barrera, San Antonio, Aug. 3, 1948, fld. 5, box 3.

77. Newspaper clipping, Escobar Scrapbook. During the war Castañeda had served as regional director of the Fair Employment Practice Commission in the Southwest.

78. Escobar to Woods, San Antonio, Sept. 4, 1948, fld. 5, box 3.

79. *San Antonio,* Jan. 12, 1950, in Scrapbook; *La Prensa,* April 30, 1950, p. 3, in Scrapbook; "School Survey of the University of Texas," in fld. 5, box 6; Gus García to Survey Committee of the San Antonio Independent School District, n.d., fld. 2, box 4; see news clipping, Jan. 12, 1950, Scrapbook.

80. *Light,* April 5, 1959, Scrapbook; Report of the Citizens' School Survey Committee, May 17, 1950, fld. 6, box 6.

81. *Express,* May 23, 1950, Scrapbook; *Light,* May 23, 1950, Scrapbook.

82. See league report, n.d., fld. 7, box 6; García radio transcript, KIWW, Sept. 21, 1950, fld. 8, box 5; league report, fld. 7, box 6.

83. *Express,* June 15, 1950, Scrapbook; *Evening News,* June 15, 1950, p. 1–A, Scrapbook.

84. *Evening News,* June 16, 1950, p. 8, Miscellaneous Newspapers; *La Prensa,* June 18, 1950, p. 1, Scrapbook; *Express,* June 20, 1950, Scrapbook.

85. News clipping, Jan. 23, 1950, Miscellaneous Newspapers.

86. Escobar to Ed. W. Ray, San Antonio, Dec. 30, 1958, fld. 8, box 3; news clipping, 1959, Miscellaneous Newspapers. Escobar died on May 10, 1970.

CHAPTER FOUR: *Mexican-American Muckraker*

1. For a short biography of López, see Ignacio López Collection Folder of Information in Ignacio López Collection in Special Collections, Green Library, Stanford University. The López Collection consists only of original as well as microfilm copies of his predominantly Spanish-language newspaper, *El Espectador,* from 1937 to 1960. López

published the newspaper out of his home throughout this time. For a brief account of López's activities see Enrique M. López, "Community Resistance to Injustice and Inequality: Ontario, California, 1937–1947, *Aztlán* (Fall 1986): 1–29.

2. *Ibid.* Also see FBI file on López secured through Freedom of Information Act; file nos. 100-200298 and 140-36569.

3. *El Espectador*, Feb. 17, 1939, pp. 1, 2.

4. *Ibid.*

5. *Ibid.*, Feb. 24, 1939, pp. 1, 7; March 3, 1939, pp. 1, 9, 11; May 17, 1940, p. 1, Oct. 23, 1942, p. 1. Also see news clipping in private collection of Leonor Varela López, hereinafter cited as López Col.

6. *Ibid.*, May 7, 1940, p. 1; Aug. 30, 1940, p. 1.

7. *Ibid.*, June 19, 1942, p. 1; July 17, 1942, p. 1; Aug. 7, 1942, p. 1.

8. See "Wooing in the Dark," undated column; see clipping in López Col.

9. *Ibid.*, Dec. 31, 1943, p. 1, and May 12, 1944, p. 1. Also see summary of Ignacio López et al. vs. W. C. Seccombe et al., District Court of the U.S. for the Southern District of California, Central Division, in "Interpreter Releases," in López Col. *El Espectador* also exposed other forms of discrimination in public facilities such as in restaurants and clubs; see *ibid.*, July 24, 1942, p. 1; Aug. 28, 1942, p. 1; Aug. 10, 1945, pp. 1, 3; Sept. 14, 1945, pp. 1, 5; and March 8, 1946, p. 1.

10. *Ibid.*, June 3, 1938, pp. 1, 2. Also see June 10, 1938, p. 1, and July 1, 1938, p. 1.

11. *Ibid.*, Aug. 25, 1939, pp. 1, 4.

12. *Ibid.*, Dec. 13, 1946, p. 1; July 26, 1946, p. 1.

13. *Ibid.*, July 12, 1946, p. 1; July 26, 1946, p. 1; May 17, 1946, p. 1; June 7, 1946, p. 1; July 12, 1946, p. 1; Aug. 9, 1946, pp. 1, 2; Aug. 16, 1946, p. 1; Jan. 24, 1947, p. 1; March 21, 1947, p. 1; Dec. 5, 1947, p. 1; Dec. 19, 1947, pp. 1, 2; Dec. 26, 1947, p. 1; Jan. 16, 1948, p. 1; Feb. 13, 1948, p. 1; and April 16, 1948, pp. 1, 3.

14. On the Westminster case see Wollenberg, *All Deliberate Speed; El Espectador*, Aug. 23, 1946, p. 1; also see June 14, 1946, p. 1; Aug. 30, 1946, p. 1; Sept. 20, 1946, p. 1; June 20, 1947, pp. 1, 3. Also see García, "Americans All," pp. 278–289; *El Espectador*, Dec. 12, 1947, p. 2.

15. *Ibid.*, Feb. 6, 1948, p. 1; Feb. 13, 1948, pp. 1, 6.

16. *Ibid.*, Feb. 20, 1948, pp. 1, 3; April 30, 1948, pp. 1, 3.

17. See *ibid.*, Sept. 7, 1951, p. 1, and April 3, 1959, pp. 1, 2.

18. *Ibid.*, Feb. 5, 1937, pp. 1, 2.

19. *Ibid.*, July 15, 1949, pp. 1, 2; July 22, 1949, pp. 1, 6.

20. *Ibid.*, July 29, 1949, pp. 1, 6.

21. *Ibid.*, Jan. 1, 1960, pp. 1, 4; Jan. 15, 1960, p. 1. Following the zoot-suit riots in Los Angeles in June 1943, López denounced the attacks on Mexican-Americans but believed that some positive results could come out of this crisis. He believed that many Anglos now realized that Mexican Americans had to be brought into the mainstream. He believed that Mexican Americans also realized that they had to lead in the struggle for full rights and not wait for someone else to do it for them. Finally, López believed that the riots had resulted in new research on Mexican Americans that would be helpful in providing guideposts for better race/ethnic relations. See López's introduction to Ruth Tuck, *Not With the Fist: Mexican Americans in a Southwest City* (New York, 1946).

22. *Ibid.*, May 3, 1940, p. 1; July 26, 1940, p. 1; Aug. 19, 1949, p. 1; Oct. 21, 1949, p. 1; Nov. 4, 1949, pp. 1, 2, 4.

23. *Ibid.*, Nov. 11, 1949, pp. 1, 5; Nov. 18, 1949, pp. 1, 10; May 25, 1951, p. 1; Feb. 1,

1952, pp. 1, 3. Also see Aug. 16, 1946, p. 1; May 7, 1948, pp. 1, 5; March 21, 1952, pp. 1, 2; March 3, 1959, p. 1; March 10, 1959, pp. 1, 4; July 31, 1959, p. 2.

24. *Ibid.*, Aug. 12, 1949, p. 1; Sept. 2, 1949, p. 1.

25. *Ibid.*, Sept. 2, 1949, pp. 1, 6.

26. *Ibid.*, Sept. 9, 1949, pp. 1, 6.

27. *Ibid.*, Aug. 11, 1950, pp. 2–3.

28. See *ibid.*, Oct. 5, 1945, pp. 1, 2, 10; Dec. 7, 1945, pp. 1, 4; April 5, 1946, p. 1; Jan. 10, 1947, pp. 1, 8; May 28, 1948, p. 1; June 18, 1948, p. 1; Oct. 22, 1948, pp. 1, 2; May 13, 1949, p. 1; July 28, 1950, p. 2; Aug. 25, 1950, p. 2; Nov. 24, 1950, pp. 1, 11; Sept. 28, 1951, p. 1; Oct. 12, 1951, pp. 1, 8; July 20, 1956, p. 8; and Aug. 3, 1956, p. 1. Also see Ernesto Galarza, *Merchants of Labor,* and Erasmo Gamboa, "Under the Thumb of Agriculture: Bracero and Mexican American Workers in the Pacific Northwest, 1940–1950" (Ph.D. dissertation, University of Washington, 1984).

29. *Ibid.*, May 16, 1946, p. 1; Dec. 30, 1949, pp. 1, 2; March 29, 1957, p. 1; April 1960, p. 1; April 25, 1952, pp. 1, 7.

30. *Ibid.*, May 2, 1952, pp. 1, 2, 7; May 9, 1952, pp. 1, 7; Aug. 8, 1952, pp. 1, 7. See news clipping in López Col.

31. *Ibid.*, Feb. 18, 1949, p. 17. The term "alambrista" refers to undocumented workers who cross the U.S.-Mexican border between San Diego and El Paso, an area where the border consists only of a fence constructed of wire ("alambre").

32. *Ibid.*, Sept. 1, 1952, p. 1.

33. *Ibid.*, Oct. 6, 1950, pp. 1, 15; June 22, 1951, p. 1.

34. *Ibid.*, May 5, 1939, p. 1; Nov. 8, 1940, p. 1. During World War II, López left Pomona for a short stint in Washington, D.C., as head of the Spanish-language Division of the Office of War Information. He later also served as Los Angeles representative of the Office of the Coordinator of Inter-American Affairs, led by Nelson Rockefeller. See press clipping in López Col. In 1945 López served for a time as field examiner in the Los Angeles office of the president's Committee on Fair Employment Practices (see news clipping in López Col.). During this time, López was investigated by the FBI as a possible security threat on the suspicion that he was either a Communist or had Communist contacts. No such evidence was obtained and the case was closed until the early 1950s, when López was again investigated because of his membership in such groups as ANMA and the Committee for the Protection of the Foreign Born. See FBI file on López.

35. See Richard M. Dalfiume, "The 'Forgotten Years' of the Negro Revolution," *Journal of American History* (June 1968), 96; López to Hon. Harry R. Sheppard, Los Angeles, May 18, 1945, in López Col.; and *El Espectador,* Oct. 4, 1946, pp. 1, 6.

36. *Ibid.*, July 29, 1949, p. 3.

37. *Ibid.*, Nov. 17, 1950, p. 3.

38. *Ibid.*, Sept. 8, 1950, p. 2; Sept. 29, 1950, p. 2.

39. *Ibid.*, Oct. 6, 1950, p. 3. During World War II, López had also attacked the Mexican Sinarquista movement in the United States, which he regarded as fascist (see López letter to *The InterAmerican* [June 1944], p. 48).

40. Undated speech by López delivered during the 1948 presidential campaign, when López was supporting former Vice President Henry Wallace (see López Col.).

41. *El Espectador,* April 27, 1951, p. 2. Also see Nov. 17, 1950, p. 3; Oct. 6, 1950, p. 1; Nov. 10, 1959, pp. 1, 11; Dec. 1950, p. 3; and July 5, 1957, p. 1. Also see FBI file on López. The FBI noted that López spoke at conferences or rallies sponsored by such "Communist-front" groups as the Los Angeles Committee for the Protection of the For-

eign Born, the Los Angeles Committee protesting the execution sentence of the Rosenbergs, the Independent Progressive Party, and the Civil Rights Congress.

42. *Ibid.*, July 3, 1942, p. 1. Also see Nov. 4, 1938, p. 1, and April 5, 1957, p. 1; López to Sheppard, Los Angeles, May 18, 1945, in López Col.; *El Espectador*, Jan. 27, 1939, p. 1, and March 4, 1949, p. 5.

43. *Ibid.* Feb. 18, 1938, p. 3. Also see López to Charles G. Ross, New York, Oct. 24, 1947, in López Col.; and *El Espectador*, May 19, 1939, p. 2; March 7, 1950, p. 1; and April 28, 1950, p. 1.

44. *Ibid.*, Sept. 8, 1950, p. 2. Also see Sept. 1, 1950, p. 2.

45. López remained a staunch New Deal Democrat and consistently endorsed FDR. In the 1948 election, López at first worked for Henry Wallace and the Progressive party until Communist involvement in the Wallace effort made López shy away. In the 1960 election, López served as Radio-Newspaper Publicity Chairman of the Viva Kennedy Clubs of California (see Edward Roybal to Whom It May Concern, Los Angeles, Oct. 12, 1960, in López Col.).

46. *El Espectador*, Feb. 1, 1946, pp. 1, 2; July 19, 1946, p. 1. Interview with Candelario Mendoza, Pomona, Sept. 6, 1983, by Mario T. García.

47. *Ibid.*, March 1, 1946, pp. 1, 2.

48. *Ibid.*, pp. 1, 3; March 15, 1946, pp. 4, 12; March 22, 1946, p. 1.

49. Mendoza interview.

50. *Ibid.*, March 22, 1946, pp. 1, 6; *ibid.*, March 29, 1946, pp. 1, 7; *ibid.*, April 5, 1946, pp. 4 and 5. Also see March 22, 1946, pp. 6, 16, and March 29, 1946, p. 6.

51. *Ibid.*, April 12, 1946, pp. 1, 2, 6.

52. *Ibid.*, April 18, 1947, pp. 1, 6; May 2, 1947, p. 1; May 16, 1947, p. 1; Feb. 20, 1948, p. 1.

53. *Ibid.*, April 16, 1948, p. 1. For other Unity League political and social activities such as voter registration, see Aug. 8, 1947, p. 1; June 7, 1946, p. 1; Oct. 11, 1946, p. 1; July 19, 1946, pp. 1, 5; April 19, 1946, p. 2; May 10, 1946, p. 3; Sept. 27, 1946, p. 1; March 21, 1947, p. 1; June 20, 1947, pp. 1, 2; and June 27, 1947, p. 4.

54. For *El Espectador's* coverage of additional Mexican-American participation in local politics see, for example, Feb. 7, 1947, pp. 1, 2; March 21, 1947, pp. 1, 8; March 19, 1948, pp. 1, 2; April 2, 1948, p. 1; April 9, 1948, pp. 1, 2, 3; April 16, 1948, pp. 1, 6; April 23, 1948, p. 1; April 1, 1949, p. 1; March 26, 1948, pp. 1, 3; Jan. 27, 1959, pp. 1, 8; Feb. 3, 1950, pp. 1, 8; Feb. 10, 1950, pp. 1, 2, 6; April 14, 1950, pp. 1, 10; May 19, 1950, p. 1; Jan. 18, 1952, pp. 1, 3; March 21, 1952, p. 1; April 11, 1952, pp. 1, 8; May 18, 1956, pp. 1, 2; May 25, 1956, p. 1; Aug. 2, 1957, p. 4; Jan. 4, 1957, p. 1; April 4, 1958, p. 3; and April 11, 1958, p. 1.

55. *Ibid.*, Aug. 2, 1957, p. 4; Jan. 27, 1950, pp. 1, 8; Jan. 4, 1957, p. 1; Jan. 11, 1957, p. 1; Jan. 18, 1957, p. 1; Feb. 1, 1957, pp. 1, 2; March 8, 1957, pp. 1, 2; March 15, 1957, p. 1; Aug. 7, 1959, p. 1; March 28, 1952, p. 1.

56. *Ibid.*, Nov. 4, 1949, p. 1.

57. *Ibid.*, p. 4; Dec. 2, 1949, p. 1; Feb. 3, 1950, pp. 1, 8.

58. *Ibid.*, Feb. 17, 1950, p. 1; March 7, 1950, pp. 1, 7; April 14, 1950, p. 1. Also see March 21, 1947, pp. 1, 8; May 23, 1952, pp. 1, 2; April 20, 1956, p. 1; May 30, 1959, pp. 1, 2; and Dec. 18, 1959, pp. 1, 2.

59. *Ibid.*, Feb. 21, 1958, p. 1. Also see April 15, 1949, p. 1, and July 26, 1957, p. 1. By no means provincial, López endorsed regional, state, and national political organizations among Mexican Americans besides supporting local Mexican-American candidates. His

involvement in such efforts included the Convention of Latin-American Civic and Political Organizations (1949), the National Council of Spanish-Speaking Peoples (1951), and the Mexican American Political Association (MAPA, 1960). Although initially supportive of MAPA, López quickly became estranged due to his belief that MAPA was politically provincial and controlled by politicians who saw MAPA as a front for the Democratic party. To López, MAPA was a "freak." See *ibid.*, Sept. 21, 1945, p. 4; Oct. 5, 1945, pp. 1, 8; July 29, 1949, pp. 1, 3; May 4, 1951, pp. 1, 2; Aug. 16, 1951, pp. 1, 7; June 1, 1951, pp. 1, 2; Oct. 26, 1956, p. 1; Nov. 2, 1956, p. 1; Nov. 9, 1956, p. 1; Nov. 16, 1956, p. 1; Dec. 14, 1956, p. 1; April 15, 1960, p. 1; April 29, 1960, p. 1; April 22, 1960, p. 1; May 13, 1960, p. 1; and May 27, 1960, p. 1.

60. Untitled and undated speech to Pan-American Optimist Club of Los Angeles, López Col.

61. *El Espectador*, June 14, 1957, p. 1.

62. *Ibid.*, April 24, 1959, p. 2. "He was very cognizant of his heritage and the language of *mexicanismo*," Mendoza recalls of López, "and yet he also knew that being an American first did not necessarily deter being a good Mexican also" (Mendoza interview).

63. *Ibid.*, Dec. 22, 1938, p. 1. According to Mendoza, López spoke immaculate Spanish and English in an educated but accented manner (Mendoza interview).

64. *Ibid.* See, for example, July 12, 1940, p. 4; Oct. 25, 1941, p. 5; Nov. 23, 1945, p. 6; Nov. 30, 1945, p. 3; Dec. 19, 1947, p. 9; Feb. 10, 1950, p. 7; and May 12, 1950, p. 1.

65. *Ibid.*, Aug. 17, 1956, p. 1.

66. *Ibid.*, Sept. 2, 1938, p. 1 (Mendoza interview).

67. *Ibid.*, Sept. 16, 1949, p. 1.

68. *Ibid.*, Dec. 8, 1938, p. 7, see *ibid.*, Feb. 18, 1938, p. 1; Sept. 26, 1946, p. 5; Nov. 21, 1947, p. 1; Jan. 26, 1951, p. 7; May 18, 1951, p. 7; April 6, 1956, p. 1; Aug. 10, 1956, p. 2; Nov. 16, 1956, p. 1; Oct. 13, 1950, p. 13; March 4, 1949, p. 16.

69. *Ibid.*, Nov. 4, 1938, pp. 1, 7.

70. See *ibid.*, Nov. 11, 1938, p. 5; Dec. 1, 1938, p. 5; Feb. 10, 1938, p. 5; Feb. 17, 1939, p. 5; March 17, 1939, p. 5; March 24, 1939, p. 5; April 14, 1939, p. 4; April 28, 1939, p. 4; June 13, 1947, p. 4.

71. *Ibid.*, April 27, 1956, p. 1.

72. *Ibid.*, May 11, 1956, p. 1. Also see May 11, 1956, p. 1, and June 26, 1959, pp. 1, 4.

73. See *ibid.*, June 17, 1938, p. 5; March 9, 1956, p. 5; Aug. 16, 1940, pp. 1, 3; July 6, 1951, pp. 2, 3; Sept. 28, 1951, p. 2; May 18, 1956, p. 2; May 25, 1956, p. 2; June 1, 1956, p. 2; June 15, 1956, p. 1; June 22, 1956, p. 2; June 29, 1956, p. 2; July 6, 1956, p. 3; July 8, 1956, p. 2; Oct. 1940, p. 6; July 30, 1948, p. 7; and Nov. 30, 1956, p. 5. Other columns in the English-language sections of *El Espectador* noted the influence of U.S. sports such as football and baseball on Mexican-American youth; see March 25, 1942, p. 2; April 1, 1949, p. 7; April 8, 1949, p. 2; April 15, 1949, pp. 2, 8; May 6, 1949, p. 2; June 26, 1959, p. 4; July 17, 1959, p. 4; July 24, 1959, p. 4; Aug. 7, 1959, p. 4; Aug. 14, 1959, p. 4; Aug. 28, 1959, p. 6; and June 17, 1960, p. 2.

74. *Ibid.*, Sept. 13, 1940, p. 1.

75. *Ibid.*, June 26, 1942, p. 1; June 10, 1949, pp. 1, 6.

76. *Ibid.*, July 7, 1949, p. 1.

77. Undated speech in López Col.

78. *El Espectador*, March 1, 1946, p. 12.

79. *Ibid.*

80. From 1961 to 1963, López served as information and relocation specialist for the

Los Angeles Community Redevelopment Agency. In 1964 he directed the Mexican-American campaign for E. J. Younger for district attorney in Los Angeles. In 1966 he was coordinator of the Viva Pat Brown committee during the campaign for governor in California. From 1967 to 1969 he served as Los Angeles director of HUD. See López biography in López Col., Stanford.

CHAPTER FIVE: *The Politics of Status*

1. Oscar J. Martínez, *The Chicanos of El Paso: An Assessment of Progress* (El Paso: Texas Western Press, 1980), p. 6.
2. See "Border Politics," in García, *Desert Immigrants,* pp. 155–171.
3. Everett Ladd, Jr., *Negro Political Leadership in the South* (Ithaca, 1966), p. 156.
4. *Ibid.*
5. See García, *Desert Immigrants,* and Oscar J. Martínez, *Border Boom Town: Ciudad Juárez Since 1848* (Austin, 1980); see also Martínez, *Chicanos of El Paso.*
6. Marsh Adams and Gertrude Adams, "A Report on Politics in El Paso," unpublished report by the Joint Center for Urban Studies of MIT and Harvard (Cambridge, 1963), pp. 1–9.
7. Martínez, *Chicanos of El Paso,* pp. 10, 12.
8. *Ibid.,* pp. 18–19.
9. Carey McWilliams, "The El Paso Story," in *The Nation* (July 10, 1948), 46; also see William V. D'Antonio and William H. Form, *Influentials in Two Border Cities: A Study in Community Decision-Making* (Notre Dame, 1965), p. 20.
10. Oral history interview with Raymond L. Telles, El Paso, Sept. 30, 1982, by Mario T. García. I wish to thank Sarah John of the Institute of Oral History of the University of Texas at El Paso for transcribing all my interviews with Raymond Telles. In six years, Telles received the following awards: the Legion of Merit of Mexico, the Distinguished Flying Cross of Peru, the National Order of the Southern Cross of Brazil, and the Medal of Merit of Aeronautics of Mexico.
11. Oral history interview with Raymond L. Telles, El Paso, Oct. 20, 1982, by Mario T. García. For the 1948 election see the *El Paso Times* and *El Paso Herald-Post* for May–July, 1948; *Times,* April 7, 1953, p. 16; March 29, 1955, p. 7–B; and Aug. 21, 1955, p. 3–D.
12. *Herald-Post,* Feb. 25, 1949, p. 25; July 20, 1950, pp. 1, 8; July 19, 1954, p. 1; Feb. 19, 1951, pp. 1, 12; Feb. 22, 1951, pp. 1, 10; Feb. 26, 1951, pp. 1–2; Feb. 18, 1955, p. 1; March 7, 1955, p. 5; Feb. 19, 1951, pp. 1, 12; Feb. 22, 1951, pp. 1, 10; Feb. 26, 1951, pp. 1–2.
13. *Ibid.,* Feb. 22, 1951, p. 1.
14. *Times,* March 4, 1951, p. 1; oral history interview with Luciano Santoscoy, El Paso, Nov. 8, 1982, by Mario T. García.
15. *Herald-Post,* March 1, 1955, p. 18.
16. *Times,* Jan. 9, 1955, p. 1.
17. Oral history interview with Raymond L. Telles, El Paso, Nov. 16, 1982, by Mario T. García.
18. Oral history interview with Francisco "Kiko" Hernández, El Paso, Nov. 9, 1982, by Mario T. García.
19. Oral history interview with Alfredo "Lelo" Jacques, El Paso, Nov. 18, 1982, by Mario T. García.

20. Telles interview, Nov. 16, 1982.
21. Oral history interview with Albert Armendáriz, El Paso, Oct. 26, 1982, by Mario T. García.
22. *Ibid.*
23. Oral history interview with Richard Telles, El Paso, Nov. 23, 1982, by Mario T. García. Also see Adams, "Politics in El Paso," p. 1–14, and Benjamin Marquez, *Power and Politics in a Chicano Barrio: A Study of Mobilization Efforts and Community Power in El Paso* (Lanham, Md., 1985).
24. Oral history interview with David Villa, El Paso, Dec. 16, 1982, by Mario T. García.
25. See John Higham's chapter on leadership in Stephen Thernstrom, ed., *Dimensions of Ethnicity* (Cambridge, 1982), pp. 69–92.
26. Villa interview; and oral history interview with Gabriel Navarrete, El Paso, Dec. 6, 1982, by Mario T. García.
27. See Steele Jones, "The El Paso Herald Post: The Pooley Years" (M.A. thesis, Texas Western College, 1968). Editor Pooley was liberal in supporting a more democratic electoral process in El Paso that would include Mexican Americans, but at the same time he considered himself an economic conservative and endorsed Dwight Eisenhower for president in the 1950s (Telles interview, Oct. 20, 1982).
28. Telles interview, Nov. 16, 1982.
29. *Ibid.*
30. Oral history interview with Ted Bender, El Paso, Dec. 13, 1982, by Mario T. García; oral history interview with Ralph Seitsinger, El Paso, Dec. 8, 1982, by Mario T. García; Telles interview, Nov. 16, 1982; *Herald-Post*, Feb. 6, p. 1, and Feb. 25, 1957.
31. *Ibid.*, Jan. 22, 1957, pp. 1, 4; also *Times*, Jan. 23, 1957, p. 1.
32. Telles interview, Nov. 16, 1982; *Times*, Feb. 6, 1957, p. 1; oral history interview with Ray Marantz, El Paso, Oct. 25, 1982, by Mario T. García; *Herald-Post*, Jan. 23, 1957, p. 2; Armendáriz interview; Hernández interview; see Telles flyer in Natalie Gross Collection, 1848–1975, box 825, Southwest Collection, El Paso Public Library.
33. *Herald-Post*, Jan. 23, 1957, p. 2; oral history interview with Conrad Ramírez, El Paso, Nov. 2, 1982, by Mario T. García; *Herald-Post*, March 16, 1957, p. 1. Also see oral history interview with Lucy Acosta, El Paso, Oct. 28, 1982, by Mario T. García, and oral history interview with Mary Lou Armendáriz, El Paso, Nov. 3, 1982, by Mario T. García; Richard Telles interview; and *El Continental*, Jan. 24, 1957, pp. 1, 6.
34. Albert Armendáriz interview.
35. Jacques interview; Acosta interview.
36. *Times*, Feb. 28, 1957, p. 1; *Herald-Post*, Feb. 26, 1957, pp. 1, 2; *Times*, Feb. 23, 1957, p. 1. The *Herald-Post* noted that the total number of county registered voters had set a record at 44,437. It stressed, however, that another 100,000 voters might have registered if not for the poll tax. "There should be no poll tax, of course," it suggested. "It is a device to restrict the number of voters. . . . Citizens should not have to pay to exercise their right to choose their officials" (*Herald-Post*, Feb. 1, 1957, p. 22).
37. *Herald-Post*, Feb. 5, 1957, p. 18.
38. *Ibid.*, Feb. 8, 1957, pp. 1–2; Feb. 14, 1957, p. 1; Marantz interview. For specific campaign issues, see *Herald-Post*, Feb. 21, 1957, p. 1; Feb. 8, 1957, p. 1; Feb. 13, 1957, p. 1.
39. Telles interview, Nov. 16, 1982.
40. *Ibid.;* Armendáriz interview.

41. Peter K. Eisinger, *The Politics of Displacement: Racial and Ethnic Transition in Three American Cities* (New York, 1980), p. 82.

42. *Times*, Feb. 26, 1957, p. 1; *ibid.*, Feb. 9, 1957, p. 1.

43. *Ibid.*, Feb. 25, 1957, p. 1; Feb. 23, 1957, p. 1; Feb. 14, 1957, p. 1; Feb. 23, 1957, p. 1; Eisinger, *Politics of Displacement*, p. 83.

44. *Times*, Feb. 23, 1957, p. 1.

45. *Ibid.*, Feb. 15, 1957, pp. 1–2; Feb. 22, 1957, p. 1; Feb. 24, 1957, p. 1; Feb. 16, 1957, p. 3; Feb. 21, 1957, p. 4; also Feb. 16, 1957, p. 1; Feb. 19, 1957, p. 4; Feb. 20, 1957, p. 1.

46. *Ibid.*, Feb. 27, 1957, p. 1; Telles interview, Nov. 16, 1982; Santoscoy interview; Telles interview, Nov. 16, 1983. Telles recalls that many businessmen threatened to curtail their advertisements in the *Herald-Post* because of its support of the People's Ticket. And Luciano Santoscoy, who worked at the large Popular Department Store run by the Schwartz family, notes that one prominent El Paso contractor advised Albert Schwartz, the head of the store, to cancel his advertisement in the *Herald-Post* because of the Pooley–Telles relationship.

47. *Herald-Post*, Jan. 24, 1957, p. 12; Feb. 27, 1957, p. 18; also Feb. 18, 1957, p. 18; Feb. 21, 1957, p. 16; Feb. 25, 1957, p. 6; Feb. 20, 1957, p. 12.

48. William J. Hooten, *Fifty Two Years a Newsman* (El Paso, 1974), p. 146.

49. *Times*, Feb. 24, 1957, p. 1; Jan 23, 1957, p. 4; Feb. 9, 1957, p. 4; Feb. 8, 1957, p. 4; Jan. 24, 1957, p. 4; Feb. 25, 1957, p. 4; also Feb. 20, 1957, p. 4; Feb. 22, 1957, pp. 4, 6; Feb. 17, 1957, p. 6; Feb. 22, 1957, p. 6; Feb. 24, 1957, p. 6; Feb. 1, 1957, p. 1; Feb. 10, 1957, pp. 1, 106. *Ibid.*, Feb. 25, 1957, pp. 1, 2; March 1, 1957, pp. 1, 6.

50. *El Continental*, Feb. 12, 1957, p. 1; Armendáriz interview; Bender interview.

51. Bender interview; Jacques interview.

52. Richard Telles interview.

53. *Ibid.;* Navarrete interview; Seitsinger interview.

54. Richard Telles interview; Hernández interview; Villa interview; Navarrete interview.

55. Richard Telles interview; Villa interview; Hernández interview.

56. Richard Telles interview; Marantz interview; Bender interview; Hernández interview.

57. Richard Telles interview; Villa interview; Armendáriz interview; Mary Lou Armendáriz interview.

58. Armendáriz interview.

59. Marantz interview; *Herald-Post*, March 2, 1957, p. 1; Telles interview, Nov. 16, 1982; *Times*, March 3, 1957, p. II-A. Eighty percent of registered voters went to the polls (Navarrete interview). Fermín Dorado, who now works for the El Paso City Planning Department, recalls that on election eve he was at the Ascarate Drive-In Theatre in the Lower Valley. The movie was interrupted for an announcement of Telles's victory. The people honked their horns and shouted in elation at the news (information supplied by Dorado, Dec. 15, 1982).

60. As cited in Hooten, *Fifty Two Years*, p. 149.

61. *Herald-Post*, March 4, 1957, p. 6; Seitsinger interview; Armendáriz interview.

62. *Herald-Post*, March 4, 1957, pp. 1, 6; *Times*, March 3, 1957, p. 1.

63. *Herald-Post*, March 4, 1957, pp. 1, 18; *Times*, March 4, 1957, p. 1; March 3, 1957, p. 6-A; March 4, 1957, p. 4.

64. *El Continental*, March 18, 1957, p. 1; *Times*, April 6, 1957, p. 1; *Herald-Post*, April 6, 1957, p. 4; *Times*, April 7, 1957, pp. 1, 4, 8, 18; also see letter to the editor in *Times*, April 9, 1957, p. 4.

65. Telles interview, Nov. 16, 1982.

66. *Herald-Post*, April 8, 1957, p. 1; *El Continental*, April 8, 1957, p. 1; *Herald-Post*, April 8, 1957, p. 18.

67. Richard Telles interview; *El Continental*, April 3, 1957, p. 1; *Times*, April 9, 1957, p. 1; *Herald-Post*, April 10, 1957, pp. 1, 8; April 9, 1957, p. 1; *El Continental*, April 10, 1957, pp. 1, 6.

68. *El Continental*, April 11, 1957, p. 1; for a comparison with the later election of black mayors in Cleveland and Gary, see Jeffrey K. Hadden, Louis H. Masotti, and Victor Thiessen, "The Making of the Negro Mayors 1967," in *Transaction*, 5 (Jan.–Feb. 1968), 21–30.

69. Oral history interview with Ken Flynn, El Paso, Nov. 16, 1982, by Mario T. García.

70. Richard Telles interview.

71. Eisinger, *Politics of Displacement*, p. xvii. Also see Charles H. Levine, *Racial Conflict and the American Mayor* (Lexington, Mass., 1974).

72. Eisinger, *Politics of Displacement*, pp. xviii, 149, 152.

73. *Herald-Post*, March 11, 1958, p. 14; Telles appointed approximately 42 Mexican Americans to various city commissions; see City Council *Minutes* in the City Clerk's Office, El Paso City Hall. For a count of Mexican Americans appointed to the police and fire departments see City Council *Minutes*.

74. *Herald-Post*, Sept. 30, 1957, p. 1; Nov. 5, 1958, pp. 1, 5; *Times*, March 3, 1959, p. 4; *Herald-Post*, March 27, 1959, p. 1; Jan. 9, 1960, p. 1; March 6, 1961, pp. 1–2; March 7, 1961, pp. 1–2; March 8, 1961, pp. 1–2, 14; March 10, 1961, pp. 1, 4; March 15, 1961, p. 18; March 17, 1961, pp. 1, 10. See also City Council, *Minutes*, March 14, 1961, pp. 476–478, and *Herald-Post*, Sept. 30, 1957, p. 1.

75. Santoscoy interview.

76. *Herald-Post*, Sept. 30, 1957, p. 1.

77. D'Antonio and Form, *Influentials in Two Border Cities*, p. 146.

78. *Herald-Post*, Sept. 30, 1957, p. 1.

79. Oral history interview with Joe Herrera, El Paso, Jan. 10, 1983, by Mario T. Garća.

80. Eisinger, *Politics of Displacement*, pp. 153, 194.

81. *Ibid.*, p. 194.

82. *Times*, Feb. 4, 1959, p. 3.

CHAPTER SIX: *The Popular Front*

1. See, for example, Albert Camarillo and Pedro Castillo, eds., *Furia y Muerte: Los Bandidos Chicanos* (Los Angeles, 1972); Juan Gómez-Quiñones, *Sembradores: Ricardo Flores Magón y el Partido Liberal Mexicano* (Los Angeles, 1973); Acuña, *Occupied America;* Gómez-Quiñones, "The First Steps: Chicano Labor Conflict and Organizing, 1900–1920," 3, *Aztlán*, 13–50; and Emilio Zamora, Jr., "Chicano Socialist Labor Activity in Texas, 1900–1920," *Aztlán*, 6, 221–238.

2. Abraham Hoffman, *Unwanted Mexican Americans During the Great Depression: Repatriation Pressures, 1929–1939* (Tucson, 1974), and Balderrama, *In Defense of La Raza*.

3. Wilson Record, *The Negro and the Communist Party* (Chapel Hill, 1951), p. 94; Mark Naison, *Communists in Harlem during the Depression* (Urbana, Chicago, and London, 1983).

4. For a different but incorrect view that argues that a potential "revolutionary" consciousness existed among Mexicans in the United States during the 1930s only to be thwarted by a "reformist" Communist party, see Douglas Monroy, "Anarquismo y Comunismo: Mexican Radicalism and the Communist Party in Los Angeles during the 1930s," *Labor History*, 24 (Winter 1983), 34–59. Also see the discourse between Monroy and Mario T. García in *Labor History* (Winter 1984), 152–156, and in *La Red* (May 1984), 2–11.

5. Oral history interview with Bert Corona, Los Angeles, Aug. 13, 1983, by Mario T. García. Also see Ruiz, *Cannery Women,* and Albert Camarillo, *Chicanos in California: A History of Mexican Americans in California* (San Francisco, 1984), pp. 58–64.

6. Interview with Dorothy Healey, Washington, D.C., March 11, 1984, by Mario T. García. Also see Naison, *Communists in Harlem,* pp. 169–192, and Laurence S. Wittner, "The National Negro Congress: A Reassessment," *American Quarterly* (Winter 1970), 883–901, and "The Plight and Struggles of the Mexican-Americans," *Political Affairs* (July 1949), 80.

7. Corona interview.

8. See "Draft Program of the National Congress of Spanish Speaking People," in Ernesto Galarza Collection, Special Collections, Green Library, Stanford University, MS 224/25/137. For more on UCAPAWA see Ruiz, *Cannery Women,* and Victor Nelson Cisneros, "UCAPAWA in California: The Farm Worker Period," *Aztlán,* (Fall 1976), 453–478. Also see Daniels, *Bitter Harvest.*

9. *Ibid.*

10. Oral history interview with Josefina Fierro, Los Angeles, July 26, 1982, by David Oberweiser. I wish to thank Mr. Oberweiser for providing me with a copy of his taped interview.

11. See *La Opinión* (Los Angeles), Feb. 26, 1939, p. 3; *La Prensa* (San Antonio), Jan. 22, 1939, p. 8. Three months later, El Congreso held its second California convention in Los Angeles on Feb. 26, 1939.

12. *La Prensa,* Jan. 22, 1939, p. 8.

13. *Albuquerque Journal,* Feb. 14, 1939, p. 5; also see *La Prensa,* Feb. 17, 1939, p. 5.

14. *Ibid.;* "Call to the First Congress of the Mexican and Spanish American Peoples of the United States," in Carey McWilliams Col., Special Col., UCLA, box 3, fld. 4–22.

15. Corona interview.

16. *La Opinión,* March 5, 1939, p. 5; March 12, 1939, p. 3; also see *La Prensa,* March 18, 1939, p. 5.

17. *La Opinión,* March 19, 1939, p. 3; April 9, 1939, p. 3; April 26, 1939, pp. 1, 8; oral history interview with Josefina Fierro, Los Angeles, Aug. 25, 1983, by Mario T. García; *La Opinión,* April 26, 1939, pp. 1, 8; also Corona interview.

18. *Ibid.,* April 29, 1939, p. 1. *La Opinión* reported an attendance of 1,000. The *Los Angeles Times* in its scant mention of the congress reported an attendance of 500. "Dedicated to improving the lot of Spanish-speaking people in the United States, a two-day conference will be launched here today by the Mexican and Spanish People's Congress" (see *Los Angeles Times,* April 29, 1939, part II, p. 1).

19. John Bright, "Las Mañanitas: A New Awakening for the Mexicans of the United States," *Black and White* (June 1939), 15.

20. See "Digest of Proceedings of First National Congress of the Mexican and Spanish American People of the United States," in Galarza MS 224/25/137; *La Prensa,* May 2, 1939, p. 2; Corona interview; *People's Daily World,* April 28, 1939, p. 3; and "Draft Pro-

gram." California possessed the most delegates: 95 from 72 diverse organizations such as UCAPAWA locals, the Workers Alliance, Comité de Beneficencia Mexicana, the United Furniture Workers of America, and the Hollywood Anti-Nazi League.

21. Bright, "Las Mañanitas," p. 15.

22. *People's World,* April 28, 1939, p. 3.

23. Bright, "Las Mañanitas," p. 15.

24. "Digest of Proceedings"; Bright, "Las Mañanitas," p. 15. The congress also denounced the use of the word "greaser" as used to define a Mexican or Spanish American and called for its elimination from dictionaries such as Webster's and Funk and Wagnall's.

25. *Ibid.*

26. *Ibid.* El Congreso also praised Warner Brothers Studio for aiding the Good Neighbor Policy through the production of such films as *Juárez.*

27. As quoted in Bright, "Las Mañanitas," pp. 14–15.

28. Emma Tenayuca and Homer Brooks, "The Mexican Question in the Southwest," *The Communist,* 18 (March 1939), 257–262. In the 1930s Tenayuca, as a young Mexican-American woman, helped organize hundreds of Mexican female workers in the San Antonio pecan-shelling industries; on Tenayuca see Blackwelder, *Women of the Depression.*

29. See Record, *The Negro and the Communist Party.*

30. Tenayuca and Brooks, "Mexican Question," p. 262.

31. *Ibid.,* pp. 266–268.

32. Maurice Isserman, *Which Side Were You On? The American Communist Party During the Second World War* (Middletown, Conn., 1982), p. 22.

33. Fierro interview, Aug. 25, 1983.

34. *People's World,* Feb. 18, 1939, magazine supplement.

35. *Ibid.;* Fierro interview, Aug. 25, 1983.

36. Nancy Lynn Schwartz, *The Hollywood Writer's Wars* (New York, 1982), pp. 15, 88. In its 1945 report the California Un-American Activities Committee (the Tenney committee) charged Bright with being a Communist:

John Bright, representing the Council of Pan-American Democracies, was a sponsor of the Committee for the Defense of Mexican-American Youth. He has been active in Communist Party circles since 1934 or 1935, according to the files of the Committee. At one time he was a member of the Hollywood John Reed Club, a Communist journalistic organization named after the first American Communist. Bright was active in raising funds for the Spanish Loyalists and the Spanish refugees and was participating in Communist Party activities in the Republic of Mexico as late as the year 1940. John Leech, a former Communist Party organizer for Southern California, testified before the Los Angeles Grand Jury on August 15, 1940, that John Bright had escorted him and Stanley Lawrence to an underground Communist group in Westwood Village in 1935 or 1936. Bright is also a member of the National Executive Board of the Communist-inspired and dominated League of American Writers. California Senate Report [of the] *Joint Fact-Finding Committee on Un-American Activities in California,* Second Report (1945), p. 193

37. Fierro interview, Aug. 25, 1983.

38. *People's World,* Feb. 25, 1939, magazine supplement. In its 1945 report the California Un-American Activities Committee (the Tenney committee) characterized Fierro de Bright as a Communist sympathizer and described her in these words: "Josephine Bright is the wife of John Bright. She has been active in Communist front Spanish-speaking organizations, congresses, Mexican congresses, Mexican agricultural workers unions and

Spanish minority groups for a number of years. In recent months she has been active in raising money for Spanish refugees in Mexico. In 1942 she endorsed the candidacy of Mrs. La Rue McCormick, a registered Communist, for the office of State Senator for the 38th Senatorial District." See *Un-American Activities*, Second Report (1945), p. 193.

39. See "Eduardo Quevedo, 1903–1964: A Biographical Presentation, March 8, 1964," in Eduardo Quevedo Col., MS 349, box 1, fld. 13, item 1, Green Library, Stanford University. Also see Quevedo Scrapbook in *ibid.*, MS 349, box 8.

40. Fierro interview, Aug. 25, 1983. Also see FBI file on Quevedo, file no. 140-31475, LA 140-5829, Oct. 5, 1965. Quevedo in the 1943 interview with the FBI also stated that he had left the congress because of its control by Communists.

41. See *La Opinión*, Sept. 29, 1940, p. 3; March 16, 1941, p. 3; May 18, 1941, p. 3; and May 3, 1942, p. 3. Also see "Proyecto De Programa Para El Congreso Del Pueblo De Habla Española De Los Estados De Norteamerica," in Galarza Col., MS 224/25/137.

42. Fierro interview, Aug. 25, 1983; July 26, 1982.

43. *La Opinión*, June 21, 1939, pp. 1, 8; June 28, 1939, pp. 2, 8; *La Prensa*, May 22, 1939, pp. 1, 2.

44. *La Opinión*, May 16, 1939, p. 8; May 21, 1939, p. 1; May 28, 1939, pp. 1, 6; June 4, 1939, p. 1; July 29, 1939, p. 3; Fierro interview, July 26, 1982; telephone oral history interview with Josefina Fierro, Santa Barbara, and Guaymas, Sonora, Sept. 7, 1983, by Mario T. García.

45. *La Opinión*, Feb. 21, 1940, p. 8.

46. *Ibid.*, Nov. 3, 1940, p. 3. El Congreso offices were located in the Music Art Building, room 405, at 233 S. Broadway (Fierro interview, Sept. 7, 1983). See also *La Opinión*, Nov. 10, 1940, p. 3, and Feb. 18, 1941, p. 3.

47. *Ibid.*, July 8, 1939, p. 5; *People's World*, Feb. 29, 1940; and "Resolutions Adopted By the Second Convention of the Spanish Speaking People's Congress of California, Dec. 9 and 10, 1939," in Galarza Col., MS 224/23/128.

48. *La Opinión*, Aug. 20, 1939, p. 1; Aug. 25, 1939, p. 5; Aug. 27, 1939, p. 3; Fierro interview, Sept. 7, 1983.

49. Fierro interview, Aug. 25, 1983. As a result of police abuses against Mexicans, three new branches of El Congreso sprang up in Belvedere, Culver City, and Carmelita.

50. *La Opinión*, Sept. 14, 1939, p. 8; Aug. 29, 1940, p. 8.

51. Fierro interview, Sept. 7, 1983. In a general essay on Mexican-American leadership, writer Gracia Molina-Pick notes that the congress staged a demonstration outside the California State Building in Los Angeles to protest the suicides of two Mexican-American boys at the Whittier Reform School. El Congreso's protest led to improvements in the reform facility. See Gracia Molina-Pick, "The Emergence of Chicano Leadership: 1930–1950," *Caminos* (Aug. 1983), 9. Also see newspaper clippings on the Whittier case in Leo Gallagher Col. at the Southern California Library for Social Studies and Research in Los Angeles.

52. *La Opinión*, Oct. 6, 1939, p. 5; Nov. 25, 1939, p. 8; Dec. 3, 1939, p. 3; Dec. 6, 1939, p. 2; Dec. 7, 1939, pp. 2, 5; Jan. 19, 1940, p. 5; July 18, 1940, pp. 1, 8; March 15, 1940, p. 5; April 12, 1940, pp. 5–6; Oct. 11, 1940, p. 5; Dec. 6, 1940, p. 5; Dec. 8, 1940, p. 3.

53. See "Special Bulletin," Second Congress of the Spanish Speaking People in California, Dec. 9–10, 1939, in Galarza Col., MS 224/25/137; and Fierro interview, Aug. 25, 1983, and Sept. 7, 1983.

54. *La Opinión*, May 1939, p. 3; see *ibid.*, May 16, 1939, p. 8; June 4, 1939, p. 3;

July 23, 1939, p. 3; Aug. 6, 1939, p. 3; Aug. 27, 1939, p. 3; Aug. 31, 1939, p. 3; Aug. 20, 1939, p. 3; Oct. 21, 1939, p. 8; Nov. 26, 1939, p. 3; June 14, 1940, p. 3. Complementing the work of the main Youth Committee in Los Angeles, several other Clubes Juveniles Pro Congreso organized in adjacent areas such as Pico and San Pedro. At the second state convention of El Congreso in December 1939, eight delegates represented the Congress Youth Clubs with a combined membership of well over a thousand (see *ibid.* and "Resoluciones Adoptados En La Segunda Convención Del Congreso De Los Pueblos De Habla Española De California," Dec. 9–12, 1939, in Galarza Col., MS 224-230-128). One additional youth club, formed in 1941, consisted exclusively of young women in East Los Angeles (*La Opinión*, Nov. 2, 1941, p. 3).

55. "Resolutions . . . Second Convention"; *La Opinión*, May 18, 1941, p. 3; Nov. 17, 1940, p. 3; March 30, 1941, p. 3; March 16, 1941, p. 3; May 26, 1940, p. 3; March 23, 1941, p. 3; March 25, 1941, p. 8; see announcement for second state convention in Galarza Col., MS 224-25-137; and Fierro interview, Sept. 7, 1983.

56. *People's World*, June 28, 1940, p. 5; on Moreno's organizing work among Mexican-American cannery workers see Ruiz, *Cannery Women; La Opinión*, Aug. 24, 1941, p. 3; "Special Bulletin;" "Resolutions . . . Second Convention." According to Molina-Pick, El Congreso boycotted Los Angeles stores which refused to hire Mexican Americans ("Chicano Leadership," p. 9).

57. "Resolutions . . . Second Convention."

58. *La Opinión*, Aug. 12, 1939, p. 8; Feb. 23, 1941, p. 3; Aug. 12, 1939, p. 8; Fierro interview, Sept. 7, 1983; *La Opinión*, Dec. 12, 1939, p. 1; Feb. 23, 1941, p. 3; Sept. 29, 1941, p. 3.

59. See "Convocatoria" in Galarza Col., MS 224-25-137; "Resolutions . . . Second Convention"; *La Opinión*, Aug. 11, 1940, p. 3; *People's Daily World*, June 28, 1940, p. 5; *La Opinión*, March 30, 1941, p. 3; "Special Bulletin"; "Resolutions . . . Second Convention." El Congreso believed in the power of coalition politics to prevent intervention in Europe and in March 1941 sent Florencia Rivera to represent it at a New York City conference sponsored by various peace groups. Popular Front politics also meant critical support for the New Deal. Taking the Popular Front into the barrios, El Congreso not only strove to establish links with labor and left organizations but with the Mexican-American middle class. It encouraged, for example, organizing Mexican-American merchants within the congress "to protect their rights and to lay the basis for a future campaign where the Mexican merchants' problems may be treated as part of a community who suffers similarly." In addition, El Congreso supported closer and friendlier relations between Spanish-speaking and English-speaking groups.

60. *La Opinión*, Jan. 18, 1941, p. 3. Like El Congreso, the National Negro Congress shifted its forces to support the war effort (Wittner, "National Negro Congress," p. 898).

61. Corona interview; *La Opinión*, March 29, 1941, p. 3.

62. *Ibid.*, Feb. 2, 1941, n.p.; *People's Daily World*, June 23, 1941, n.p. Other groups in the Council included the Korean Club, American Peace Mobilization, Democratic Youth Federation, and the California Youth Legislature. Fierro interview, Sept. 7, 1983; *La Opinión*, April 5, 1942, p. 3; April 12, 1942, p. 3; April 20, 1942, p. 1; April 19, 1942, p. 3; April 16, 1942, p. 8; April 19, 1942, p. 3; April 20, 1942, p. 1; April 22, 1942, p. 1; Fierro interview, Sept. 7, 1983. Bert Corona recalls that 50,000 people registered in the census (Corona interview). Also see Mario T. García, "Americans All."

63. *La Opinión*, April 26, 1942, pp. 1, 6. For the adverse effects of the Bracero Program see Galarza, *Merchants of Labor.*

64. *The Nation*, April 3, 1942, p. 487; *La Opinión*, Feb. 11, 1943, p. 3. Also July 13, 1941, p. 3.

65. *The Nation*, April 3, 1942, p. 487; see McWilliams, *North From Mexico*, p. 265; "The Sinarquista Movement in Mexico—June, 1943," in Sinarquista File, Office of Strategic Services—Research and Analysis Branch, R & A No. 843, sub-file 289, box 9, National Archives, Washington, D.C.; *La Opinión*, Nov. 24, 1940, p. 3; and Jean Meyer, *Le Sinarquisme: Un Fascisme Mexicain? 1937–1947* (Paris, 1977), p. 54.

66. As quoted in Salvador Abascal, *Mis Recuerdos: Sinarquismo y Colonial María Auxiliadora* (Mexico City, 1980), p. 390.

67. *La Opinión*, March 23, 1940, p. 3; March 2, 1941, p. 3.

68. Fierro interview, Sept. 7, 1943; Fierro de Bright article is entitled "American-Mexican and New Deal" and appeared in *Pic* (Aug. 1942). See quotation from article in *Un-American Activities*, Second Report (1945), p. 201.

69. See "Call!"; *La Opinión*, Aug. 13, 1942, p. 1; Aug. 15, 1942, p. 1; Fierro interview, Sept. 7, 1943; also see McWilliams, *North From Mexico*, p. 295.

70. Fierro interview, Sept. 7, 1943.

71. *Ibid.*; Fierro interview, July 26, 1982. On Sinarquista activity in California which downplays the threat from the "right," see California, *Senate Report [of the] Joint Fact-Finding Committee on Un-American Activities in California*, First Report (1943), pp. 1342–1359.

72. Fierro interview, Aug. 25, 1983; July 26, 1982.

73. Isserman, *Which Side*, p. 119. Isserman also notes: "The Communists did not abandon the struggle for black rights during the war, but rather forced that struggle into narrow channels," p. 141.

74. Fierro interview, July 26, 1982; Sept. 7, 1983.

75. Isserman, *Which Side*, p. 111; Fierro interview, July 26, 1982. Albert Camarillo in his coverage of El Congreso concludes that the demise of the congress was the result of the lack of elected public officials in the ranks of El Congreso's leadership who could translate the organization's program into legislation; red baiting of the congress due to the presence of radicals and Communists in the leadership; the lack of funding; and, finally, the induction of much of the leadership into the war effort. See Camarillo, *Chicanos in California*, pp. 227, 229.

76. McWilliams, *North From Mexico*, pp. 227, 229.

77. Fierro interview, Sept. 7, 1983; undated transcript of interview with Bert Corona in possession of Corona.

78. McWilliams, *North From Mexico*, pp. 231–232. In the recent play and movie *Zoot-Suit*, writer Luis Valdez incorrectly omits the central role played by Mexican-American activists in organizing the Sleepy Lagoon Defense Committee (see George E. Shibley to editor, *Los Angeles Times*, Los Angeles, Sept. 25, 1978). A copy of the letter was provided to me by Bert Corona. The Tenney Un-American Activities Committee in California charged that the Sleepy Lagoon Defense Committee "is a typical Communist front organization" (see *Un-American Activities*, First Report [1943], p. 1358; also see *Un-American Activities*, Second Report [1945], pp. 174–182). Likewise see Carey McWilliams, *The Education of Carey McWilliams* (New York, 1978), pp. 108–115; Citizens' Committee for the Defense of Mexican-American Youth, "The Sleepy Lagoon Case" (June 1943); and Guy S. Endore, *The Sleepy Lagoon Mystery* (Los Angeles, 1944). On the Tenney committee see Ingrid Scobie, "Jack B. Tenney and the 'Parasitic Menace': Anti-

Communist Legislation in California, 1940–1949," *Pacific Historical Review* (May 1974), 188–211.

79. McWilliams, *North From Mexico*, p. 234.

80. For a good account of the riots see *ibid.*, 244–258; also Mauricio Mazón, *The Zoot-Suit Riots: The Psychology of Symbolic Annihilation* (Austin, 1984), and Fierro interview, Sept. 7, 1982. The Communist party in the United States also believed that similar riots in Detroit and Harlem were the work of pro-Nazi fifth-columnists (Isserman, *Which Side*, p. 157). Also Joe Marty, Citizens' Committee for the Defense of Mexican American Youth, to Friends, Los Angeles, Aug. 7, 1943; copy provided by Bert Corona. Also see *Inter-American*, 2 (Aug. 1943), 5–6.

81. See U.S. House of Representatives, *Investigation of Un-American Propaganda Activities in the United States*, 78th Congress, 1st session, vol. 16, 1944, p. 10340; James K. Hall to Mario T. García, Washington, D.C., June 6, 1984, in possession of Mario T. García. Also see Edward L. Barrett, Jr., *The Tenney Committee: Legislative Investigation of Subversive Activities in California* (Ithaca, 1951).

82. See *Un-American Activities*, First Report (1943), pp. 1304, 1313; *ibid.*, Second Report (1945), pp. 182, 193. One FBI agent in 1942 referred to El Congreso as "allegedly a communist front"; see R. B. Hood to Director, FBI, Los Angeles, May 5, 1942, in FBI file on LULAC; also see FBI Report 100–4303, Los Angeles, June 26, 1943, and E. E. Conroy to Director, FBI, Dallas, April 14, 1939, in FBI file on LULAC.

83. Fierro interview, Sept. 7, 1983.

84. Corona interview; undated newspaper clippings on Luisa Morena provided by Bert Corona. Also see Ruiz, *Cannery Women*, p. 116.

85. Fierro interview, July 26, 1982.

86. Wittner, "National Negro Congress," p. 901.

CHAPTER SEVEN: *Border Proletariats*

1. See Arroyo, "Industrial Unionism and the Los Angeles Furniture Industry"; Daniel, *Bitter Harvest;* Monroy, "Mexicans in Los Angeles"; Nelson-Cisneros, "La Clase Trabajadora"; and Ruiz, *Cannery Women*.

2. On Mine Mill see Vernon H. Jensen, *Nonferrous Metals Industry Unionism, 1932–1954* (Ithaca, 1954); D. H. Dinwoodie, "The Rise of the Mine-Mill Union in Southwestern Copper," in James C. Foster, ed., *American Labor in the Southwest: The First One Hundred Years* (Tucson, 1982), pp. 46–56. Also see Richard E. Lingenfelter, *The Hardrock Miners: A History of the Mining Labor Movement in the American West, 1863–1893* (Berkeley and Los Angeles, 1974); Vernon H. Jensen, *Heritage of Conflict: Labor Relations in the Nonferrous Metals Industry up to 1930* (Ithaca, 1950); James W. Byrkit, *Forging the Copper Collar: Arizona's Labor-Management War of 1901–1921* (Tucson, 1982); Mike Solski and John Smaller, eds., *Mine Mill: The History of the International Union of Mine, Mill and Smelter Workers in Canada Since 1895* (Ottawa, 1985).

3. On El Paso, see García, *Desert Immigrants*. On labor segmentation and "colonized labor" see Barrera, *Race and Class in the Southwest;* Almaguer, "Class, Race, and Chicano Oppression"; Bonavich, "A Theory of Ethnic Antagonism"; Edwards et al., eds., *Labor Market Segmentation;* García, "Racial Dualism in the El Paso Labor Market"; and Staples, "Race and Colonialism."

4. See Hoffman, *Unwanted Mexican Americans;* Balderrama, *In Defense of La Raza.*

5. *El Paso Times,* Jan. 28, 1930, in El Paso Vertical File-Smelting Industry in Southwest Collection, El Paso Public Library.

6. Dinwoodie, "Rise of the Mine-Mill Union in Southwestern Copper," p. 47.

7. Interview with Humberto Sílex, El Paso, Dec. 11, 1982, by Mario T. García.

8. See interview no. 505 with Sílex by Oscar J. Martínez and Art Sadin, El Paso, April 28, 1978, in Institute of Oral History, University of Texas at El Paso (hereinafter cited as IOH).

9. Sílex interview, Dec. 11, 1982.

10. As quoted in Frank Arnold, "Humberto Sílex: CIO Organizer from Nicaragua," in *Southwest Economy & Society* (Fall 1978), 5.

11. *Ibid.* and Sílex interview, April 28, 1978, IOH, pp. 15–16; interview with Sílex, El Paso, Dec. 13, 1982, by Mario T. García.

12. See García, *Desert Immigrants,* pp. 127–154; Mark Robinson to Harold [no last name listed], El Paso, Jan. 14, 1941, in Archives of the International Union of Mine, Mill and Smelter Workers, Western History Collection, University of Colorado, box 553, folder-Local 501 (hereinafter cited as UMMSW).

13. Sílex interview, Dec. 11, 1982; *Labor Advocate,* Jan. 27, 1939, p. 1. The *Advocate* was the newspaper of the El Paso Central Labor Council.

14. As quoted in clipping from El Paso Vertical File-Industries-American Smelting and Refining Co., Southwest Col.

15. Interview with J. B. Chávez, El Paso, Jan. 18, 1983, by Mario T. García. When Chávez suffered a severe injury to his arm, which had to be amputated, he had no recourse to any type of compensation nor could he get a lawyer to file suit against Phelps-Dodge (Sílex interview, Dec. 13, 1982).

16. Sílex interview, Dec. 11, 1982. In 1935 Mine Mill was one of the charter unions of the CIO. That year Mine Mill possessed a membership of 15,000. Mine Mill had its origins in the Western Federation of Miners, founded in 1883. In 1905 the federation helped organize the Industrial Workers of the World (IWW). In 1916 it changed its name to the International Mine, Mill and Smelter Workers Union as part of the American Federation of Labor. See Benjamin Stalberg, *The Story of the CIO* (New York, 1938), pp. 27 and 62.

17. Chávez interview.

18. Sílex interview, Dec. 11, 1982.

19. *Ibid.,* and Sílex interview, April 28, 1978, IOH, p. 17.

20. *Ibid.,* IOH, p. 18; Dinwoodie, "Mine-Mill," p. 4.

21. Sílex interview, April 28, 1978, IOH, p. 20.

22. Chávez interview. Union dances also were held as a recruiting tool.

23. Sílex interview, Dec. 11, 1982.

24. Chávez interview.

25. Sílex interview, Dec. 11, 1982, and April 28, 1978, IOH, p. 4.

26. As quoted in Arnold, "Humberto Sílex," p. 7.

27. *Ibid.,* p. 8; *Labor Advocate,* Aug. 23, 1940, p. 1.

28. *El Paso Herald-Post,* March 11, 1940, pp. 1–2; March 22, 1940, p. 16; March 7, 1940, pp. 1, 11; March 8, 1940, pp. 1, 16. J. B. Chávez recalls that Fox had six deputy sheriffs as informers inside the P–D plant (Chávez interview, Jan. 18, 1983). For the relationship between the CIO and the Communist party see Bert Cochran, *Labor and Communism: The Conflict that Shaped American Unions* (Princeton, 1977).

29. *Herald-Post,* March 8, 1940, pp. 1, 16. For the brown scare, see Romo, *East Los Angeles.*

30. *Ibid.*, March 9, 1940, pp. 1, 6. According to Sílex, Sheriff Fox around this time told James Robinson: "If God wanted to make men equal he wouldn't have made whites, browns, and blacks" (Sílex interview, Dec. 11, 1982).

31. *Herald-Post*, March 12, 1940, p. 4; March 11, 1940, p. 4. Sheriff Fox later testified before the Dies committee and reiterated his charge of Communist ties between Juárez and El Paso labor leaders (*ibid.*, March 26, 1940, p. 1; March 27, 1940, p. 1; July 24, 1940, p. 1; *Times,* July 21, 1940, p. 8).

32. *Herald-Post*, March 12, 1940, pp. 1, 4.

33. *Ibid.*, March 19, 1940, p. 1. Of the remaining three men in jail, Pedroza was turned over to U.S. immigration officials and repatriated from the country; Oaxaca was released from county jail and given a "voluntary departure" by U.S. immigration officials; finally, Frank Sener was tried and convicted on a charge of "vagrancy," fined $200, and sentenced to 74 days in jail. See *ibid.*, March 11, 1940, pp. 1, 12; March 12, 1940, pp. 1, 11; March 13, 1940, p. 9; March 15, 1940, p. 1; March 18, 1940, pp. 1, 8; March 19, 1940, pp. 1, 7; March 21, 1940, pp. 1–2; March 22, 1940, pp. 1, 16; and March 23, 1940, p. 1.

34. Sílex interview, Dec. 13, 1982.

35. *Herald Post*, April 12, 1940, p. 2; Nov. 4, 1940, pp. 1, 12; *Times,* Nov. 8, 1940, p. 9; *Herald-Post,* Nov. 13, 1940, pp. 1, 8; Nov. 6, 1940, pp. 1–2; Nov. 9, 1940, pp. 1, 6; Nov. 12, 1940, pp. 1, 12; Nov. 15, 1940, p. 1; Nov. 4, 1940, pp. 1, 12; May 7, 1940, p. 7; Feb. 6, 1941, p. 1.

36. *Ibid.*, Feb. 1, 1941, pp. 1, 6; Feb. 3, 1941, pp. 1, 10; Feb. 4, 1941, pp. 1, 12; Feb. 7, 1941, p. 1; Robinson to "Harold," El Paso, Jan. 25, 1941, UMMSW, box 553, fld.-Local 501; *Herald-Post,* Sept. 4, 1941, p. 10.

37. *The Union,* Sept. 27, 1943, p. 8. For the role of the CIO during World War II see Nelson Lichtenstein, *Labor's War at Home: The CIO in World War II* (Cambridge, 1982).

38. Sílex et al. to Robinson, El Paso, Aug. 9, 1941, UMMSW, box 131, fld. 501.

39. As quoted in *Mine-Mill Union,* May 4, 1942, p. 10.

40. Sílex to Robinson, El Paso, May 18, 1942, UMMSW, box 41, fld. 15. Also see Allan D. McNeil to Sílex, Denver, Jan. 5, 1942, box 41, fld. 15; same to same, March 27, 1942; same to same, May 9, 1942; same to same, May 11, 1942; same to same, May 20, 1942; and Sílex to McNeil, El Paso, May 18, 1942, all in box 41, fld. 15.

41. Fewer than a handful of the women remained in these jobs after the war. Some had been "cantineras" [barmaids] before working at the refinery (see Chávez interview, Jan. 18, 1983). Gabriel Cedillo recalls that most of the women were single and some performed semiskilled jobs as operatives (see interview with Gabriel Cedillo, El Paso, Nov. 18, 1982, by Mario T. García).

42. As quoted in *Mine-Mill Union,* May 25, 1942.

43. *Ibid.*, July 6, 1942, p. 3.

44. See agreement, May 6, 1942, in UMMSW, box 131, fld. 509.

45. Sílex to Reid Robinson, El Paso, July 14, 1942, in UMMSW, box 41, fld. 15; Sílex to Allen D. McNeil, El Paso, Oct. 19, 1942, UMMSW, box 41, fld. 15; same to same, El Paso, Nov. 14, 1942, UMMSW, box 41, fld. 15; Leo Ortíz to McNeil, El Paso, Aug. 3, 1942, and same to same, El Paso, Aug. 6, 1942, in UMMSW, box 41, fld. 3; Jess Nichols to Reid Robinson, El Paso, March 24, 1943, UMMSW, box 41, fld. 1; report of Jess Nichols, Dec. 3, 1942, UMMSW, box 41, fld. 1; Anchondo to Robinson, El Paso, Jan. 9, 1943, UMMSW, box 131, fld. 509; Nichols to Robinson, El Paso, March 24, 1943; same to same, March 10, 1943, UMMSW, box 41, fld. 1.

46. *Mine-Mill Union,* Aug. 28, 1942.

47. See flyer in UMMSW, box 41, fld. 1.

48. See Leo Ortíz to Reid Robinson, Miami, Arizona, Feb. 16, 1943; Robinson to Ortíz, Denver, March 18, 1943; Ortíz to McNeil, El Paso, Aug. 3, 1942; and same to same, El Paso, Aug. 6, 1942; Ortíz to Robinson, El Paso, Sept. 11, 1942, all in UMMSW, box 41, fld. 3. Also see Nichols to Robinson, El Paso, June 23, 1943; same to same, El Paso, July 10, 1943, box 41, fld. 1. Robinson to Sílex, Denver, June 8, 1945; same to same, Denver, July 19, 1945; and Sílex to Robinson, El Paso, July 3, 1943, all in UMMSW, box 134, fld. 509.

49. Ceferino Anchondo to Reid Robinson, El Paso, Jan. 9, 1943, UMMSW, box 131, fld. 509; Nichols to Robinson, El Paso, March 15, 1943, and Robinson to Nichols, Denver, March 12, 1943, in UMMSW, box 41, fld. 1; Nichols to John R. Steelman, El Paso, n.d., UMMSW, box 41, fld. 1; *The Union*, Oct. 11, 1943, p. 15; *Union News*, Sept. 26, 1944, in UMMSW, box 136, fld. 616.

50. Arthur Martínez and Nichols to J. B. Beaty, El Paso, July 26, 1944, UMMSW, box 134, fld. 501; Robinson to Nichols, Denver, May 6, 1943, UMMSW, box 41, fld. 1; same to Sílex, Denver, May 18, 1943, and Sílex to Robinson, El Paso, May 10, 1943, in UMMSW, box 41, fld. 15; R. F. Gafford to Robinson, El Paso, June 4, 1945, UMMSW, box 134, fld. 509; NLRB document, June 25, 1945, in UMMSW, box 134, fld. 501; contract, Jan. 24, 1944, in Archives of U.S. Steelworkers, El Paso; Sílex interview, Dec. 13, 1982. According to J. B. Chávez, the contract froze seniority for Anglos while advancing Mexican Americans into more skilled jobs and reducing the dual wage gap (Chávez interview).

51. See "Abusos, Discriminación En El Suroeste," in *The Union*, Aug. 28, 1944, p. 12; also R. F. Gafford to Reid Robinson, El Paso, June 4, 1945, box 134, fld. 509. For other CIO strikes in 1946 see Cochran, *Labor and Communism*, pp. 248–271. Also see Art Preis, *Labor's Giant Step: Twenty Years of the CIO* (New York, 1964), pp. 257–383.

52. *Herald Post*, March 2, 1946, pp. 1, 2; Feb. 16, 1946, p. 1; Feb. 25, 1946, pp. 1, 8; Feb. 26, 1946, p. 1; Feb. 27, 1946, p. 14; Feb. 28, 1946, p. 3; March 2, 1946, pp. 1, 2; March 11, 1946, p. 1.

53. *Ibid.*, Feb. 28, 1946, p. 3; Feb. 16, 1946; Feb. 25, 1946, pp. 1–8; Feb. 26, 1946, pp. 1, 4, 7.

54. *Ibid.*, March 4, 1946, pp. 1–2; Feb. 28, 1946, p. 3; March 2, 1946, pp. 1–2; March 9, 1946, p. 1; March 18, 1946, p. 1.

55. *The Union*, April 3, 1946, p. 2; *Herald-Post*, March 13, 1946, pp. 1, 11; March 28, 1946, p. 1.

56. *The Union*, May 13, 1946, p. 19, and May 27, 1946, p. 4.

57. *Herald-Post*, March 14, 1946, p. 1; March 11, 1946, pp. 1–2; Humberto Sílex, J. B. Chávez, and Ignacio Tovar Financial Report, July 1, 1946, in Humberto Sílex Private Col.; *Herald-Post*, March 4, 1946, pp. 1–2; March 13, 1946, pp. 1, 11.

58. *Herald-Post*, Feb. 26, 1946, pp. 1, 7; Sílex interview, Dec. 13, 1982.

59. *Herald-Post*, Feb. 26, 1946, pp. 1, 7; March 8, 1946, pp. 1, 15; *The Union*, April 3, 1946, p. 2.

60. *Herald-Post*, Feb. 26, 1946, pp. 1, 7; March 12, 1946, p. 3; Sílex interview, Dec. 13, 1982.

61. *Ibid.*, March 16, 1946, p. 12, and March 29, 1946, p. 9. Ceferino Anchondo of Local 509 served on the executive committee of the Citizens Committee. Also see Ignacio Tovar to Brother Montgomery, El Paso, April 2, 1946, UMMSW, box 134, fld. 509, and May 27, 1946, p. 4.

62. Tovar to Brother Montgomery, El Paso, April 2, 1946, UMMSW, box 134, fld. 509.
63. *The Union,* April 3, 1946, p. 2.
64. *Herald-Post,* March 22, 1946, p. 4; April 3, 1946, p. 4.
65. *Ibid.,* March 6, 1946, pp. 1–2; March 28, 1946, p. 1; April 30, 1946, p. 1; May 13, 1946, p. 1; *The Union,* May 27, 1946, p. 4; Chávez to Robinson, El Paso, March 17, 1946, UMMSW, box 134, fld. 509.
66. *Herald-Post,* May 30, 1946, p. 3; June 11, 1946, p. 1; June 12, 1946, pp. 1, 10; June 13, 1946, pp. 1, 5; June 17, 1946, p. 1; Sílex to Morris Wright, June 17, 1946, UMMSW, box 134, fld. 509.
67. *Herald- Post,* June 21, 1946, pp. 1–2.
68. *Ibid.*
69. *Ibid.,* June 28, 1946, pp. 1, 18; June 29, 1946, p. 1; *The Union,* June 24, 1946, p. 2.
70. *Ibid.,* June 24, 1946, p. 2; Sept. 16, 1946, p. 3; Sílex interview, Dec. 13, 1982.
71. See Juan Gómez-Quinoñes, "The First Steps: Chicano Labor Conflict and Organizing, 1900–1920," *Aztlán* (Spring 1972), 13–49; Gómez-Quinoñes and David Maciel, *Al norte del rio bravo (pasado lejano), 1600–1930* (Mexico City, 1981); Maciel, *Al norte del rio bravo (pasado immediato), 1930–1981* (Mexico City, 1981).
72. On efforts to deport Sílex see Sílex Private Col.
73. Sílex interview, Dec. 13, 1982. In 1967, owing to declining membership and other causes, Mine Mill did merge with the U.S. Steelworkers. Many of the Mine Mill veterans are still active today with the Steelworkers. See Robert S. Keitel, "The Merger of the International Union of Mine, Mill and Smelter Workers into the United Steel Workers of America," *Labor History* (Winter 1974), 36–43.

CHAPTER EIGHT: *Mexican-American Radicals and the Cold War*

1. Rodolfo Acuña, *Occupied America,* p. 213. For an earlier version of this chapter see Mario T. García, "Mexican American Labor and the Left." For a research note on ANMA see Liliana Urrutia, "An Offspring of Discontent: The Asociación Nacional México-Americana, 1949–1954," in *Aztlán* (Spring 1984), 177–184. For a discussion of Mexican-American conditions in the late 1940s see Ernesto Galarza, "Program for Action," in "The Mexican American: A National Concern," in *Common Ground* (Summer 1949), 27–38.
2. See FBI report 100-3464, Phoenix, Oct. 9, 1950. All FBI reports cited were obtained through the Freedom of Information Act. Mexican-American support for Wallace was evident at a May 16 rally in Lincoln Park in East Los Angeles, where Wallace spoke in Spanish to about 10,000 Mexican Americans (see Curtis D. MacDougal, *Gideon's Army* [New York, 1965], 2:373).
3. See "Breve Historia del Pueblo Mexicano en E.U.," in *Progreso,* June 1952, in ANMA file located in Natalie Gross Col., Southwest Collection, El Paso Public Library; interview with Alfredo Montoya, Washington, D.C., July 3, 1984, by Mario T. García; and "Segunda-Convención Nacional de la Asociación Nacional México-Americana," in Southwest Col.
4. "Constitución de la Asociación Nacional Méxicana-Americana," in Southwest Col.; Montoya interview; FBI Prosecutive Summary Report on ANMA, Dec. 5, 1952, p. 28 (hereinafter cited as FBI Summary); interview with Dorothy Healey, Washington, D.C., March 11, 1984.

5. *Progreso*, Dec. 1950, p. 1; see "Asociación Nacional Méxicana-Americana," in Southwest Col.; see Alfonso Sena, "Discurso Principal Conferencia Estatal de Colorado," in Southwest Col., and Montoya interview.

6. FBI Summary, p. 39; *Eastside Sun*, Oct. 27, 1949, p. 1; see letter from FBI agent [name deleted] to J. Edgar Hoover, Nov. 17, 1958, location deleted in FBI files on ANMA.

7. *Eastside Sun*, Oct. 20, 1949, p. 1; also *People's Daily World*, Aug. 22, 1949.

8. See various FBI reports on ANMA; FBI report PX 100-3464, Phoenix, May 17, 1951; FBI Survey, p. 33; *The Union* (Mine Mill), Jan. 16, 1950, p. 4, and Oct. 23, 1950, pp. 7–8; FBI report LA 100-30990, Los Angeles, Sept. 15, 1950; and Montoya interview. Mauricio Terrazas recalls about 1,000 members in ANMA in Southern California (interview with Mauricio Terrazas, Los Angeles, Aug. 13, 1983). Also see *Progreso*, Dec. 1950; Oct. 1950; April 1950; and "Convención Nacional Fundadora de ANMA," p. 6, in Southwest Col. Also see E. B. Fincher, "Spanish-Americans as a Political Factor in New Mexico, 1912–1950" (Ph.D. thesis, New York University, 1950), pp. 95–99.

9. See ANMA Constitution in FBI report LA 100-30990, Los Angeles, March 29, 1951.

10. See Kenneth Waltzer, "The New History of American Communism," *Reviews in American History* (June 1983), 259–267.

11. See "The Mexican-Americans—Their Plight and Struggles," *Political Affairs* (May 1949), 71–80.

12. See Montoya and Flores, "Towards the Unity of the Mexican People in the United States (1949), in FBI Survey, p. 111; "Breve Historia"; and Isabel Gonzáles," Step-Children of a Nation" (pamphlet issued by the American Committee for the Protection of the Foreign Born, 1947).

13. Statement by Montoya in 1949 as quoted in FBI Survey; *Progreso*, Oct. 1950, pp. 2, 6.

14. FBI report LA 100-30990, Los Angeles, March 29, 1951.

15. Sena, "Discurso Principal."

16. *Progreso*, April 1952, p. 7; Oct. 1950, p. 5; Sena, "Discurso Principal."

17. As quoted in report submitted by special agent in charge to Director, FBI, El Paso, April 20, 1949, in FBI files.

18. *Progreso*, June 1952, pp. 5–6; FBI report SF 200-32497, San Francisco, Oct. 31, 1952.

19. *Progreso*, June 1952, p. 2.

20. FBI Report DN 100-5176, Denver, Feb. 21, 1952.

21. See 1950 ANMA document in FBI report LA 100-30990, Los Angeles, Sept. 15, 1950, and ANMA Constitution in FBI report SF 100-31499, San Francisco, April 10, 1953; see also report by Alfonso Sena in UMMSW, box 206, fld. 11.

22. Montoya interview.

23. "Mexican-Americans," pp. 71–80, and as quoted in FBI Summary and "Resolutions on Party Work Among the Mexican People," Communist Party Convention, Aug. 3, 1948, and as quoted in FBI report DN 100-5176, Denver, June 15, 1949. The CP, while flirting with the concept of nationhood for Mexican Americans in the late 1940s, soon shifted its analysis to one that conceptualized Mexican Americans as a "national minority" and discounted the concept of nation for Mexican Americans. By national minority, the CP meant that Mexican Americans were exploited both as an essentially working class and as members of a distinct ethnic minority. In this sense they shared a similarity with blacks in the urban North. Blacks in the Deep South, however, the CP regarded as a "na-

tion" possessing all the economic and cultural characteristics of a nation as defined by Stalin in his discussion of the "National Question." On these distinctions see "The Plight and Struggles of the Mexican Americans," *Political Affairs* (July 1949), 75–84; J. D., "On Chauvinism Against the Mexican-American People," in *ibid.* (Feb. 1952), 51–56; James Burnhill, "The Mexican People of the Southwest," *ibid.* (Sept. 1953), 43–53; and Burnhill, "The Mexican American Question," *ibid.* (Dec. 1953), 50–63.

24. Montoya interview; also see *The Union,* July 28, 1952, p. 7. ANMA's slogan at the convention was "Unity for first class citizenship."

25. See 1950 ANMA report in FBI report LA 100-30990, Los Angeles, Sept. 15, 1950, and see "Brief History" in FBI Survey.

26. *Progreso,* Jan. 1953, p. 3, in UMMSW, box 118, fld. 3.

27. *Progreso,* Dec. 1950, p. 2, in Southwest Col.

28. *Ibid.,* p. 5; see FBI report SF 100-31499, San Francisco, April 10, 1953, and ANMA Constitution in FBI report LA 100-30990, Los Angeles, March 29, 1951.

29. *Progreso,* Dec. 1950, p. 2, in Southwest Col.

30. *Ibid.,* June 1950, p. 8.

31. Sena, "Discurso Principal."

32. See quotation from Montoya speech, May 20, 1950, in FBI Survey, p. 124.

33. *Ibid.,* pp. 125, 94, 90; FBI report SF 100-31499, San Francisco, Aug. 20, 1951.

34. As quoted in the *People's Daily World,* Feb. 8, 1951, in FBI report SF 100-31499, San Francisco, Aug. 20, 1951.

35. "La Voz de ANMA," Oct. 1951, in FBI Survey, p. 128.

36. *Ibid.,* p. 126.

37. FBI report DN 100-5176, Denver, Feb. 21, 1952. Casualty figures were taken from the press from Jan. 1 to June 23, 1951. Also see "La Voz de ANMA," Oct. 1951, in UMMSW, box 206, fld. 11.

38. *Progreso,* April 1952, p. 4.

39. See FBI report DN 100-5716, Denver, Feb. 21, 1952, and "La Voz," Oct. 1951, p. 3 in UMMSW, box 206, fld. 11.

40. *Progreso,* April 1952, p. 4.

41. *Ibid.,* pp. 1, 3; June 1952, p. 4; *The Union,* Dec. 7, 1951, p. 4. Also see *Eastside Sun,* Jan. 31, 1952. On the *Salt of the Earth* strike, which lasted in southern New Mexico from October 1950 until January 1952, see *The Union* from 1951 to 1952; also Herbert Biberman, *Salt of the Earth: The Story of a Film* (Boston, 1965); Deborah Silverton Ronsenfelt, ed., *Salt of the Earth* (New York, 1978); Jack Cargill, "Empire and Opposition: The 'Salt of the Earth' Strike," in Robert Kern, ed., *Labor in New Mexico: Union, Strikes, and Social History Since 1881* (Albuquerque, 1983), pp. 183–267.

42. Sena, "Discurso Principal"; FBI Survey, p. 134.

43. As quoted in FBI report DN 100-5176, Denver, Feb. 21, 1952, and "La Voz," Oct. 1951, in UMMSW, box 206, fld. 11.

44. See document "Atención!" in Southwest Col. and *Progreso,* Dec. 1950, p. 4. Long-time organizer Bert Corona recalls that as a member of ANMA he worked with braceros and migrant workers and at times mediated between braceros and their former employers (undated interview with Corona by Jesús Mena in possession of Corona).

45. FBI Survey, p. 111; FBI report EP 100-4596, El Paso, 1949; DN 100-5176, Denver, June 27, 1950; LA 100-30990, Los Angeles, Sept. 15, 1950; SF 100-31499, San Francisco, March 27, 1952; AL 100-51, Albuquerque, Dec. 26, 1950.

46. *Progreso,* Oct. 1950, in FBI Survey, p. 129; FBI report EP 100-4596, El Paso,

Nov. 10, 1952; FBI report, SF 100-31499, San Francisco, April 10, 1953; interview with Clint Jencks, San Diego, Aug. 11, 1983, by Mario T. García; *The Union*, Sept. 25, 1950, p. 5.

47. On Operation Wetback see Juan Ramón García, *Operation Wetback*. Also see series of articles on plight of undocumented Mexican workers in *People's Daily World*, April 25, 1949; May 11, 1949; May 18, 1949; May 27, 1949; May 31, 1949; June 1, 1949; June 2, 1949; June 3, 1949; June 24, 1949; June 27, 1949; June 28, 1949; June 29, 1949; June 30, 1949; and July 5, 1949.

48. Undated in FBI Survey, p. 116. Also see David Caute, *The Great Fear: The Anti-Communist Purge under Truman and Eisenhower* (New York, 1978).

49. FBI report LA 100-30990, Los Angeles, March 29, 1951.

50. *Ibid.;* FBI report SF 100-31499, San Francisco, Oct. 31, 1952; and FBI Survey, p. 116.

51. FBI Survey, pp. 118–119; FBI report SF 100-31499, San Francisco, March 27, 1952, and June 10, 1950; also *People's Daily World*, Aug. 9, 1949; *Eastside Sun*, March 13, 1952; and FBI Survey, p. 120. Also see Louise Pettibone Smith, *Torch of Liberty: Twenty-Five Years in the Life of the Foreign Born in the U.S.* (New York, 1959), pp. 417–424.

52. *Progreso*, Oct. 1950, p. 2; Dec. 1950, p. 5; April 1952, pp. 4, 6. For deportation of Mexicans under the McCarron Act also see Acuña, *Occupied America*, pp. 215–216. For the national application of the McCarron Act and the McCarron-Walter Act see Caute, *Great Fear*, pp. 224–244.

53. FBI Survey, pp. 90–91.

54. *Progreso*, Oct. 1950, p. 4. For the effects of the cold war antisubversive hysteria see McWilliams, *Witch Hunt*. Also see FBI report LA 100-20990, Los Angeles, March 29, 1951. In addition, see Peter L. Steinberg, *The Great "Red Menace": United States Prosecution of American Communists, 1947–1952* (Westport, Ct., 1984), and Ellen W. Schrecker, *No Ivory Tower: McCarthyism and the Universities* (New York, 1986).

55. Hoover to Special Agent in Charge, Washington, D.C., Feb. 1, 1952, in FBI files.

56. W. F. Kelly to Hoover, Washington, D.C., Jan. 22, 1952, in FBI files on ANMA.

57. *Progreso*, Jan. 1953, p. 3, in UMMSW, box 118, fld. 3; *ibid.*, March–April 1953, p. 4, in UMMSW, box 118, fld. 3. Bert Corona recalls that many other Mexican-American activists were likewise deported during this period, including labor leaders such as Fernando Dávila and Frank Vásquez of the furniture workers, Frank Corona of the dock workers, and Frank Martínez of the cannery workers (undated interview with Corona in Corona's possession).

58. *The Union*, July 28, 1952, p. 7; *Progreso*, Jan. 1953, pp. 3–4.

59. FBI report, Los Angeles, Jan. 1–May 19, 1952, in FBI files.

60. *Progreso*, April 1952, p. 6.

61. "La Voz," Oct. 1951, p. 1, in UMMSW, box 206, fld. 11.

62. Sena, "Discurso Principal." Also see "Report of Alfonso Sena," in UMMSW, box 206, fld. 11.

63. *Ibid.;* ANMA news release, Dec. 2, 1951, in UMMSW, box 200, fld. 11.

64. See "Resolution on Plan of Action for Boycott Campaign of Judy Canova Show," in UMMSW, box 206, fld. 11; also FBI report DN 100-5176, Denver, Feb. 21, 1952; Sena, "Discurso Principal"; *Progreso*, April 1952, p. 4; June 1952, p. 4; *The Union*, Feb. 25, 1952; and *El Paso Herald-Post*, July 14, 1952, p. 1.

65. "La Voz," Oct. 1951, p. 1, in UMMSW, box 206, fld. 11; FBI report AL 100-51, Albuquerque, Dec. 26, 1950.

66. *Progreso*, Jan. and Feb. 1951, p. 2, in UMMSW, box 206, fld. 11.

67. *Ibid.*, Jan. 1953, p. 4, in UMMSW, box 118, fld. 3.

68. FBI report SF 100-31499, San Francisco, April 10, 1953.

69. *Ibid.*, and LA 100-30990, Los Angeles, Sept. 13, 1950.

70. *Progreso*, Dec. 1950, p. 4; April 1952, p. 8; June 1952, pp. 3, 7; Oct. 1950, pp. 1, 5; Terrazas interview.

71. FBI Survey, p. 122; *People's Daily World*, April 10, 1950.

72. FBI report AL 100-51, Albuquerque, Dec. 26, 1950.

73. *Progreso*, Dec. 1950, p. 3.

74. FBI report AL 100-51, Albuquerque, Dec. 26, 1950.

75. *Ibid.;* CH 100-22449, Chicago, July 2, 1951; EP 100-4596, El Paso, 1949; LA 100-30990, Los Angeles, Feb. 8, 1950.

76. *Ibid.*, LA 100-30990, Los Angeles, March 29, 1951.

77. *Ibid.*, AL 100-51, Albuquerque, Dec. 26, 1950.

78. Terrazas interview; FBI report, AL 100-51, Albuquerque, Dec. 26, 1950; FBI Survey, pp. 37, 58–59; Special Agent in Charge to Director, FBI, El Paso, July 15, 1952; FBI report LA 100-30990, Los Angeles, Sept. 15, 1950; SF 100-31499, San Francisco, Oct. 31, 1952; CH 100-22449, Chicago, July 2, 1951. Also interview with Julia Luna Mount, Los Angeles, Aug. 12, 1983, by Mario T. García.

79. Luna Mount interview. For more on Luna Mount see Ruiz, *Cannery Women.*

80. FBI Survey, pp. 44, 103; FBI report PX 100-3464, Phoenix, May 17, 1951; *Progreso*, Jan.–Feb. 1951, in UMMSW, box 206, fld. 11; FBI report, EP 100-4596, El Paso, 1949; FBI Survey, p. 106; Terrazas interview.

81. FBI report SD 100-7084, San Diego, Dec. 16, 1949; FBI Survey, p. 102. Also *People's Daily World*, Oct. 6, 1949; Oct. 18, 1949; Oct. 25, 1949.

82. FBI Survey, p. 103.

83. *Ibid.*, pp. 103–104; Terrazas interview.

84. *Ibid.*, pp. 104–105; see FBI report LA 100-30990, Los Angeles, Sept. 15, 1950, and *Eastside Sun*, March 9, 1950. Also see *People's Daily World*, Feb. 7, 1950; Feb. 8, 1950; Feb. 14, 1950; March 22, 1950; and April 27, 1950; *Progreso*, Jan.–Feb. 1951, p. 5.

85. *Ibid.*, April, 1952, p. 3; *Eastside Sun*, Nov. 29, 1951, p. 1; Montoya interview; *Progreso*, Jan. 1953, p. 2, in UMMSW, box 118, fld. 3; undated interview with Bert Corona in possession of Corona; see "Convención Nacional Fundadora," and "Segunda Convención" in Southwest Col.

86. FBI Summary, p. 109, and FBI report SF 100-21499, San Francisco, Aug. 20, 1951.

87. FBI report LA 100-30990, Los Angeles, Sept. 15, 1950; *Progreso,* Jan.–Feb. 1951, pp. 1, 4; "La Voz," Oct. 1951, in UMMSW, box 206, fld. 11; also see FBI Survey, p. 130.

88. *Herald Post*, July 11, 1952, pp. 1, 12.

89. Special Agent in Charge to Director, FBI, San Francisco, Feb. 14, 1950. Approximately 3,000 pages of documents pertaining to ANMA were located in FBI files (James K. Hall to Mario T. García, Washington, D.C., June 6, 1984).

90. FBI report LA 100-30990, Los Angeles, Feb. 8, 1950.

91. Deleted name to FBI, deleted location, Nov. 15, 1949.

92. FBI report SF 100-31499, San Francisco, April 10, 1953; Aug. 10, 1951; undated interview with Corona.

93. FBI Survey, pp. 71–79.

94. Deleted name to Hoover, deleted location, Nov. 17, 1958. The report was made in 1949 but summarized in 1958.

95. FBI report CH 100-22449, Chicago, July 2, 1951.

96. FBI Survey, p. 22; FBI report SF 100-31499, San Francisco, June 16, 1950.

97. *Ibid.;* LA 100-30990, Los Angeles, March 29, 1951; FBI Survey, pp. 80–89.

98. FBI report EP 100-4596, El Paso, 1949; FBI Survey, pp. 101–102, 2–27; FBI report DN 100-5176, Denver, June 18, 1949.

99. Hoover to Denver Special Agent in Charge, Washington, D.C., Sept. 29, 1952; Hoover to New York Special Agent in Charge, Washington, D.C., May 29, 1953; see Olney statement in FBI 100-361179-141. For the wider use of the attorney general's list to harass left organizations see Caute, *Great Fear*, pp. 169–178. For other Mexican-American organizations investigated by the FBI, see Gutiérrez, "Chicanos and Mexicans," pp. 29–58.

100. See Montoya's letter dated May 11, 1953, in Hoover to Denver Special Agent in Charge, Washington, D.C., June 26, 1953. For a comparison with Afro-American responses to the cold war see Gerald Horne, *Black and Red: W.E.B. Du Bois and the Afro-American Response to the Cold War, 1944–1963* (Albany, 1986).

101. FBI report DN 100-5176, Denver, April 5, 1954; *Herald-Post*, Feb. 5, 1954, p. 1; May 13, 1957, pp. 1–2; May 17, 1957, pp. 1, 20. Also see Harvey Matusow, *False Witness* (New York, 1955).

102. Terrazas interview.

103. *Progreso*, Jan. 1953, p. 3, in UMMSW, box 118, fld. 3.

104. Special Agent in Charge to Director, FBI, San Francisco, Sept. 10, 1953.

105. Terrazas interview.

106. Montoya interview.

107. Terrazas interview.

108. See Waltzer, "New History."

109. Montoya interview.

110. FBI report DN 100-5176, Denver, April 5, 1954.

CHAPTER NINE: *Carlos E. Castañeda and the Search for History*

1. Félix D. Almaraz, Jr., "Carlos Eduardo Castañeda, Mexican-American Historian: The Formative Years, 1896–1927," *Pacific Historical Review* (Aug. 1973), 320–322. Also see Carlos E. Castañeda, "Why I Chose History," *The Americas* (April 1952), 477.

2. Almaraz, "Castañeda," pp. 322–334; Castañeda, "Why I Chose," p. 476. Also see Almaraz, "Carlos E. Castañeda's Rendezvous with a Library: The Latin American Collection, 1920–1977—The First Phase," unpublished paper in the Carlos E. Castañeda Collection, Benson Latin American Library, University of Texas at Austin, unnumbered folder; Almaraz, "The Making of a Boltonian: Carlos Castañeda of Texas—The Early Years," *Red River Valley Historical Review* (Winter 1974), 329–350; interview with Castañeda in *La Prensa* (San Antonio), Jan. 22, 1939, p. 3; and eulogy to Castañeda in *ibid.*, May 29, 1958, pp. 3, 23.

3. Almaraz, "Castañeda," p. 319.

4. Castañeda, "Why History Today," unpublished essay in Articles-Castañeda Folder, Castañeda Col., p. 5.

5. Castañeda, "The Rhythm of History," in *Man* (Feb. 1949), 27–28; also see Castañeda, "The Lessons of History," unpublished essay in Articles-Castañeda Folder, Castañeda Col.

6. Castañeda, "The First American Play," *Catholic World* (Jan. 1932), 1.

7. Castañeda, "Origins of Culture in the Americas," unpublished essay in Castañeda

untitled folder, box 1, Castañeda Col., p. 3. On Bolton see Herbert Eugene Bolton, *Wider Horizons of American History* (New York, 1939); also see John Francis Bannon, ed., *Bolton and the Spanish Borderlands* (Norman, 1964).

8. Castañeda, "The Broadening Concept of History Teaching in Texas," unpublished essay in Castañeda untitled folder, box 1, Castañeda Col., p. 2.

9. *Ibid.*

10. Castañeda, *Our Catholic Heritage*, vol. I, *The Finding of Texas* (Austin, 1936), preface, n.p.; pp. 22, 244–245; Castañeda, "Broadening of History," p. 7. On Barker see, for example, *Mexico and Texas, 1821–1835* (New York, 1928).

11. Castañeda's typescript review of Whitaker's book, p. 1, in Castañeda Col. See published review in *Catholic Historical Review* (Oct. 1942), 402–403.

12. Castañeda, "Our Latin American Neighbors," *Catholic Historical Review* (Jan. 1940), 424–425.

13. *Ibid.*, p. 423; Castañeda, "Earliest Catholic Activities in Texas," *Preliminary Studies of the Texas Catholic Heritage Society* (Oct. 1931), 2; *Catholic Heritage*, vol. 2, *The Winning of Texas* (Austin, 1936), preface, n.p.; vol. 3, *The Missions at Work* (Austin, 1938), p. 75; "The Six Flags of Texas," in *Preliminary Studies of the Texas Catholic Historical Society* (Jan. 1932), 11; "Pioneers of Christian Culture in Texas," essay published by Editorial Jus (Mexico City, 1950), p. 8.

14. Castañeda, "Our Latin American Neighbors," p. 426; Castañeda, "Contrastes," unpublished essay in Castañeda untitled folder, Castañeda Col., p. 11.

15. Castañeda, *Missions at Work*, p. 3.

16. Castañeda, "Our Latin American Neighbors," pp. 424–427.

17. Castañeda, "The First American Play," *Catholic World* (Jan. 1932), 429.

18. *Ibid.*, p. 434.

19. Castañeda, "The First Printing Press in Mexico," typescript manuscript in Castañeda—articles folder, Castañeda Col. See published essay in *Publisher's Weekly* (Jan. 1940), 50–53; Castañeda, "The Beginning of University Life in America," unpublished manuscript in Castañeda untitled folder, box 2, Castañeda Col. (see published version in *Preliminary Studies of the Texas Catholic Historical Society*, 3 [July 1938]); Castañeda, *Catholic Heritage*, vol. 5, *The End of the Spanish Regime* (Austin, 1942), pp. 409–410; Castañeda, "Why I Chose History," p. 477, and "Pioneers of Christian Culture," p. 11.

20. Castañeda, "The Fight for Democracy," unpublished essay in Castañeda untitled folder, box 2, Castañeda Col., pp. 3–4.

21. *Ibid.*, pp. 4–5.

22. Castañeda, "Six Flags of Texas," p. 10.

23. Castañeda, "Pioneers of Christian Cultures," p. 5. On Turner, see Frederick Jackson Turner, *The Frontier in American History* (New York, 1920), and *Rise of the New West, 1819–1829* (New York, 1906). Also see Wilbur R. Jacobs, ed., *The Historical World of Frederick Jackson Turner with Selections from His Writings* (New Haven, 1968). In his recent analysis of the failure of borderland historiography to employ Turner's frontier thesis, David Weber omits a discussion of Castañeda's work, which implicitly suggests a Turnerian analysis of the Spanish-Mexican colonization of Texas (see David J. Weber, "Turner, the Boltonians, and the Borderlands," *American Historical Review*, 91 [Feb. 1986], 66–81).

24. Castañeda, "Beginning of University Life," and "Latin America's First Great Educator," *Current History Magazine* (May 1925), 223–225.

25. Castañeda, "Broadening Concept of History," p. 12.

26. Castañeda, "Fight for Democracy," p. 2.

27. *Ibid*. Also see Castañeda, *Catholic Heritage*, vol. 6, *The Fight for Freedom* (Austin, 1950), and "Six Flags of Texas."

28. See, for example, Castañeda's critical review of Owen P. White's Anglo-centered *Texas: An Informal History* in *The Americas*, 2 (April 1946), 531–532.

29. Castañeda, "The Problem of the Mexican," unpublished essay in Articles—Castañeda, Castañeda Col., pp. 1–2, and Castañeda, "The Second Rate Citizen and Democracy," unpublished typescript in folder "Mexican-Americans," in Castañeda Col., p. 2, and published in Perales, *Are We Good Neighbors?* pp. 17–20.

30. Castañeda, "Problem of the Mexican," p. 2.

31. Castañeda, "Second Rate Citizen," p. 4.

32. Castañeda, "Old Americans and Their Reincorporation: A Challenge to Texas Schools," unpublished address delivered Sept. 4, 1951, at Edgewood School District Workshop, San Antonio, in Castañeda Col.

33. Castañeda, "Problem of the Mexican," p. 11.

34. Castañeda, "Second Rate Citizen," p. 3.

35. Castañeda, "Problem of the Mexican," p. 12; Castañeda, "Statement on Discrimination Against Mexican-Americans in Employment," unpublished typescript, 1947, folder "Mexican Americans," in Castañeda Col.; published in Perales, *Good Neighbors?* pp. 58–63.

36. Castañeda, "Problem of the Mexican," p. 7.

37. *Ibid.*, pp. 7–11; Castañeda to Judge Hardman, Del Rio, Feb. 24, 1934, in Castañeda Col.

38. Castañeda, "Problem of the Mexican," pp. 12–13; "Statement of Discrimination," p. 7.

39. Castañeda, "Statement of Discrimination," p. 8.

40. Castañeda, "Second Rate Citizen," p. 5, and "Statement of Discrimination," p. 7.

41. Castañeda, "Inter-American Cultural Relations," p. 2, unpublished typescript in untitled folder, Castañeda Col., published in *Catholic Library World* (Oct. 1947), 26–30.

42. Castañeda, "Modern Language Study and World Peace," p. 3, unpublished essay in Castañeda Col.

43. *Ibid.*, pp. 3–6.

44. Castañeda to Mrs. Thoms. Head, Del Rio, March 28, 1934, in Castañeda Col.

45. See "Recommendation for Bi-Lingual Library Service," in Castañeda to Miss Lucia F. Powell, Austin, April 2, 1935, Castañeda Col.

46. Castañeda, "Modern Language Study," pp. 10–11; Castañeda to Mrs. T. J. Martin, Del Rio, Sept. 27, 1934, Castañeda Col.

47. Castañeda, "American Ways of Life and Higher Education," unpublished speech, April 19, 1953, pp. 1–3, untitled folder, Castañeda Col.

48. *Ibid.*, p. 12.

49. Castañeda, "The Educational Revolution in Mexico," *Educational Review* (Oct. 1924), 123–125.

50. Castañeda, "Is Mexico Turning Bolshevik?" *Catholic World* (June 1926), 336–372.

51. Castañeda, "The First Pan-American Congress," *North American Review* (June–July–August 1926), 249–255.

52. Castañeda and Horace Virgil Harrison, "Latin America and the New World," typescript, pp. 1, 7, in untitled folder, box 2, Castañeda Col.

53. *Ibid.*, p. 3.

54. Castañeda to Mrs. Esther Pérez Carvajal, San Antonio, Jan. 13, 1935, Castañeda Col.

55. Castañeda to Leonard, Austin, May 18, 1938, Castañeda Col.

56. Lecture by Miguel León-Portilla, Feb. 1987, University of California, Santa Barbara.

CHAPTER TEN: *George I. Sánchez and the Forgotten People*

1. For more on Sánchez's life see Américo Paredes, "Jorge Isidro Sánchez y Sánchez (1906–1972)," as well as other essays in Paredes, ed., *Humanidad: Essays in Honor of George I. Sánchez* (Los Angeles, 1977), pp. 120–126. Also see Gladys Ruth Leff, "George I. Sánchez: Don Quixote of the Southwest" (Ph.D. thesis, North Texas State, 1976). For Sánchez's role in a controversial dispute in the early 1930s over racial attitudes at the University of New Mexico, see Gonzáles, "Perfect Furor."

2. George I. Sánchez, "Bilingualism and Mental Measure: A Word of Caution," *Journal of Applied Psychology,* 18 (Dec. 1934), 769.

3. Sánchez, "Spanish-Speaking People in the Southwest—A Brief Historical Review," *California Journal of Elementary Education,* 22 (Nov. 1953), 107.

4. Sánchez, "New Mexicans and Acculturation," *New Mexican Quarterly,* 11 (Feb. 1941), 62.

5. *Ibid.,* pp. 63–64.

6. Sánchez, *Forgotten People: A Study of New Mexicans* (Albuquerque, 1940), p. vii.

7. Sánchez, "New Mexicans and Acculturation," p. 67.

8. Sánchez, *Forgotten People,* p. 12.

9. Sánchez, "New Mexicans and Acculturation," pp. 67–68. Also see Acuña, *Occupied America,* and Barrera, *Race and Class in the Southwest.*

10. Sánchez, "Pachucos in the Making," *Common Ground* (Fall 1943), 13, 18.

11. Sánchez, "Spanish-Speaking People," p. 109; also see, Sánchez, "Spanish in the Southwest," unpublished paper available in the Chicano Studies Library, University of California, Berkeley.

12. See, for example, Gilbert G. González, "The System of Public Education and Its Function within the Chicano Communities, 1910–1930" (Ph.D. thesis, UCLA, 1974); González, "Racial Intelligence Testing and Mexican Children," *Explorations in Ethnic Studies,* 5 (July 1982), 36–49; and González, "Racism, Education, and the Mexican Community in Los Angeles, 1920–1930," *Societas* 4 (Autumn 1974), 287–302.

13. Sánchez, "Bilingualism and Mental Measure: A Word of Caution," *Journal of Applied Psychology,* 18 (Dec. 1934), 765.

14. *Ibid.,* p. 766, and Sánchez, "Significance of Language Handicap," in Marie M. Hughes and Sánchez, "Learning a New Language," *1957–58 General Science Bulletin* (Washington, D.C., 1958), p. 28.

15. Sánchez, "Bilingualism and Mental Measure," pp. 765–768.

16. Sánchez, "New Mexicans and Acculturation," p. 61.

17. Sánchez, "Bilingualism and Mental Measure," p. 767.

18. Sánchez, "New Mexicans and Acculturation," pp. 61–62; "Group Differences and Spanish-Speaking Children—A Critical Review," *Journal of Applied Psychology,* 16 (Oct. 1932), 556.

19. Sánchez, "The Education of Bilinguals in a State School System" (Ph.D. dissertation, University of California, Berkeley, 1934), p. 32.

20. Sánchez, "Bilingualism and Mental Measure," p. 767.

21. Sánchez, "A Study of the Scores of Spanish-speaking Children in Repeated Tests" (M.A. thesis, University of Texas, 1931), pp. 5, 13.

22. Leff, "Sánchez," p. 294. Mowry in his study of Sánchez comments: "He seemed to move from a position in the 1930's in which he stressed the Hispanic cultural influence in the ethnic identity of Spanish-speaking people to a recognition in the 1940's and 1950's of the cultural and racial heterogeneity of the Spanish-speaking people which made generalizations concerning their ethnic identity difficult" (see James Mowry, "A Study of the Educational Thought and Action of George I. Sánchez" [Ph.D. thesis, University of Texas, 1977], p. 92).

23. Sánchez, "Scores of Spanish-Speaking Children," pp. 15, 18–21. Also see H. T. Manuel, *The Education of Mexican and Spanish-speaking Children in Texas* (Austin, 1930).

24. *Ibid.*, pp. 25, 34; "Bilingualism and Mental Measure," p. 767; Leff, "Sánchez," p. 82.

25. Sánchez, "Bilingualism and Mental Measure," p. 767.

26. Sánchez, "Scores of Spanish-Speaking Children," p. 68.

27. Sánchez, "Bilingualism and Mental Measure," p. 771. Also see Richard E. López and Julian Samora, "George Sánchez and Testing," in Paredes, ed., *Humanidad*, pp. 105–107.

28. Sánchez, "Education of Bilinguals," p. 30.

29. Sánchez, "Bilingualism and Mental Measure," pp. 769–771.

30. Sánchez, "Scores of Spanish-speaking Children," p. 3. "Sánchez wrestled with the language problem of the Spanish-speaking child," one writer notes, "thirty years before many other scholars began to examine this question" (see Leff, "Sánchez," p. 262).

31. Leff "Sánchez," p. 70. Also see Sánchez, "The Implications of a Basal Vocabulary to the Measurement of Abilities of Bilingual Children," *Journal of Social Psychology*, 5, no. 3 (1934), 395–396.

32. Sánchez, "Scores of Spanish-speaking Children," pp. 19–20.

33. Sánchez, "Group Difference and Spanish-Speaking Children," p. 550.

34. Sánchez, "Bilingualism and Mental Measure," p. 770.

35. Sánchez, *Forgotten People,* pp. 32–32.

36. Sánchez, "Basal Vocabulary," pp. 395–397.

37. Sánchez, "The Crux of the Dual Language Handicap," *New Mexico School Review,* 38 (March 1954), 13–15.

38. *Ibid.*

39. See Sánchez, "Latin America and the Curriculum," *Curriculum Journal,* 11 (Nov. 1940), 303–305.

40. Leff, "Sánchez," pp. 135–136.

41. Sánchez, "North of the Border," *Proceedings and Transactions of the Texas Academy of Science* (1942), p. 84. Over twenty years later, Sánchez conceded that bilingual education was not yet a reality. In 1965 in testifying in Senate hearings on bilingual education Sánchez observed that Spanish still represented a native language for 5 million residents of the Southwest who were not immigrants. He reminded the Senate that the ability to communicate in Spanish enabled Americans to function more effectively in Latin America and that Spanish should be considered a natural resource of greater worth than either oil or cattle. See Leff, "Sánchez," p. 441.

42. Sánchez, "Education of Bilinguals," p. 33

43. Sánchez, "Spanish Name Spells Discrimination," *Nation's Schools,* 41 (Jan. 1948), 22.

44. Leff, "Sánchez," p. 411. In the Hernández case, Sánchez wrote the appendix to the brief and helped attorneys develop the "class apart" theory (*ibid.*, p. 539).

45. Sánchez, *Concerning Segregation of Spanish-Speaking Children in the Public Schools* (Austin, 1951), p. 16.

46. *Ibid.*, p. 17.

47. *Ibid.*, pp. 17–22.

48. Sánchez, "Spanish Name Spells Discrimination," p. 22.

49. Sánchez, "Concerning Segregation," p. 23.

50. *Ibid.*

51. *Ibid.*, p. 24.

52. *Ibid.*, p. 38.

53. Sánchez, "North of the Border," p. 81.

54. As quoted in Mowry, "Educational Thought," p. 176.

55. Sánchez, "North of the Border," p. 77.

56. Sánchez, "School Integration," p. 10.

57. *Ibid.*

58. Sánchez, "The American of Mexican Descent," *Chicago Jewish Forum*, 20 (Winter 1961–62), 120.

59. Sánchez, "New Mexicans and Acculturation," p. 172.

60. Leff, "Sánchez," pp. 172, 402; San Miguel, *Let All of Them Take Heed*, p. 96.

61. Sánchez, "Latin America and the Curriculum," p. 303.

62. *Ibid.*, p. 305, and "Inter-American Education Problems," *Phi Delta Kappen* 24 (Nov. 1948), 98–99.

63. Sánchez, "Cultural Relations Within the Americas," *Childhood Education*, 18 (April 1942), 342. Sánchez, however, cautioned against portraying Latin America and its people in a folkloric and unrealistic fashion (*ibid.*, p. 341). Also see Sánchez, "A New Frontier Policy for the Americas," *The Alcalde*, 19 (March 1961), 9–11. For more on Sánchez and inter-American educational policies see San Miguel, *Let All of Them Take Heed*, pp. 91–108.

64. Sánchez, "Spanish in the Southwest," p. 6. Also see "Spanish-Speaking People," p. 11, and Sánchez's introduction to Lyle Saunders and Olin E. Leonard, "The Wetback in the Lower Rio Grande Valley of Texas" (Inter-American Education Occasional Paper, Austin, 1951). Also see Sánchez and Saunders, "Wetbacks: A Preliminary Report to the Advisory Committee Study of Spanish-speaking People" (Austin, 1949). For controversy surrounding the Saunders and Leonard study see De Leon, "Sunbelt Hispanics," chap. 7.

65. Leff, "Sánchez," p. 84. Also see Paul R. Ehrlich and S. Shirley Feldman, *The Race Bomb: Skin Color, Prejudice, and Intelligence* (New York, 1977).

66. Sánchez, "Concerning American Minorities," in *Proceedings*, Fifth Annual Conference, Southwest Council on the Education of Spanish-Speaking People (Los Angeles, 1951), p. 54.

67. Mowry, "Educational Thought," p. 174.

68. *Ibid.*, p. 170. Also see Steven Schlossman, "Self-Evident Remedy? George I. Sánchez, Segregation, and Enduring Dilemmas in Bilingual Education," *Teachers College Record* (Summer 1983), 871–907. While conceding that Sánchez experimented with ideas on what Schlossman calls "vernacular education" or bilingual education, he contrasts Sánchez's qualified embrace of bilingual education with what he asserts, perhaps unfairly, was the uncritical support for bilingual education by Chicano educators and activists in the 1960s and 1970s. For a view that sees Sánchez more as a precursor of Chicano educational and psychological thought see Nathan Murillo, "The Works of George I.

Sánchez: An Appreciation," in Joe L. Martínez, Jr., ed., *Chicano Psychology* (New York, 1977), pp. 1–10.

69. Sánchez, *Forgotten People*, p. 13.

70. *Ibid.*, p. 98. In 1970, two years before his death, Sánchez, in looking back over his struggles to achieve quality education for Mexican Americans, still expressed disappointment. Mexican Americans continued to lag behind other Americans in educational attainment, although he conceded that the recognition of the value of bilingual education represented a step forward. He told an interviewer: "The relative position of Mexican Americans in the Southwest, educationally speaking, is essentially the same as it was ten years ago. This doesn't mean that they have not reached a higher grade of attainment. However, the rest of the population has not stood still either, so the situation is essentially the same" (see "An Interview with George I. Sánchez," in the *National Elementary Principal* [Nov. 1970], pp. 102–104).

CHAPTER ELEVEN: *Arthur L. Campa and the Cultural Question*

1. See Anselmo F. Arellano and Julian Josue Vigil, eds., *Arthur L. Campa and the Coronado Cuarto Centennial* (Las Vegas, New Mexico: 1980), pp. 4–5. For more on Campa's life see bio-file folder on Campa at Penrose Library, Special Collections, University of Denver.

2. For an excellent study of Aurelio M. Espinosa as well as a bibliography of his studies published from the 1910s to the 1940s, see Aurelio M. Espinosa, *The Folklore of Spain in the American Southwest: Traditional Spanish Folk Literature in Northern New Mexico and Southern Colorado*, ed. J. Manuel Espinosa (Norman and London, 1985).

3. Campa, "Folklore and History," *Western Folklore*, 24 (Jan. 1965), 5.

4. Campa, "The Spanish Folksong in the Southwest," *University of New Mexico Bulletin*, 4 (Nov. 15, 1933), reprinted in Carlos E. Cortés, ed., *Hispanic Folklore Studies of Arthur L. Campa* (New York, 1976), p. 5.

5. Campa, "Sayings and Riddles in New Mexico," *University of New Mexico Bulletin*, 5 (June 15, 1934), reprinted in Cortés, ed., *Folklore Studies*, p. 10.

6. *Ibid.*, p. 23.

7. Campa, "People, Land and Culture," *El Nuevo Mexicano* (no specific date, but published in 1939), in Arellano and Vigil, *Campa*, p. 50.

8. Campa, *Spanish Folk-Poetry in New Mexico* (Albuquerque, 1946), p. 7.

9. Campa, "Folksong," p. 32.

10. See Campa, "The Churchmen and the Indian Languages of New Spain," *Hispanic American Historical Review* (Nov. 1931), 542–550; "Chile in New Mexico," *New Mexico Business Review* (April 1934), 60–63; and "Some Herbs and Plants of Early California," *Western Folklore*, 9 (Oct. 1950), 337–347.

11. Campa, "A Bibliography of Spanish Folk-Lore in New Mexico," *University of New Mexico Bulletin*, 2 (Sept. 1930), in Cortés, ed., *Folklore Studies*, pp. 3–4.

12. See preface in Campa, *Folk-Poetry*.

13. Campa, "Bibliography," pp. 3–9.

14. Campa, *Folk-Poetry*, pp. 18–19.

15. Campa, "Spanish Traditional Tales of the Southwest," *Western Folklore*, 6 (Oct. 1947), 322. Also see his later *The Treasure of the Sangre de Cristos* (Norman, 1962).

16. Campa, "Spanish Religious Folktheatre in the Southwest," *University of New Mexico Bulletin*, 5, nos. 1, 2 (Feb. 15 and June 15, 1934), in Cortés, ed., *Folklore Studies*, p. 128.

17. Campa, "Bibliography," p. 25.

18. Campa, "Folktheatre," 5, no. 1, p. 8.

19. Campa, "Folktheatre," 5, no. 2, p. 6.

20. Campa, "Bibliography," p. 25.

21. Campa, "Folktheatre," 5, no. 1, p. 12.

22. *Ibid.*, 5, no. 2, p. 156.

23. Campa, "Sayings and Riddles," introduction, pp. 5, 13, 27.

24. Campa, "Bibliography," p. 27.

25. Campa, "Folktheatre," 5, no. 1, p. 7.

26. *Ibid.*, p. 12.

27. Campa, *Folk-Poetry*, p. 12.

28. *Ibid.*, p. 189.

29. *Ibid.*, pp. 95–100, and "Bibliography," p. 13.

30. Campa, "Folktheatre," 5, no. 2, pp. 6–7.

31. Campa, *Folk-Poetry*, pp. 189–190.

32. *Ibid.*, p. 11.

33. *Ibid.*, pp. 29–30, 92, 130, 190.

34. Campa, "Spanish Folksongs in Metropolitan Denver," *Southern Folklore Quarterly* (Sept. 1960), 180–181.

35. Campa, *Folk-Poetry*, pp. 12, 15. See Carey McWilliams, *North From Mexico.*

36. *Ibid.*, p. 13.

37. Campa, "Juan De Oñate Was Mexican: The Coronado Cuarto Centennial and the 'Spaniards,'" *El Nuevo Mexicano*, Oct. 12, 1939, in Arellano and Vigil, *Campa*, p. 35.

38. Campa, *Folk-Poetry*, p. 14. See also Fernando Ortíz, *Cuban Counterpoint: Tobacco and Sugar* (New York, 1947).

39. *Ibid.*, pp. 15–16.

40. Campa, "Our 'Spanish Character,'" *El Nuevo Mexicano*, Dec. 21, 1939, in Arellano and Vigil, *Campa*, pp. 43–44.

41. Campa, "The New Generation," in *ibid.*, pp. 25–26. For more on the Spanish Fantasy see Gonzáles, "Perfect Furor."

42. Campa, *Folk-Poetry*, p. 9.

43. *Ibid.*

44. *Ibid.*, p. 214.

45. Campa, "The Return of the Conquistador," in Arellano and Vigil, *Campa*, p. 37.

46. Campa, *Folk-Poetry*, pp. 190–191.

47. Campa, "Anglo versus Chicano, Why?" *Intellectual Digest*, 3 (Jan. 1973), 80.

48. *Ibid.*, p. 81.

49. Campa, "Even if I Should Resemble the Devil, I Am Who I Am," *El Nuevo Mexicano*, Jan. 19, 1939, in Arellano and Vigil, *Campa*, p. 7.

50. Campa, "Business Is Business," *El Nuevo Mexicano*, May 4, 1939, in *ibid.*, p. 22.

51. Campa, "Mañana is Today," *New Mexico Quarterly* (Feb. 1939), p. 294.

52. Campa, "Everything in the Past was Better: 'Back In My Day,'" *El Nuevo Mexicano*, Feb. 9, 1939, in Arellano and Vigil, *Campa*, p. 16.

53. Campa, "Mañana," p. 294.

54. *Ibid.*

55. Campa, "Language Barriers in Intercultural Relations," *Journal of Communication* (Nov. 1951), 44–45.

56. Campa, "Mañana," p. 295.

57. *Ibid.,* p. 298.

58. Campa, "Cultural Variations in the Anglo-Spanish Southwest," *Western Review,* 7 (Spring 1970), 8–9.

59. Campa, "Mañana," pp. 298–299.

60. Campa, "Anglo versus Chicano," p. 82.

61. Campa, "El Héroe Popular Norteamericano," *Revista Hispánica Moderna,* 34 (July–Oct. 1968), 561.

62. Campa, "Cultural Variations," p. 5.

63. *Ibid.,* p. 9.

64. Campa, "On the Banks of the Rio Grande," *El Nuevo Mexicano,* Jan. 26, 1939, in Arellano and Vigil, *Campa,* p. 11.

65. See Bruce-Novoa, *Chicano Poetry: A Response to Chaos* (Austin, 1982).

CHAPTER TWELVE: *The Chicano in American History*

1. Emory Bogardus, *The Mexican in the United States* (Los Angeles, 1934); Manuel Gamio, *Mexican Immigration to the United States: A Study of Human Migration and Adjustment* (New York, 1930); Paul S. Taylor, *Mexican Labor in the United States,* 3 vols. (Berkeley, 1928–34).

2. McWilliams, *North From Mexico.*

3. See Albert Camarillo, "Chicanos in the American City," in Eugene E. García et al., *Chicano Studies: A Multidisciplinary Approach* (New York, 1984), pp. 23–39.

4. Bolton, *Wider Horizons.*

5. Milton Gordon, *Assimilation in American Life: The Role of Race, Religion, and National Origins* (New York, 1964).

Index